Beyond Affirmative Action

Beyond Affirmative Action

Reframing the Context
of Higher Education

Robert A. Ibarra

The University of Wisconsin Press

The University of Wisconsin Press
2537 Daniels Street
Madison, Wisconsin 53718

3 Henrietta Street
London WC2E 8LU, England

Library of Congress Cataloging-in-Publication Data
Ibarra, Robert A.
   Beyond affirmative action : reframing the context
of higher education/Robert A. Ibarra.
      340 pp.   cm.
Includes bibliographical references and index.
   ISBN 0-299-16900-6 (cloth: alk. paper)
   ISBN 0-299-16904-9 (pbk.: alk. paper)
   1. Education, Higher—Social aspects—United States.
2. Affirmative action programs—United States. 3. Hispanic Americans—Education (Higher)—Social aspects.
4. Minorities—Education (Higher)—Social aspects—
United States. 5. Education, Higher—Aims and objectives—United States. I. Title.
   LC 191.9 .I23   2001
   378.1'9829—dc21   00-008920

Publication of this book has been made possible in part
by a grant from the Evjue Foundation.

To my mentor, colleague, and friend, the late Arnold "Arnie" Strickon, professor of anthropology emeritus at the University of Wisconsin–Madison and a faculty member at Walden University July 19, 1932–July 20, 1997

Contents

Tables

Foreword

The movement to rescind affirmative action by court decisions or state mandates is forcing leaders in higher education to rethink their strategies and to explore new ways to achieve diversity. Public institutions in California, Florida, and Texas are experimenting with undergraduate admission policies that automatically admit the top few percent of in-state high school graduates. This is only one solution, a kind of quick fix that helps only undergraduate students in states with high-density minority populations. But conditions in society have changed so much today that the legal means for achieving equitable access to higher education are becoming far more complex than some numerical formula. The issue now is not about the value of affirmative action, for that has been proved. The important question is, how should we value and ensure diversity on our campuses so that everyone benefits? Learning new ways to see and value diversity will be more productive for higher education in the long run than any stopgap measures now in place.

This is an underlying premise in Robert Ibarra's book *Beyond Affirmative Action*, in which he introduces a novel theory about diversity that could fundamentally change higher education in America. Others share this perception of it as well. One reviewer claimed that Ibarra's were the best new ideas he had seen as an administrator in higher education in more than ten years. One reason for my enthusiasm comes from watching these ideas emerge as he wrote his preliminary report on Latinos in graduate education. I saw how they grew from useful concepts for understanding why people do what they do into a powerful model for change. I think Ibarra is onto something quite new and important.

His book explores the premise that higher education has not evolved its thinking about affirmative action since the program was first implemented. In the early 1960s the goal was to eliminate barriers—by creating active recruiting and retention programs—that had limited or barred altogether minority students' access to higher education. The continued focus on these goals, he suggests, hid the fact that the culture of higher education is a major contributor to the persistence of underrepresentation of minorities in our institutions. Educators have always known that academic culture can negatively affect all students to some degree, not just minorities. Some graduate students are simply turned off by it and leave. What Ibarra found is a new perspective on how culture, context, and cognitive teaching/learning conditions in academia affect the achievement of many students and faculty, especially women and ethnic minorities. The breakthrough comes in showing, for the first time, why and how the cultural context of academia creates or destroys these conditions for success. What you have here are ideas that go beyond current thinking on affirmative action and multiculturalism. Rather than discard these models, however, Ibarra builds a multicontextual theory upon their foundations.

One reason I find Ibarra's book so valuable is his rich discussion of academic culture and the value of diversity. His ideas are helpful for gauging how gender and ethnic differences play a vital role in the intellectual life of a university. For instance, many of the women and minority faculty members we have hired at the University of Wisconsin–Madison have made striking contributions to the research and teaching mission of this institution. In many cases they are at the forefront of newly emerging fields or they are leading many of us into new areas in traditional departments and colleges, such as law, anthropology, sociology, education, psychology, literature, and music, to name but a few.

Quite apart from this we have powerful academic reasons for valuing diversity—it opens up new ways of thinking, teaching, learning, and conducting research that result in new knowledge from viewing the world through different cultural contexts and cognitive learning styles. What Ibarra shows us is that we often fail to recognize these important events. Instead we are content with seeking diversity because "it's the law" or "it's the right thing to do." This book will change that perspective to one that promotes diversity because it is the only way to tap the full spectrum of human potential and experience and to open up new ways to advance knowledge.

JOHN D. WILEY

Chancellor, University of Wisconsin–Madison

Acknowledgments

Gathering the data and completing this book would not have been possible without the cooperation of an informal network of people at many institutions around the country. I especially wish to extend my appreciation to all the deans and staff members at graduate schools who helped immeasurably in locating participants, scheduling, and providing locations for the interviews. I also wish to thank Christine O'Brien at the Ford Fellowships for Minorities Program; Hector Garza, formerly vice president of minority issues at the American Council on Education (ACE); Eileen O'Brien, who provided advice and data from her research on Latinos in higher education for ACE; Amalia Duarte, formerly an editor of *Hispanic Outlook in Higher Education,* and Elizabeth Veatch, formerly of the Smithsonian Institution's Office of Fellowships and Grants, for helping to identify potential interviewees. Special recognition goes to my dear friend and colleague Alicia González, former director of the Office of College and University Relations at the Smithsonian Institution, for helping me to identify participants and pilot the original question set for the study.

Many on the staff of the Council of Graduate Schools (CGS) gave their time and suggestions along the way, especially for my preliminary report for CGS. I thank Peter D. Syverson for help with data questions, Nancy A. Gaffney for constant feedback and final editing, and my colleague Anne Pruitt for listening, encouraging, and offering advice. Special acknowledgment goes to Philomena Paul for the many hours of transcribing interview tapes for both the 1994–1995 and 1996–1997 segments of the Latino study and for offering her valuable insights about the interviews. I would also like to thank the many readers who gave their time and thoughts for the original CGS report. Among them were students, faculty, staff, colleagues, friends, and family: Akbar Ally, Ivan Pagán, Cathy Middlecamp, Clifton

Conrad, Eligio Padilla, Sarita Brown, Joe Corry, King Alexander, and Consuelo López-Springfield.

A great number of new friends and colleagues, even acquaintances, contributed in a variety of ways to the final manuscript. I wish to thank Luis Piñero, Michael Olneck, Maury Cotter, Greg Vincent, Hardin Coleman, Bob "Don Plátano" Skloot, Herb Lewis, Edna Szymanski, Mark Curchack, John P. Bean, and Eden Inoway for listening, commenting, and offering feedback on significant portions of the work. I also wish to thank Brian Foster, Armando Arias, and Carlos Rodriguez who reviewed the original manuscript and offered their input. I am deeply indebted to several special friends who helped me reshape the book: Sheila Spear, who graciously suffered reading through an overly long draft and who skillfully prodded me with her coaching and editing; Jeanne Connors, who was exceedingly helpful in establishing editing priorities; and John Center, who not only helped tweak various sections but provided invaluable help in formatting the drafts. I especially want to thank Akbar Ally, not only for reading some of the text but also for really listening and being a good friend when I needed it the most. I want to thank Adam Gamoran and the gang at the sociology of education brown bag lunches for allowing me to join the group and helping me try out ideas.

I am grateful to Jeff Iseminger, a fellow anthropologist, for allowing me to lift his article nearly word for word from *Wisconsin Week* (December 10, 1997; reprinted with permission from Wisconsin Week, University of Wisconsin–Madison). Gene Rice, at the American Association for Higher Education, in many respects set the tone for the book and provided essential information and feedback about the new American scholar. I could not have completed the work on Latinas and gender issues without the guidance and direct participation of Alberta Gloria, Nancy Gaffney, Tanya Thresher, Betsy Drain, and Yolanda Garza. A special thanks to Tona Williams from the brown bag gang, who commented on the first report.

Some of the most important feedback, however, came from the psychologist Manuel Ramírez, my new colleague, who not only read early versions of the introductory chapters but also cofounded and developed the field of bicognition, one of the foundations for this book. I wish to thank other new colleagues, including Miguel Ceballos and Al Cohen, who helped enormously by guiding me through the unfamiliar territory of quantitative research and psychometric testing and analysis. I also wish to recognize a relatively new colleague, Mercedes de Uriarte, professor of journalism at the University of Texas at Austin, who not only read an early version of the book but also was the first to join me in presenting its theoretical findings.

Special thanks go to my mentor and friend, the late Dr. Arnold Strickon, who read the proposals for the study and book as well as a rough first draft of the preliminary report. Shortly before he succumbed to cancer, his encouragement convinced me to write this book. Three important people need special recognition for helping me in different ways to create and write this book: my wife, Marilyn Knudsen, who reviewed and edited many complete drafts of this book and helped me find the time to complete the work; John D. Wiley, then provost and vice chancellor for academic affairs at the University of Wisconsin–Madison, now chancellor, for supporting my year in Washington, D.C., granting me time to work on the manuscript, and reading drafts of the work in progress; and finally, Polly Kummel, whose editorial guidance was invaluable. It was a joy to work with someone as skilled as Polly because she really grasped the nuances of my ideas and knew exactly how to push and direct the book in progress. She made a difficult process a lot more fun.

I wish to express my gratitude to Dr. Edgar Beckham and the Ford Foundation for both the grant support that made the study a reality and for allowing me the opportunity to share the research with other scholars. My deepest appreciation goes to Dr. Jules B. LaPidus, president of the Council of Graduate Schools, for reading and editing the original study proposal and final drafts of the CGS report and for supporting the study from inception to completion. Finally, a special grácias goes out to the many Latinos and Latinas who gave their time and shared their lives with me to bring life to the study and make this study meaningful.

Part I

Reframing the Context
of Higher Education

1

Critical Junctures
for Change

Proponents view it as leveling the playing field. Opponents see it as bureaucratized inequality. Whatever they call it, most people think affirmative action in higher education will disappear. Some hope to abolish it; others believe it is evolving. The latest transformation is in the hands of politicians. For example, as this book went to press, Jeb Bush, Florida's governor, was facing crowds and picket lines of angry African American and Latino legislators, students, parents, and other voters.[1] They were unified against his "One Florida" plan, which would abolish affirmative action policies in college admissions and replace them with guaranteed college admission for those students graduating in the top 20 percent of their high school class.

Bush acted in the fall of 1999 after Ward Connerly, the California conservative, had decided to bring his crusade against affirmative action to Florida and to try to place on the state's ballot a referendum for abolishing affirmative action policies, not only on campus but in state contracts. Statewide polls showed Florida voters overwhelmingly in favor of the Connerly proposal, a version of which was approved by California voters in 1996. And, in the wake of the *Hopwood* decision from a federal appellate court, also in 1996, George W. Bush, the governor of Texas and the Florida governor's brother, had instituted guaranteed college admissions for the top 10 percent of Texas's high school graduates.

These political decisions represent a dramatic shift for American higher education. They were made amid recurrent cries of discrimination and institutional racism on college campuses across the country, accusations that always leave bitter feelings and no small amount of puzzlement among the majority males who continue to hold the preponderance of faculty and administrative positions.[2]

These decisions have also left politicians, attorneys, and college administrators alike scrambling to find ways to maintain and even improve diversity on campus. One of the early attempts occurred at Harvard University in 1997 when leading proponents of affirmative action in higher education held a series of closed meetings. Their goal was to come up with research on diversity that would help preserve the system and make a case that would counter the increasingly conservative bent of the U.S. Supreme Court (Lederman 1997a). Participants were dismayed to realize that in the twenty-odd years since the *Bakke* decision (which permitted consideration of race or ethnicity as one factor in admissions), no research (at least none the courts would be likely to accept) had been done that could confirm the social value of increasing the diversity of our college and university student populations. Affirmative action had simply become the morally right thing to do, and no one had been concerned about justifying its value in some quantifiable way. The reward for complacency was the debacle of the 1990s.

Today, most college and university administrators see the need to ensure that students, faculty, and staff represent a cross-section of society in order to meet the expectations of a rapidly increasing, ethnically diverse national population. What no one can figure out is why, despite well-directed efforts by affirmative action programs over the years, many segments of the national population still are grossly underrepresented on campus, although their numbers are growing rapidly.

For example, among the fastest-growing populations today is the thirty-one million Latinos of various national origins who, according to U.S. Census Bureau estimates for 1999, represent 11.7 percent of the total U.S. population. Demographers project that, in the next half-century, current birthrates alone will make Latinos the largest ethnic population in the country (U.S. Census Bureau 1996, 2000). Despite this growth, 1995 data—the most recent available—show that Latinos accounted for only 7 percent of total U.S. college enrollment in 1995 (D. Carter and Wilson 1997); by 1999 estimates, only 11 percent of all Latinos aged twenty-five or older had earned at least a bachelor's degree (U.S. Census Bureau 2000). Like other minority groups, they do not appear to be catching up in proportion to their population growth. The overriding question for educators is, what can be done to improve these numbers?

This book studies this critical juncture from inside academe, and it is unique in several ways. First, it examines the people and the processes that produce our graduates and scholars and how dynamic internal forces shape them, especially graduate education. It also describes this process and the issues involved through the experiences of Latina and Latino graduate students, as well as faculty members or administrators near the peak of their careers. Above all, this book aims to provide a unique theoretical construct of academic organizational culture and diversity that could alter current perspectives on research, teaching, and learning in higher education. This is more than just an analysis of educational systems, or an anthropological study of diversity and change; it is the analysis of and explanation for a new paradigm for education that is emerging from the synergy of ethnicity and academic culture. It begins with a new cultural model that reframes current theories about diversity and ends with a discussion of concrete ideas for improving academic culture and the acquisition of knowledge in ways that will make everyone in higher education more comfortable and productive.

In the process, I apply to the problem findings from studies of cultural context and cognition by combining parallel schools of thought in anthropology, psychology, and education. Looking at the literature of three disciplines provided me with fresh insights for explaining the conflicts and chronic academic difficulties and performance differentials registered by minorities and women throughout higher education. This construct also led me to formulate guidelines and adaptive strategies for reframing and enhancing the culture of the academy. The model-building process, a central framework for this book, required questioning and challenging the prevailing paradigms from the varying perspectives of students and faculty. Ultimately, it demanded stepping outside the traditional box of theory to explore for new ideas. The result is *Beyond Affirmative Action: Reframing the Context of Higher Education,* part blueprint for modifying our educational structures and part cultural road map for traversing the changing social landscape in the next century. We begin the journey in this first chapter by looking at the current challenges for enhancing campus diversity in general and then the demographic conditions for Latinos in higher education.

"Shaping the River": Academic Performance Gaps and Demographic Change

Demonstrating the benefits of affirmative action is a major theme in Bowen and Bok's *Shape of the River* (1998). Theirs was the first major study to provide longitudinal data that show affirmative action works for minorities who attend highly selective Ivy League schools. But their data on "academic performance gaps," a pattern they call "underperformance" among ethnic minorities, are most important for this discussion, for it is a core issue I tackle here. In their study of more than forty-five thousand students of all ethnic groups from twenty-eight highly selective colleges and universities, Bowen and Bok tracked students' progress through higher education and beyond. Their data show that ethnic minorities, and especially African Americans, benefited greatly from race-sensitive admissions policies since 1968. Their data on average cumulative grade-point average (GPA) by groups also show that after controlling for all variables—gender, ethnicity, socioeconomic status, standardized test scores, high school grades, and the like—African Americans' and Latinos' GPAs ranked them in only the 23d and 36th percentiles, respectively, in their college graduating class. This is relatively low compared to Bowen and Bok's majority student cohorts, whose average class rank by GPA was in the 53d percentile (1998, 72).

Some individuals could construe this academic gap, or, more accurately, performance differential, as proof of inherent genetic variation between whites and blacks, thus confirming the belief that affirmative action is nothing more than an unfair policy that favors unqualified ethnic groups. But Bowen and Bok tracked down the factors that led to gaps in academic performance and found that a variety of qualitative experiences—before college and in college—seemed to be significant determinants, although these were not easily quantifiable and thus less than satisfactorily explained. In the end, Bowen and Bok could substantiate little other than an association of performance differentials and some combination of variations in the admissions process and/or differing campus environments (1998, 72–86).

Academic performance gaps are even more difficult to discern among graduate students than undergraduates. Here Bowen and Bok measure success by such factors as admission to prestigious graduate programs and degree completion but little else. This includes comparisons of how long it takes different cohorts and groups to complete an advanced degree, a relatively common measure of academic progress in graduate school.

The most salient features of the Bowen and Bok study for my work are their recommendations for minority programs and the factors they found that have been successful in reducing academic performance gaps among ethnic minorities. The latter include a number of contextual components—people-oriented relationships, family engagement, psychological environment, working in groups, a collaborative learning environment—that are directly related to criteria that I use to formulate a new theoretical construct in chapter 3. These key criteria help reduce the gaps in academic performance, thereby enhancing other conditions for ethnic minorities to succeed in higher education. Implementing them means instituting an effective theoretical framework, a new perspective on the context of higher education, and a rationale for changing academic cultures that reaches beyond mere programmatic initiatives.

Since the publication of Bowen and Bok's study, other scholars have described the educational benefits of affirmative action (Orfield 1999). But proponents fear that nothing may convince the courts, especially if the argument that diversity enriches teaching, research, and intellectual campus life "is based largely on intuition" and principles of faith (Price 1998, B4). These conditions, according to Hugh B. Price, president of the Urban League, underscore the "urgent need for fresh thinking to prevent higher education from reverting to the days when it recruited only a few, token minority-group students" (Price 1998, B4). The demographic change now profoundly affecting the country will "provide the moral, economic—and constitutional—justification necessary for viewing as compelling state interest the inclusion of minority-group students in colleges and universities," according to Price (B4). He adds that in the next fifty years, "our country's economy increasingly will be carried on the backs of African-American and Latino workers, entrepreneurs, and consumers." Given these pronouncements on the condition of affirmative action in transition, one essential question is how to use the studies of campus diversity and demographic change to find solutions.

Challenges for Increasing Campus Diversity

Research that examines the academic success levels for ethnic minorities and women must look beyond the assigning of blame. Theories that blame women and minorities for failure to advance, as well as those that blame institutions for impeding the advancement of minorities and women, fail to fully account for why qualified, highly capable ethnic minorities and women are becoming less attracted to traditional graduate education and are seemingly less enamored with pursuing faculty careers. The nation's hot economy surely has played a role in the declining numbers in graduate enrollments, but the situation may reflect a cultural dimension that has been hidden by the concern about academic performance differentials.

For example, retaining Latino students is a serious problem for our colleges and universities. My interviews with Latinos across the country unearthed a growing disenchantment with academia in general. Regardless of the institutions involved, these students, faculty, administrators, and even nonacademics described their student or faculty experience as either turbulent or missing important academic and/or cultural values. Many commented that values regarding research, publication, teaching, or community service, for example, are so locked into a standard and dominant academic model that other relevant cultural value systems are excluded (Tennant 1997). According to Moses, universities have improved in recruitment and outreach but not in retention of significant numbers of underrepresented populations. Students and staff turn away because "they perceive the university as cold, indifferent, uncanny [*sic*], and *not* a place they want to be" (Moses 1990, 403; see also Carroll and Schensul 1990). This growing discontent reaches to the core of graduate and professorial training in our universities today. To make matters worse, few academics are responding to the issues, and fewer still see the need to change or improve the current educational paradigm.

Much of the current research on higher education presumes that ethnic and gender conflicts are a consequence of subtle bias, injustice, or overt sexism and racism by individuals within institutional systems who maintain power and control over others (see, for example, H. Adams 1993; American Council on Education 1992; R. Kerlin 1997; Scheurich and Young 1997; Spann 1990; Wagener 1991). Individual interactions and attitudes are likely to be covert, perhaps even unconscious, so they are difficult to identify and eliminate in an organization. Time-honored solutions for combating these inequities (see D. Burgess 1997; Richardson 1989) rely on three essential ingredients: access (student recruitment and college orientation and admissions programs), retention (financial support, academic support or advising, and sometimes cultural support programs), and increasing the critical mass of historically underrepresented populations (programs for hiring women and minority faculty).

This recipe of essential ingredients and programs is often called the "educational pipeline" by many of those involved in campus minority affairs. The image evoked is that the main stream of majority students in higher education travels through a pipeline from admissions through graduation with fewer barriers to success than minority students. Colleges and universities create minority programs to eliminate the barriers that impede the progress of minority students toward their degree. For decades access or admission to and through this pipeline has been the biggest concern on our campuses. It still is the driving force behind programs created to build new pipelines from our campuses to the affected ethnic minority communities to allow them greater access to higher education. Consequently, the three essential components in the "pipeline model" place greater emphasis on process, or the business functions, of colleges and universities (e.g., recruiting and retaining minority employees and students) than on the content and methods of delivering education to all kinds of students, which is the actual business of education within these institutions.

To be sure, these solutions combat racism and sexism and often help reduce their incidence. But the current analogies about educational pipelines and the perceptions about access (Brown 1987) are giving way to concerns about improving the culture and environment for women and minorities, a small shift in thinking to include the business of education

8

among the other concerns of minority affairs (see American Council on Education 1992; R. Kerlin 1997). The time may be right to alter the programmatic solutions created more than thirty years ago in order to deal with pressing needs and take advantage of institutional conditions for change. Some educators concede that the programmatic remedies address only part of the problem or, at best, treat only the symptoms.

Whenever colleges or universities implement new programs or update comprehensive recruiting targets and retention plans, they usually see immediate and positive results from their efforts. Depending on the target, ethnic student enrollments may increase or more women may join the faculty. But the initial gains tend to level out or drop off over time. On campuses fortunate enough to provide significant and sustained funding for minority students and faculty, such programs will continue to have positive results (see "Affirmative Action" 1995; Whatley 1996). But without significant and open-ended funding, such efforts rarely, if ever, maintain their initial momentum, especially on predominantly majority campuses (Schweitzer 1993; University of Wisconsin–Madison 1988, 1991). In the short term, the improved results offer a false sense of accomplishment at best.

Let me be clear on this point. I am convinced that adequately staffed and funded minority access, retention, and financial support programs *are* important for improving diversity and *do* maintain the minority presence on predominantly majority campuses (see H. Adams 1993; Chapa et al. 1993; Richardson 1989; Whatley 1996). The problem is that the programs and their function have changed little over the years. These programs are designed mainly for recruiting and maintaining a minority presence on campus. Most programs focus on secondary educational missions, such as student services or activities aimed at changing current structures and improving campus conditions. Consequently, they are often marginalized programs within the minority student affairs office.

Every once in a while, a well-intentioned faculty member launches a study and rediscovers a different angle on the barriers-to-graduate-school-for-minorities problem (D. Burgess 1997, B7–8). But these scholars offer only tried-and-true advice and little information about *how* to do it; all of it focuses on technical improvements, and none of it ever looks at real problems. Few faculty reexamine the fundamental values of academia. Few programs have clear mandates to review and revise those academic cultures. Consequently, few initiatives sustain their momentum over time.

Daniel Seymour suggests that institutions of higher learning are gripped by "paradigm paralysis" and are reluctant to change because they have "no alternative models to pursue" (1996a, 23). Although higher education has been trying to diversify for thirty years—and to figure why it has such difficulty doing so—today's economic, political, and demographic realities mean it is time to try substantially new solutions from different perspectives. Student complaints are increasing and faculty tensions are rising with accusations of racist cultures and chilly climates on campus. Student protesters, though less militant than in the past, continue to debate the same issues regarding the lack of diversity, or they demand more recognition for ethnic and gender-based programs (Martell 1997). In many parts of the country rollbacks resulting from anti–affirmative action legislation are exacerbating campus conflicts (Mangan 1999; Selingo 1999). But on campuses where this is not the case, the constant tensions suggest that other problems exist and continue unabated.

To summarize, the central conflict regarding campus diversity and demographic change is between culturally different populations and traditional academic values—those that involve how things are done in academia. Now the pressures for change—the incentives—are mounting. Voters, state legislatures, and court rulings are dismantling thirty years of affirmative action and antidiscrimination legislation, while women and ethnic populations on campus argue that the barriers they have always faced in academia remain unchanged. This is a crucial point in the debate about educational reforms. Despite steady increases by underrepresented populations, especially women, real equity and diversity remain elusive on campus. A case in point: the tenure rate for all Latino full-time undergraduate faculty declined nearly 19 percent between 1989 and 1996, the largest decline among all the underrepresented populations surveyed in higher education. For Latino males the tenure rate is about 44 percent, but for Latinas the rate is even lower, not quite 38 percent in 1996 (D. Carter and Wilson 1997). It is crucial to understand the current circumstances before we develop solutions.

The Crossroads of Cultural Change in Higher Education

The numbers of minority students enrolled in U.S. colleges have shown steady increases since the mid-1980s; they now account for approximately 25 percent of total enrollment (Gose 1996, 1997). In fact, the number of minority students has doubled since 1976. The largest gains come from Latino student enrollments, which increased 3.7 percent from 1996 to 1997 and have grown steadily—by 4 to 5 percent annually from 1993 through 1997 (Carlson 1999; Gose 1996, 1997; Wilds and Wilson 1998).

Declines in total student enrollment between 1995 and 1999 reflect the steady drop—1 to 5 percent—in majority student enrollments every year since 1991. These changes appear to represent a demographic shift among those graduating from high school in the 1990s—increasing numbers of minority graduates and decreasing numbers of majority students attain their diplomas (Gose 1996, 1997). Despite these shifts, the demand for higher education among all U.S. residents aged eighteen to twenty-four is expected to increase by 30 percent in the first decade of this century (Macunovich 1997).

However, the growth in the number of Latino scholars is deceptive. Despite declines in total enrollments of majority students across all age groups since 1991, 43 percent of the majority population aged eighteen to twenty-four was enrolled in college in 1995, an all-time high nationally (Gose 1996, 1997). Latino enrollment rates in that cohort are 20 percent lower for all age groups and 40 percent lower among the twenty- to twenty-four-year-olds (Macunovich 1997, 44). Sustaining Latino student enrollment in the future will be highly dependent on such slippery factors as available funding, access to higher education, and regional enrollment trends for ethnic students in general.

Research on Latino graduate students and faculty suggests that their foothold in higher education remains tenuous (Cuádraz 1992, 1993; Gándara 1982, 1993, 1995; Ibarra 1996; R. Padilla and Chávez Chávez 1995). Trends in graduate enrollment during the 1990s show ethnic minority enrollment grew at the same 2 percent annual rate as did overall graduate student enrollment (Syverson and Welch 1997, 23). But percentages mask the real problem. For example, despite a 6 percent increase in the number of Latino graduate students in 1995, Latinos do not enter graduate schools or join the faculty in numbers great enough to effect cultural change. Increasing the critical mass of minority students is important, but increasing the number of minority faculty may be the critical factor in effecting academic change to meet the future needs of ethnic population growth in this country.

The latest figures highlight the problem for Latinos in higher education.[3] If we take a snapshot of 1995, we find that

• Only 7.6 percent of college undergraduates were Latinos.
• Fifty-six percent of all Latinos in higher education were attending two-year institutions.
• Only 6 percent of Latinos attending two-year institutions went on to four-year schools.
• Only 9 percent of all Latinos had bachelor's degrees, compared to 23 percent for non-Latinos.
• Graduate school enrollments increased by 6.8 percent for Latinos, but they accounted for only 4.2 percent of all graduate students in 1996.
• Only 3 percent of all doctoral degrees awarded to U.S. citizens went to Latinos.

- The number of Latinos awarded doctoral degrees had grown by only 3.6 percent since 1985.
- Only 2.4 percent of all faculty were Latino, representing a mere 1 percent increase since 1985.
- The tenure rate for all Latino faculty had dropped by 4 percent since 1985.

The statistics are revealing and the consequences disturbing. Latino populations grew 53 percent in the 1980s, more than seven times faster than the rest of the nation's population. Latinos are expected to number more than forty-four million by 2015, becoming the largest minority group in the United States (Hodgkinson and Outtz 1996, 5). Yet Latinos, like other underrepresented populations, are simply not getting into higher education in adequate numbers to make a difference in academia. Even at the doctoral level, Latinos trail Anglos and African Americans in obtaining degrees in the social sciences, humanities, and education (Solorzano 1995).[4] The problem is lack of growth in the intellectual elite in proportion to the overall size of the rapidly growing ethnic minority populations.

For example, figures for total minority population enrollments in higher education are appallingly low. The total enrollment of minority students in higher education rose only 3 percent from 1994 to 1995 (Gose 1997, 1; Marklein 1997). Completion rates for minorities hovered around 10 percent each for associate, bachelor's, and master's degrees in 1995 (Marklein 1997). Data from the Council of Graduate Schools show that despite the slowdown in overall graduate school enrollments since 1992, ethnic student enrollment shows significant increases, especially from Latinos and Asian Americans (Syverson and Welch 1997). Yet the percentage of doctoral degrees awarded by ethnic group changed very little from the mid-1980s to the mid-1990s (D. Carter and Wilson 1997; Solorzano 1995).

Access no longer seems to be the main problem; flattening enrollments may now be a greater concern (D. Burgess 1997). In recent surveys of first-year undergraduates (see Alicea 1997), Latino respondents said that money and social stress are major issues. With the costs of education increasing, 31 percent of Latinos said a major concern was money, whereas about 17 percent of all students surveyed felt this way. Thirty-three percent of Latinos said financial aid was a very important factor in choosing their college (Alicea 1997). Surveys also showed that all students considered stress a big problem. But the highest percentage of students feeling stress were Latinos, who registered concerns about emotional and physical health. As fiscal and social costs rise, many ethnic populations enter college only to become discouraged; they may be leaving higher education at alarming rates, as the figures I have cited tend to suggest.

The problem today remains complacency more than conflict. The failure to find viable ways to attract, maintain, and increase the enrollment of women and minorities in higher education means fewer students are enrolling at a time when the mechanisms we have long relied on are under political fire. After the dismantling of affirmative action in California, Florida, and Texas, it was inevitable that politicians would fill the void with quick-fix solutions in return for political gain (or to staunch political losses). It is too soon to tell whether their policies for admitting top high school graduates will have any real effect on diversity in their public institutions. But we do know that class-ranking systems fail to address the real problems of disparity in academic performance among various kinds of students.

The essence of my argument is that complacency by those involved in higher education is partly the result of a lack of incentives and partly a lack of direction. As I intend to show, most of us have been looking at the wrong methods or in the wrong places for new solutions. The current paradigm for explaining the conflict focuses on discrimination, such as institutional racism. We need to look closely at this because, from a variety of perspectives, institutional racism does not always appear to be a sufficient explanation. This book explores an alternative explanation.

An Overview of the Study

This alternative explanation is a new perspective on diversity that in many ways takes us beyond affirmative action. My ideas emerged from a study I completed on the problems of Latinos in graduate school (Ibarra 1996). In searching for answers, I broadened the study to include women and students and faculty throughout higher education who come from other minority groups. This book is not about demystifying Latinos, although explaining terms and describing culture are essential parts of it. It is about demystifying higher education, the traditional structures and cultures for creating knowledge and learning new ideas. The spotlight to a large extent is on graduate education, but the examples will be Latino—not just my insights but those of the many Latinos I interviewed. And, as I will show, their take on the world of graduate education is not unlike that of other minorities, of women, and even of some majority men.

The basis of this book is a group of seventy-seven individuals, forty-one Latinos and thirty-six Latinas, whom I interviewed for a project for the Council of Graduate Schools (CGS) in 1994 and 1995. I published portions of the research as a monograph entitled *Latino Experiences in Graduate Education: Implications for Change* (1996).[5] The interviews were

13

designed to highlight the social backgrounds and relevant experiences of participants before, during, and after completing their graduate education. The study focused on selected samples of Latino faculty, administrators, and graduate students working on master's or doctoral degrees. I also interviewed nonacademics, individuals with doctoral degrees who either left academe or never pursued an academic position. Most nonacademics were employed by private organizations either directly or indirectly affiliated with higher education. Because of time constraints and variable interview conditions, the field study could not include ethnographic observations of student or faculty campus activities.

I selected the participants to reflect, as much as possible, a cross-section of ethnicity, national origin, gender, generation, region, type of institution (large research universities and small institutions that granted only master's degrees, for example; see appendix 1), academic disciplines, and cohort groups (students, faculty, administrators, and nonacademics). I did not choose them because they experienced either a particularly pleasant or unpleasant experience in graduate school. In general, students came from a variety of backgrounds and were at all stages in their degree program when I interviewed them. Latino faculty and administrators were those both new and tenured, as well as seasoned deans, vice chancellors, and presidents of institutions. The majority were born between 1940 and 1960, but their years of birth spanned almost five full decades, beginning in the 1930s.[6]

My primary goal in selecting participants was to sample populations by ethnicity and region. For example, the forty-one Mexican Americans whom I interviewed came primarily from the western and southwestern states of California, Arizona, New Mexico, and Texas, although a few were from the east coast and the Midwest. Among them, four had emigrated from Mexico. The sample included sixteen Puerto Ricans, half of whom were from the island and the other half from New York, New Jersey, Washington, D.C., and Florida. The twelve Cuban Americans were primarily living in Miami and included seven born and raised in Cuba. The eight "Other Latinos" were people I encountered at random throughout the selection process, and they gave the following as their origins: three were from Costa Rica (including one international student); one each from Colombia, Venezuela, and the Dominican Republic; one from California and one from New Mexico. The last two individuals, both of whom referred to themselves as Spanish Americans, traced their ancestry two hundred years to the original Spanish land-grant families from Mexico and did not initially identify as Mexican Americans in the interviews.

All but one were U.S. citizens. Though 20 percent were immigrants who became naturalized U.S. citizens, the majority of respondents (62 percent) were from predominantly first-generation (immigrant) and second-generation backgrounds. However, within each group only half the Mexican Americans, and most of the Puerto Ricans, Cubans, and "Other Latinos," were from first, or immigrant, generations.

The Scope of the Latino Study

New ideas often evolve when models with a demonstrated history of usefulness in one field are applied and transformed in a way that becomes useful or advances the thinking in another field. Integrating models into new constructs first requires clarifying a number of concepts. The first part of this book, "Reframing the Context of Higher Education," focuses on building a foundation for the new theoretical paradigm that I develop in chapter 3. For instance, chapter 2 clarifies how important concepts of culture and ethnicity fit current conditions in academia. Much of the research on ethnicity in higher education oversimplifies and aggregates the data, sometimes making it useless for learning about different cultures. I will reexamine these problems and other anthropological theories on culture and ethnicity and apply them in new ways to explain the dynamics of ethnic groups and their boundaries in academic settings. Research on academic cultures is growing, but the interactive dynamics involving different ethnic populations is not yet fully understood in traditional academic institutions (see Tierney 1990).

As I analyzed the interviews, I was reminded of the cultural models developed by the anthropologist Edward T. Hall, a pioneer in the field of intercultural communication (1959, 1966, 1974, 1977, 1984, 1993). Hall's ideas describing culture, context, and cognition matched closely the comments and patterns of behavior expressed by my interviewees. Contrasting Hall's model of ethnic minority cultures with Euro-American cultures led me to insights that expand the current paradigm about teaching and learning in colleges and universities (see chapter 3). The clinical psychologist Manuel Ramírez (1983, 1991), along with his colleague Alfredo Castañeda (1974), among others, generated a parallel theoretical model. Their work, which contrasts the learning styles predominant among Mexican Americans and other minorities with the learning styles of Euro-American males, produced the theory of bicognition that preceded Hall's cognitive model by nearly fifteen years. Synthesizing cultural context, cognitive styles, and ethnic identity generated a multicontextual configuration that explains cultural dissonance in academia.

This new theory of multicontextuality offers a more comprehensive explanation for academic dissonance than institutional racism. In fact, my argument here is that for quite some time popular beliefs that academic conflict originates in racial prejudice have masked conflict-oriented models that involve culture or cognition. Interactions not easily explained by racism—such as minorities or women who appear to discriminate against other minorities or women—are by default attributed to institutional racism. This mind-set overlooks or ignores the influence of cultural context and cognition.

Part II, "Latinas and Latinos in Graduate Education and Beyond," puts aside these common assumptions that correlate ethnic and gender conflicts with racism or sexism and begins to sift out patterns of multicontextuality among Latinos in their graduate school and professional experiences. Chapters 4, 5, and 6 examine the transformation from graduate students into faculty and, for some, administrative leaders. These chapters focus primarily on cultural patterns and issues derived from my interviews with Latinos and current research in education and anthropology. Explicit cultural knowledge is information that is widely shared and discussed among a self-identified group of people and passed on to others about how to behave and get along successfully in life. Tacit cultural knowledge is shared information that is so ingrained that people do not and cannot talk about it (Spradley and McCurdy 1980, 16–17). These chapters examine the explicit and tacit nature of Latino cultures in general and in the context of our graduate educational systems through the interviewees' accomplishments as faculty members.

The concepts are complex and varied. Our colleges and universities have a constellation of cultures and subcultures that influence their social systems. These chapters explore the dynamic interactions that involve both the cultural diversity of Latino students of different national origins and the patterns of shared behavior and values within the cultures and subcultures of academia. For most Latinos and Latinas who are completing their degrees, this process is intensified by the turbulence of ethnic enculturation into academia. Stressful transformations seem to activate overt or covert inclinations toward graduate studies that relate to ethnicity. For some, ethnic research is an adaptive strategy that maintains their ethnic identity while buffering the forces of academic enculturation.

Cultural context and cognition play roles that go beyond the assumption that academic turbulence originates only between different ethnic individuals and faculty members. In fact, one of my primary objectives here is to show how the struggle for academic success directly relates to the conflict between contextually different populations and the specific contextuality and value systems historically ingrained within the institutional cultures themselves. Chapter 5 also uses a multicontextual strategy to examine the nature of academic organizational cultures and the origins of doctoral education in the United States. Graduate education traces its roots to a German research model, which in turn incorporates the values of academic cultures that evolved within institutions dedicated to a singular contextual format—scientific exploration—for exploring knowledge. That is, new knowledge is gained by open exploration that uses only those contexts and processes that are appropriate for scientific experimentation. But the learning modes created by and for the cultural needs of specific national origin populations, such as those found in Germany, shape and limit some ethnic minorities' ability to use the scientific methodology, communication, and educational systems that generate and deliver that knowledge in this country.

However, the model of Western analytical science is not the center of concern here. Indeed, without it we would not have achieved what we have in our society today. The concern instead is about imbalance, the overly dominant role that our analytical research models play in higher education to the exclusion of other legitimate learning modes and styles. Boyer (1990), among others, says that scholarship today may be out of sync with differences in learning styles and knowledge acquisition among students and faculty (see J. Anderson and Adams 1992; Kolb 1981, 1984; Rice 1996). This disynchronicity affects many individuals adversely, especially most ethnic minorities and women, who must learn more than one mode in order to succeed in higher education.

One perspective on these issues suggests that the professional bureaucracy of higher education is shaping academic cultures and restricting cultural change. Universities are organizations run by trained and indoctrinated specialists (faculty members) who are given considerable individual control over their own work. According to Daniel Seymour, professional bureaucracies are usually very conservative and less likely to change than other bureaucracies, such as those found in government and the private sector, because they are either unwilling or unable to adapt quickly to the demands of a changing environment. Because faculty members control the work in higher education, the system is unable to correct problems that faculty choose to ignore (D. Seymour 1996a). In short, many Latinos in academia are imprinted with cultural contexts and cognitive skills that are at odds with the cultural contexts and predominant cognitive designs found throughout academia.

While the transformation for graduate students is fraught with conflict, the experiences of Latino and Latina faculty are even more difficult. Latino faculty who enjoyed a relatively uneventful graduate school experience are surprised when they become embroiled in cultural issues about hiring, student admissions, minority service load, professional development, research interests, governance, retention, and, more frequently, tenure. In chapter 6 I detail my findings from the interviews with Latino and Latina faculty and show that faculty/administrator participants throughout the country face significant conflicts with academic cultures regardless of their background, type of institution, or academic discipline. Many describe their entry into the professoriate as a metamorphosis into a dominant ethnic group rather than a transition into a profession. The transformation can be so overpowering that Latino faculty have accused other Latino colleagues of turning their backs on the community and forgetting their cultural heritage. This phenomenon occurs among other ethnic minority populations as well.

Is there any evidence that the theory of multicontextuality plays a part in other ethnic/academic interactions? Can the theory be confirmed by methodological analysis? (see McCall 1996, 44). In part III, "The Engagement of Cultural Context in Academia," I show how the results of additional analysis and data from faculty surveys by the Higher Education Research Institute (HERI), which lend support to my hypothesis, correlate significant and sustained contextual and cognitive differences within ethnic or gender groups to the influence of various aspects of academic culture.

The analysis in chapter 7 compares a variety of ethnic and women faculty members' responses to selected questions about instructional methods and goals against a benchmark of survey responses from majority faculty males. Preliminary results show that certain contextual and cognitive preferences, among other characteristics, may be a major distinction between majority males and women faculty members and those from certain ethnic groups.

These pedagogical cultural differences and comparative analyses of academic culture offer new ideas, as well as challenges, for changing the face of higher education. The final chapter pulls together other findings and data to conceptually reframe the cultural context of higher education. I don't expect to end the muttering about the influence of racism and sexism, but the implications of this new theoretical model could improve upon our academic cultural systems and, in turn, improve the climate for diversity that continues to be such a chimera for institutions of higher learning. This new model also offers cultural guidelines for teaching, learning, and assessment in higher education. Applying both new and rediscovered models of cultural context to academic cultures shows how successful universities in the future can adopt a balanced combination of context and cognition when implementing change in their institutional structures and cultures.

Explaining a new paradigm is not an easy process. This model-building process, which favors comprehensiveness over succinctness, may also challenge one's patience. By its nature it requires more compiling and comparing of familiar ideas than readers are accustomed to. But when new constructs must be built and presented for others to understand, the nature of that process is to think expansively and systemically. Each chapter will guide readers from a basis of familiar ideas toward new sets of images that may sometimes take awhile to fully comprehend. That journey also may seem divergent, digressive, even unclear at times, yet it is all essential for mapping out new territory. Even with guidance, leaving a world of comfortable assumptions to take up new ways of perceiving that world does not come without some effort. For that reason, this book provides ample discussion of familiar ideas and constructs to help readers see and absorb the new principles of multicontextuality from different perspectives.

2

The Latino Study

Reconceptualizing Culture and Changing the Dynamics of Ethnicity

The Spanish colonial origins of the United States have yet to be woven into the fabric of American history. Although the United States has always been a multi-ethnic society, in American popular culture and in most general histories, the American past has been understood as the story of English America rather than as the stories of the diverse cultures that make up our national heritage.

David J. Weber, "Our Hispanic Past"

Very little is known about Latinos and Latinas in graduate education. We know the total Latino population in the country is growing rapidly, and we have some quantitative data about Latinos in higher education, but are we making the correct assumptions about their progress through graduate school? Are we making accurate interpretations of the data we collect? Graduate programs have little qualitative information about the student experience in general, so are we asking the right questions when we collect data on Latinos, or on any graduate students we study, for that matter?

The Latino study, as it was initially conceived for the Council of Graduate Schools (CGS) in 1994, revolved around two essential questions: Why are so few Latinos and Latinas entering graduate education or the professoriate? And, from a variety of perspectives, what are the Latina and Latino students' experiences both during and after their graduate programs? CGS wanted to find out more about Latinos in graduate school to guide graduate institutions toward improving recruitment and retention programs for minority students, faculty, and staff in general. My part of the study was to collect new information that could determine why Latinos, Latinas, and other ethnic minorities had such chronic difficulties in higher education. For instance, what strategies are helpful in successfully completing an advanced degree? What role does ethnicity play in this process? Are these factors different for subgroups within the Latino population itself? How do the cultures of academic institutions, disciplines, and departments affect the passage through graduate school and beyond?

The pages that follow begin to address some of these issues, first by providing baseline data on the current condition of Latinos in graduate education. This includes a discussion of the Latino study's research strategies, data collection issues, and an overview of findings by other researchers in the field. The central purpose of this chapter is to establish the concepts of culture, including organizational culture and ethnicity, that are at the heart of the difficulties faced by higher education and Latino graduate students, faculty, and administrators.

Latinos in Graduate Education

Only a handful of researchers are actually studying Latinos in U.S. graduate education.[1] Most researchers focus on specific ethnic populations such as Mexican Americans, or Chicanos (see Cuádraz 1992, 1993; Gándara 1982, 1993; Lango 1995; Solorzano 1993, 1995).[2] Research about Latino faculty seems to be more generic and tends to examine statistical trends (see Aponte and Siles 1996; H. Astin et al. 1997; HACU 1996; HERI 1991; O'Brien 1993), or it focuses on broader themes about conditions of employment or status (Anzaldúa 1990; Nieves-Squires 1991; R. Padilla and Chávez Chávez 1995). Overall, research on Latinas and Mexican Americans predominates.

Specific studies of Latino graduate students recognize the significance of sociocultural conditions and family-community influences in shaping their cultural perspectives, even within higher education. In her case study of the first affirmative action generation, the sociologist Gloria Cuádraz interviewed forty Chicanas and Chicanos in the doctoral program at the University of California, Berkeley, between 1967 and 1979. She found that, for most of the subjects, "racial, gender, class, and political dislocation personified their experiences" (1993, 170).

21

She shows that the first Chicana and Chicano graduate students at Berkeley were disconnected from majority students in a variety of ways that reflect dislocation or gender and class differences. Most were uncomfortable being the "only one," or "one of a few," Chicanos or students of color in their departments (race or ethnic dislocation). Mainly, Chicanas felt uncomfortable "with the break from their traditional family ideology" (gender). Those from low-income families felt educationally underprepared (class). Many others resented the criticism from faculty members who said they were focusing too much on Chicano studies and politics or incorporating this "questionable subject" into their scholarly research (ethnic, political, and scholarship dislocation). Cuádraz notes that in order to cope with their marginalized conditions, these students adopted an effective survival strategy by forming and/or participating in a variety of academic and social support networks centered around the Mexican American graduate student community (1992, 41; 1993, 170–200).

Patricia Gándara (1995), also interested in the phenomena of Latino student achievement and success, interviewed fifty high-achieving Chicanos and Chicanas who completed doctoral or professional graduate degrees. But unlike the study by Cuádraz, Gándara's research was framed in an educational perspective and focused narrowly on individuals from low-income Mexican American families with little formal education. Looking for insights about "students who don't fail" (1993, 9), Gándara found acculturation-like patterns in their family, social, and precollege educational experiences that were consistent with achievement patterns in most middle-class majority families. In her book, *Over the Ivy Walls* (1993), Gándara reports that she found that—despite conditions of poverty, low parental education, large families, and limited English at home—each subject had developed a strong sense of cultural identity, "self-efficacy," and motivation for achievement as a result of consistent and continual exposure to dual cultural experiences (Mexican American and majority) that shaped his or her worldview toward upward mobility.

For example, these Mexican American families held to more traditional values of authoritarianism, especially for females, but mixed in with this was strong support and encouragement for educational success for all offspring (1993, 26–55). Her subjects also tended to come from public school systems on the edges of the Latino community, and they consequently developed good relationships within dual reference groups. The two groups were their ethnic peers, who were unlikely to go to college, and middle-class majority student peers, who were highly motivated toward college and had experienced parents to guide them. Her study emphasizes that the key to academic success, especially among Latino ethnic minorities, is to deeply ingrain bicultural values and identity within youth by providing them with appropriate bicultural anchoring experiences at critical formative points in their lives.

A review of the current literature highlighted research gaps and trends and yielded important clues about Latinos and Latinas in education. However, I found few qualitative studies of any kind that examined graduate student experiences and no comparative or cross-cultural studies of Latino graduate students or faculty. More than anything else, I noted that none of the Latino-focused studies examined the effects of institutional or academic culture on Latinos or Latinas in graduate education. Though some scholars, such as Cuádraz (1993) and Gándara (1993), recognized the problem, researchers rarely incorporated concepts about academic culture or institutional climate into their research designs (R. Kerlin 1997). From this analysis a framework for my initial Latino study began to take shape.

Current Data on Latino Graduate Degrees

To establish a framework for the research, I needed reliable data in addition to those presented in chapter 1 that show Latinos are not progressing into academe in significant numbers. Most resources confirm that little has changed for Latinos since the 1980s despite their growth in numbers (President's Advisory Commission 1996). I also learned to be cautious about using these data because many sources derive their figures from different data pools or from different configurations of the same data—producing results that are not always easily comparable.[3] Although the data and analysis are accurate, each source has particular idiosyncrasies that prevent researchers from using the data to address a variety of questions. For instance, CGS data from the participating member graduate schools show Latinos accounted for only 5 percent of total student enrollment in 1996 despite a 7 percent average annual increase from 1986 to 1996 (see appendix 2).

One of the important changes shown in the CGS data is the increase in the number of female graduate students. Women today are the new majority, representing almost 55 percent of the total graduate student enrollment among the CGS members surveyed (Syverson and Welch 1997). Latinas and Asian women, who account for 9 percent and 10 percent, respectively, of all graduate students, are increasing faster than any other group, including men (Syverson 1997b, 10; Syverson and Welch 1997, 10; Syverson 1997a).

The U.S. Census Bureau estimates the current Latino population at 3.7 million (or 11.7 percent of the total U.S. population, excluding residents of the Commonwealth of Puerto Rico[4]) and divides it into three categories,

23

the last of which can be subdivided again. According to the bureau, 65.2 percent of all Latinos are of Mexican origin; people of Puerto Rican origin (living on the mainland) account for 9.6 percent of the total Latino population; Cuban Americans, Americans of Central and South American origin, and "other Hispanics" account for 4.3 percent, 14.3 percent, and 6.5 percent, respectively (U.S. Census Bureau 2000, 1).

The increasing number of graduate degrees awarded to Latinos since the late 1980s appears promising despite variations among some Latino ethnic groups. Latinos who were U.S. citizens and permanent residents earned 617 more doctoral degrees in 1998 than in 1989, an increase of 47 percent. The number of doctoral degrees awarded to Puerto Ricans increased by 123 from 1989 to 1998, an increase of 41 percent. Mexican Americans registered an increase of 243 degrees, or a 42 percent, and "Other Latinos" received 251 more doctoral degrees in 1998 than in 1989, an increase of 58 percent, the biggest increase registered (National Science Foundation 2000). This suggests that some progress is being made toward increasing the number of Latinos with doctoral degrees, but is that the best measure of the improvement in Latino diversity in higher education?

For example, a primary goal of most colleges and universities is to increase the diversity of their faculties. One way to measure success is to monitor the awarding of doctoral degrees; recipients of doctoral degrees are more likely to enter the professoriate than are the recipients of other postgraduate degrees (see National Science Foundation 1994, 1996, 1997).[5] But whether Latinos and other minorities are making any headway in the process depends on how you look at available data. Table 2.1 highlights the problem. (The NSF data contain figures for each year between 1989 and 1998, but only the first and last years are included here for comparative purposes.)

Between 1989 and 1998, the number of all doctoral degrees awarded increased annually at a steady pace. While the actual number of degrees awarded increased significantly in almost every group, the percent of majority students receiving doctoral degrees declined steadily over the years. From the numbers of doctoral degrees awarded over the ten-year period, it appears that minorities, especially Asian Americans and Latinos, are making great strides toward enhancing the diversity of the professoriate in the United States. But even that assumption is suspect given that people who were not U.S. citizens—that is, international students for the most part—made the greatest gains of all.

The real problem for minorities is revealed in the percentages. No matter how many more doctoral degrees are awarded to them each year, the percentage of minorities receiving degrees in ratio to the total number awarded is still quite low. Among Latinos the annual data show that the

Table 2.1. Doctoral degrees awarded in all fields by U.S. colleges and universities by ethnicity and citizenship, 1989–1998

Group	Ph.D.s awarded 1989	Ph.D.s awarded 1998	Difference in awards 1989–98	% of total 1989	% of total 1998	Percentage change 1989–98
Majorities	20,894	23,338	+2,444	62.0	57.0	−5.0
Hispanic/Latinos	582	1,190	+ 608	1.7	2.9	1.2
African Americans	822	1,467	+ 645	2.4	3.6	1.2
Asian/Pacific Islanders	633	1,168	+ 535	1.9	2.9	1.0
American Indian/ Alaskan Natives	94	189	+ 95	0.3	0.5	0.2
Non–U.S. citizens*	8,274	11,338	+3,064	24.4	27.8	3.4
Citizenship/ethnicity unknown	2,583	2,164	− 419	7.6	5.3	−2.3
Total	33,882	40,854				

Source: National Science Foundation et al. (1999), *Summary Report 1998: Doctorate Recipients from United States Universities,* appendix table B-2a.

*Includes permanent and temporary visa holders.

percentages have inched up only slightly each year and in 1998 barely attained 3 percent (see also National Science Foundation et al. 1999; NSF 2000). Those data show that percentages have actually remained relatively flat in the ten years considered, suggesting that, contrary to what many believe, Latinos and other minorities have not been keeping up with the increases in doctoral degrees awarded and may actually be losing ground overall.

The most recent data for all master's degrees awarded shows similar patterns. In 1995 only 3 percent went to Latinos, 6 percent to African Americans, 4 percent to Asian Americans (who tend to go straight for doctoral degrees, only rarely stopping to pick up a master's along the way), and 69 percent to majority non-Latinos. American Indians received less than 0.5 percent of all master's degrees in 1995 and 1996 (D. Carter and Wilson 1997; National Science Foundation 1997). Although the percentage of master's degrees going to Latinos has increased 42 percent since 1989, the annual percentage increase in all master's degrees awarded to Latinos has remained at a relatively flat rate of 5 percent since 1989. In real numbers this means that in 1995, 5,772 more Latinos received master's degrees than in 1989, and 397 more Latinos received doctoral degrees in 1996 than in 1987. Yet these numerical gains do not increase the percentage of Latinos who obtain advanced degrees. The data suggest that Latinos are treading water in the graduate degree pools.

A Qualitative Versus Quantitative Research Strategy

In designing my study of Latino graduate students, I chose a slightly unorthodox research strategy and modified design. First, I chose a qualitative approach because few researchers have collected information through personal interviews or observations. I selected a semi-structured interview protocol to allow for more consistency in data collection and flexibility for unbounded inquiry. Finally, instead of aiming the study at one target, that is, a bounded set of characteristics, such as one group (Chicanos), or location (in California), or cohort (current students or completed students only), I expanded my research to cover a broad spectrum of characteristics simultaneously. This expansion included, for example, a variety of Latino groups, generations, occupations, regions of the country, and types of institution.

The only characteristic shared by research participants, other than their ethnicity, was that each had been accepted to and enrolled in a graduate program. Thus all participants were deemed successful because they at least had reached the highest levels of our educational system. Participants were at varying stages in the completion of their graduate programs and on many rungs of the career ladder. Following a semi-structured interview process, and using an appropriate question set, I linked each participant to a common set of graduate experiences. This approach proved more illuminating than I had imagined; the expanded research design created a snapshot of experiences common to five generations. The study not only confirmed the findings of other investigators but its overall design generated a breakthrough for explaining the problems plaguing Latinos and other groups in higher education.

My other reason for choosing a qualitative approach relates to my concerns about finding consistent and reliable data and data that would give me good answers to the kinds of questions I was exploring. Qualitative researchers liken quantitative research to analyzing footprints on a sandy beach. One gathers a great deal of information about what people were doing there, but one can deduce little about why they behaved as they did. Quantitative sociological methodologies have had a major influence on the research on Latinos and other minorities in graduate education, and the analysis of data tends to be highly problem oriented (see, for example, H. Astin et al. 1997; D. Carter and Wilson 1997; Brown 1987, 1988; HERI 1991; Herrnstein and Murray 1994; Justiz et al. 1994; Nettles 1990; Wyche and Frierson 1990; Zwick 1991). Quantitative survey methods seem to yield results faster and provide data that quickly determine trends in what people are doing; this sometimes leads to new insights. But why people are motivated to behave as they do is not so easily determined by quantitative survey methods. Unless researchers re-contact a significant sample of surveyed respondents for in-depth interviews or use other ethnographic observations to validate the findings, quantitative data carry a high risk of misinterpretation. This is especially true among populations of national origins that are different from those in the majority group.

Qualitative analysis, in comparison, takes more time, is more labor intensive, and the results appear to be more subjective. Unfortunately, educators and administrators perceive qualitative issues, such as diversity or student progress, as difficult to measure and evaluate because the various disciplines and departments have no uniform standards for graduate training (S. Kerlin and Smith 1994, 7). Critics claim that qualitative studies generally limit the study of human culture to small groups. Because qualitative studies exclude numerical or statistical measurements, and rely on only one individual's observations and perceptions, quantitative investigators believe qualitative research can lead to the invalidation of the cultural reality of an ethnic group simply because the study lacked objectivity. Anthropologists, however, are careful not to discount the behavior patterns and practical knowledge that non-Western people use to explain and cope with their social worlds. Anthropologists regard these theories as having the same explanatory potential as those ideas we derive from our own academic knowledge and social theory (McCall 1996, 44). But anthropologists must apply rigorous analytical testing even to these seemingly unscientific constructs.

Despite a growing trend toward more qualitative ethnographic research (see F. Padilla 1997), my concern is that current research on ethnic populations in postsecondary education remains too heavily dependent upon too few numerical data to provide the answers we seek about diversity. For example, Bowen and Rudenstine's study, *In Pursuit of the Ph.D.* (1992), now considered a benchmark for research on graduate education, provides more than four hundred pages of data and analysis about degree trends, outcomes (completion and attrition rates), fields of study (programs), and policy recommendations about doctoral degrees and recipients. The authors, however, dedicate only eight pages to analyzing educational patterns among gender and ethnic groups, warning readers that the data are subject to misinterpretation because important differences exist among ethnic populations (1992, 37).

Researchers studying ethnic populations find that data "are rarely collected or disaggregated by ethnic groups, even though significant differences exist between these groups" (O'Brien 1993, 1). In reports that do disaggregate ethnic populations, the data provide useful information about intragroup socioeconomic variations among Latinos—unless, of course, the data are drawn from U.S. Census Bureau reports that do not include residents of Puerto Rico (see NCES 1995; U.S. Census Bureau 2000). Beginning in the early 1980s, various organizations, such as the National Research Council (Thurgood and Clarke 1995), the Ford Foundation (National Research Council 1996a, 1996b, and 1996c), and eventually the Educational Testing Service (Grandy 1994) and the National Science Foundation (1997, 2000), became cognizant of the negative consequences of lumping underrepresented populations into single categories and began to disaggregate ethnic data as much as possible. But quantitative research, even with disaggregated ethnic data, suffers from the limitations of inconsistent collection techniques (see Brown 1987, 1988; Nettles 1990; Wagener 1992; Zwick 1991). Consequently, some research on minority students or faculty in graduate education tends to be predictable, often draws its conclusions from aggregated data, and is usually targeted toward validating the need for pipeline programs and the solutions they offer.

Other Data Collection Problems

The collection of ethnic data on incoming students in higher education has changed little over time and is still a problem for campus administrators as well as researchers. In the past, educational institutions collected data through a voluntary check-box system on appropriate forms, and individuals simply self-identified by checking their "minority," "race," or "ethnicity" status. Today colleges and universities commonly collect and report ethnic data by semi-aggregated race and ethnic categories labeled "African Americans," "Asian Americans," "American Indian and Native Pacific Islanders," "Hispanics," and "other nonwhite populations," in accordance with the categories originally established by the U.S. Census Bureau. Many researchers find semi-aggregated data somewhat useful, even though the sample sizes of ethnic cohorts are still too small for significant sampling and analysis (National Science Foundation 1994, 1996).

Efforts to improve ethnic data collection on campuses are now in jeopardy. For instance, in 1997 the University of Michigan came under pressure from critics of affirmative action when a majority individual sued the institution for discrimination in failing to offer her admission. Shortly thereafter, the university ceased a two-year-old study analyzing by race and ethnicity the grades and test scores of all applicants and those offered admission (Strosnider 1997b).

Data collected in U.S. colleges and universities often ignore cultural differences and assume all ethnic populations act and think alike. The mistake here is assuming that all "minority" behavior is the result of common experiences, such as poor educational opportunities and low socioeconomic status. Thus administrators merge data collected on Mexican Americans, or Chicanos, for example, with that from other distinct Latino populations (e.g., Cuban Americans, Spaniards of European origin, Argentinians, etc.) and then categorize the results under such labels as "Latino and Hispanic" or simply "Minority." Some institutions simply lump students inappropriately, for example, by counting citizens with noncitizens or including groups like Brazilians with Portuguese heritage, who are neither Hispanic nor minority by federal government definitions. Thus the entire data collection process tends to homogenize a great diversity of people and cultures, to conceal important differences between these diverse subgroups, and to lead to dubious inferences about Latinos in general.

Reconceptualizing Culture

Anthropology is renowned for ethnographic research that interprets complex societies. Anthropologists have been criticized justifiably for being too complex, esoteric, and abstract but rarely for being simplistic. Reifying culture, that is, treating cultural abstractions as real, or making them into concrete material things, is an example of the cultural simplicity that permeates the general research perspective in higher education. Concepts of culture, diversity, and ethnicity are treated as solid, uncontested realities about the world. *Culture,* as educational research often defines the term, consists of values, traits, or lists of characteristics that are used to define people. Thus educators interpret culture in their own popular fashion. The term *ethnicity* is never questioned; it is simply defined by using static categories of people with specific identities and characteristics to differentiate one from another. At one extreme "the process of reification has made cultures into cohesive, hard-surfaced units, inside which we picture groups of people as living and thinking in separate worlds" (Limerick 1997, A76). This vision of culture lacks a certain interrelatedness with other cultures and ignores the fact that culture, ethnicity, and diversity are dynamic and changing concepts of human behavior, not pieces of iron.

Fortunately, some anthropologists are studying postsecondary education in the United States, although the majority of educational anthropologists stick close to issues within public and private K–12 systems. In general, nonanthropologists studying higher education use cultural models that have some functional and explanatory power, but most are calcified concepts fixed in time and defined by characteristics that change very little. For instance, campus culture is often perceived as "sets of experiences and traditions that define the characteristics of a particular campus" (Justiz

1994, 12). Thus campus culture consists mainly of concrete things such as curriculums and activities like mentorship that can be inventoried and evaluated. Campus culture is like a barrier that can be overcome, in most cases by increasing the number of minority students and faculty on a campus (Justiz 1994). These are constructs of culture that cannot appropriately describe the dynamics involved in educating culturally diverse populations and, as such, need to be reconceptualized.

Some educational anthropologists pursue an administrative perspective, writing about decision making, systems change, or graduate and academic cultures (Basch et al. 1999; Mitchell-Kernan 1995; Peterson and Spencer 1990; Spain 1995; Upham 1994; Wiedman 1990, 1992). Others examine academic culture from the perspective of the faculty or a department (Tierney 1990; Tierney and Bensimon 1996; M. Williams and Price 1993). All begin with a definition of *culture;* here I use Spradley and Mc-Curdy's definition, which is simply the "acquired knowledge that people use to interpret experience and to generate behavior" (1980, 2). This is a human social heritage that reflects ways of acting and doing things and that is passed on from one generation to the next through both formal and informal methods of teaching and demonstration.

For anthropologists the study of organizational cultures is similar to the study of other complex societies, and, with some exceptions for corporate cultures (see Hamada 1994; Hamada and Sibley 1994), the general concepts of culture and analysis still apply (Aquilera 1996). A more detailed discussion of academic cultures appears in chapter 5 with a discussion about Latino faculty. For now it is enough to define the anthropological perspective as one that examines "deeply embedded patterns of organizational behavior and the shared values, assumptions, beliefs, or ideologies that members have about their organization or its work" (Peterson and Spencer 1990, 3). Academic organizational culture is manifested in a number of arenas, such as the department, the school or college, the institution, and even the discipline within which cultural transactions and interactions take place. Thus within an organization we find not a single culture but a constellation of cultures, or more accurately, subcultures that generate the sociocultural systems of academia.

Of utmost importance is analytical style, which is critical for setting the theme and direction of research outcomes. Anthropology has at least two influences on analytical context, "postmodernism" and "interpretive anthropology"; for different reasons these generate some concern for researching Latinos in higher education. Interpretive anthropology has not influenced me greatly; it suggests that rather than analyze the patterns of cultural behavior, cultural analysis should engage in the "study of the symbolic/expressive dimension of social life" (Wuthnow et al. 1984, 259; see also Geertz 1973). Interpretive anthropology is less involved in learning about why people do what they do and more focused on how to interpret culture through symbolic expressions of culture. (For instance, rather than study the social-cultural conditions that may be implicated in schizophrenia and the effect of this neurological disorder on its victims, one anthropologist has studied the delusional language of homeless schizophrenics [Lovell 1997].) Today this research context pervades the social sciences, especially anthropology. However, interpretative anthropology, as currently construed, is insufficient for the research I undertook.

It is time to reconceptualize culture with new and more explanatory concepts about systems, social process, and cultural patterning from various sources. Such a reconceptualization must begin by establishing empirical and operational methods that are more appropriate for studying diverse groups of people in complex societies. The next step is to identify a dynamic model of social systems and processes that explains *why* people do what they do and couple it with descriptive models to explain *what* they do and *how* they do it. Fredrik Barth offers a useful set of assertions for the analysis of culture in complex societies (1989, 134–41). I have synthesized four of his propositions about culture to use as guidelines for the Latino study, and they became recurring themes for this book:

1. *Cultural meaning is linked to an individual's particular experience, knowledge, and orientation in society.* In terms of studying Latinos in academia, we must pay particular attention to the social context, or the meaning of social interactions between Latino students and/or faculty or any other interactive population within the cultures of higher education. We must identify the social processes within which these populations "intermesh, sometimes with interference, distortion and even fusion" (Barth 1989, 133). Moreover, each Latino group may be characterized by different cultural dynamics. It is in our interest to characterize salient patterns within academia, determine how these patterns are produced and reproduced, how boundaries between groups (e.g., Latinos, Latinas, faculty, administrators, etc.) in academia are maintained, and, finally, to figure out what makes these populations become coherent cultures and subcultures in the community.

2. *Culture is distributed in a population; it is shared by some but not by all others.* People in academia, for instance, may be involved in sets of multiple reality (e.g., international students, tenured faculty, ethnic and gender groups, etc.), and they create different or partial realities for moving in and out of these worlds (Barth 1989, 130). These realities provide a variety of cultural patterns over time, depending on current conditions and circumstances within the institutions. Therefore, cultural reality in academia does not come from any one source or person within the organization. It is our task to identify the systems, models, and processes in order to build a theory about the cultural phenomena we observe (1989, 122).

3. *A person's life experiences and interactive patterns between groups govern that person's position in society* (Barth 1989, 134). No one person can tell us what everything in his or her culture really means—particular concepts within any community are a composite of overlapping perspectives. In the academic community, like society in general, we either relate or do not relate to people with multiple cultural traditions. Positioning is a first step toward devising a model for a number of important social processes. Interactions, associations, and principles of learning are all related to positioning (context) and have important implications for Latinos in academia.

4. *Cultural events are the result of interplays between the material world and social interaction and thus are always in conflict with the intentions of individuals.* In other words, a dynamic view of individual experience and creativity is the result of how actors construe events and how they intend to or actually overcome resistance from others about how culture is generated.

Reconceptualizing Ethnicity

Ethnicity is an increasingly important concept to comprehend in our complex society today. For nonacademics and academics alike, the changing dynamics of ethnicity create challenges for defining and understanding it. When one attempts to incorporate ethnicity within the constructs of culture, context, and cognition, the task becomes even more demanding. Misconceptions about the phenomenon called ethnicity in the United States usually derive from either of two perspectives: one projects ethnicity as some sort of fixed sociocultural entity whose diacritica we can list and whose reality and legitimacy we can evaluate (Patterson 1979; Barth 1969); the other viewpoint believes ethnicity is a modern myth or a purposeful invention (Sollors 1989). In the latter viewpoint, ethnicity is a fictional category that, if taken too seriously, could inflict damage on our society. From this perspective, some authors still propagate the myth that cultural differences are diminishing and ethnicity will disappear over time because of cultural assimilation (Alba 1985; Appiah 1997; Bork 1996; Fox 1996).

The model of ethnicity as a fixed sociocultural entity is the more common perception. It is concrete, reifies cultures, and strives to objectify individuals who identify with populations of different national origins. This model of ethnicity simply assumes that ethnic groups are a cultural reality and, as such, frequently are the underlying mental model of diversity in higher education research. The model of ethnicity as myth posits the opposite view. None of this is real or reified, nor is it some ancient, deep-seated, primordial force located in one's heart that conjures innate bonding among people. Instead, it is a modern invention created for a variety of purposes, not the least of which is economic or political gain and survival. From this postmodern standpoint, ethnicity is represented by transactions between individuals but not perceived as casting people into cohesive ethnic groups. Rather, ethnicity is simply a "perspective onto psychological, historical, social, and cultural forces" (Sollors 1989, xx). Proponents of the idea that ethnicity is a social myth think the concept exists only in the heads of social analysts and not in the hearts of the people they study. Consequently, they would have us believe that the ethnic solidarity associated with events like the recent Cuban American protest to keep a six-year-old Cuban refugee in Miami, or the struggle by Mexican American students in Texas to keep affirmative action policies alive, are not evidence of a functioning and cohesive ethnic group and are nothing more than tools to capture economic gain or political advantage. Such motives certainly drive many activities like these but not enough to disclaim ethnicity as simply a window on social forces.

Among those who discount ethnic identity in our society are those who tend to disregard the need for diversity and multiculturalism in higher education (Bork 1996). Many are convinced that ethnic identity in any form (i.e., Hispanicization, Afrocentrism, tribalization, etc.) is a desperate attempt by "racial groups" in this country to demand socioeconomic parity in the face of diminishing cultural differences and disappearing cultural heritage (Appiah 1997). One example of this limited perspective comes from the Ghanian immigrant K. Anthony Appiah, who wishes to do away with ethnic identity entirely. His attempts to do so demonstrate how he misunderstands the nature of culture and the concepts of ethnicity in this country. He suggests that Americans should dispose of our preoccupation with diversity and cease to use the terms and concepts that define culture as well. "Culture is not the problem, and it is not the solution," he tells us. "So maybe we should conduct our discussions of education and citizenship, toleration and social peace without the talk of cultures" (Appiah 1997, 35).

Another misconception about ethnicity is the belief that cultural heritage and the prominence of ethnic group identity are on the wane or perhaps should be. Stories about how well different immigrant groups assimilated in North America underpinned the teaching of U.S. history during the late 1800s and represent one of the founding myths of American society. The story, we are told, is that shortly after their arrival, immigrant groups and individuals learned English quickly and gave up their old cultural ways for new ones, or at least their children and grandchildren did, and became part of the melting pot of humanity from which was cast a new and powerful nation. This probably never happened as many imagined and, given the adaptive strategies of the humans who voluntarily or involuntarily resettled here, it probably never will. Even tribal populations, with their societies established long before the arrival of any European settlers, were not prone to assimilating multicultural customs. In fact, despite intense proselytizing by Western religions in the southwestern United States, most tribal nations there have held on to their own belief systems.

The reality of our European immigrant history in the United States is more myth than history. Instead of giving up their cultural ways, immigrant groups selectively adopted cultural customs that suited them while maintaining their original ones. For instance, some ethnic communities in the late 1800s were in fact bilingual (English and language of origin), even in school. But the impression given to outsiders was of a predominantly English-speaking community. This phenomenon continued well into the twentieth century, and some communities have changed little in this regard since their founding (Ibarra 1976).

Rather than assimilate, many immigrants were motivated by cultural, social, or economic incentives to create adaptive strategies to enhance or preserve their cultural resources, their cultural capital. Adopting bilingualism with a monolingual façade is simply one successful strategy for preserving a native language. These dynamics are still occurring today. Bennett (1969, 1975) describes similar adaptive behaviors in his study of ranchers, farmers, tribal populations, and Hutterites who coexist in a rural community in Canada. The strategies became coping mechanisms for dealing with various people, situations, and resources. If given a choice of alternative economic strategies, for instance, living off the land or using it for animal husbandry or collective cultivation to increase its productivity, individuals will try to create effective ways to adjust to their social and economic situations by any number of processes related to "problem-solving, decision-making, consuming or not consuming, inventing, innovating, migrating or staying," and so on (Bennett 1969, 11). For instance, choosing which system of food production is best for the ranching-farming community in Canada is greatly influenced by ethnic cultural predilections. This model does not assume that every decision or strategy is entirely rational from every perspective, for the strategies that groups and individuals adopt might in fact *seem* illogical and ill suited for either their success or survival in the long term. Hutterites farm collectively, for example, and much like Amish communities in the United States, they appear to be cultural anachronisms with limited economic futures. They prefer a less technologically advanced lifestyle and tend to shun modern conveniences. Yet their communities, like many Amish communities in North America, continue to thrive and grow.

However, risk aversion is one assumption usually built into adaptive strategies. For the most part, people who select cultural strategies generally do so in hope of reducing risk and minimizing adverse outcomes. Avoiding maladaptive strategies or even adopting radically new ones could prove less risky if people track the success or failure of other groups and individuals. If they can learn successful strategies from others with similar cultural backgrounds, like the Amish and the Hutterites, so much the better. This somewhat entrepreneurial model views "ethnicity as a variable affecting a variety of behaviors rather than some sort of fixed socio-cultural entity" (Strickon and Ibarra 1983, 174).

The fluctuating nature and character of ethnicity is not a cultural anomaly. For example, it might be incorrect to suggest that the loss of Spanish among second-generation Latinos in California confirms that they are "thinning out culturally" in the same way that majority ethnic groups have in the past (Appiah 1997, 32). This phenomenon does not necessarily signal the eminent decline of ethnic identity or that cultural heritage is disappearing among Latino populations. Rather, it could reflect fluctuating cultural differences, in this case between generations, that are a natural outcome of choice and changing adaptive strategies. Unfortunately, these cultural variances are often prejudged by others as either bad or good. In fact, they are neither. They are merely adaptive strategies for coping with and adjusting to the social, cultural, and economic situations and available resources.

Ethnicity can be perceived as sets of strategies and behaviors that are currently successful for particular groups or individuals, and they can be changed rather quickly. Let me clarify this concept by restating what my colleague and I have presented elsewhere:

We consider ethnicity to be a general term for a wide variety of social phenomena which are exhibited by people who share (or believe they share) a common cultural-historical background (Greeley 1972, 7–9) and who contrast themselves with other people of a different background within the same socio-political order. From this point of view no effect can be attributed to ethnicity *per se,* as a dimension in its own right, but only to the manifestations of the shared heritage. These manifestations may include one or more of the following: (a) an expressed self-identification by some or all of the individuals constituting an "ethnic" population; (b) the cultural content not shared with surrounding populations such as artifacts, symbols, values and institutions which represent (or are believed to represent) the persistence of a shared cultural heritage; (c) formal organizational arrangements such as political and/or economic interest groups. (Strickon and Ibarra 1983, 174)

The fundamental principles in our construct are choice, flexibility, and adaptation. One way to actively demonstrate these functions among Latinos is to compare them to the latest model for explaining ethnic variability. Based on somewhat contradictory concepts of assimilation and creative adaptations, Fox (1996) proposes that a new national ethnic identity is being constructed, the "Hispanic Nation." The author claims that old regional, racial, and political differences among Mexican Americans, Puerto Ricans, Cuban Americans, and other Spanish language-sharing groups are giving way (assimilating) to a new consciousness now forming into a single ethnic community. New nationalists—he labels them *pan-Hispanicists*—are intentionally using a variety of forces to unify the different ethnic populations. Fox claims the various media (e.g., television, newspapers, radio) are the powerful influences that plant these ideas and then nurture them into a sense of unity among Latinos. He believes the Latino media help construct the Hispanic Nation in four ways: by creating the imagery of an imagined community; by hiring Latino professionals; perhaps by mobilizing listeners or viewers to take appropriate action; and, finally, by shaping a continent-wide, North American Spanish dialect (Fox 1996, 65).

In essence, Fox proposes that Latinos are forming a new adaptive strategy that is symbolized by the emergence of a new nation and a new pan-ethnic identity. Then he writes:

Even so, Hispanics may eventually go the way of their predecessors, the German Americans, who long clung to their language and distinctive customs. As recently as the 1950's, after two wars against Germany and forty years since the end of large-scale German immigration, there were still towns and counties in the United States where a modified form of German was the language of community life. But with the exception of these pockets, by mid-twentieth century the German Americans "would become the only large ethnic group to disappear as a serious ethnic political force." (1996, 65–64)

In light of our model of ethnicity, Strickon and I would agree with Fox on only a couple of points. A national consciousness could be forming among Latinos in this country, and a concerted effort by various media could play a significant role in achieving that end. However, we differ in the belief that this transformation signals any cultural displacement by way of assimilation or that Latinos will "go the way" of their German American predecessors and disappear as a "serious ethnic political force." In the first place, contrary to popular belief, many northern European populations that settled in various pockets throughout the country, including the German Americans, did not disappear from the fabric of our national cultures. In fact, they are still viable ethnic communities today; in the case of German Americans, I would speculate some may still play a significant political role, though not as overtly as many would expect.

These arguments are based upon my own research findings among Norwegian Americans in Wisconsin. That work not only substantiates my propositions but also, oddly enough, provides important insights that confirm the transformational nature of Latino ethnicity in graduate education (Ibarra 1976; Ibarra and Strickon 1989; Strickon and Ibarra 1983). For the nearly 150 years since their arrival in the Midwest, Norwegian Americans, who like to call themselves Norwegians, have been living in a geographic swathe of communities from southern Wisconsin to the Dakotas, roughly following the course of the Mississippi River toward the north-west. Wisconsin, like many states in the region, is dotted with communities of northern European settlers in this predominantly rural region of family-run farms.

My research among Norwegians in Westby, Wisconsin, a small dairy and tobacco-growing community near La Crosse, discovered rich layers of ethnic identities, including "immigrant Norwegian," "rural American," and "commercialized Norwegian" cultures that at first seemed mutually exclusive (Ibarra 1976).[6] In fact, they were far more inclusive and some-what flexible ethnic transformations. Each of these identities was a per-fectly acceptable cultural adaption displayed in one way or another by nearly everyone in the community. The three Norwegian cultural adapta-tions are a microcosm of ethnic dynamics in this country. Norwegian im-migrant culture never really disappeared; it simply transformed into new modalities as second, third, and fourth generations adopted a variety of rural American lifestyles.

What does all this have to do with Latino ethnicity? Probably a great deal. It is very likely that if Latino populations continue to grow in this country, a form of Latino national consciousness, similar to the commer-cialized Norwegian culture, would be appropriate and actually may be emerging among Latinos now in their twenties and thirties, according to a recent issue of *Newsweek* (see Larmer 1999; Leland and Chambers 1999). It would simply become another variety of social phenomenon to share with others. Establishing such a national consciousness does not preclude the demise of other social phenomena, as Fox would have us believe, be-cause it is exhibited by people who share (or believe they share) a common cultural-historical background. That is a stylized exhibition of assumed cultural phenomena. Among Latinos, this would mean continuance of Mexican American, Puerto Rican, Cuban American, and other identities of national origin. This is no different than the Norwegians around Westby who exhibit sharp distinctions among themselves, depending upon which region in Norway their ancestors came from—Gudbrandsdal, the Sogn, Flekkefjord, and so on.

Even if the social phenomenon we call ethnicity transforms into a com-mercialized ethnic phenomenon, it is no less legitimate and no less ethnic than county fairs or other commercial ventures that play upon cultural phenomena for economic or social gain. What I argue here is that, like the Norwegians of Westby, a national consciousness, be it American or La-tino, is one of a number of potential adaptive strategies for incorporating a repertoire of behavioral phenomena. Given that premise, Latinos will not likely "go the way of their German American predecessors," as Fox suggests. As Latinos, we carry multiple identities with us and use them to identify with a variety of cultural constituents in our society. It is the nature of our multicultural world (Trueba 1999).

The anthropologist Susan Keefe and the psychologist Amado Padilla (1987) did an excellent study of Chicano ethnicity that confirms the interconnectedness of Latino culture and ethnic identity. They examined the complex interrelationship of assimilation, acculturation, and ethnic identity among Mexican Americans from several counties in southern California. Their conclusions closely align with my findings among Norwegian Americans in Wisconsin. That is, Keefe and Padilla see "culture change *and* ethnic persistence occurring simultaneously" within their study group (1987, 191). Among their respondents, Keefe and Padilla found "situational ethnicity," which is similar to the Norwegian Americans I found to have immigrant, rural American, and commercialized Norwegian identities. Sometimes Keefe and Padilla's respondents were part of the larger society, demonstrating their knowledge of American culture as "Mexican *Americans*," and other times they were "American *Mexicans*," carrying on traditional cultural values and reflecting ethnic pride in their heritage. But in other contexts they were "Chicanos, practicing new and emerging cultural patterns and sustaining an ethnic community set apart [from] both Anglos and recent immigrant Mexicans" (1987, 190).

Their data found limited support for acculturation processes or no support for assimilation models. What Keefe and Padilla found is that if Mexican Americans exhibit acculturation, it is selective and multidimensional. Rather than apply the term *bicultural,* to suggest a duality of ethnic traits, Keefe and Padilla preferred to introduce the term *cultural blends* to describe their respondents. From interviews they found Mexican Americans clearly favor those things associated with their Mexican heritage but selectively participate within all three ethnic identities—American, Chicano, and Mexican American (1987, 80). The authors noted that individuals, with certain preferences toward variable cultural characteristics selected within several situational ethnic identities, felt no less Mexican American, for example, if they were less proficient in Spanish or if they identified less with Chicano politics and had more non–Mexican American friends. Yet cultural blends were neither marginalized members of their ethnic group nor equally proficient in both Anglo and Mexican cultures (1987, 95–96).

These important distinctions suggest that across an array of ethnic groups are individuals who exhibit a variety of cultural preferences within perhaps at least two cultural contexts and at least two cognitive learning styles. The intermixture of these patterns found among Latinos in academia, for instance, is likely to be closely associated with similar findings among the Mexican American respondents in the study by Keefe and Padilla. Thus cultural blending is one adaptive strategy for accommodating multiple ethnic identities (e.g., Mexican, American, or Mexican American) that many ethnic populations exhibit in this country today.

The evidence for a collective ethnic identity drawn from a unique historical ancestry is more common in this country than we realize. Our national perspective, our tunnel vision about the historical blending of ethnic identities, prevents us from seeing these phenomena beyond certain segments of our society, like the isolated enclaves of Norwegian Americans in Wisconsin or the struggling Chicano communities in California. Ethnic blending is characteristic of many groups, including African Americans as well as Irish or English Americans. The last are often among "those people written about on the social pages of the *New York Times* who trace their ancestry to pre-Revolutionary America" (Walens 1975, 276). Neville (1975) suggests that a sense of collective ethnic identity can be found among mainstream southern Presbyterians in this country. Walens depicts the romanticized version of the "Old West" in America as a collective ethnic identification that blends myth with historical reality (1975). The growth of Old West tourism in many locations, such as Virginia City, Nevada; Dodge City, Kansas; or Durango, Colorado, is founded on principles identical to those that sparked the Norwegian American ethnic revivals in Westby, Wisconsin, and the developing multiple ethnic identities among Chicanos in California. Thus, even in the mainstream of American culture steeped in the Old West lies an adaptive strategy for blending historical reality, myth, and commercialization into multiple ethnic realities.

For Latinos in academia these fundamental concepts of ethnic identity also hold true. That there are multiple and concurrent ethnic identities was one of the constructs I knew to be a vital dynamic among rural Norwegian Americans in Wisconsin, and it appears that the same holds true for Mexican Americans. Even more critical is the growing literature that clearly shows the importance of ethnic identity. Latinos, for example, are "interested in education, but not at the expense of losing their Latino identity or culture" (Hurtado et al. 1992, 36). Trueba suggests the emergence of this new solidarity and resiliency among young Latino professionals is "profoundly related to the construction of a new ethnicity and a new identity, without necessarily rejecting other identities" (1999, 9). It has evolved beyond the principle of accommodation without acculturation to produce "a complex change of personal identities and collective identities over several generations for economic and political goals" (1999, 90). Signs of this change are surfacing in a variety of ways: the successful attempts by Latinos in southern California to vote out of office entrenched members of Congress, the growing popularity among general U.S. audiences of Latino music and major films about Latino or Mexican culture, and, finally, the obvious political influence of Cuban Americans in Miami to maintain the U.S. embargo of Cuba (see Larmer 1999).

The Conflict over Identity Pools Versus Identity Pigeonholes

My research on ethnic identity in the United States examines Latinos from all across the nation, across decades of experience, and in a variety of schools and institutions. From their perspective, *ethnicity* is a general term for a wide variety of social phenomena expressed as any combination of self-identification and cultural content (i.e., values, artifacts, institutions) not shared with other populations. These social phenomena are not some static primordial construct that comes merely from the heart (Banks 1996); rather, from what I have seen, these are fluid and dynamic and are derived from adaptive strategies (Barth 1967). But I soon realized that graduate education is ignoring the ethnic diversity among Latino populations, and the process of completing an advanced degree tends to homogenize Latinos ethnically. Consequently, the entire process misses some important cues about why they are having difficulties.

When Latinos enter higher education, they have most likely been influenced by a socially constructed group associated with an identity of national origin (i.e., Mexican, Puerto Rican, Cuban, etc.). That process is an accumulation of experiences and social transactions in which they learned about who they are compared to others and how they should deal with people outside their ethnic group. At this social boundary between groups, behavioral episodes define and shape one's adaptive cultural strategies (Barth 1969; Bennett 1969; Ford 1992). The boundaries are not walls that contain cultural content but are merely useful devices for distinguishing between two or more other things or groups (Banks 1996). Ethnic groups depend on this interchange for identity, even though it is the boundary that defines the group and not the cultural content. Ultimately, the activity of making transactions and decisions among individuals or groups of individuals leads to successful strategies in using ethnicity and the ethnic group as a resource in adapting to the larger society.

The concept of ethnic identity that education imposes on Latinos and other ethnic minorities creates conflict in those who enter universities or graduate schools. This conflict originates from contradictory mind-sets that perceive ethnicity as being either static or fluid groupings—identity pools or identity pigeonholes. An identity pool is a cognitive identity structure determined by a multitude of behaviors and many conditions—cultural values, preferences, language, intellectual interests, and so on—that Latinos, among others, perceive and use almost unconsciously on a daily basis. This is clearly an adaptive construct with changing boundaries. Its fluid and changing nature can be likened to a pool, or pools, of identity in which ethnicity, gender, social roles, social status, and the like are interrelated. The combination of conditions and behaviors is much like a mixture of different kinds of liquid in a container or a pond (e.g., viscous, opaque, colored, heavy with suspended particles, hot, boiling, cold, frozen, etc.) that can react to changes in the environment and fit or form its boundaries to accommodate situations. It may or may not always adapt well to meet all conditions, however.

Pigeonhole ethnicity, on the other hand, represents the rigid identity system that Latinos encounter when they enter the world of academia, among others, and it places them in contrived categories and endows them with preconceived characteristics and stereotypes. Those who perceive ethnicity as a pigeonhole of compartmentalized identity have difficulty comprehending the changing nature of identity pools. The systems use similar terminology but represent very different concepts of ethnicity. Consequently, for Latinos both identity systems cause tension and conflict, sometimes for entirely different reasons. The result is confusion and misunderstanding between groups, for no one posts cultural rules or road maps to show these differences.

Many Anglos are oblivious to the confusion and ethnic stereotyping that surrounds them. Comments about how well someone speaks English or how they don't appear to be Latino (or African American, or Asian American, and so on) are reactions to some common misperceptions about ethnic groups in this country. For instance, many Anglos assume that most ethnics are foreigners or recent immigrants and are surprised when someone has no accent or cannot speak his language of ethnic origin fluently. Few Anglos are aware of ethnic differences among groups. Latinos should appear and act like Mexican Americans, or all Asian Americans like Japanese, or all Native Americans like Plains Indian tribes in the Midwest, and so on, because those are the images most commonly used to portray specific ethnic populations in this country. Most confusing are the cultural blends, with identities and behaviors that represent a variety of ethnic and cultural characteristics. Latinos who perform successfully in multiple languages, or who are not typecast as ethnic actors, are usually skilled in cultural blending. The entertainment industry calls them "crossover" stars, and their success is open to ethnic confusion, as Marc Anthony, a Puerto Rican who is a rising star in Latin pop music, can relate. When a magazine placed a jalapeño pepper beside his picture, he exclaimed, "Jalapeños are Mexican. I've never eaten one in my life. . . . This whole crossover wave thing really displaces me," he says. "Like I'm coming in and invading America with my music. I was born and raised in New York" (Leland and Chambers 1999, 54).

The fact is, minorities are exposed to the identity system at a very early age and may confront it before they enter school. They simply are not aware of it until they are challenged about who they are and about their ethnic identity in the educational system, or they become fully conscious of it by crashing headlong into the rigid walls of the school system. That can happen at any time and at any place during their primary, secondary, or postsecondary education. Sometimes they may not even realize what is happening at the time. What they experience is often described as an uncomfortable sense of being pigeonholed, or circumscribed, by a concept of identity that has little relationship to how they actually behave or perceive themselves in society.

This concept of sociocultural identity labels and boxes groups of students in presumed categories with static behavioral characteristics. Such rigid, often ill-fitting, constructs mislead some researchers into believing that ethnicity is fiction, invented for sociopolitical purposes (see M. Burgess 1978; Hobsbawm 1983; Hobsbawm and Ranger 1992; Sollors 1989; Steinberg 1989). Quite the opposite construct, which I will discuss again in part II, suggests that turbulence and discord between individuals as they interact and transact with each other is not only a conflict of different cultural contexts and cognition but also in part a conflict generated within students who come from identity pools yet must reckon with identity pigeonholes within an educational system.

The chapters that follow highlight the experiences of these Latinos throughout the educational system and beyond. Although they belong to a combination of groups fast becoming the largest ethnic population in the United States, we still have little information about them in higher education. We have seen data that show that, despite slight increases in recent decades, Latinos are essentially treading water in academia. I will argue this is partially the result of two conflicting cultural forces: the influence of culture and ethnicity imprinted on individuals in childhood by family and community, and a second set of cultural forces that reshapes them throughout their precollege and postsecondary educational experiences. I develop the dynamics of this concept, which I present as a new empirical model, in chapter 3. The findings come from students, academics, and nonacademics as they reflect upon their educational or career experiences and how they believe those experiences affected them. The consensus about their individual experiences seems to validate their collective perceptions and provides a starting point for discussing and reassessing graduate education in general.

3

Multicontextuality

A Hidden Dimension in Higher Education

> It is *not* that [people] must be in sync with, or adapt to [their] CULTURE but that CULTURES grow out of sync with [*people*]. . . . *PEOPLE* must learn to transcend and adapt their CULTURE to the times. . . . To accomplish this . . . [people need] the EXPERIENCE of other CULTURES.
>
> Adapted from Edward T. Hall, *Beyond Culture*

Common Assumptions

Something is unique about the difficulties experienced by some Latinos in graduate education. In a preliminary report of my findings for the Council of Graduate Schools, I noted that more than half the Latino participants, both students and faculty, completed their degree with relatively few educational setbacks (Ibarra 1996). Yet a little more than half said they experienced "difficulties" in graduate school in dealing with the differences in how they and the majority of their colleagues perceived the world. These issues were unrelated to health, finances, family, or other life circumstances, but they were brought on by friction with majority individuals. Many Latino students found that something about their cultural experiences contrasted sharply with the cultural experiences of their majority colleagues in graduate education. As respondents became more involved with academia, the conflicts intensified. Even then, they did not consider them obstacles to their educational progress.

Latino students often expressed these conflicts as intense ethnic and gender tensions beyond the usual problems encountered by graduate students. They frequently associated the problems with the graduate faculty, which is not unusual. The apprenticeship model in graduate school rests on the skill of faculty advisers to remold their graduate students and prepare them for advanced research, teaching, and perhaps even an academic career. Among university faculty and administrators, it is common knowledge that many diverse populations have more educational difficulties than majority populations. What is not commonly understood is why these difficulties occur and how to prevent them.

The current widely held assumption is that difficulties encountered by minorities, including Latinos, are the result of barriers and obstacles that, if removed, would allow success. To help remove barriers institutions may advance multicultural initiatives that heighten cultural awareness, change the curriculum, or provide cultural centers that celebrate diversity. Based on the dominant assumptions, I originally set out to identify the barriers. But I found that, while the barriers are still pervasive (see Gloria and Pope-Davis 1997), removing them did not necessarily lead to success.

Minorities on campus often assume that chronic tension between cultures emanates from either individual or institutional discrimination. As a result, they associate prejudice with any behavior, from preference to overt hatred and even violence. Prejudice could explain individual behaviors, of course, but I propose another theory of institutional discord. Other forces—in a hidden dimension—are at work and they exhibit characteristics similar to the venerable *isms* of discrimination. Our ability to distinguish them, however, is clouded by the common belief that racism, sexism, and classism are the primary discordant forces that permeate our institutional cultures. Because we have no viable data or alternative models to explain it, by default "racial disharmony" has become locked in the academic psyche as the only explanation for the institutional disorder of chronic cultural dissonance.

Why are these problems so pervasive? Why is there still conflict when the barriers and obstacles are supposedly removed? Is institutional racism the only answer after all? For answers to these questions we must search for explanations from another perspective. What if the problems are not only "things" that are there—barriers and obstacles—but also "things" that are not there, factors that do not involve multicultural issues and that are missing from our educational systems in general? We always look at the words on a page when we read, and some of us are adept at reading between the lines, but what about examining the white spaces, the gaps between words and letters? That approach would examine the gaps between cultures, to see what is there or whether anything is missing.

Many of us in higher education take for granted that our traditional models of reality are still valid because they appear to explain cause and effect. We may be reluctant to acknowledge that we have grown accustomed to thinking that racism is a predominant condition in higher education. This chapter begins to reexamine that model of reality by looking at research transcripts with a new perspective to try to determine what is missing from the academic systems that cause conflict for Latinos and Latinas—and, by extension, members of other minority groups.

The Complexity of Defining Racism

Nearly everyone in the study touched upon issues or personal experiences relating to some kind of cultural conflict in their lives. A little more than half the participants described targeted forms of discrimination such as racism, sexism, xenophobia, or the like. About one-third of them actually labeled their experiences as racism, although interviewees described clear examples of gender discrimination and others that may have been class discrimination.

But other subjects were simply not sure. For example, Anita, a Puerto Rican student from New York, told me, "When you talk about issues like racism, it's so complicated and so subtle. It wasn't really direct, but it was just all the little things that happened. I am not sure if it's only an issue of racism because I know other students had trouble too, and they weren't people of color, so it's complicated" (Ibarra 1996, 47). Some were less concerned about racism than they were about conflicting values, specifically academic cultural values. Discrimination seemed to be an insufficient explanation for their experiences.

Racism is a slippery concept, especially when tied to common ideas about race. Most anthropologists discard the idea of various biological human "races" because the term is loaded with inaccurate biological connotations that conflict with social concepts of culture and ethnicity. The concept of race is a social phenomenon throughout the world (M. Cohen 1998b), but hardly anyone can agree on what sociocultural characteristics constitute a human race or how to distinguish that from the concept of ethnicity.[1] From a historical and sociological perspective, race in its current social context seems appropriate for distinguishing certain populations from others in this country, with the exception of Hispanics. But Latinos, unlike all other groups, are not defined by race and are the only officially designated ethnic group in the U.S. Census (OMB 1997; U.S.

Census Bureau 1995).[2] Thus *Hispanic* is simply an ethnic category that lumps together groups differentiated by their various national origins.

Building an Alternative Perspective

As I sifted through the transcripts of my interviews with Latinos in higher education and looked at them with a different perspective, trends emerged that related to discrimination between Latino students and Latino faculty. Not surprisingly, students' complaints centered around faculty, though they did not always attribute racism, sexism, or other types of discrimination as the cause for their conflicts. One reason for this was their reluctance to suggest that Latino professors are racist or discriminate against Latino students. Yet I heard stories that criticized Latino and Latina faculty for overt racism and sexism in regard to Latino students. A number of female students described how their female faculty advisers took advantage of them or their research. In each case students were perplexed and unable to explain why Latino or women professors behaved contrary to the students' expectations of socially sensitive people.

In contrast, the Latino faculty I interviewed were forthright in their claims of discrimination by members of the majority. Regardless of class or ethnicity, Latino faculty, and especially women, faced more conflict and felt more tension within academia than they did as graduate students. Faculty are faced with a different process—negotiating their way into the academic culture as colleagues. And it seems to be even more difficult than life as a graduate student. But in discussing their experiences, they were using different explanatory terms. They were talking about culture rather than racism.

Thus something other than racial tension was creating conflict and dissonance for both Latino students and faculty. Because of the existing tensions between Latino students and Latino faculty as well as between Latino faculty and their colleagues, what they were talking about appeared to be associated with academic cultural values. It centered around transformations of ethnic and gender identity. As I concluded in my preliminary report:

For Latino graduate students, the transition toward completing the degree begins by recognizing that a cultural gap exists between their specific ethnic/cultural values and the dominant values of academic subcultures: departmental, disciplinary, institutional, and so on. Whether because of ethnicity, gender or other conditions, this transition is intensified by the turbulence of acculturation into academe. For some, ethnic research bridges the cultural gap by providing a means to maintain their specific Latino ethnicity while simultaneously adopting the mantle of the academy. For others, ethnic interests can only surface after completing the degree.

Utilizing a successful adaptive strategy, many Latinos pursue ethnic research to ameliorate the forces of academic acculturation by becoming ethnic cultural brokers and professors too, thus attempting to create a successful blending of cultures. Shaped by the cultural grinding wheel of academia, only a few Latinos and Latinas, imbued with successful adaptive strategies for accumulating multiple ethnic identities, emerge from their graduate experience ready to pursue a commitment to both their cultural and academic communities. (1996, 57–58)

Roberta-Anne Kerlin describes similar findings in her dissertation, "Breaking the Silence: Toward a Theory of Women's Doctoral Persistence" (1997), in which she followed women through one year of their graduate education. In the process of gaining an "academic self-identity," her subjects were "reluctant to submit to a process" that would make them "the kind of person who puts a private agenda first and the needs of the larger academic community, including students, last" (13). For Kerlin this discord was symptomatic of a competitive power relationship between advisers and students.

Contributions of Anthropology—The "Hidden Dimension"

But inequitable power relationships explain only a small portion of the puzzle. It was Pedro who revealed the first set of clues for decoding the rest of it. Pedro was a Mexican American graduate student studying for his degree at a university in Texas. He was frustrated by "the system" and during his interview acknowledged that he had been trying to educate his professors about the nuances of Latino culture. He also questioned whether he should stay in the program. In his own words he interpreted "communication breakdowns" between him and his professors as cultural gaps, which I have underlined in the following passage:

I had difficulty with one assistant professor in my area about cultural things. We've had some <u>communication breakdowns.</u> . . . It is hard for me to try to explain this because he was saying some very rude things like "[Pedro] you ought to consider dropping out of the program. You need to write [your papers in] active voice.". . . I said, . . . "I know I need to write in active voice, but . . . I think in passive voice. . . ." I tried to explain something like "the bullet fell," rather than "I dropped the bomb . . ." and he wasn't interested in that. I remember once telling him . . . "Maybe my communication hasn't been too direct." I [explained] about how Mexicans tend to [talk] around [the subject using] <u>indirect communication.</u>

. . . There's [saving] face involved in all this, and he says, . . . "<u>[Pedro] I prefer to be very direct; that way there's no backstabbing.</u>" . . . It was just a series of things, one comment after another. Then he talked to the [department] chair and said, . . . "I don't think [Pedro] is a very good candidate." . . . He's been the only person in the whole department that I have had problems with, who I felt was actively thinking, . . . "[Pedro] is really not the person we want to have here." I remember one time he said, . . . "You may know a lot about Mexico, but that's not going to get you through the program,". . . comments that weren't even elicited, and I wondered what I had said or done that prompted him to say that. There was one time that he said, . . . "[Pedro] when I used to be [in the private sector], I would spell out the worst scenario for the people who are going to be my assistants . . . and those people who listened to the darkest things, and stuck around, found out it wasn't really that bad and they became top performers."

[He is] a very <u>competitive</u> type guy. . . . I was thinking he probably didn't have too many Mexican Americans or women work for them [the private sector], because <u>there's a certain amount of relationship building.</u> He's very cold at times. I just haven't been real happy with him. Crazy as it is, I have a comp [comprehensive exam] about a week from tomorrow, and he is writing the questions. . . . I know that he had problems with [international] students . . . with language abilities and I think . . . this is just open hostility. . . . I brought it up to my department chair and he said, . . . "<u>This is not a cultural problem. What you're talking about is a personality problem."</u> . . . And I said, . . . "I'd like for them to treat me the way I'd like to be treated, because I know that the people that he's worked with are <u>very competitive</u> . . . there isn't that <u>emotional tie between people.</u> . . ." I said, "I'd like some nurturing and this is the way I work," and so on. . . . "Well, [Pedro], you're not going to get that here. It just doesn't work. . . ." That's what my department chair told me. . . . I find insensitivity, just the lack of bringing sensitive people in. You see <u>people [here] that are just not sensitive to Mexicans."</u> (Ibarra 1996, 45–46)

Pedro attempted to explain to his professors the differences between Mexican Americans and Anglos in regard to communication, competition, and relationships between people, so that they could understand the hidden dimension of the conflict that is engaging him. Implicit in his comments are profound differences in fundamental cultural values regarding human interaction, associations, and learning. Pedro clearly understood the nuances of his Mexican American ethnic culture and how they contrasted with the academic cultures associated with the faculty in his department. Pedro spoke English fluently and exhibited all the appropriate visible cultural cues for living seamlessly within the dominant academic cultural community. Yet Pedro, and many other Latinos like him, assumed the imprint of Mexican cultural values was not noticeable to the professors in his department. He was motivated to explain his behavior only when he believed his professors misinterpreted these values and when these hidden cultural elements appeared to be undermining his academic success in graduate school.[3]

Later in his interview, when I asked him about major issues for Latinos on his campus, Pedro responded, "Sensitivity to the culture, level of development and a sense of . . . where our community is coming from. But I don't see it as a race issue. . . . I think it's cultural in the way of . . .

48

cognitive-type things, and the way that you perceive them." Transcripts from other students' interviews revealed similar underlying patterns and concerns. This was no longer just reading the words, or reading between the lines; this was reading what was missing in the white spaces of graduate education. In telling his story, Pedro pointed to an alternative explanation, one that finds support in two bodies of theory. He was describing patterns of *cultural context* as first described by the anthropologist Edward T. Hall, a pioneer in the field of intercultural communication in the late 1950s and early 1960s. Pedro was also reflecting patterns of *bicognition,* a cognitive learning pattern described by the clinical psychologists Manuel Ramírez and Alfredo Castañeda that they developed about the same time Hall began his work on cognition.

Implications of Cultural Context

Hall's construct of culture is basically descriptive and somewhat organic. He believed that patterns of cultural behavior are extensions of our basic biological processes, including the senses (vision, olfaction, touch) and cognition (perceptions of time and space). As such, culture is not a single entity but a complex set of associated and interlinked systems that mold and shape (in ways that are not unlike imprinting) individuals within groups, and this process begins at birth (1974, 1993). Thus, he says, people raised in different cultures live in different sensory worlds usually unconscious of how these worlds differ (1959). For Hall, one framework for shaping one's perceptual world is the process of learning how people are expected to think and behave within a specific cultural or ethnic group. Another framework is a function of social transactions, relationships, activities, or emotional interactions between various people both inside and outside the group. He notes that when "people of different cultures interact, each uses different criteria to interpret the other's behavior, and each may easily misinterpret the relationship, the activity, or the emotions involved" (1974, 2). Until they learn otherwise, such individuals assume they share a "correct" interpretation of reality from within their respective worldviews, whether or not they really know how things work.

Hall launched the multidimensional science of proxemics, which studies how people use personal and public space as a function of culture—social distance, interior and exterior design, urban planning, and so on (Hall 1966, 1984, 231; Hall and Hall 1990). Very briefly, it entails observing in context sequences of common or frequent human interactions, such as personal conversations, formal interviews, or greeting behaviors between strangers or friends. These behaviors may be embedded in activities associated with learning situations at school or ordinary daily transactions such as purchasing items in a store. The ultimate purpose of the observation is to uncover new cultural meaning and knowledge. Hall wanted to know *how* people in the context of their different worldviews would communicate, interact, associate, and learn. He seemed particularly interested in culling new insights by focusing on the unconscious cultural behaviors embedded in nonverbal communication.[4] His work generated new fields of study and important concepts about communication, cognition, ethnicity, and cultural context.

I used two interrelated concepts for analyzing the interviews: Hall's ten cultural systems of human activity and their interplay within his binary model of high- and low-context cultures. These are described in table 3.1 at the end of this chapter. Pedro's comments suggest the cultural systems Hall called "primary message systems," which concentrate on language and nonverbal forms of communication (1959, 45–60). Hall identified ten basic elements, or sets, of learned cultural behavior that lend themselves to observation and the communication of *overt* and *covert* meaning.[5] Overt behaviors are the outward, visible, and mainly conscious components of culture, such as speech, dress, art, customs, and so on. These are often associated with formal, structured, and expected social behaviors, the "rules of the game," be it poker, writing, football, or driving a car. Covert behaviors are the less obvious components of culture that contain "the most important paradigms or rules governing behavior, the ones that control our lives, function below the level of conscious awareness and [are] not generally available for analysis" (Hall 1977, 43).

These hidden dimensions of cultural elements and meaning, no less structured than overt behaviors, are usually informal ways of doing things. They are generated by unspoken rules or expected codes of behavior within societies. They may even consist of informal customs that allow individuals to bend the rules or go around the official way of doing things in society. These unwritten rules communicate what, when, why, and how to do things or signal relationships between individuals. For example, overt greeting behavior, in private or public places, may include a handshake, a bow, a hug, or a combination of these among different cultures. But how they are executed, by whom or to whom, contains cultural codes that reveal status, intent, or other relationships that are understood by those who can read the signals.

Sometimes even obvious social rules conflict with those of other cultures. For Pedro and others in the study the tension between Latinos and academics is a conflict of the rules within their respective cultural systems. The events, as Pedro recalled them, were multidimensional. He described his "communication breakdown" with one particular professor as a series of interactions in which Pedro felt forced to defend himself against rude, insensitive, and even hostile remarks. Despite the overt suggestion that he drop out of the academic graduate program, Pedro denied that the behaviors were anything but cultural "insensitivities," even after his department chair called them a "personality problem." Pedro's attempts to explain himself in the context of Mexican culture reveal his overt and covert levels of communication. On the surface Pedro is frustrated by the professor's lack of understanding and his disinterest in the origins of Pedro's writing style. When Pedro explains that his third-person style is generated in part by his Mexican heritage, he relates the professor's preference: "to be very direct; that way there's no backstabbing." If this response is accurate, the cultural implications are very serious at a deeper level. The professor not only discounted Pedro's communication style but considered it a deadly form of social game playing.

Pedro was further challenged by the professor in two ways. First, the professor discounted Pedro's acknowledged understanding of Mexico with a warning that relying on community-based knowledge does not lead to academic success. Then the professor told the story of his own management style, which included sharing with others his views about potential problems at work. The implied moral of the story is that being direct in communicating to colleagues, even in "the worst [case] scenario," is considered being open and honest and leads to success for those who are committed and loyal. Indirect communication, by implication, is considered dishonest and "backstabbing." Although these events are told only from Pedro's perspective, they are similar to stories told by other Latinos in the study.

At a deeper level of understanding, other less obvious messages emerge from the white spaces in the passage. Pedro's dialogue is interlaced with direct or implied comments about competition and nurturing and judgments about how professors fail to establish an "emotional tie between people." These seemingly unrelated comments are all directly related to the conflicting primary message systems associated with gender roles in Latino and non-Latino cultures. Hall found that significant differences in core values may exist within cultural systems (context) between populations of different national origins and that these differences are often reflected (overtly and covertly) in transactions between various cultures and groups (see Hall 1959, 1977, 1993).

For example, Hall found that the context of many Mediterranean-based cultures, such as those of Latin Americans, North American Latinos, and even some Middle Eastern populations, tends to be oriented more toward people and community than are some populations from northern Europe (e.g., Germans, Scandinavians, Norwegians, etc.). Among Mediterranean-based cultures, it is not out of character for males to be openly expressive, communicate emotionally with words and gestures, and even value a "nurturing" role, as evidenced in the emotional ties they display toward other members of the family and community.

Most academics in North America tend to avoid at all cost "emotional ties between people," especially with students. For example, the unwritten rule among many graduate faculty is that graduate students must prove themselves to be at least academic junior colleagues before advisers invest in social or emotional relationships with them. Despite changing values about gender roles in the United States today, many individuals in the mainstream of our society may harbor stereotyped beliefs that "nurturing" and "emotional ties" are primarily female characteristics. Thus the covert rationale for maintaining social distance between faculty advisers and students, combined with unconscious and misapplied gender stereotypes, permeates the attitudes toward many ethnic students who are attending graduate schools in the United States.

Many Latinos in academia also are characterized as being less competitive than members of other ethnic populations, such as African Americans (E. Seymour and Hewitt 1997). Latinos place a high value on maintaining strong family and community ties. To achieve this, in academia they tend to avoid certain types of confrontation or competition. The tension between majority academics and Latino academics is subtle, almost invisible, and can build to a breaking point. Hall tells us that, if possible, Latinos avoid face-to-face unpleasantness and confrontation with colleagues at work or with whom they have a relationship (1977, 158). As a result, outsiders misperceive Latinos as being passive and unassuming in their work.

The truth is that Latinos, both males and females, are quite assertive, competitive, even protective when the situation involves important cultural values such as those related to the family, the community, society, and the like. The differences lie in the context—the when or where such behavior is deemed necessary or appropriate. For example, Latinos and Latinas soon discover that graduate student training encourages them to think very critically about other scholars and to analyze scientific ideas in culturally unfamiliar ways. Consequently, for the first time in their lives many Latinos and Latinas find themselves in competitive graduate research programs that adopt academic cultural behaviors that are often diametrically opposed to their own. Thus graduate school customs may be difficult for Latinos to learn and, for some, even harder to endure through completion (see Ibarra 1996).[6]

"Context," according to Edward Hall and Mildred Hall, "is the information that surrounds an event and is inextricably bound up with the meaning of that event. The elements that combine to produce a given meaning—events and context—are in different proportions depending on the culture" (1990, 7). Hall could identify and sort populations throughout the world based on how groups and individuals perceive and communicate with one another within their concepts of time and space, interaction, and association or how they establish modes of learning about the world. He could scale cultures on a continuum from "high" to "low," signifying the importance or intensity of these cultural patterns within groups. Individuals from a "high-context" culture tend to use the multiple streams of information that surround an event, situation, or interaction (e.g., words, tones, gestures, body language, status, or relationship of speakers) to determine meaning from the context in which it occurs. Communication is within the context itself, whereas very little is in the actual message transmitted.

For individuals in a "low-context" culture the pattern is just the opposite. They tend to filter out conditions surrounding an event, situation, or interaction to focus as much as possible on words and objective facts. They put great care into explicitly stating the message and review the details in linear step-by-step fashion as necessary. Failure to state information explicitly can distort the message. "Contexting," either high or low in a culture,

refers to the fact that when people communicate they take for granted how much the listener knows about the subject under discussion. In low-context communications, the listener knows very little and so must be told practically everything. In high-context communication, the listener is already "contexted," and so does not need to be told very much. (Hall and Hall 1990, 158)

At one end of the continuum of cultural context Hall found that high-context populations are likely to be Asian and Asian Americans (especially Japanese and Japanese Americans), Arab or Middle Eastern groups, Mediterranean-based peoples, Africans and African Americans, Latin Americans and Latinos in North America, native North American Indian groups, and North American women in general. In contrast, northern European populations, such as the Germans, Swiss, and Scandinavians, are usually low-context cultures. Hall placed at the low-context end of the continuum most North American populations with national origins derived from northern Europe, as well as Anglo males. The primary cultural difference between men and women is that men have greater association with more formal levels of culture (i.e., business formality), whereas women have greater association with informal levels of culture (i.e., family and community). The epitome of high-context cultures in the United States are the Native Americans living in the Southwest; German Americans are the best representation of low-context culture. Hall never assigned positive or negative values to these binary groups, for they were simply labels that differentiate cultural and cognitive characteristics of various domestic ethnic populations and international cultures.

The essential distinctions between these contexts trigger the cultural dynamics. Compared to low-context cultures, high-context cultures place a much higher value on developing and maintaining "extensive information networks among family, friends, colleagues, and clients, and they are involved in close personal relationships" (Hall 1984, 8). Following a logical progression, high-context cultures are more likely than low-context groups to develop social systems and organizations that are people oriented. Thus family, kin, community, and even close collegial relationships become extremely important in the core of their lives.

Hall further characterized low-context populations as tending to have a fixation on time—spending it, losing it, making it up, carving it out, and so on. He labeled these populations "monochronic" because they tend to be driven by schedules and prefer to complete one task at a time in sequential order. High-context populations are the opposite. Time flows for these individuals; events happen when they are ready and take their own course. Among most tribal populations, according to Hall, time is a very different concept than it is for nontribal cultures. Many U.S. tribal languages, for example, communicate primarily with verbs only in the present tense. Hall labeled high-context populations "polychronic," characterized by a facility for juggling many activities simultaneously and involving a great number of people in the process. Low-context cultures tend to organize thinking in linear fashion and make plans, theories, and designs for action in calculated ways by using primarily the logic of written words and mathematics to communicate. High-context cultures focus less on schedules and tend to think comprehensively, expecting others to understand implicit social needs. Written contracts are less important than bonds of personal trust between people (1984, 97–98).

While reviewing Hall's publications, my understanding of his ideas grew more complex and extended beyond the original bounds of communication. Hall included criteria that not only differentiate people and cultures by how they deal with time, space, interactions, and other cultural systems but also how these systems further generate culturally distinct preferences about how societies deal with such things as authority and control, decision making, information and strategies, image, personal relationships, propaganda and advertising, the media, and so on (Hall 1984, 117–23). His ideas about nonverbal interactions began with constructs about the various meanings behind gestures and body language (Hall 1959) and grew into far more complex interrelations associated with "interpersonal synchronicity." In *The Dance of Life* Hall described certain populations of high-context people as needing to stay in physical synchronicity with each other on a regular basis or suffer from dissonance in their lives, becoming accident prone or even increasing their susceptibility to disease (1984, 163). Interpersonal synchronicity is important for high-context individuals. It is often evidenced by the intense need of Latinos and other ethnic student populations to push for multicultural centers or special ethnic student housing on campus (see Parker 1997) in order to associate with each other and recharge the cultural batteries. This need for physical synchronicity is both conscious and unconscious and goes largely unrecognized by the majority of administrators on our campuses today.

In summary, Hall's work detailed the binary oppositions between high-context cultures, which are usually associated here with underrepresented ethnic and gender populations in higher education, and low-context cultures, represented by the predominantly Euro–North American populations that shaped higher education and academic cultures in the United States. To help readers focus on these primary cultural dynamics, the end of this chapter contains a selection of high- and low-context characteristics of culture culled from thirty years of Hall's research. I will be making reference to these comparisons throughout the book.

The Contribution of Cognitive Studies

Hall's model establishes important benchmarks for explaining the conflicts for Latinos in academia. Yet his model did not resolve inconsistencies in the research puzzle I encountered. Among the Latinos I interviewed, many did not exhibit all the high-context characteristics I expected. Some Latinos were more, or even less, high context in certain respects than others. No single ethnic group or individual in the study fit perfectly into one end or the other of the spectrum of cultural context.

Shortly after Hall's first book, *The Silent Language* (1959), became popular in the 1960s, the psychologist Herman Witkin, working with colleagues on spatial orientation in humans (Oltman, Goodenough, and Witkin 1973; Witkin and Oltman 1967; Witkin, Goodenough, and Oltman 1979; Witkin, Moore, et al. 1977), discovered interesting cognitive differences in people with clearly opposite visual orientation patterns. Witkin constructed specially designed environments and visual tests to distract and disorient subjects. Then he directed experiments that revealed that certain individuals, primarily men, can accurately resume an upright position, even in the absence of external visual cues for guidance. Others, usually women, cannot do this without some external visual cues to assist them. Initially, researchers assumed that some individuals rely on internal cues to orient properly and thus labeled them "field independent," whereas they labeled "field dependent" those people who need external cues for proper orientation.

Further research in object-oriented testing (i.e., block designs, picture completions, and object assembly) revealed that the overall organization of the testing environment dominates field-dependent subjects and that they are highly influenced by the human or social elements involved (R. Cohen 1969). In addition, field-dependent people tend to perform better on "verbal tasks and intelligence tests; learn materials more easily which have human, social content, and which are characterized by fantasy and humor; are sensitive to the opinions of others; perform better when authority figures express confidence in their ability; and, conversely, perform less well when authority figures doubt their ability" (M. Ramírez and Castañeda 1974, 65). Field-independent individuals tend to do well in impersonal environments and learn easily from inanimate objects or testing materials and are adept at segmenting parts of the environment or separating parts from whole objects, and their performance is not affected by the opinion of others. Field-independent subjects favor analytical testing because the nature of these experiments is abstract and impersonal. In fact, the defining characteristics of these two distinct cognitive styles relate to preferences in how one integrates, classifies, and organizes the environment.

By the mid-1960s researchers had concluded that women tend to be more field dependent and males more field independent. Rosalie Cohen's work with public school children revealed many other cognitive and intellectual differences that she believed contribute directly to cultural conflict for women and other low-income populations in public schools, including unspecified ethnic groups (1969).[7] Areas of significant conflict or incompatibility, including perceptions of time, social space, and causality, are directly associated with analytical abstractions within school testing and evaluations. In fact, Cohen observed the method of information transfer in field-independent analytical thinking. She noted that schools embody an analytical (field-independent) style not only in test criteria but also in their overall institutional ideology. Schools, as she noted, reward development of the analytical (field-independent) style of processing information in the learning environment, so much so that children with relational (field-dependent or high-context) styles are likely to be considered confused, anxious, deviant, and disruptive in this environment (1969, 830). However, because the student population included unknown numbers and types of ethnic groups, it is nearly impossible to determine how these cultural differences contribute to her findings.

The Parallel Evolution of "Bicognition"

The theories on cultural context and cognition came together when in the early 1970s cognitive studies focused on specific cultural groups. The most important development emerged when psychologists developed a branch of cognitive studies that focuses specifically on their findings that Mexican Americans in general are more field dependent than Anglo-Americans (Díaz-Guererro 1977; Holtzman 1977; Kegan and Zahn 1975). The preeminent researchers in this field are the clinical psychologists Manuel Ramírez and Alfredo Castañeda, who first established in 1974 the interrelationship between the conflicting cognitive styles of Mexican American cultural values and socialization systems, and public school learning styles and environmental systems. Building on the work of Witkin and others, Ramírez and Castañeda revised previous findings and developed new ideas about ethnic culture and cognition.

These parallel developments in anthropology and psychology seemed to compliment each other by validating basic concepts while providing unique insights. The cognitive research of Ramírez and Castañeda, like Hall's work with context, generated important breakthroughs in understanding the cultural dynamics of Latinos in academia. One major development, for instance, was the attempt by Ramírez and Castañeda to discredit the notion that one cognitive style is better than the other, a significant misconception that continues today in education. Witkin first postulated that everyone is undifferentiated, or field dependent, from birth and that as individuals mature they move from that rudimentary stage toward a more developed stage of field independence (1974, 73–74).

Ramírez and Castañeda demonstrated that different cognitive styles are reflections of group cultural values shaped by the socializing forces of family and community. Individuals are taught with certain cultural learning, incentive-motivational, human-relational, and communication styles. These are not a rudimentary stage in maturation, nor are they genetically predetermined. The socialization or acculturation process, Ramírez and Castañeda claimed, encourages preferences for one or the other cognitive style but does not preclude the development of either style concurrently. This, in fact, explains why successful bicultural individuals continue to develop appropriate cognitive styles to accommodate and coexist in bicultural environments (1974; see also R. Cohen 1969). These are learned ways of behaving bicognitively.

The early tests designed by Witkin and others measured only field independence, not dependence. Thus they had no way to determine whether children were becoming less field dependent as they were developing more field independence. Ramírez and Castañeda recognized the negative sense of the term *field dependence* and replaced it in their work with the term *field sensitive*. The new term more accurately describes the tendency for these individuals to register their greater sensitivity to the social and physical environment. Describing women or Mexican Americans as field sensitive, for example, is certainly an improvement over the older terminology. But from the perspective of real-world applications, the term *sensitive* still has potential for contributing another stereotype and becoming oversimplified, overgeneralized, and even misunderstood (T. Carter and Segura 1979, 114, 118).

Bicognition in K–12 Education

In their book, *Cultural Democracy, Bicognitive Development, and Education* (1974), Manuel Ramírez and Alfredo Castañeda proposed that bicultural individuals, and especially field-sensitive children, do learn to become field independent. But they also learn cognitive switching, or *flex*—an ability to draw upon both cognitive styles at any given time to adjust or adapt to a variety of activities, tasks, or social environments. This *bicognitive* (somewhat neurological, or bicameral) versatility allows individuals to interact selectively, and their "behavior can reflect either cooperation or competition; they can solve problems which require inductive or deductive thought; they can respond to or effectively ignore the social environment" (M. Ramírez and Castañeda 1974, 130).

Manuel Ramírez also found that Mexican Americans, for example, exhibit tendencies to combine both cognitive styles to produce new coping behaviors and adaptive strategies to resolve life's problems (1998, 155). His study of adolescents and young adults found that

active involvement in two or more cultures (biculturalism/multiculturalism) does not result in severe value conflicts or in identity crises; rather, such involvement tends to foster flexibility of personality functioning and development of skills as cultural facilitators and leaders in mixed ethnic group situations. Thus, active involvement in different cultures seems to make the person more adaptable by virtue of introducing him/her to different coping techniques, different problem-solving strategies, and different ways of perceiving life problems and challenges. (63)

Multiple socialization processes of school, family, and community, and dual cultural participation, then, produce not deficit but a complex set of behaviors for adapting to the need to function effectively in at least two cultural worlds. Ramírez and Castañeda called this *bicognitive versatility* (1974, 29). Although most people have personalities that exhibit a definite preference for one style or the other, many individuals are a unique combination of cognitive styles, choosing to be sensitive in communication style, for example, but using a more independent style regarding their motivations. Over time, Manuel Ramírez recognized the similar dynamics of flex within personalities and cultures as well as cognition, and this development eventually formed the basis of his work on multicultural personality development (1991, 21–26; 1998).

Only since the mid-1980s have other models emerged and focused on gender and ethnic minorities using similar fundamental concepts of bicognition (Anzaldúa 1987; de Anda 1984; Stanton-Salazar 1997). The ground-breaking work of Ramírez and Castañeda among successful Mexican American and non–Mexican American schoolchildren and college students revealed that regardless of ethnicity, "they tended to be more flexible in their styles as compared to their less successful peers. It was also discovered that the more successful students were flexible in both cultural and cognitive domains. That is, these children, adolescents, and young adults could shuttle between the different cognitive and cultural styles" (M. Ramírez 1991, 20). Intensive "studies of these children and their families in both the Anglo and the Latino groups revealed that most of them could shift between field independent and field-[sensitive] behaviors" (M. Ramírez 1998, 99). The most important observation was that

the most flexible children tended to have been socialized in bilingual/bicultural families. That is, both Anglo and Mexican American children who had been socialized in mainstream American middle-class and Mexican American or Mexican culture, and who had learned both English and Spanish demonstrated that they were the most bicognitive. They could function in both the Field Sensitive and Field Independent cognitive styles, and they could use elements of both styles to arrive at new problem solving and coping styles. (1998, 99–100)

Implications for Higher Education

The implications at the K–12 level are also important for understanding variations in student performance at the college/university level. Preliminary results from pilot studies of the cognition, cultural flexibility, and academic performance of almost two hundred students at the University of Texas at Austin show that "students who match their preferred cognitive style with their major tend to have higher G.P.A.'s" and "expressed more life satisfaction than those students whose cognitive styles and majors were mismatched" (Kim 1997, 7). Other researchers say they have found "a significant relationship between biculturalism and a number of measures that serve as indicators of positive mental health and adjustment" (A. Ramírez 1988, 147). Even bicultural Cuban Americans show better psychological adjustment than other Cuban Americans who participate primarily with Cuban or Anglo culture (Szapocznik et al. 1978; see also A. Ramírez 1988).

Cognitive styles, and by association high-context/low-context cultural situations, must be viewed as multidimensional and not unidimensional variables. In the 1999 edition of his book Manuel Ramírez clearly defined the characteristics of cognitive styles found specifically among children and college students and in the personalities of people in general. Table 3.2 at the end of this chapter describes field-sensitive and field-independent characteristics associated with communications, interpersonal relationships, and motivation and with teaching, parenting, supervisory, and counseling relationships among adults. Among children, Manuel Ramírez compared characteristics associated with relationship to peers, personal relationship to teachers, instructional relationship to teachers, and thinking style.

Manuel Ramírez and Castañeda advocate adopting a philosophy they call *cultural democracy,* which is intended to legitimize field-sensitive and field-independent cognitive differences as valid products of cultural and community value systems. As such, the authors encourage our sociocultural institutions to incorporate both cognitive styles. According to Ramírez and Castañeda and other researchers (including R. Cohen 1969 and Hall 1977, 1984, 1993), educational systems in the United States are biased toward field-independent learners (i.e., analytical, or low context). "American public education has tended to develop one hemisphere of the brain at the expense of the other" (M. Ramírez and Castañeda 1974, 156).[8] Consequently, "the interpretation of cultural democracy appears to assume an *unresolvable conflict or incompatibility* between the 'dominant' sociocultural system and other sociocultural systems" (M. Ramírez and Castañeda 1974, 28). In other words, Manuel Ramírez and others believe that both K–12 education and higher education are imbalanced to the advantage of field-independent learners and to the detriment of field-sensitive individuals.

A New Synthesis toward Cognition in Multiple Contexts

Thus the discovery of culturally different cognitive styles and the adaptability and versatility of bicognition suggest that, in the words of Manuel Ramírez and Castañeda, the education establishment is using only half its brain. The issue here is not that certain populations defined as "Anglos" perform better academically than others because they possess a certain "innate" ability or educational advantage, or that Latinos and other ethnic minorities perform poorly because they lack certain "inherent" abilities or are educationally unprepared. The real issue is educational achievement. Ramírez and Castañeda imply that our educational system, and not necessarily the people within it, may contribute to the problems associated with student academic performance. What it boils down to is that our educational system (K–18 and beyond) is literally teaching only half the knowledge base—the information that tends to be readily absorbed by roughly half the population—and it continues to do so with only half the information about learning methodology and pedagogy currently available to it. Consequently, all students, including low-context field-independent learners, are missing out on the benefits.

Educators are fully aware that other cognitive learning styles exist.[9] The problem is that they have not validated anything other than the pre-dominant educational format. Low-context field-independent knowledge and learning may be so ingrained and so prevalent in education that any alternative is unimaginable. If so, our educational system has not just an "unresolvable conflict" but is quite simply out of balance.

Meanwhile, Latinos and others from high-context cultures enter our educational systems with various cognitive learning styles. Many are pre-pared to learn in groups, think comprehensively, and cherish the commit-ment to family and community above all. To succeed, Latinos must then learn to think and do things in both high and low contexts, must become field independent as well as field sensitive, and must maintain these learn-ing styles throughout their educational experience. As a result, too many drop out in high school and few continue into higher education. But until now U.S. education has never been faced with the urgency, or the crisis conditions, to push it to revise and reform our learning systems.

The majority of schoolage children and college-bound individuals came from, or were socialized among, populations favoring and advocat-ing predominantly low-context cultures with preferences toward field-independent learning. Furthermore, until the midtwentieth century almost all southern European immigrant cultures, and other populations with tendencies toward high-context characteristics or field-sensitive styles, pre-ferred to adapt quickly and become part of the "American" cultural fabric. Achieving the "American dream" meant learning to acculturate, fit in, and learn the ways of the majority culture quickly. Learning to become low context and perceive field independently was part of the challenge and a major ticket to success.

That is all changing today with the influx of new kinds of students in higher education; more than half of those now enrolled are women. The increase in the number of women getting degrees is clearly market driven and a reflection of the changing composition of the labor force. Labor and employment projections for 2008 show that the number of occupations requiring an associate degree or higher will increase from 14 percent to 31 percent of all jobs by 2008, while women in all age groups, and especially baby boomers aged forty-five to sixty-four, will be entering the labor force in greater numbers. The enrollment trends for men in higher education are projected to remain steady or decrease slightly (Fullerton 1999, 25).

Many ethnic groups now entering higher education in greater numbers bring with them a different set of social and cultural aspirations than their predecessors; they have no intention of adapting, acculturating, or fitting in quickly. On the contrary, Latinos, among others, are not accepting the dictum to learn in only one way, nor are they willing to give up their own cultural contexts and cognitive styles as did earlier immigrant groups in this country. The national media are watching the unique characteristics of *Generation Ñ* (pronounced EN-yay), the term used by *Newsweek* to define this rapidly growing and influential population of young Latinos in their twenties and thirties (Leland and Chambers 1999). Although they are "changing the way this country looks, feels and thinks, eats, dances and votes, . . . they are not 'crossing over' into mainstream America" (Larmer 1999, 48, 51).

For earlier generations, being Latino was a negative, and most tried to acculturate. But those attitudes are changing, Jaime Cortez, the son of a migrant farm worker, told *Newsweek*. Cortez believes that "America has this weird optimism that dictates that we have to leave the past behind" (Leland and Chambers 1999, 54). Today, being Latino means celebrating a rich blend of ethnic identities and interests and expecting the rest of the country to adapt or eventually accept Latinos on their terms. Being bilingual is a plus, and this younger generation enjoys switching identities from American to Latino and back. And it seems to be working, for the nation is recognizing Latino accomplishments in sports and entertainment, and politicians across the country are increasingly aware of the power wielded by Latino voters in Texas, California, Florida, Nevada, and even the Midwest (1999).

Nor does this generation leave its aspirations and social characteristics back home. The members of this cohort prefer to learn in multiple ways without compromising their cultural preferences in their academic communities too. Cultural context and bicognition models help explain why Latinos and other minorities are running into conflict in higher education. Thus academic underperformance among various populations is merely a symptom of a deeper problem (see Bowen and Bok 1998). The real issue is how to deal with the deficiencies in our educational system, in our organizational structures, and in the cultural values of higher education itself. Correcting these problems requires more than installing a form of "cultural democracy"; it requires reframing the current cultural context of academia altogether.

Reframing Academic Cultures

The anthropologist Michael Agar offers interesting suggestions for how to frame cultures (1994a, 1994b). To understand a new culture he suggests "making sense out of human differences in terms of human similarities" (1994b, 231). These similarities become benchmarks and act as backdrops against which we see the differences in the way individuals actually do things in different cultures. Most of these differences surface in the languages (both verbal and nonverbal) used in transactions and communication between people (1994b).

My earlier analysis of Pedro's dilemma is based on similar concepts. Pedro associated his frustrations directly with faculty who misunderstood the differences between Mexican American culture and their own academic cultural values. The hidden dimension in his comments revealed that the misunderstandings formed a complex web of associations and connotations that highlighted the cultural differences. To grasp the subtle meanings, Agar suggests creating new "frames," or boundaries, "around the details [which] highlights how those details are related to each other" (1994a, 130). Hall called them "situational frames," the common settings and behavioral situations found in all cultures (e.g., greeting behavior, eating, working, classroom behavior, and the like) in which cultural activity can be analyzed (1977, 129). Multitudes of situational frames are possible, as are ways to reframe the new knowledge about others that we gain. "Themes" then tie these frames together with concepts and ideas.

However, my examination of graduate education and academic cultures involves more than just language or communication. The patterns of cultural context, ethnic identity, and academic culture are in themselves "situational frames" and are found within the organizational structures of our colleges and universities. We must learn how to see and understand how these different situational frames relate to cultural dissonance for Latino students and faculty—as well as students and faculty from other ethnic groups—within academic culture. One means for doing this is to reconfigure the cognitive and contextual models to view the current world of academe through a new cultural frame of reference.

The question is how to begin the process. The first task is to reconfigure a complex set of cultural and behavioral models, pulling together their inherent strengths for explaining phenomena. Hall's model, for example, functions best at a macro level of human behavior and is not often clear about the origins of conscious and unconscious differences in cultural context. Manuel Ramírez's bicognitive model supplies the micro perspective of human behavior, explaining individual personality styles and their variations as observed at the macro level of society. Bicognition fills in some of the picture between the two ends of the continuum of cultural context. The bicognitive model explains *why* some Latinos and Latinas exhibit variable patterns of high- and low-context behaviors and preferences: Hall recognized that in different domains individuals will exhibit both high- and low-context behaviors, depending on the circumstances.

The best illustration of how this new theoretical combination works is through Pedro's story. Pedro, for example, was fully aware of both Mexican American and Anglo culture and contexts. But he apparently had been socialized first in the values of Mexican American culture, which dominated his perspective on the world. He was to some extent bicognitive, but this was not easy to tell from outward appearances. The real stumbling block for Pedro, and in fact for all the Latino students and faculty I interviewed, was the embedded low-context culture and the field-independent or analytical style that dominates nearly all educational systems, especially higher education. Graduate school is an intense socialization process into the professoriate—an intensely low-context world. Combining bicognition and constructs of cultural context could offer a better model for explaining why certain students encounter turbulence in our educational systems.

A Theory of Multicontextuality

As a micro model of the human condition, bicognition represents a variable in individual personality and cultural styles generated by two distinct cognitive (field-sensitive and field-independent) conditions within individuals. As such, it takes the psychological characteristics of individuals and turns them into labels that characterize larger cultural groups and populations within which society validates individual identity. Cultural context is a macro model of human culture. It represents a range of cultural characteristics that identify and reflect differences in various cultural groupings. As such, it takes the characteristics of larger groups and populations and turns them into labels that characterize individuals who consider themselves members of those groups. Indeed, these characteristics of cultural context may be what shape part of one's ethnic identity.

It seems logical, therefore, that these highly compatible and complementary constructions be conjoined for a greater purpose. With that in mind, it would be appropriate to identify this amalgamation as *multicontextuality,* representing the admixture of multiple human conditions and sociocultural contexts. Throughout the remainder of this book I will use the dynamic models by Hall and Manuel Ramírez to help develop this construct. I will also apply these tools for micro or macro analysis, or both, as appropriate. This new construct represents only the beginning of scientific inquiry. Consequently, I have generated no statistical design for analysis, and I will use numerical data to illustrate what appear to be patterns of multicontextuality rather than patterns that show statistical significance. As I identify the characteristics and conditions of Latinos and Latinas in higher education, it will become apparent why the recombination of these qualitative models is more appropriate here than quantitative data for developing a theory of multicontextuality.

Multicontext individuals reflect the characteristics of a growing number of people in our education systems today. They are bicognitive individuals, able to demonstrate flex by interacting selectively across cultural contexts and cognitive styles. They are equipped with a versatility that enables them to adjust or adapt at any time to a variety of activities, tasks, or social environments. Latinos and Latinas who have learned this successful adaptive strategy maneuver through the predominantly low-context environment of higher education. They know when to signal who they are culturally, and they know what to do to perform well as students and faculty, depending on the circumstances and the people around them. Adapting is not always easy and requires additional concentration and academic work. Furthermore, multicontextual individuals are not only ethnic minorities or women; some Anglo males demonstrate this ability as well, but only additional research will provide the evidence that this is so.

What this suggests is that multicontextuality is not a process of acculturation. It is not like a one-way street that directs the flow of cultural adjustment and demands that a less-dominant culture or ethnic group adopt the ways of a dominant culture. In fact, a multicontextual individual is likely to have a pluralistic ethnic identity and be sensitive to both gender perspectives. Moreover, their behavioral patterns are not necessarily fixed or associated entirely with any one particular ethnic group. Multicontextuality sometimes cuts imperceptibly across culture and gender lines. Some Anglo males clearly are multicontextual, and some recognize that their repertoire allows them to be high and low context and field sensitive and independent. They are not simply adopting a set of ethnic or gender characteristics but are exhibiting an adaptive strategy that reflects their ability to learn several sets of cultural, gender, and cognitive styles, regardless of the dominant culture and cognitive style imprinted in their early childhood.

In fact, many high-context Anglo males do just as poorly on standardized tests as their minority peers and for similar reasons—those associated with context and cognition. We simply ignore them in the quest to find out why a greater proportion of minorities does so poorly in comparison to the majority. As a result, what we observe is that the extremes of high and low context and field sensitive and independent are more prevalent among certain ethnic groups and among women and that these tendencies have more negative consequences for these groups. Chapter 4 further explores this ethnic relationship.

As the multicultural and bicognitive models both suggest, measuring all the characteristics of individuals and groups would show cultural patterns that tend toward either high- or low-context cultural preferences. If an evaluation tool were devised to determine individual cultural context and cognition, it might not immediately reveal an individual's contextual patterns. However, if Hall and Manuel Ramírez are correct, compiling those individual sets of choices from larger sets of self-identified ethnic populations probably would reveal a pattern of preferences. Given changing conditions over time, such as the constant infusion of cultural values from in-migration, group characteristics among Mexican Americans may not change as quickly as they might for individual Mexican Americans, for example. Furthermore, I will show that institutional and organizational cultures also exhibit high- and low-context cultural characteristics with which individuals both inside and outside the organizations can identify.

Although the characteristics that identify the various models may show a preference or predominance among various individuals or groups, none of the models I used would generate rigid stereotypes or permanently assign individuals to either end of the spectrum of possibilities. In fact, within the models of cultural context, bicognition, and multicontextuality, individual characteristics and group dynamics change over time. Thus neither culture nor context should be perceived as static. I will clarify or redefine each of these concepts as needed throughout the book.

For example, academics may wish to redefine the basic meaning of *context,* as anthropologists have done, to accommodate a fluid model of culture and cognition. Lave, Murtaugh, and de la Rocha describe it as a "relationship rather than a single entity. For on the one hand, context connotes an identifiable, durable framework for [an] activity, with properties that transcend the experience of individuals, exist prior to them, and are entirely beyond their control. On the other hand, context is experienced differently by different individuals" (1984, 71–72). This view of context requires an understanding of both the stable aspects and features of cultural context and how individuals define it. As a result, many individuals probably would self-identify as having or exhibit a combination of high- and low-context cultural characteristics, or field-sensitive and -independent styles. Depending on the immediate sociocultural conditions or long-term life-changing circumstances, such as mobility, generation, life partnerships, and education, many individuals may be multicontextual. Chapter 4 further explores this ethnic relationship.

The second factor operating here relates to the difficulty of cultural adjustment for field-sensitive individuals, either women or people from high-context ethnic backgrounds. Hall found that "in a schedule-dominated monochronic culture like ours, [some] ethnic groups which focus their energies on the primary group and primary relationships such as family, and human relationships, find it almost impossible to adjust to rigid schedules and tight time compartments" (1984, 204). Moreover, for Pedro and other Latinos in graduate school, other hidden conditions within institutions of higher learning and their academic cultures cause difficult adjustments to the community of scholars. This is the essence of the problem and the central reason ethnic minorities find it difficult to adjust to higher education as easily or as quickly as others.

By using a multicontextual model, new perspectives emerge for analysis. First, this model yields a new relationship between racism and cultural conflict. It may provide a better vehicle for at least diminishing, if not eliminating, racism, as the columnist William Raspberry suggests (1998). If "race" is synonymous with other social phenomena, what develops here could well have an indirect, even direct, benefit in eliminating some of the problems ascribed to racism. Shifting the battle to maintain diversity and equality in higher education from the current discord over race to a debate about ethnicity will shift the argument from racism to ethnocentricism. If one of our goals is to eliminate discrimination, it is far easier to revise socially developed misconceptions about culturally learned behavior and group values than it is to reverse socially presumed misconceptions about genetically predetermined group behavior *and* cultural values. Within the models of cultural context and cognition are implicit concepts of imbalance and inequality, central issues for reframing the current paradigm.

Finally, Hall's high- and low-context criteria and the work on bicognition by Manuel Ramírez and Castañeda are useful descriptive models for a first approximation of cultural differences. I will expand them to incorporate new models of cultural change and to accommodate the changing dynamics of ethnicity. Hall focused on *how* people with different worldviews could communicate, interact, associate, and learn, but he did not delve into *why* people behave the way they do. Manuel Ramírez and Castañeda offered new insights into that same question.

But gaps in the research remain. For instance, Hall was not involved in the study of institutions and their cultures per se, although he assumed they were involved in culture on a higher organizational level (1959; Hall and Hall 1990). A major objective here is to develop a new perspective that assumes that the organizational cultures of institutions, like most human social systems and groups, contain patterns of high- and low-context culture imprinted by the individuals who first created and then sustained them. Although Hall was not prepared to proceed down this path at the time, we must if we are to reframe the cultural context of higher education.

To summarize the main ideas in part I, my study of Latinos in graduate education led me to look at their experiences through the fresh lenses of cultural context and bicognition, which in turn led me to an examination of the role of the culture of academia in the problems Latino graduate students encounter. The resulting multicontextual perspective includes new frameworks for observing the interactions of ethnicity and academic organizational cultures. Because the current paradigm for cultural diversity in higher education may actually impede our understanding, I search beyond these predominant assumptions to query and analyze what happens to individuals before they enter and proceed through graduate school to take up new careers beyond.

In parts II and III, I begin to examine academia from three interrelated perspectives: as a complex society; as a society made up of organizational cultures, subcultures, genders, and ethnic groups; and as a society involved in transformations and transactions leading to graduate degrees and sometimes the professoriate. Part II focuses on the dynamics of ethnic transformations using the experiences of Latinos and Latinas, and on the process of becoming multicontextual in graduate education (see chapter 4), and as faculty (chapters 5 and 6). The questions examined are not just *how* they do this but also *why* and with *what* consequences for achieving success.

Table 3.1. Selected characteristics of high and low context

Low context (LC)	High context (HC)
1. Interaction	1. Interaction
Low use of nonverbal signals. Their messages rely more on words than nonverbal cues. Body language is less highly developed, with little attempt to synchronize with words.	**High use of nonverbal signals.** Voice tone, facial expression, gesture, and eye expression all carry significant parts of a conversation. Body language is highly developed and synchronized with words.
Communication is direct. They appear to be blunt, even rude, in their directness. LC people spell things out exactly and value being specific. Getting to the main point quickly is highly valued.	**Communication is indirect.** They avoid getting to the main point of discussions quickly and talk around them to avoid being pushy. They embellish discussions and expect others to gather the main ideas from the context provided.
Messages are explicit and elaborate. Their verbal message is highly articulated with accurate distinctions; context is less important. The information is in explicit code (words, directions, publications, lectures).	**Messages are implicit and restricted.** Their verbal message is implicit, associated with informal intimate language, and context is important (situations, people, nonverbals). Words are collapsed and shortened to create simple messages with deep meaning that flow freely.
Messages are literal. Communication is a way of exchanging information, ideas, and opinions but is not intended to unify (identify or associate) culturally with others. Conversations reflect the occasion, but only one linguistic code is used.	**Messages are an art form.** They see communication as a form of engaging another person, a unifying cultural activity that may include bilingual code switching (beginning or ending sentences or conversations in two languages).
Long-term interpersonal feedback. They avoid interfering with or intervening in others' lives. They take colleagues' mood shifts for granted, attributing them to personal problems that should be ignored.	**Short-term interpersonal feedback.** Constant checking on emotional status of others is important for group morale. Though this characteristic is attributed to women, HC people in general are especially attuned to slight mood changes among friends and colleagues.

Continued on next page

Table 3.1.—*Continued*

Low context (LC)	High context (HC)
1. Interaction (cont.)	1. Interaction (cont.)
Disagreement is depersonalized. They withdraw from conflict and get on with the task. They depersonalize disagreement with a "tough it out" rather than "talk it out" approach. They defuse confrontation by quiet separation. (Force means communication breakdown.)	**Disagreement is personalized.** They are sensitive to conflict and criticism expressed by another's verbal and nonverbal communication. They must resolve conflict before work can progress. They use a "talk it out" approach to defuse confrontation and unpleasantness, especially at work. (Force means communication.)
2. Association	2. Association
Personal commitment to people is low. Relationships start and end quickly. Many people can be inside one's circle, but boundaries are blurred. They are accustomed to short-term relationships and are often highly committed to their job or career. Written contracts are important.	**Personal commitment to people is high.** Relationships depend on trust, build up slowly, and are stable. They are careful to distinguish who is in their circle. People are deeply involved with each other. They have a strong tendency to build lifetime relationships. Written contracts are less important than bonds of personal trust.
Task orientation. Things get done when everyone follows policies and procedures and pays attention to a goal. Being nice to people is not necessary nor is it as important as completing the job.	**Process orientation.** Getting things done depends on one's relationship with people and attention to the group process. Being nice, courteous, and kind to people is more important than completing a job.
Success means being recognized. They seek publicity and to stand out among their peers to "get ahead" in society. They value individualism and may ask for more information about someone's accomplishments.	**Success means being unobtrusive.** They seek less attention for their accomplishments. Talking about one's achievements is considered brash and boastful. They value humility, and such passive behavior may be misinterpreted by LC people as being unassertive.

Table 3.1.—*Continued*

Low context (LC)	High context (HC)
3. Temporality	3. Temporality
Time is monochronic (M-Time). They emphasize schedules, compartmentalization, and promptness. They do one thing at a time and may equate time with money and status. Change happens fast.	**Time is polychronic (P-Time).** They emphasize people and completion of transactions. They do many things at once (multiple tasking) and do not equate time with money or status. Change happens slowly, for things are rooted in the past.
• They do work on a schedule and do one thing at a time. Their intent is to do things quickly and see immediate results.	• Because life has its own flow, they are reluctant to schedule time, cognizant that the needs of people may interfere with keeping to a schedule.
• They value speed and efficiency in work. The objective for learning and training is "getting up to speed."	• They value accuracy and completion of a job. How well something is learned is more important than how soon or how fast.
• They concentrate on the job at hand.	• They are highly distractable and subject to interruptions at work.
• They take deadlines and schedules seriously.	• They regard deadlines and schedules as goals to be achieved if possible.
• They adhere religiously to plans.	• They change plans often and easily.
• They emphasize promptness. Being late sends a message about status or importance.	• They value promptness if they know it is important to the relationship. Being late does not send a message.
• They see people who juggle several tasks at once (P-Time) as being totally disorganized.	• They perceive people who work in sequence as obsessive. Working collegially is more important than achieving work goals.

Continued on next page

Table 3.1.—*Continued*

Low context (LC)	High context (HC)
3. Temporality (cont.)	3. Temporality (cont.)
Time is a commodity. Time can be spent, saved, or wasted. One's time is one's own.	**Time is a process.** Time is part of nature; it belongs to everyone.
Synchrony is not important and tempo of life is faster. They are less likely to consciously or unconsciously synchronize body movements while interacting with others (kinesics). The pace of life is hurried and individualized; synchronizing with others is not valued.	**Synchrony is important and tempo of life is slower.** Body movement while interacting with others is consciously and unconsciously synchronized. The absence of synchrony at work or performing with others may cause stress and tension. The pace of life is slower and synchronizing with others is highly valued.
Culture relative to time is superficial. They perceive culture as something that one can change, put on, or take off. Change means discarding (excluding) old ways for new ones. Because they regard culture as a superficial difference, they have trouble accepting difference in others. They tend to expect others to be as willing to reshape their culture as they are.	**Culture relative to time is ingrained.** They perceive culture as an integral part of everyone and everything. Change means incorporating or adopting (including) new ways with old ones. Because they regard culture as ingrained, they are receptive to what is different in others, and they seldom expect others to reshape their culture.
4. Gender and LC culture	4. Gender and HC culture
M-Time cultures are formal (male oriented). Formal culture is technical, highly scheduled, task oriented, concentrated, and imposing. The official worlds of business, government, entertainment, and sports are shaped by men. Formal wisdom in professions like business and the law give minimal importance to informal culture.	**P-Time cultures are informal (female oriented).** Informal culture evolves over time from shared personal experiences that tie individuals to the group and its identity. It exists in all cultures. Communication is an informal process with no specific senders, receivers, or identifiable messages. Wisdom is group oriented.

Table 3.1.—*Continued*

Low context (LC)	High context (HC)
4. Gender and LC culture (cont.)	4. Gender and HC culture (cont.)
Formal culture is team oriented. Teams consist of individuals with specific skills who are brought together to work on projects or tasks. Their work may be linked, but it is sequential and compartmentalized (handed off to others).	**Informal culture is group oriented.** Individuals with general and/or specific skills come together to work as a group to complete projects. Work is interactive, and individuals are not territorial about specific tasks.
5. Territoriality	5. Territoriality
Space has more boundaries. LC people need more social distance for interaction, with little if any touching or contact during conversation. Personal space is compartmentalized, more individualized, and private.	**Space is more communal.** HC people are comfortable interacting within close social distances, and constant nonintimate touching during conversation is normal. Personal space is shared, and involvement with others is encouraged.
Privacy is more important. They are concerned about not disturbing others and following social rules of privacy and consideration.	**Privacy is less important.** HC people are involved with those who are closely related (family, friends, close business associates) and have few concerns about privacy.
Personal property is shared less. LC people tend to show great respect for private property. They seldom or reluctantly borrow or lend things.	**Personal property is shared more.** They respect private property but tend to borrow and lend things often and easily. My home is your home.
6. Learning	6. Learning
Knowledge is obtained by logical reasoning. A rational step-by-step model of scientific analysis yields information. Reality is elemental, fragmented, compartmentalized and thus easier to isolate for analysis.	**Knowledge is obtained by a gestalt model.** Facts are perceived as complete units (gestalts) embedded in the context of situations or experiences; they can be recalled as wholes, and they are not easily separated for analysis. Things are interconnected, synthesized, and global.

Continued on next page

Table 3.1.—*Continued*

Low context (LC)	High context (HC)
6. Learning (cont.)	6. Learning (cont.)
Analytical thinking is important. They prefer an inductive reasoning process, to go from the specific to the general. They focus on compiling details. They have difficulty translating their thinking process into symbols so that comprehensive thinkers can easily understand it.	**Comprehensive thinking is important.** They prefer deductive reasoning, to go from general to specific. They use expanded thinking ("big picture" actions, ideas, and/or complex forms). They have few problems translating their thinking processes symbolically (nonverbally) for others to understand.
They learn best by following directions. They assemble or combine facts according to rules they memorize. Things are spelled out with explicit explanations, even in an apprenticeship model. Theoretical and philosophical problems are treated as real.	**They learn best by demonstration.** They learn by hands-on methods: observing and mimicking others, practicing it mentally and physically, demonstrating it to others, and by apprenticeship. Real-life problems are as important as theoretical and philosophical ones.
Learning is oriented toward the individual. They prefer to approach tasks and learning individually. They tend to work and learn apart from others. Teamwork means individuals are assigned specific tasks to accomplish.	**Learning is group oriented.** They prefer to work in groups to learn and solve problems. Some groups prefer constant talking (interacting) in proximity when working or learning.
Creative learning process is externalized. They prefer to learn or create complex knowledge like mathematics externally—with the aid of pens, paper, books, computers, and so on. The learning process is highly visible and accessible for others to evaluate and correct. Externalized creative processes help to speed up change, but they are slower and less productive than internalized processes.	**Creative learning process is internalized.** They may be capable of learning or creating complex knowledge like mathematics or music in their heads rather than by using learning extensions like pen and paper. The creative learning process is comprehensive, and integrating complex ideas can happen all at once. Internalized creative processes are less visible for others to evaluate and correct, but they are much faster and more productive than externalized processes.

Table 3.1.—*Continued*

Low context (LC)	High context (HC)
7. Information	7. Information
Information does not flow freely. Data are highly focused and compartmentalized. They make relatively low use of personal information networks.	**Information spreads rapidly.** It moves as if it has a life of its own. They make relatively significant use of multiple personal information networks.
Information can be separated from context. They can separate the two, an artifact primarily of Western analytical science.	**Information without context is meaningless.** They prefer information in context; otherwise, it is unreliable.
8. LC academic systems	8. HC academic systems
LC disciplines. They may favor traditional scientific fields that tend to conduct analysis with methods that often eliminate context (separate information from context). Research analysis usually deals with large numbers of quantitative and easily measured variables; results are more deterministic and context is less important. New research projects are directed toward strongly projected predetermined outcomes.	**HC disciplines.** They may favor disciplines that are more directly involved with contextual thinking and research about living systems and people. Research analysis is more qualitative and probabilistic and requires attention to variables in which cultural context is important. New research projects are clear about the direction and methods of analysis, but projected outcomes are less predetermined and more open ended and flexible.
Scientific thinking is emphasized. They value examining ideas rather than broad comprehension of real-world applications. Linear thinking is ultra-specific and inhibits a broad mutual understanding of multilayered events. Scientific thinking uses words and math to communicate.	**Practical thinking is valued.** They value application of knowledge in real-world events (social skills). Interconnected thinking fosters creativity and broad comprehension of multilayered events.

Continued on next page

Table 3.1.—*Continued*

Low context (LC)	High context (HC)
8. LC academic systems (cont.)	8. HC academic systems (cont.)
Academic/teaching style is technical. Their style is individual, less interactive, and teacher oriented. Research interests include people or communities, but they focus on theoretical and philosophical problems. Writing style uses fewer pronouns.	**Academic/teaching style is personal.** Their style is more open, interactive, and student oriented. Research interests are directed to real-life problems with people and the community. Writing style tends toward more use of personal pronouns.
Science relies on Linnean-style taxonomies. Scientific taxonomies favor linear analysis that classifies living things mainly for information retrieval. Taxonomic systems emphasize the processes of collecting specific information more than its integration into usable, intelligible patterns.	**Science includes folkstyle taxonomies.** Taxonomies function beyond information retrieval to communicate *about* the living things being classified. The communication is among those who already understand the cultural significance of the things being discussed. The intent is to integrate the information and contextual thinking to open new areas for research.

Source: Adapted from the work of Edward T. Hall (1959–1993) and Edward T. Hall and Mildred R. Hall (1990).

Table 3.2. Characteristics of field-sensitive and field-independent children and adults

Field-independent (FI) children	Field-sensitive (FS) children
1. Relationship to peers	1. Relationship to peers
Prefer to work independently	Like to work with others to achieve common goals
Like to compete and gain individual recognition	Like to assist others
Are task oriented; are inattentive to social environment when working	Are sensitive to feelings and opinions of others
2. Social relationship to teacher	2. Social relationship to teacher
Avoid physical contact with teacher	Openly express positive feelings for teacher
Interact formally with teacher; restrict interactions to tasks at hand	Ask questions about teacher's taste and personal experiences; seek to become like teacher
3. Instructional relationship to teacher	3. Instructional relationship to teacher
Like to try new tasks without teacher's help	Seek guidance and demonstration from teacher
Are impatient to begin tasks; like to finish first	Seek rewards that strengthen relationship with teacher
Seek nonsocial rewards	Are highly motivated by working individually with teacher
4. Thinking style	4. Thinking style
Focus on details and parts of things	Function well when objectives are carefully explained or modeled
Deal well with math and science concepts	Deal well with concepts in humanized or story format
Like discovery or trial-and-error learning	Function well when curriculum content is relevant to personal interests and experiences

Continued on next page

Table 3.2.—*Continued*

Field-independent (FI) children	Field-sensitive (FS) children
5. Communications	5. Communications
Tend to be impersonal and to the point	Tend to personalize communications by referring to own life experiences, interests, and feelings
Tend to focus more on verbal than nonverbal communications	Tend to focus more on nonverbal than verbal communications
6. Interpersonal relationships	6. Interpersonal relationships
Are reserved and cautious in social settings	Are open and outgoing in social settings
Present as distant and formal	Present as warm and informal
7. Motivation	7. Motivation
Seek nonsocial rewards	Value social rewards that strengthen relationships with important others
Are motivated in relation to self-advancement	Are motivated in relation to achievement for others (family, team, ethnic/racial group, etc.)
8. Teaching, parenting, supervisory, and counseling relationships	8. Teaching, parenting, supervisory, and counseling relationships
Focus on task or goal	Focus on relations with student, child, supervisor, or client
Are formal and private	Are informal and self-disclosing

Source: Manuel Ramírez III (1999), *Multicultural Psychotherapy: An Approach to Individual and Cultural Differences,* 2d ed. (formerly titled, *Psychotherapy and Counseling with Minorities: A Cognitive Approach to Individual and Cultural Differences*) (Needham Heights, Mass.: Allyn and Bacon), table 3.2, p. 25.

Part II

Latinas and Latinos
in Graduate Education
and Beyond

4

The Graduate School Experience

Ethnicity in Transformation

> My identity depends on who I'm talking to. It depends on which setting I'm in. If I'm writing, I call myself a Chicana. If I'm in a group of people who are in the community, who are the people who really are involved in community affairs like arts, those kinds of things, writers, literary people, *Chicana* is what I use so it's more politicized in those circles. At home and talking to other people I would say *Mexican American,* and with people who speak Spanish I would say *Mexicana.* Within the university, *Hispanic,* so these terms are used all the time.
>
> Marta, an administrator from California

My interviews usually started with a nostalgic tour of the subjects' past. Where did their families come from? What were their early educational experiences? I continually searched for clues to what may have sparked their interest in pursuing graduate work and, when appropriate, an academic career. When we shifted to graduate school issues, the participants' moods sometimes changed, or the tension increased noticeably. It was the first time that some had examined that part of their lives, and reliving it even briefly surfaced a variety of emotions. Anger and pain were evident in some of their expressions. These memories brought a few to tears, yet all wanted to share their story to help others. The interviews revealed that completing graduate school, especially with a doctoral degree, was a complex transformational process that began during the undergraduate years. I knew many of my subjects would find the interview difficult, but their level of intensity surprised me.

By the end of my study I had concluded that many Latinos and Latinas undergo at least two different transformations in graduate school: one is learning to become a scholar or an academic; the other is preparing for entry into the professoriate. Many interviewees can describe the difficult steps one must endure to obtain an advanced degree and become a scholar—the graduate school experience. This is the process most educators study and analyze. Few of us describe the personal and less obvious transformations some must make to become members of the faculty. For some Latinos and members of other ethnic groups, this means learning to subordinate, rather than culturally blend, one set of identities for another in order to succeed in academia. Unfortunately, few of us write about the painful process of exchanging ethnicity and/or gender for membership in the academy.

Here I begin with an overview of conditions in primary and secondary education, followed by research findings related to undergraduate circumstances, and, finally, graduate school conditions and the adjustments a minority student makes to adapt and survive in a majority culture. I intend to show how much these identity transformations define the educational process for Latinos and Latinas.

Preconditioning for Success in Graduate School

For Latinos school plays as important a role as the family in determining an individual's educational expectations (Cuádraz 1992, 32). Although this statement sounds obvious, it carries significant implications. For instance, high schools are important arenas for acculturating Latinos and others from high-context cultures into an educational system dominated by a low-context culture. Many Latinos first encounter different class values and other ethnic cultures in predominantly Anglo or middle-class public schools. But a definitive factor in their success is how well they acquire the different modes of learning and perceiving the world.

In most cases Latinos must absorb learning skills that may be antithetical to those skills they learned from their family or community. In these schools Latinos and other ethnic populations either learn how to become multicontextual and work effectively within the dominant low-context culture, or they gain admission to college ill prepared to succeed. Thus, people from high-context cultures need to learn more in our public schools than just middle-class values or low-context thinking skills. They must learn how to communicate and associate with people who evaluate the world through predominantly low-context cultural criteria. For Latinos that entails learning and integrating the less obvious low-context characteristics into a repertoire of their own behavioral patterns, or "scripts" (Ford 1992), while maintaining their ethnic identity and customs for interacting successfully at home.

This process is more complex if our educational institutions do not recognize or question the low-context concepts (for related research see de Anda 1984; Hale-Benson 1986; Stanton-Salazar 1997). In most cases the less obvious characteristics within a culture are those that outsiders never fully absorb or integrate well. The consequences of failing to internalize these new behaviors may be poor academic performance, cultural misunderstandings, or worse—students may drop out of school. Despite the increasing number of Latinos who are enrolling in the public schools, educational conditions for Latinos in general are deteriorating rapidly. Recent reports show that in 1995 Latinos aged sixteen to twenty-four accounted for the highest percentage of high school dropouts (more than 30 percent) in the population, a rate that is increasing faster than that for any other group in the United States; by comparison, dropout rates for African Americans range from 16 percent to 28 percent, depending on the source (President's Advisory Commission 1996; Puente and Sanchez 1995; Viadero 1997; WCER 1996; Wilds and Wilson 1998).

The dropout issue underscores the importance of secondary and postsecondary preparation for Latinos seeking access to higher education. The quality of precollege preparation can vary greatly, but the kind of school and the socioeconomic mix of students have a direct bearing on Latinos' educational outcomes. I found that two factors in the primary and secondary years stand above others as likely indicators for success in higher education: taking advanced placement courses within a college preparatory curriculum (college prep track); and/or attending a predominantly Anglo high school. Most of the seventy-seven Latinos I interviewed, including 90 percent of the Mexican Americans, had taken college prep courses. Sixty percent of my Latino subjects, including more than 70 percent of the Mexican Americans, had attended a predominantly Anglo or integrated high school (more than 50 percent Anglo). These findings are among the data from my study that concur with Gándara's study of successful Chicano graduate students (1995).

The high dropout rate, which may be caused by poverty, poor schools, racism, low educational expectations, and/or cultural alienation, is a major cause of leaks in the so-called educational pipeline and obviously reduces the Latino pool of potential college freshmen. These are important factors, but they are much too complex to treat here and are far beyond the scope of this book.

First Experiences in Undergraduate Education

Because Latinos have the highest high school dropout rate, the number of Latinos who enroll in college each fall is relatively small (T. Smith et al. 1996, table 4.5). And when they do enroll in higher education, they tend to be overrepresented in two-year institutions (Almanac Issue 1997; Chacón, Cohen, and Strover 1986, 298). Those in the Latino study had numerous reasons for pursuing postsecondary education. One theme was clear: most had wanted to go to college, but they had few clues as to what to expect and even less information about how to gain admission. Except for a few of the women, most participants, regardless of ethnicity or family socioeconomic status, reported a high level of parental encouragement to attend college. But their parents were notably reluctant for their offspring to pursue a graduate degree.

The majority of participants (62 percent) also discussed the limitations that affected their college experiences. These included being close to home, lack of financial support, family experience that ranged from difficult socioeconomic conditions to no experience with college, lack of certain academic skills, and poor high school counseling. Approximately 32 percent of the study group—and, again, Mexican Americans primarily—faced circumstances that caused them either to transfer to another undergraduate school or to temporarily drop out of college altogether. Nearly 70 percent transferred between institutions, causing minor but unwanted disruptions in their progress. This finding illustrates a central theme noted in my interim report in 1996: parents who are concerned that their offspring succeed do whatever they can to instill high educational aspirations. However, because the parents often lack experience with and have little understanding of higher education in the United States, their well-intentioned efforts go only so far. Most Latinos in the study group were prepared academically, but they were unaware at first of the degree to which they lacked information vital and educational preconditioning essential to success in college or graduate school (1996, 26). The consequences can prove costly: poor academic performance, inconsistent or poorly planned academic programs, or even a time-out—which sometimes became permanent—to totally redesign their lives.

But I found that participants had something else in common—persistence and determination to overcome adversity. The dogged pursuit of a college degree, sometimes over long periods of time, was a primary survival strategy. Tenacity may be the single most important factor in Latinos' success in graduate education. According to Gloria and Pope-Davis, Latino undergraduates must deal with "stress, confusion, and dissonance about belonging to an academic culture incongruent with their own cultural attitudes, beliefs, and behaviors" (1997, 248; see also Gloria 1997 and Gloria and Robinson-Kurpius 1996).

In the past, admissions officers seldom took such characteristics into consideration when deciding whom to admit to college or a graduate program. But today more and more state universities are barred from using racial preferences in student admissions following a spate of recent decisions to outlaw affirmative action in Texas by mandate of U.S. Court of Appeals for the Fifth Circuit (Mangan 1998a), by voter referenda in California and Washington State (Selingo 1999), or by the regents' decision at the University of California (Mangan 1999). Florida may set a trend by voluntarily banning preferences through a governor's decree and action by the state board of regents (Nickens 1999). Many universities, such as those in Texas, Florida, and California, are resorting to class-rank admissions strategies that give automatic acceptance to a top percentile of all graduating high school seniors in the state, or they incorporate new criteria that partially select students on some evidence that demonstrates their persistence, determination, or tenacity (Healy 1999). Unfortunately, this admissions alternative works only at the undergraduate level and is effective primarily in states with significant minority populations. Until other plans emerge, graduate school admissions policies would benefit greatly by using a broader review of an applicant's experiences and ability to overcome adversity, both personally and in academic life (see Ibarra 1996).

The Graduate School Challenge

Once admitted to graduate work, Latinas and Latinos may face a veritable obstacle course of forces, institutional and personal, through which they must maneuver to get through and beyond their graduate programs. Ethnic conflict and transformation are only the most obvious obstructions on the course.

To all outward appearances, Latinos in the study seemed to be relatively typical graduate students. Table 4.1 illustrates the graduate degree status of the Latino study group at the end of the project in 1995. Twenty participants had completed only a master's degree or were working on their master's. Of those, thirteen were expecting to complete their degrees by 1996. Almost 12 percent of the participants—three Latinos and six Latinas (predominantly Chicanas)—either had no interest in seeking a doc-

Table 4.1. Latino study, 1994–1995: Degree status of participants by gender and ethnicity (June 1995)

Degree status	Males $n=41$	Females $n=36$	Mexican American $n=41$	Puerto Rican $n=16$	Cuban $n=12$	Other Latino $n=8$	Totals and (%) $n=77$
Ph.D. completed	25	17	20	9	8	5	42
(% of group)	(61)[a]	(47)	(49)	(56)	(67)	(63)	(55)
Ph.D. expected	6	9	10	3	1	1	15
							(19)
M.A. completed or expected	10	10	11	4	3	2	20
							(26)
Average completion time for Ph.D. (years)[b]	6	8	6.7	6.2	4.5	5.8	5.5

[a] Percentages are based on group totals and do not equal 100 percent due to rounding.

[b] Elapsed time to degree (ETD) calculated from graduate school enrollment date to completion date, Ph.D. only.

torate or were not sure they would pursue one. Those planning to stop with their master's were involved in their careers, pursuing other goals, or felt school would take too much time and money away from their families. Of the remaining fifty-seven participants, forty-two had obtained their doctoral degrees, fifteen had doctoral programs in progress, and all but two expected to finish by 1998. Several had taken a sabbatical of at least ten years after completing their master's degree; only one felt she was unlikely to complete her doctoral degree (Ibarra 1996, 8).

In contrast to their undergraduate experiences, however, a majority remarked how uncomfortable they were in graduate school. Of course, nearly all students who uproot their life or family and relocate to an unfamiliar place to live in low-income student housing are uncomfortable. Acclimating to a new community or struggling with rigorous graduate work is an ordeal common to Latinos and Anglos alike. But such commonalities can mask important cultural differences.

Graduate school is essentially a remolding process. From a minimalist's point of view, "the research university model (originally copied from Germany)—with its graduate doctoral programs and autonomous, professionalized disciplines—has been established in this country for more than a century. It's an apprentice system, a compact: Your advisor and other professors mentor you, and if you pass the required hurdles of scholarship—and to a far lesser extent, teaching—their recommendations get you a tenure-track job" (Weisbard 1997, 121). Some describe it as an "academic boot camp" with undertones of monastic life. Instead of turning students into clerics, graduate schools turn students into scholars by various means of mental pushing, probing, shaping, and grinding until the inductees become candidates worthy of joining the inner circle of the professoriate. It is somewhat akin to being initiated into a secret society, but the psychological stress of initiation is sustained over many years, and much more pressure is involved. Ann Matthews captures the inherent conditions of academe in *Bright College Years: Inside the American Campus Today:*

It is a place enormously knowing, but almost never reasonable, situated in the United States but not entirely of it. Laws, customs, language all run differently there. Time does too. . . . The world of academe is strongly territorial, but not very social. Its three tribes—those who learn, those who profess, and those who arrange—carry a great deal of baggage, visible and invisible. . . . But for seven centuries, the basic alchemy of the venture has held. Learn, or leave. Be willing to be changed, or get out. (1997, 36–7)

Graduate students cannot avoid interacting with faculty. In fact, they soon learn to emulate faculty members as much as possible. Their strategy is the reverse of undergraduates', who tend to do the least amount of work required for a degree. There is no ceiling on the effort required for completing a graduate degree. Graduate students must attend seminars always prepared to discuss salient issues and make significant contributions—or suffer the consequences. Others are indentured—as project or research assistants, they work alongside their professors and other students in the labs every day, or they must spend hours with colleagues and faculty as teaching assistants in undergraduate classes. Lave and Wenger might identify this as "situated learning," or a learning community (1991, 15). Graduate students are in fact "peripheral participants" in this process. As apprentice-like learners, they are physically located at the periphery of the work space; graduate students must observe and interact to gain an understanding of the beliefs of their particular discipline, their "community of practice" (1991, 93). Learning is never merely the "transmission" of knowledge or the "acquisition" of skill, for "learning and a sense of identity are inseparable" (1991, 114–15). Graduate students, then, must not only emulate their professors but must identify with their discipline in a way that resembles ethnic group cohesiveness.

In fact, graduate students soon learn that being changed means they must bend to the faculty's definitions of what constitutes hard work and success. As we shall see, problems surface because Latino and other minority students do not always define those terms as the faculty does. For example, most faculty members select graduate students by how well they demonstrate their intellect on standardized tests, or how well they fit in to the department or how strongly they are motivated to pursue the faculty member's research interests. In many universities students' motivation is measured by their competitive drive to pursue a doctoral degree and become a member of the faculty. Anything less than that is considered failure, for the efficient provision of new minds for the research maw determines the success or failure of academic departments in almost all research-driven universities. Women and minorities, on the other hand, may hold different views of what constitutes success or failure. Developing their intellect may be more important than demonstrating their brilliance, their research interests may not always coincide with the faculty's interests, and "working hard" may have nothing to do with cutthroat competition and everything to do with collaboration and progress toward a goal that leads somewhere other than the professoriate or a career in academe. Most graduate students learn these hidden meanings about academic work after they are accepted to apprentice with the faculty.

Entry into academe is a tricky event. New students do not expect to be treated as junior colleagues in their department, but they do expect some sort of academic guidance. Instead, they may encounter a tradition of sink or swim. Most quickly find they have been left to fend for themselves without clear information about what to do until someone, usually an advanced graduate student, shows them the ropes. However, from the outset many new graduate students find their major professor distant and detached rather than encouraging and supportive. That pattern usually continues until students have proved their academic worth in the mind of the mentor. Granting newcomers, especially those with different cultural perspectives, the right to participate in the department—the local community of practice—would cause tension. To avoid the displacement of long-held academic beliefs, old-timers use their power to mute but not extinguish the newcomers (Lave and Wenger 1991, 116). Faculty thus tend to play a game of wait-and-see. Why invest time and effort developing a relationship unless the inductees can demonstrate their abilities and somehow prove they are likely to complete the program successfully?

If mentor and student eventually establish an apprenticeship compact, it neither guarantees mutual understanding nor eliminates cultural or interpersonal conflicts. It only ensures that close social transactions between mentor and mentored will maximize the one-way transformation process that the "candidate for degree" must make. For graduate students, gaining the right to participate with professors is very much like learning to identify with an ethnic community. Learning and meaning do not come from precisely defined community boundaries—academia, in this case—but from interactions between communities, from "multiple interconnections with persons, activities, knowing and the world" (Lave and Wenger 1991, 121). They either learn to be scholars or leave; they become willing to change into professors or they get out. These are familiar conditions for graduate students, especially for those enrolled at competitive research institutions.

Graduate schools, however, are notorious for not providing social support systems for most students. In fact, minority undergraduates, and even international graduate students, have better support systems than do minority graduate students. Many campuses allocate student fees toward maintaining support groups that cater almost exclusively to ethnic undergraduates' social and academic needs. Ameliorating the situation for graduate students requires finding appropriate ways to mentor, counsel, and help students adjust to graduate school culture.

Minority graduate populations on most campuses are so small—smaller still within departments—that isolation and loneliness become magnified. This pushes students to form their own support groups, a process that forces them to spend their time, money, and emotional energy or to go begging to their departments or graduate school administrators for help in starting such a group. On campuses with international students, international graduate students often take advantage of their numbers to establish informal support networks in addition to those established by the institutions.

In comparison, domestic minority graduate students, mostly from the United States and often among the smallest student populations on campus, are too dispersed and too few in number to form appropriate informal groups or to be able to network effectively. Latinos and graduate students from other ethnic groups often transfer out of large research universities, especially those with predominantly Anglo campuses, or drop out of programs altogether because they feel so isolated (see E. Seymour and Hewitt 1997). Latinos and Latinas who are people oriented and gravitate toward family and community life find graduate school can be the least attractive, least friendly, and sometimes the coldest community they encounter in their entire educational experience.

Among participants in my study, the first generation of Latinos and Latinas, who entered graduate school during the early 1970s, described struggles with their departments in a stoic, matter-of-fact way; they simply did what they had to do to survive and succeed. Twenty years or more later the current crop of Latino graduate students is dealing with the same issues, except they are less tolerant and more demanding than their predecessors. They are also realists who acknowledge that despite their conflict, they must endure graduate school culture. These overt characteristics merely inflame the invisible academic conflicts that constitute some of the turbulence for Latino graduate students. These circumstances continue today, unrecognized or ignored by faculty, staff, and even their non-Latino colleagues.

In general, Latino study participants seemed to focus on the hidden dimensions of the academic metamorphosis, often describing the process as one of transformation from one ethnic group into another. In most cases transformation into the professoriate was even more of a challenge for women. At first, I thought that graduate school could be "watering down" the ethnicity of my interviewees, making them almost "homogenized." After further analysis I realized that at least two interrelated transformations were taking place. On one level, Latino graduate students were losing their ethnic identity or they were downplaying it, perhaps in an effort to absorb new academic cultural values. Meanwhile, they were also showing increased interest in ethnic research topics or ethnic academe in general. For example, interest in ethnicity as a focus of study jumped from 25 percent to 75 percent between the subjects' initial graduate school enrollment and the completion or near completion of their highest degree (Ibarra 1996). Latinos and Latinas apparently undergo a significant ethnic transformation in graduate school.

The Graduate School Transformation

Many Latinos described their time in graduate school as being "cut off" from the rest of the *real* world, where culture and identity matter. Some entered graduate school with strong cultural identities that had been enhanced by the undergraduate environment itself. Even predominantly majority campuses (such as the Ivies) attempt to provide cultural centers or sponsor the development of minority student groups. Fresh from these undergraduate experiences, or from the nonacademic world of work, Latinos enter graduate school and encounter a no-nonsense work environment in which the remolding process begins immediately. Sealed off from much of campus social life by departments, and segmented further by disciplinary fields and subdisciplinary research interests, graduate students find little free time for participating in the rich social life of campus and community. They learn that new values are rewarded here: specialization, fragmentation, attention to minute detail, and accuracy. And they learn that experts are the most valued and venerated. No longer is it enough to regurgitate information on tests and term papers; they must now completely absorb it.

Graduate students quickly learn that knowledge and comprehension are their swords and shields in the open arenas of theoretical argument within their discipline. The small graduate seminars are verbal testing grounds in which they learn the jargon and exchange the venerated names and works of both predecessors and contemporary scholars in the discipline. Seminars are the dynamic interactive core of apprenticeship. Clustered around the professor, small groups of neophytes load and reload information for the real battles that lie ahead—qualifying examinations and publication of seminar papers, dissertations, articles, and, ultimately, books.

A graduate program is in fact a very small world, often humorously described as a place where one learns more and more about less and less. The primary goal, at least in the realm of research institutions, is to create new knowledge through rigorous research procedures. This knowledge does not necessarily need real-world applications or any application at all, for that matter. In the academic culture of departments and disciplines the faculty is cloistered and determined to diminish those influences and preconditions that may distract them and their students from pursuing the knowledge that scholars are creating. The analytical, linear process of finding answers and new knowledge is highly prescribed in the biological and physical sciences. Even the social sciences and humanities have little room for alternative methodologies.

Consequently, some traditional faculty members perceive cultural and ethnic values and perspectives as injecting bias into the learning-knowledge processes within a discipline. Ethnic identity and culture have their primary place as the focus or object of study in some social science departments or humanities disciplines. Some disciplines, like anthropology, frown on researchers' studying their own ethnic community in the belief that such a practice leaves their work vulnerable to biased data and interpretations. Even then, ethnic research rarely has achieved high intrinsic academic value unless it can be popularized. Before it can gain recognition and value it must become a subject interesting to a broad range of people or homogenized so that many benefit from applying the research finding to the larger society. The underlying attitude that ethnicity can get in the way of true scholarship is one reason so many ethnic populations tend to hide or downplay their ethnic and gender values and absorb the new academic culture of the discipline. Many intend, after completing their degrees, to reemerge in academia with their identities intact and their personal missions still aimed at changing the system. Instead, they discover, or fail to discover, that they have been significantly transformed.

Even when graduate departments make special efforts to assist the progress of Latinos and other minority students toward completion of their advanced degrees, the transformation may require these students to submerge or discard their cultural values. Sometimes even their own community calls students' ethnic and gender identity into question, and this is a large price to pay. As one Chicana administrator from Texas described it, "In Austin being female was an advantage. . . . A young Hispanic female with a doctorate in that field was quite marketable. [Back home] it was just the opposite. . . . What was interesting for me was the contrast that I was marketable [with a Ph.D.] outside [my home community] and back home I was not."

The main point is that ethnicity becomes the central feature, the main characteristic undergoing change in graduate students. Few understand the dynamics or implications of this transformation. Identity, research interests, and academic cultural conflict are all relatively different ethnic interactions and transactions in higher education. We need to understand the dynamics of ethnicity in the cultural contexts—the situational frames—of graduate education in order to understand the processes of this educational transformation.

The Educational Process and Latino Student Issues

Admissions

Like many other minority students, more than half the Latino study group selected a high-risk admissions strategy and applied to only one or two graduate schools. Most felt very positive about their admission to graduate school, that is, they did not recall encountering many difficulties in the process. From their perspective, three factors facilitated their entrance to a program: their ethnicity, especially as it related to their bilingual capabilities and the school's affirmative action initiatives; letters of recommendation from undergraduate faculty; and their undergraduate careers, especially unique research experiences or the type of school they attended. In general, all the Latinos and Latinas I interviewed gave ample evidence that ethnicity played a role in preparing them for or influencing their entry into graduate school.

Factors that they perceived as having hindered them the most were low standardized test scores (mainly, the Graduate Record Exam, or GRE), a problem that tended to be clustered by state, with the largest and most serious complaints coming from participants who attended graduate schools in Texas; departmental reluctance or discrimination, reflecting negative attitudes as well as actual inequities in the admissions process, as some students discovered; and, above all, financial support—80 percent of respondents could not have attended graduate school without some form of internal or external funding through fellowships and family support. At some point during their graduate school experience, 75 percent used personal resources, 65 percent were awarded fellowships, and 55 percent received assistantships or grant support (Ibarra 1996).

Acclimation

Once they had acclimated to a new community, the majority of respondents felt comfortable on campus. Asked what the campus attitude toward Latinos was, their answers split almost evenly: roughly 30 percent felt the campus attitude was favorable, 35 percent felt it was "okay," and 35 percent felt the attitude was negative. Asked about their department's attitude toward them, 28 percent felt it was favorable, and 31 percent said it was "okay" or that they had not spent enough time there to tell. But more than 41 percent felt the attitude was negative. Those perceiving a positive attitude generally noted that the university had made positive changes, seemed supportive and helpful, or that it had demonstrated it was behind affirmative action initiatives. Those who felt it was "okay" said they saw little change in negative faculty attitudes and behaviors toward them while in graduate school but described the general climate as tolerant, indifferent, and ambivalent. Those who felt the climate was negative described attitudes that ranged from "benign neglect, sink-or-swim, stereotyping" to overt attitudes such as "discrimination, hostile environment and culture, or racism."

Such "campus climate" questions tend to measure degrees of conflict and to assume that the issues are between obviously different groups or reflect expected differences of opinion between groups.[1] But that assumption is not entirely correct, for it is not always the obvious differences that surface. In qualitative follow-up questions about campus issues, I asked participants a number of questions, such as what the major issues among Latino graduate students were. As questions shifted from "climate" or attitudinal issues to cultural issues, the differences became more evident.

For example, sixty-eight of the seventy-seven individuals in the study responded to the question about major issues; 33 percent felt there were either no Latino graduate issues or none they could recall. A few described pleasant experiences and nurturing environments, but the majority of those who could not recall any Latino graduate student issues acknowledged that they had been too busy—with studies, work, or life—to notice. But forty-six participants (67 percent) recalled major issues Latinos encountered and commented on the problems. Their responses generated the following general categories, listed in descending order by total number of comments in each category. Almost all their comments are listed; the italics highlight the top two or three issues.

- Institutional or general issues (31 responses)—Nine cited *financial support,* and seven thought *too few Latinos on campus* were the most important problems in this category. The other fifteen comments covered problems about affirmative action; insufficient institutional funding to develop graduate education; few Latino/Latina faculty; lack of ethnic studies program (i.e., Chicano, Puerto Rican, or Latino studies); inequities in education; lack of support systems (nonfinancial); and GRE problems (i.e., low scores, difficult access to test sites, multiple test-taking issues, and so on).
- Academic culture issues (14 responses)—Five cited *curriculum issues,* and five cited *departmental culture* (ethnic research problems, retaining

identity while getting Ph.D., cultural isolation, insensitivity to culture, inattention to minority status of Latinos) as the most problematic areas in this category, whereas only four cited *racism*.

• Ethnic conflict issues (11 responses)—Five specifically cited *intracultural or class issues* (i.e., minority programs too politicized for undergraduates, island versus mainland conflicts among Puerto Ricans, Mexican versus Mexican American conflicts), while others mentioned unspecified ethnic conflicts as problems they saw or encountered.

• Personal or individual issues (9 responses)—Six referred to *social/cultural issues* (i.e., family, clash with traditional campus and community cultures, gender issues) as major problems in this category. Other problems cited included feelings of grief, feelings of pressure to prove themselves, and feelings of inadequacy or of being in the wrong place, like an impostor who did not belong in graduate school.

In general, their stories revealed episodes of conflict in adjusting to academic culture. Most participants found their adjustment often began with a clash between their ethnic identity and cultural values on the one hand and, on the other, the academic value system within the department.

Latinos in the study reacted by adjusting in a variety of ways. Some said they experienced a kind of academic culture shock within the department. For example, many felt the absence of community and family values and commented on their difficulty establishing personal relationships with faculty they perceived as strangely distant. Roberto, a Cuban American professor in Florida, stated, "I guess the farther away you are from the community, the stronger the need for the connection, because you feel so isolated. At [Ivy league institutions] you're out, you're a minority, your networks must get strengthened." Consequently, a majority of those interviewed tried to establish social groups, either formally or informally, among colleagues and with other Latino graduate students. In many instances what started as casual study groups developed into strong bonds of social support to cope with the situation. For a few these bonds came to resemble those in an extended family.

Puerto Ricans from the island found the competitiveness among colleagues at research institutions particularly unnerving. In general, the scarcity of Latino research interests or Latino faculty caused many to make major adjustments. Juliana, a social science professor who grew up in the Southwest, was in a program at a large research university in Texas. Not long after she was admitted, she was upset to find that in her department "one of the things that was a barrier was being the only Hispanic there, and having [my research] agenda that dealt with multicultural issues. No one on the faculty or even the university was prepared to deal with it. So I had to change my research topic because there was no one available."

Apparently, no faculty member had sufficient experience in multicultural approaches or research to guide her doctoral program.

Cultural Adjustments—Ethnicity and Minority Status

Other Latinos in the study found that the adjustment and transformation process touched upon sensitive areas of ethnic identity. Many participants wanted to describe their first experiences as "minorities" on campus.

Only five participants, or roughly 7 percent of the total study group, identified themselves either with the pan-ethnic term *Hispanic* or with *Latino.* Central and South Americans and/or those with parents from mixed ethnic backgrounds (i.e., Latino/Anglo) preferred pan-ethnic identity markers. Some felt their identity was confusing or too complicated to explain so they used pan-ethnic terms to facilitate interactions with non-Latinos. Mexican American and Puerto Rican respondents showed signs of ethnic polarization related to sociopolitical struggles within the dominant U.S. culture. They evinced a strong preference for using specific terms. In general, approximately half the Mexican American participants preferred to use the term *Mexican American* exclusively, and a third preferred to use only *Chicano* or *Chicana.* Puerto Ricans seemed consistent about their identity.

In regard to patterns evidenced in the responses to the question on minority status, 68 percent of those Latinos responding ($n = 66$) said they clearly perceived themselves as a minority, 24 percent said they did not, and 8 percent gave mixed responses. Those who do not consider themselves "minority" were predominantly Cuban American (83 percent) and "Other Latinos" (50 percent) and a smaller number of Puerto Ricans (25 percent). Some Cuban Americans made the point that "to expect special treatment as a minority implies victimization, injustice, and second-class status, which, for most Cuban Americans, seems not to be a part of Cuban culture. Indeed, many Cubans revealed it was only upon entering higher education that they first experienced being a minority" (Ibarra 1996, 13). Although many respondents within these groups claimed they experienced marginalization and discrimination, most held fast to their self-perception as "foreigners"—not "minorities," as defined by other "North Americans."

The Influence of Academic Culture

The entry of Latinos and Latinas into graduate school is marked by major changes in their lives. Their transformation into graduate students, not an easy process for anyone, is accompanied by complex issues involving ethnic identity and academic pressures to change and conform. In addition to the adjustments that all students endure, Latinos must acclimate to alien academic values and departmental cultures that conflict with their own. Romo, a Chicano who is now a professor, shared his experience in doing ethnic research and maintaining his ethnic identity:

There was some effort to get Chicanos in [to the program], but there was no effort to keep us. There was no effort to support the kind of research we wanted to do, so . . . you were on your own. . . . It was the subtle things which were ways of negating any kind of importance for Latinos. For example, in American politics, when you talked about politics it was always regarding voting—there was never any inclusion of data regarding Latinos, and we were told in some classes Latinos were insignificant, that's why the data wasn't included. . . . So if you wanted to [do research or] write papers dealing with Latinos, it was discouraged. . . . I think we all shared a desire to retain Chicano identity through this grueling process of becoming either a Ph.D. or lawyer, an educator, or whatever, and a desire to resist the efforts to not care about Chicanos. . . . We wanted to see the kind of work we were doing was related to Chicanos and that it was going to have some kind of benefit to the Chicano community.

For Latinos in graduate or professional schools, ethnic boundaries give way to new identities: "graduate student," "doctor," "professor," or "dean" as the roles shift and evolve. The consequences of these transformations are evident in the tension and conflict voiced by the Latinos in the study. On the surface Latinos react to the initiation into graduate school and their discipline in ways similar to all other populations: some adjust, some adapt, and some leave. However, for those who stay, one survival strategy is to focus their research on something of personal interest. For Latinos and other ethnic populations the interest in studying ethnicity seems to emerge from the graduate education process itself (see Ibarra 1996, 56–57).

More than half the Latinos I interviewed encountered difficulties in graduate school. Some problems would be familiar to all graduate students: learning tensions, performance anxiety, stress associated with academics and finances, and problems with difficult professors. However, Latinos described additional cultural turbulence that is more commonly associated with underrepresented populations than with majority graduate students in general.[2] Some told stories about covert attitudes and real or imagined "lack of empathy with ethnic research topics" (Ibarra 1996, 47). Some provided horror stories of overt attitudes of discrimination or detailed the sarcastic and humiliating comments made openly to them by the faculty. In one case a faculty adviser took advantage of the student's bilingual and bicultural abilities to enhance her own research agenda. When the student became suspicious and backed away from the pressures, the faculty adviser made life difficult for the student both inside and outside the department (Ibarra 1996, 46).

The most serious difficulties for Latino graduate students were those associated with professors. This is not surprising, given the relatively close interactions involved in the graduate school apprenticeship model. Some professors were simply insensitive to all students, graduate or otherwise, regardless of ethnicity or gender. A few faculty advisers left their department for new positions elsewhere, abandoning graduate students in the middle of their programs. The more interesting pattern here, however, is that Latino faculty caused serious problems. One Latina described how she was told by someone on her thesis committee that a Chicano professor on the committee not only tried to undermine her work but then tried to use it for his own research. She was puzzled by this but simply had to shrug it off as another experience typical of graduate school. Intracultural or even intraethnic issues like this one occur quite frequently among the ethnic populations on campus, yet these events are rarely discussed openly.

The episodes with Latino faculty are one of the conundrums of what many take to be racism. The circumstances are identical to the attitudes and actions labeled "racist" when minorities run into conflicts with majority faculty. But what happens when a minority faculty member has serious conflicts with members of her or his own ethnic group? And is it racism? I believe that the suspicion that Latino faculty treat Latino students badly is justified. In my experiences these conflicts often are rooted in differences in social class or culture and/or in a misunderstanding of the course requirements and goals rather than racism.[3]

However, not all incidents involving Latino faculty are rooted in class conflicts; these interactions revealed something else that is quite important. Latino students' interpretations of their confrontations showed differences in their cultural values and those of Latino faculty, which often amounted to conflict between cultural context and academic culture. For instance, Raul said he was confused by his Latina faculty adviser's general approach:

Sometimes, even with the faculty member I work with, I am not getting the respect I feel I should get or the support. . . . Where I [come] from, being real, sincere, and genuine are very important [qualities] because people can see through you. . . . I didn't get much of that from the person I worked with. I think she was trying to help me, but in her way. . . . I just think the strategy she took is different from the strategy I want to take to become successful. I think she felt that . . . you [should] internalize everything from the department and . . . either do what you want to do and struggle all the way through, or do what another faculty member is doing and hopefully it will go with what you want to do. "Don't worry about being mentored—get your degree and do what you want afterwards." I think that's pretty sound advice, but the way it was being given . . . it confused me more.

She's Latina but much more assimilated culturally than I am in terms of frame of mind, outlook, perception. She grew up in difficult circumstances too. I admire her for the obstacles she's overcome. But again, in one of our conversations, she said, . . . "I'm not here for those students who don't give a damn. I'm here for those students who work hard." . . . A lot of times I think [her] assumption is that those students who fail are the ones that didn't work hard. That's not true, because there were a lot of instances for me to fail, not in school, in [my urban community]. . . . The students who work hard will be fine, and I will be there for them. But I think the students who are walking that fence like I was need to have some positive reinforcement because they are the ones struggling with the self-doubt like I was. I think that's the fundamental difference between her and me. The assumption of hard work and the work ethic. (Ibarra 1996, 49–50)

In other words, Raul saw the differences between academic culture and his ethnic values as conflicts in cultural context. He noted that different perspectives on the appropriate goals for a graduate student are complicated by contrasting strategies for advising and helping graduate students within the department. Raul seemed surprised to see a Latina professor, especially someone he knew had grown up in difficult circumstances similar to his own, using a low-context approach to advising graduate students. He saw her as advising students to ignore conflicts rather than address them openly and sincerely as someone from his community would expect and value.

He was especially offended by her statement that "I'm not here for those students who don't give a damn. I'm here for those students who work hard." Though Raul did not explain what he thought she meant by hard work, they clearly had different definitions of the phrase. Their definitions reflect the contrasts in ethnic and academic culture, at least in the social sciences. First, social science professors define hard workers as those who are voluble in seminars and can demonstrate a firm grasp of the material or research methodology and analysis. Graduate school is a competitive environment in which students become scholarly critics, adept at finding flaws and arguing for or against the ideas, logic, and theories proposed by other scholars. For instance, active participation in seminars, even for those who have good command of the material, often is culturally foreign to many minority graduate students. And majority professors often become testy and condescending to those students who do not immediately demonstrate a relish for being in the thick of either written or verbal intellectual battles.

This phenomenon, called "argument culture," is endemic in academe, according to Deborah Tannen (2000). It is counterproductive for students because rather than have them learn the more difficult processes of integrating ideas and putting them in historical or disciplinary contexts, faculty encourage them to demonstrate intellectual prowess by tearing apart scholarly work. This process, in fact, fosters oversimplification, misrepresention, or never letting the facts get in the way of a good argument.

From his own experiences Raul knows that high-context minority students have the ability for graduate work, but they can be consumed with doubt about their abilities. This—along with culturally ingrained reticence—can lead them to hold back when participating in graduate seminars. If their reticence is greeted by superciliousness and patronizing comments, which tend to be the "motivators" of choice among low-context tenured faculty—personified by Professor Kingsfield in *The Paper Chase*—the students' self-esteem becomes undermined. Minority graduate students who are made to feel inadequate tend to mask that reaction with behaviors that vary widely, from being overly aggressive and fighting with colleagues in professional settings to becoming shy, withdrawn, and isolated.

Raul also understood that Latinos feel personally obligated to overcome the stigma of their ethnic minority status, compelled to prove by their actions, attitudes, and sheer hard work that they are just as good as or better academically than their peers. He recognized that many people use these behaviors regardless of ethnicity, but he believes they are more prevalent among "students of color because they don't see people like them[selves]. Because once you achieve [in graduate school], you have [to overcome the stigma associated with] your last name or color" (Ibarra 1996, 42). Whether Latinos' reaction to criticism is overaggression or withdrawal, non-Hispanics often use those behaviors to characterize minority graduate students as those "who don't give a damn." In other words, Raul saw his professor as associating an apathetic affect with failure, a reaction he equated with betrayal. He, on the other hand, saw those students as crying out for help and guidance. To Raul, the Latina professor has been so assimilated into the faculty culture, which shies away from students who need special attention to cultivate their abilities, that she has turned her back on her own culture. One of the unstated messages here is Raul's profound disappointment in the Latina professor.

According to Manuel Ramírez (1991), field-sensitive Latinos tend to be motivated by "social rewards which strengthen relationships with important others" and are "related to achievement for others (family, team, ethnic/racial group, etc.)," whereas field-independent people "seek nonsocial rewards" and their "motivation is related to self-advancement" (1991, 20, table 3.2). This is a telling point, for one of the fundamental differences in the values held by Anglo faculty and those held by ethnic minorities is the critical difference between academic culture and ethnic values. In *The New Faculty Member* (1992) Robert Boice, an authority on faculty development, notes that most college teachers come from educated families. "They value displays of brilliance (that is, verbal fluency and productivity in research and scholarship) in students and in colleagues. So it is, [Alexander] Astin [1985] concludes, that professors value the demonstration of intellect over the development of intellect; we favor students and colleagues who arrive with the proper intrinsic motivation, manifest brilliance, and social tone" (262).

Raul confided to me after the interview that because of his conflict with the professor, he was going to transfer to a different graduate school to complete his doctoral degree. To repeat Matthews's dictum about college: "Be willing to be changed or get out."

Raul represents many Latinos and Latinas in the study who were trying to cope with very new and uncomfortable situations. According to Ford's "living systems framework" (LSF), they were constructing new frameworks and systems for living under these new conditions (1992). During their interviews Latinos and Latinas compiled their experiences, each a new behavioral episode, into useful "scripts" for succeeding in graduate school. Multicontextual individuals, whose scripts contain the repertoires of both high-context cultural behaviors and field-sensitive cognitive styles, learn to adapt to graduate school culture while enduring the difficult process of becoming low-context, field-independent academics. This fits the model of behavioral change described by Ford (1992). The dynamics of systems analysis in his LSF model breathe life into Hall's model of cultural context and Manuel Ramírez's concept of bicognition.

Extrapolating from Ford's model, Latinos in the study were undergoing any number of changes. The change was most likely transformational— some stable behavior patterns were altered, and the original patterns of Latino ethnic values were superseded or, more accurately, were set aside and became dormant. The students adopted new cultural patterns, those valued by the professoriate. "This kind of change process is illustrated by concepts such as metamorphosis, insight, identity crisis, emotional decompensation, personality reorganization, and religious conversion," according to Ford (1992, 56).

Ford's model illustrates cognitive transformations that lead to becoming multicontextual. In academia this is an adaptive strategy that requires adopting a new lifestyle with significant cultural differences from the student's ethnic family and original community. Latinos in the study were not just learning or teaching in low-context, field-independent academic environments but were faced with actually thinking and being in those modes in order to don their new ethnic identity, the professoriate. The real surprise for multicontextual individuals comes after their academic transformation, when they realize that teaching, learning, and research styles in higher education are contextually deficient, or, more accurately, dominantly low context. This does not necessarily mean they are incorrect modes of teaching and learning. It simply means that half the learning modalities are either missing or dormant. This educational deficiency becomes evident when high-context students learn that graduate school discounts and discredits comprehensive thinking and analysis in deference to linear, sequential, low-context thinking. The realization of this educational bias does not fully set in until graduate students enter the professoriate, as we shall see in the chapters that follow.

Many characteristics in conflict are between the high-context, field-sensitive values of Latino graduate students and the low-context, field-independent values of the professoriate. But the professoriate is not just a subculture; it is itself an "ethnic group." It is the primary group, the alpha group, in graduate school. It demands that students transform themselves and accept academic cultural values before they can be accepted into the community of scholars—the community of practice. Much of this could be said of the military as well, and I would agree. The military in many ways also serves as family, community, and ethnic group in the extreme. The learning transformation of a graduate student is not unlike a cultural identity shift on the order of magnitude of intense military training. According to Lave and Wenger, two things may happen: first, as the identity of learners changes, changes in their cultural identity and social relations are inevitable; second, change may ensue in the shift that occurs from "learning to display knowledge" as student apprentices to the more advanced level of "learning to know" as professors and scholars (1991, 112; also see Lave 1993).

Identity shifting is one of many adaptive strategies that multicontextual individuals learn early. Even so, can the training to become a member of the professoriate overshadow the ethnic identity associated with national origin? It can and it does. Burton Clark, a foremost scholar on higher education, observes: "By the time young academics are committed to a discipline and embedded in an institutional setting, the beliefs and identities they import from their social-class background also fade" (1987a, 107). Clark believes the overriding power of the academic discipline instills a new sense of individual status that realigns one's points of view. Other scholars agree. In their research on ethnic identity and change, de Vos and Romanucci-Ross claim:

A less general and sometimes conflicting form of present-oriented social belonging is identity through participation in an occupation. This identity may conflict with a national identity. When an individual acquires competence in a skill or a profession, his primary commitment shifts to his occupation, or to the social class of his profession. He may identify himself by status as a nobleman or a commoner, or by occupation, as a merchant or a worker, or more specifically as a scientist, a physician, and so on. This identity may be much stronger and more compelling than a national or ethnic allegiance. However, in time of conflict an ethnic or national allegiance may assume priority, such as in the case of some German and Japanese social scientists who distorted professional knowledge in the direction of ethnic-national ideologies in World War II. (1975, 19)

If Ford's transformational theory is the cognitive principle at work here, Latino graduate students may set aside some of their ethnic values. More likely, these values just become hidden or submerged so that the students can adopt a new set of academic cultural values alongside their originally imprinted Latino community values; thus they form a new set of adaptive strategies. Latino graduate students can selectively maintain, modify, or reject some of their cultural values to better accommodate the appropriate academic values for perceiving and transacting within the academic world. According to Barth (1967, 1969), they become ethnic entrepreneurs. According to Ford's model, they are motivated to do so by academic goals, the goals of a professorial career rewarded with research grants, scholarly recognition, and tenure. If the academic culture of research values these rewards, teaching, community service, and student services play a much lesser role in academic life.

Faculty roles and rewards realign high-context, field-sensitive ethnic values with low-context, field-independent academic values. This pattern creates conflict between people from different cultural contexts. This is what Latino students perceive and describe as most uncomfortable about faculty, especially Latino faculty, who "act as if they forgot who they are." For some Latinos it is less a matter of forgetting than simply subordinating their ethnicity while in graduate school. Elenita, a Puerto Rican graduate student, described it succinctly: "In undergrad college, people often went to their own ethnic pools, they strongly identified with their ethnicity. . . . I felt more of a sense of that as an undergrad than here in graduate school. Everyone's so busy with other things that it's very difficult to focus primarily on your culture and your ethnicity."

Latino students are not the only ones from high-context cultures who are uncomfortable with and concerned about the transformation to faculty. Boice found corroborating evidence regarding the special problems of African Americans who had just entered the ranks of faculty:

They may refer to earlier events, often graduate school. Feelings of anger about academic careers often begin before the doctorate. The discriminations are subtle and painful; over time, they make their recipients feel crazy. While still in graduate school, as in their later professorial experiences, Afro-Americans *often feel pressured to give up their racial and ethnic identities.* There, as later, they are discouraged from studying their own cultures and problems as colleagues express doubts about whether such research is "real." (1992, 257; emphasis added)

Latinos in my study described identical circumstances. As I said earlier, only 25 percent entered a graduate program with an interest in studying their ethnic heritage. During the interviews nearly 70 percent of the group said they had completed or intended to complete a master's or doc-

Table 4.2. Latino study, 1994–1995: Field of study of participants by ethnic group (June 1995)

Field of study	Mexican American $n=41$	Puerto Rican $n=16$	Cuban $n=12$	Other Latino $n=8$	Totals and (%) $n=77$
Education	13[a]	2	2	1	18 (23)[b]
Social science	17	7	5	3	32 (42)
Humanities	6	2	3	1	12 (16)
Physical science	3	1	2	2	8 (10)
Biological science	2	4		1	7 (9)

[a] Figures include both master's and doctoral degrees.

[b] Percentages are based on group totals and do not equal 100 percent due to rounding.

toral thesis on an ethnic topic. More than 33 percent described some form of struggle with their department or faculty adviser in regard to focusing their research project on ethnicity. As might be expected, the first generations of Latinos to enter graduate schools had many more difficulties than their successors.

For others, the influence of ethnic group interests varied according to whether their discipline was in a physical or social science (see table 4.2). Some Latinos in the humanities or social sciences met with resistance from their advisers or encountered informal rules within their discipline that discouraged them from studying a topic related to their ethnic heritage. For instance, a number of participants in my study were highly critical of faculty in departments of cultural anthropology, a field known for developing the concept of multiculturalism and encouraging cultural sensitivity. The faculty had dissuaded the respondents from researching a topic associated with their ethnic group. For Latino scientists the concern is not as relevant, although a large majority of them spent a significant amount of personal time involved in special ethnic sections of national science organizations or other academic associations. Most dedicated their time to encouraging minority students to become scientists (Ibarra 1996).

The common denominator among students in the Latino study group was perseverance to complete the degree, as well as the motivation to become a professor or a professional. But the social and cultural costs of becoming a professor could be quite high. Juliana made an interesting comment that illustrates a multicontextual strategy in regard to the transformation.

I think [what] I had to do . . . here in academia deals with the language issue. I've had to learn to talk like an academician—there is a particular language that you use in [social science]. You find yourself shifting into the jargon of . . . the language of the community. That was very difficult for me because I had been in [clinical] practice for so many years, and I had been dealing with what I refer to as "real people." Suddenly I get into academia, and you're supposed to cite your references when you speak, and you're supposed to use particular jargon, and you're supposed to use empirical research. And it was, like—who cares? But that was the socialization into the [social science] academic community.

And I transition in and out of it very easily. Once I learned how to play, I viewed it as a—I hate to use the term *game,* because it's almost as if I'm not doing it as a real person—but once I learned the rules of the interaction, I'm very good at shifting from one to another. It's survival.

Although Juliana seemed to take her experience in stride, she is an exception. The issues are far more serious and deeply unsettling for some. Yolanda, for instance, was nearing completion of her doctoral degree. As she discussed the troubling conditions associated with the hostile culture and environment she encountered in graduate school, she revealed mixed feelings about becoming a professor:

YOLANDA: I think it's a hostile environment, and it gets very difficult to continue to motivate yourself to persevere. Graduate school is already difficult enough without its being a hostile environment.

IBARRA: Can you describe that hostile environment?

YOLANDA: I think they have a very rigid narrow perspective, and when I say "they," I'm talking more about the administration, with the management decisions about dealing with the program, the class schedules, and the propaganda. If you recruit working professionals, you should have a schedule that understands that they are working. Most working professionals have day jobs.

A second hostile condition is all of the management that I see is pretty much handled by white males who have been at the university for a long time. . . . It's not that they have a different perspective so much as they don't understand another perspective. I feel like it is a different culture that I have to learn how to navigate . . . everyday . . . and learn how to be with.

IBARRA: Can you describe that culture?

YOLANDA: A culture that values bureaucratic adherence to the existing policies rather than focusing on learning or students.

IBARRA: And these are the kinds of influences or patterns that are affecting the Latinos and Latinas?

YOLANDA: Right, because for me interacting with other people is what it's about. . . . So if you bring Latinos in, by and large, if there is any one similar characteristic, it's about their relationships with people and that's very important. It's discounted to a large extent. That's what makes it so oppressive to be there, because you're not really considered a person.

> ... I can see the advantages of being a university professor, which I
> think is interesting. . . . I went to school so that I could impact a greater
> number of people, and while I think that the potential is there as a uni-
> versity professor, I think that I value the practitioner role more highly,
> and I'm exploring that debate with myself now. . . .

IBARRA: Why do you feel that the practitioner side is more attractive than the academic side?

YOLANDA: The practitioner side is more attractive because it's more hands-on,
there's more immediate feedback, there is opportunity, and I think it's
less of a struggle [for] acceptance and inclusion.

Metamorphosis, identity crisis, reorganization, or conversion—
throughout the study each transformation closely involved Latino ethnicity associated with groups of different national origins: Mexican American, Puerto Rican, Cuban American, or "Other Latino" origins. For many
Latinas in the study group, transformations included issues about gender
identity as well. It seemed that graduate school was indeed like a battle-
ground, a fight about conflicting identity pools or pigeonholes. The concept of ethnicity is constant and changing for Latinos. As they are transformed through graduate education into a new group, the professoriate,
the pigeonholing lessens or the ethnicity is crowded out by more pressing
concerns. As Elenita said, "It is difficult to focus primarily on your culture
and your ethnicity."

At the end of this process the focus turns to those who complete advanced degrees and move toward their careers. As academics, even those
Latinos and Latinas who felt little or no conflict during graduate school
suddenly confront a new and more formidable challenge—gaining full acceptance into academe. Success here requires a thorough orientation into
academic culture and becoming adept at traversing internal organizational
structures. The first inkling of the problem came from Ilda, a Chicana
graduate student from Texas. Ilda, who was nearing completion of her
doctorate, was astutely aware of the larger concerns with organizational
culture, especially the differences in context between her cultural values
and those of academia:

ILDA: I don't know how this institution compares to other schools, but I have found
it lacking. . . . I think the personal connections that I made have been very
valuable, but they are few and far between and discontinuous. I found over
the years that I'm also very motivated by personal relationships, but institutions of higher education are like machines. I don't know if it's a gender issue
or not, but they are not people oriented, at least this one is not. I had some
issues even at my place of work, so it may be a gender issue, but my frame
of thinking always considers who is involved, how would it affect them,
what is the effect on people and on the relationships with people, whether
they are community relations, or whatever. Organizationally, it's bureaucratic

and hierarchical, and the focus tends to be more on—I'm talking about my work now more than school—what rules are being followed. Are they being followed correctly, are they being broken rather than taking the people [-oriented] side of things? Much more than I would have expected, I find a lack of attention to people as well, even in the school. I would have expected . that because we are student oriented and we teach classes, that the work and school environments would be much different, and I find that they're not.

IBARRA: The work and school environments have the same kind of cultural dominance, and it is different from that of the growing Latino population?

ILDA: Right, the cultural dominance and also the organizational cultural dominance—it's not people oriented and I'm surprised at that.

"Organizational cultural dominance, it's not people oriented." I was surprised by her words too. She had almost completed her graduate work, and on the eve of her entry into academe she found it "lacking" in something. Ilda's comment led me to rethink what we understand about academia and the professoriate. Cultural context, cognition, and ethnicity are inextricably intertwined. High-context characteristics among Latinos seem to be in conflict with low-context characteristics of academe: "It's not people oriented." And it seems that when Latinos and other ethnic minorities prepare for entry into the professoriate, they experience a transformation into a new ethnic group. For individuals with more high-context cultural values and field-sensitive cognitive values, the transition would be difficult at best. Those who could accommodate or combine both sets of characteristics would likely be more multicontextual in their ways of acting and doing things. Ilda felt the institution—the university—was lacking something, and she associated the organizational culture of her work environment—the bureaucracy and the hierarchy—with the "organizational cultural dominance" of her university. (Part III takes a closer look at academia through the eyes of Latino and Latina faculty, administrators, and nonacademics across the country.)

Focusing increasingly on the patterns of organizational culture, bureaucracy, hierarchy, and change, I began to look for what is lacking in our institutions of higher education.

5

"They Really Forget Who They Are"

Latinos and Academic Organizational Culture

> If we continue to teach our graduate students in ways that perpetuate the systems that have contributed to our personal infernos, then we can never expect to remedy the problems we so eloquently and frequently lament. For me, being Chicana brings with it the cultural legacy of an awareness of the interconnectedness of generations. That applies to academia as well. We suppress our voices through conformity, through mindless repetition of scripts, through the indirect devaluing of that which is important to us each time we give in to the aspects of academia that forced us to compromise our core values.
>
> María Christina González, *The Leaning Ivory Tower*

Graduate education is a formidable process of professional socialization. This point was reinforced at an annual meeting of the Council of Graduate Schools in 1994, when Claudia Mitchell-Kernan, an anthropologist, described a number of these formative social/cultural processes. Drawing from a variety of academic studies (see Becker et al. 1961; Granfield 1992; Jones 1980; Klamer and Colander 1990; Leijonhufvud 1973; Traweek 1988), she noted that success is almost entirely based on mastering disciplinary techniques that may or may not have anything to do with understanding the real world. In fact, faculty members often discourage graduate students from seeking to apply their knowledge in a nonacademic career.

Also, "the aspirations, anxieties, and perceptions that students bring to their graduate training are transformed and . . . most adopt the accretion of peculiarities common to the normative demeanor, image and folkways of their group" (Mitchell-Kernan 1995, 4). She pointed out to the assembly of graduate deans that a major function of academic socialization is to "disabuse students of their prior interests and expectations" in their discipline. "Those students who question the relevance of their training experience high levels of isolation and stress and eventually either submit to the dictates of their elders or drop out." Given such conditions, we should not be surprised to find that those graduate students who survive tend to become "more or less indignant or disagreeable" (1995, 4).

Her message captures the forces of academic enculturation—a process of learning how to participate in a culture. The main thrust of her remarks is well taken: if the process of professional socialization is intended to expunge students' prior interests and expectations, what takes their place and how is that change achieved? Reviewing my interviews with faculty for clues to their success, I noted two distinct features: all had found a faculty or administrative position within a year of receiving their degree; and no other distinct patterns or advantages reflecting potential for success emerged from the interviews. The number of Latinos who attended private versus public schools was not unusual among those who joined the professoriate, and equal numbers began college at two- and four-year institutions. Nor could I discern significant patterns in regard to socioeconomic differences, the relative prestige of their undergraduate institutions—or anything else. Where or how they started their college career made no difference. What stood out among them, in uniquely different ways, was their strength of character. All were motivated and goal oriented despite life traumas and academic difficulties. But my attention kept returning to the academic conflict that the interviewees described.

I knew from personal experience that issues among faculty and administrators would surface, but I never realized how intense they would be. The first hint of major issues surfaced early and unexpectedly. I was surprised to hear faculty, even new faculty, remembering graduate school as relatively positive, in sharp contrast to the current conflicts in their faculty careers. Latinas had especially difficult experiences, and even Latino faculty at predominantly Latino schools, or Hispanic Serving Institutions (HSIs), which are not usually associated with ethnic tensions, were describing cultural problems.[1] I noted that the problems were not always cultural conflicts between Anglo faculty or administrators and my research subjects; rather, the conflicts more often involved conflicts with academic culture and academia in general.

Only after I analyzed the transcripts did I find that faculty issues also seemed to relate to the concepts of context and cognition. In fact, the evidence that points to such conflict is probably stronger for faculty and administrators than it is for graduate students. Part III discusses that evidence. This chapter tackles a series of distinct but interrelated perspectives on the nature of academic culture and its influence on higher education.

The Latino Studies Program

Not all Latinos in my study found graduate student life difficult. Some found that academic enculturation often heightened their awareness of cultural contradictions, but others found fewer or less striking contradictions. Depending on their perspective, enculturation into the value system of the professoriate either dulled or sharpened their perception of faculty roles and rewards, especially at large universities where research drives academic culture. The following story embodies the Latino faculty issues that emerged from my original interview project, and it advances my hypothesis about the dominance of academic cultural values over ethnicity.

A relatively small Latino studies program at a midwestern research university has for decades had a tradition of serving both students and faculty. It was founded both as an interdisciplinary offering and to provide a mechanism for actively recruiting Latino undergraduate and graduate students as well as Latino faculty. Latino political activists pushed the university to create the program during the 1960s. But the activists could not convince campus administrators to award Latino Studies the degree-granting status that only one other ethnic studies program has received. Consequently, the Latino faculty hired through the program received tenure only in the 1990s, and most received tenure only in the latter half of the decade.

These faculty members have joint appointments, split between Latino Studies and another academic department in the College of Arts and Sciences, which also houses Latino Studies. The joint appointments, which are standard practice nationally when nondegree programs hire faculty, are a double-edged sword. These transdisciplinary partnerships provide academic credibility and variety to Latino Studies. But new faculty must spend their first seven years or so focused on research and teaching, seeking to achieve tenure in the academic discipline of their degree-granting department. As a result, the partnership structure severely drains the strength of the Latino Studies program, diffuses loyalties, and tends to undermine the program's efforts to achieve legitimacy as a degree-granting department. According to Evelyn Hu-DeHart (1995), this is actually a common pattern for ethnic studies programs in higher education.

The program, staffed almost entirely by Latinos and Latinas, has a rotating directorship, usually held by a tenured professor who also teaches Latino Studies courses; office support, which consists mainly of students hired as staff; and a full-time nonfaculty university employee. Hired almost ten years earlier, the university employee was functioning primarily as a recruiter and retention specialist with significant but informal influence over the student services component of the program.

When the last director, whom I will call "Andres," took over, he acknowledged that he had no clear understanding of the recruiting, retention, and student services component of the program. Almost immediately, Andres attempted to end recruiting and retention activities and reallocate those funds toward more appropriate "academic pursuits," such as paying outside speakers and underwriting other cultural events. He assigned the recruiting-retention specialist to other duties. The Latino faculty members believed neither the specialist nor his recruiting and retention services should continue to play such a large and influential role in a program they perceived as predominantly academic. They believed the program should be rededicated to a greater emphasis on teaching, research, and cultural events—that is, the components important to faculty. Although the program had long had a dual mission, the faculty now saw the student service component as distracting from the primary research and teaching mission of the program.

During the final year of Andres's two-year term, he reviewed the situation and attempted to shore up the maligned student services component on and beyond the campus. The Latino students were discontented, complaining frequently about how the Latino faculty were distant, uncaring, and failed to consider students' perspectives on program issues. Most faculty for the Latino Studies program believed the recruiting-retention specialist had caused the discontent by instigating unrest among the Latino students. The professors grew impatient and wanted to put the matter to rest. Soon after students left campus for the summer, and before a new director was named, Andres met with college and university officials to tell them the majority of the Latino Studies faculty wanted the specialist and his services to be severed from the program immediately. It seemed that the professors wanted no part of the community component or the student services representative. From Andres's perspective, divorce was imminent.

A few Latino students learned about the reorganization plan and were not surprised by the faculty's position. They had long felt that the Latino faculty had underestimated the program's cultural significance for them, the campus, and the community at large. The students believed the faculty had behaved like "Anglo professors focused more on their research than the people or the community." One student was overheard to comment: "They really forget who they are. They don't understand the Latino community anymore, or the importance of the culture and the students in it."

After some discussion among university administrators about how to handle this dilemma, Antonio, the newly appointed Latino Studies director, returned to campus in the fall completely opposed to the reorganization plan. He had recognized the importance of maintaining the dual mission of academics and community service and insisted that the recruiting-retention employee stay in the program and that the infrastructure remain unchanged.

This contorted situation is emblematic of the social/cultural conditions that many Latino faculty and staff face. It is also an example of the kind of transactions that take place in the various academic fiefdoms of administrators, faculty, and students. In this case students played a secondary role; the faculty's objectives overrode the students' preferences for the outcome. Students' voices were heard only after Antonio arrived. University administrators tried to ameliorate the situation, but it was nonetheless handled in a low-context fashion: make a quick, decisive, unilateral move to control the outcome and avoid involving too many people in the process. The process was contrary to the premise of the Latino Studies program, which was founded in a high-context mold to serve *all,* most particularly Latino students. In that regard, the decision process should have been more group oriented and inclusive rather than unilateral.

Additionally, administrators were well aware that the academic culture of traditional institutions in higher education favors the faculty mission over all others, for self-governance drives many universities and almost always takes priority in these situations. For example, during a meeting to discuss the ramifications of separating the recruiting and student service components from the Latino Studies program, hardly anyone questioned the faculty's motives. In fact, administrators merely assumed and remarked openly that it was important that the program's structure not hinder teaching and research. Few facts or allegations need to be presented in such circumstances. Although the program was founded with a dual mission and had had significant success in recruiting, retaining, and graduating a high percentage of Latino students, everyone assumed student services and the recruiting specialist would be moved if his presence created tension among faculty members in their mission of teaching and research in Latino Studies. Like oil and water, student services and the faculty mission do not mix together well. These are not value judgments, contradictions, or exceptions to the rule; these are facts of academic life.

Embracing the Status Quo

The lesson from all this is the need to recognize the full power of academic enculturation and how academic values can override ethnicity. From its beginning the Latino Studies program was balanced between the ethnic community and the community of scholars. How, then, do we account for the Latino faculty's attempt to dismantle a successful and high-context component of its program? Andres, to his credit, was a strong advocate for the program and Latino issues and took the initiative to speak out whenever possible about the inequities he observed that affected Latino students, faculty, and staff. Certainly, tense relationships between the Latino Studies faculty, the staff specialist, and students were the acknowledged catalyst for these events, but the underlying academic faculty culture was the driving force.

Andres and program faculty were acting in accordance with primary faculty values at a research university. One could argue with their methods, but it is hard to fault faculty for realigning and strengthening the program toward academic priorities. They were simply guided by the roles and rewards of faculty culture in which research, publication, and teaching take precedence, in that order, over most other campus concerns. Mariflor, a Latina professor at a large research university, summarized the issue nicely:

We should have Chicano professors who don't all get together and try to turn themselves into models of white professors, who sit around and talk about how we're a big research institution and we only want students who are research oriented. [We] look at students only in terms of how they will reflect upon us rather than how we as professors will reflect upon the community and its well-being. We all knew that . . . we [Latinos and Latinas] are career oriented much too often, with everybody trying to be another white administrator.

After joining the professoriate, Latinos find their allegiance lies somewhere between two adaptive strategies: to "buy in" to the faculty value system and become a stakeholder in traditional concepts of academia, or "hold fast" to their own cultural and ethnic values. There is a third strategy they can choose—to switch back and forth between the two as necessary. However, the focus here is on only the first two strategies. Those who choose to buy in do so to pursue membership in the professoriate and become faculty members. This entails following faculty and academic priorities to gain the rewards of a research institution. Pablo, a Chicano scientist at a research university in the Southwest, commented in regard to Latino faculty retention: "I think we do lose a lot of faculty, and some of these faculty are getting very bad advice [about how to secure tenure]. . . . To become involved in the Chicano [student] issues while you're a faculty member is, I think, academic death. It's the department that's going to give you tenure, and the only thing that's important at a research university is the kind of research that you're doing. Everything else is extraneous."

In contrast, Maria, now chair of her department, chose to hold fast. She offers this advice to faculty:

If the cost of getting into those positions is too high, you can't do it, and if it means you've got to stay on third base, then I guess that's where you have to stay and do what you can on third base. These universities can take your soul away from you, they can take who you are, who you think you are, what was I thinking when I started out, what was I going to do in life, what was my mission, what was my vision. They'll take it all. Universities are tough places.

Embedded in the Latino Studies episode was another familiar theme: marginalization, as represented by faculty who were struggling for ethnic self-validation, recognition, and academic value in their programs. Their loyalties, meanwhile, had become stretched between the program and their departments, between comprehensive values focused on culture and community and time-restricted values focused on research and publications to achieve tenure. When the Latino Studies situation reached a boiling point, its constituents had to choose which path to take.

This story also shows how the values of the professoriate drove the Latino Studies faculty. They either did not recognize the critical implications of Latino community issues embedded in the student services component, or they were fully aware of the implications and chose to ignore them. This may seem incongruous, antithetical, even hypocritical, but it is not necessarily racist. It's fairly clear that the faculty were simply acting as faculty, not as Latinos or even Latino faculty. Latino Studies students saw the faculty as cultural contradictions—as Latinos "who forget who they are." Yet they may be acting in ways that are quite consistent with faculty cultural values overall.

Did they really forget who they are? I think not. Anthropologist Renato Rosaldo might suggest that the tale of the Latino Studies program reflects the consequences of Latinos' existing within the "culture in the borderlands" where "cultural forms shape or are shaped by human conduct" (1993, 207). We constantly encounter these interactions and transactions, these apparent cultural contradictions, in academia.

Andres, for example, was guided by the reward system, which reinforced his decision to orient the program toward research and teaching and was imprinted on him in graduate school. Yet he is a strong advocate for Latino recognition and a combatant against perceived inequities, speaking out openly against the same academic culture and system that chronically disconnects from and ignores the culturally different, the Latino students and faculty, among many others. Agreeing with and opposing the academic cultural system simultaneously is not the same as biting the hand that feeds you; rather, it demonstrates the responses of multicontextual individuals to the inner patterns of cultural values imprinted by primary communities of family *and* faculty culture. Latinos and Latinas are neither assimilating (see Chapa 1988) nor acculturating; they are becoming multicontextual, selectively responding to new cognitive imprints and choosing activities that may be reinforced by new cultural reward systems, as many other ethnic minorities are doing in higher education today.

Academic Organizations, Cultures, and Systems

The concept of organizational culture has been troublesome for anthropologists to define. Part of the problem is that anthropologists have difficulty agreeing on a definition of *culture*. Another part of the problem is that the term has become popular in the corporate world, which has misused it for decades. When the concept of culture was first introduced in the business sector during the 1970s, it was a new way for management consultants to manipulate organizational change (see Davis 1971). Davis, for instance, defines corporate culture as a simplistic dichotomy of guiding beliefs comprised of the business philosophy espoused by upper management and launched by strategic plans, and of the quotidian beliefs—the rules and feelings about everyday behavior, such as rites and rituals—that all employees embrace (1971; 1984). Because guiding beliefs give direction to daily beliefs, Davis argues that upper management can ignore the latter as less important and inconsequential (1984). Corporate culture is merely a disembodied pattern of shared values and beliefs that senior management can manipulate to reduce such workplace behavior to a homogeneous, monolithic entity. This serves as the basis for a number of misguided research trends: culture became a concept related primarily to leadership (Schein 1985); it can be changed or managed at will to fit the current strategic plan (Davis 1984); and culture is merely something an organization "has," and it becomes manifested through its myths and rituals (Deal and Kennedy 1982).

Soon business gurus like Peters and Waterman (1982) popularized the term *organizational culture* by extolling the virtues of corporations with "strong cultures" driven by strong leaders with dynamic vision, as compared to corporations with "weak cultures" that needed revitalization for optimal performance. Thus *culture* became a euphemism for exploring the relationship between change and efficiency (Wilkins and Ouchi 1983;

Zeira and Avedisian 1989). Since then the term has evolved into a ubiquitous concept for labeling nearly every behavior pattern in the workplace today. As a result, the concept of organizational culture has become diluted and confused in the mind of the general public.

Further, social scientists, especially anthropologists, never clearly defined the concept of organizational culture (see Baba 1986; Briody 1989; Jordan 1994; Sachs 1989; Schwartzman 1993; Sharff, Jagna, and Saunders 1994; Trice and Beyer 1993). The consequences have been problematic, for the majority of popular works on the topic appear to be anthropological (see Adizes 1988; Deal and Kennedy 1982; Miller 1989; Pettigrew 1979). Unfortunately, the research on organizational culture conducted outside anthropology generated oversimplified models, superficial analysis, and misleading expectations (Giovannini and Rosansky 1990).

The first step toward clarifying these concepts is to determine how anthropologists view an organization. If, according to Baba (1989), organizations are "societies writ small," what are some general conditions that help define them? Hamada developed the following list of useful anthropological assumptions about organizations:

(1) Organizations are socio-cultural systems embedded in larger socio-cultural environments; (2) The management culture of an organization is not necessarily *the* organization culture. . . . (3) Organizational life is more fluid than linear. . . . (4) Values are often subconsciously perceived, and yet they influence organizational members' behaviors, decision-making patterns, and emotional and affective reactions to organizational phenomena; (5) Therefore, we must look at *not only* what happens, but *what it means;* . . . (6) Significant events and processes in organizations are often *ambiguous* (multivocal) and *uncertain* (unpredictable); (7) Socio-political alliances of organizational members are not necessarily the same as the cultural integration of their ideational worlds; (8) The same events can have very different meanings for different people because of differences in their cognitive schema; . . . (9) People create, reinvent, and manipulate symbols in order to increase predictability and control over organizational phenomena; (10) Organization is filled with internal contradictions and conflicts, formal and informal realms, double talk and parodies. Organizational rituals often symbolize underlying forces for disintegration as well as integration. (1994, 26–27; emphasis his)

One definition of organizational culture, presented in chapter 2, defines it as shared organizational norms and values containing deeply embedded patterns of behavior, assumptions, beliefs, or ideologies that members have about their organization or its work (Peterson and Spencer 1990, 3). Trice and Beyer expand on the idea by saying that norms and values are "relatively coherently interrelated sets of emotionally charged beliefs . . . that bind some people together and help them to make sense of their worlds" (1993, 33). But now that I have refined the definitions of culture and ethnicity as concepts of fluid multiple identities, contexts, and cognition, I think these somewhat flexible but static definitions need further modification to accommodate the conditions of organizational structures. Though the concept "of an authentic culture as an autonomous internally coherent universe no longer seems tenable," it is still a fact and not a "useful fiction" (Rosaldo 1993, 217). It is simply no longer possible to assume that everyone shares the same set of values and perspectives within the cultures of an organization.

A Revolution in Organizational Theory

Organizational theory has undergone a revolution of sorts, one that has led to a profound change in how we see the nature of organizational planning and even the nature of organizational life. It was simply a shift in thinking and understanding about how organizations function, a transformation of familiar ideas from an orderly world built in the industrial age and centered around nineteenth-century science to a less orderly world of dynamic, interrelated organizational systems founded on the new physics of the twentieth century and a unique theory that the universe consists more of chaos than order (Wheatley 1992). Since the late 1950s this paradigmatic shift had taken hold in a host of formal disciplines, ranging from the natural sciences to the social sciences and linguistics (Schwartz and Ogilvy 1979). By the mid-1980s researchers were applying these ideas to organizational theory where the paradigm was shifting from a positivistic approach to a naturalistic approach (Lincoln 1985).

The positivistic view is the orthodox Newtonian view of the world. It is a world comprised of mechanical and machinelike systems that are rational, predictable, simple and that, when aggregated or compiled, form into hierarchical structures that can be analyzed objectively and ultimately controlled (D. Clark 1985; Guba 1985; Lincoln 1985). Organizational success is measured by maintaining stability—"a strong culture." The naturalistic paradigm, synthesized here from Lincoln (1985, 34–35) and Guba (1985, 86–88), posits a worldview with approximately seven axioms that, coincidentally, permeate many of the principles of the theory of multicontextuality:

- Organizational systems are *complex* entities in their own right. They are separate, diverse, dynamic, and interactive and are not just comprised of the sum of their parts.
- Organizations are not based on some orderly sense of natural hierarchy driven from the top down. Rather, organizational systems contain multiple (heterarchic) orders that can exist side by side, and the predominant

order shifts according to the frequency of interactions and transactions, and shifting social factors.

- Metaphorically, organizational systems are holographic, not machinelike or clocklike but multidimensional and interconnected. Each part contains information about the system as a whole.
- The world and organizations are indeterminate, unpredictable, and uncontrollable. Some current and future conditions are ambiguous, and they are only partially knowable among the individuals involved.
- Organizational systems are based on mutual causality rather than direct causality—the "if-then" notion of causal relationships in which action and outcome are linear. Mutual causality is a symbiosis of nonlinear systems that make cause and effect indistinguishable. They cannot be separated into a linear sequence, for they grow and evolve in such as way as to make cause and effect meaningless.
- Organizations are shifting from mechanical, assembly-like systems for instituting change to systems of change based on morphogenesis, wherein dramatic and unpredictable change generates new, higher-order forms (e.g., virtual organizations).
- A worldview based on pure objectivity is illusional—no process is neutral—and the emerging organizational worldview is based on perspective. It recognizes multiple perspectives in which no single viewpoint, or in this case academic discipline, provides more than a partial picture.

Proponents of the predominant positivistic form of academic culture tend to focus on cultural coherence and homogeneous institutional properties (Kuh and Hall 1993; Manning 1993). Opponents may find little to like about such forms of academic culture and disdain even the standard administrative process. Both perspectives exist concurrently, though not always openly, in organizational culture. Martin (1992) suggests that at least three cultural perspectives are at work in most organizations: the integration perspective, usually associated with leadership and tending to perceive cultural patterns of harmony and homogeneity; the differentiation perspective, which notes separation into groups and conflict as part of organizational reality; and the fragmentation perspective, which recognizes that chaos, complexity, fluctuation, and ambiguity also exist within an organization. These perspectives are not always shared, nor are they immutable, for they may shift according to circumstances.

Tierney (1997) examines higher education from a similar point of view. He suggests that the concept of organizational culture and the process of socialization into higher education are literally up for grabs. These are neither coherent nor shared by everyone involved, and thus socialization has no single format. He argues that "we ought not think of socialization as a series of social acquisitions that occur in unchanging contexts irrespective of individual and group identity. Individuals do not 'acquire' static, sedentary concepts. Socialization is not simply a planned sequence of learning activities where recruits learn one fact and then another" (1997, 7). Tierney also suggests that such a perspective helps create "academic communities that honor differences rather than assimilation" (1997, 7).

This idea originates from an earlier study by Tierney and Bensimon, *Promotion and Tenure: Community and Socialization in Academe* (1996), which depicts faculty culture and the dynamics of academic organizational systems and reveals the importance of human "difference," which is too often ignored in academe. Their goal is to create what they call "communities of difference" in academia that recognize organized change and do "not demand the suppression of one's identity in order to become socialized to abstract norms" (1996, 16). Tierney and Bensimon suggest that, "rather than assuming that 'new recruits' must learn to deal with their situations, we consider how the organizational culture might be changed. Unified, consensual notions of reality are rejected in favor of communities in which it is understood that different individuals and groups will always have competing concepts of reality" (1996, 17).

Academic Organizational Structures

I believe that three cultural domains best describe the overall academic culture of higher education. National culture of education focuses on broad education issues and organizations and is differentiated by institutional type, loosely following the Carnegie classification.[2] These types include public and private institutions that range from research universities to two-year institutions. The other two domains are campus cultures and campus subcultures. It is safe to assume that campus culture includes at least three major interactive, highly stratified groups: students, faculty, and administration (see also Austin 1990; Bensimon 1990; Gilliland 1997; Kuh 1990, 1993; Kuh and Hall 1993; Moffatt 1989). Within institutions of higher learning a variety of groups are associated with campus subcultures—departments, academic units (programs and institutes), nonacademic units (i.e., sports programs, hospitals), schools and colleges, the institution, and so on.

Some suggest a college or university is the institutional equivalent of a honeycomb (D. Seymour 1995). The culture promotes separateness; the policies encourage the building and nurturing of inviolable cells. Hard divisions exist between various parts of the campus (student affairs and academic affairs; faculty and administrators). The greatest fragmentation is between and among the academic units (D. Seymour 1995). But academic disciplines are important and perhaps the most dominant of all subcultures. Because they wield so much power and influence over faculty socialization, academic standards for research and teaching, and even tenure, the disciplines are often called the "invisible colleges" on a campus. Academic cultures are very much like components—organic components—within an organizational system and structure. The structures, components, and even systems of higher education may vary greatly throughout the world (Becher 1984, 1989; B. Clark 1984, 1987a). For insights about Latino faculty we must assume this structure and analysis are relevant to academic organizations only in the United States.

One of the more interesting patterns in the organizational structure of colleges and universities is the tendency toward polarity (binaries) and hierarchy. Academic culture seems to be permeated with these two constructs, which play a significant role in shaping value systems in higher education. The distinguished anthropologist and former college president Yolanda Moses establishes a baseline perspective on hierarchy in university culture: "Universities and colleges, though different, in many ways are basically hierarchical. There are faculty hierarchies, program and degree hierarchies, administrative hierarchies, and student hierarchies, to name a few" (1990, 403–4). Besides hierarchies, cultural binaries also are embedded within university organizations. For example, masculine characteristics of achievement and objectivity are valued much more than cooperation, connectedness, and subjectivity, qualities traditionally associated with women and minorities. Traits associated with wealthy majority males before World War II now tend to generate tension between groups of working-class women and minorities.

Binaries and hierarchies embedded in the cultures of academic disciplines reflect similar values and problems for ethnic minorities and women involved in higher education. Matthews observes that binary oppositions generate priorities throughout university culture. One of those binary opposites tends to separate minorities and women from the majority. Comparing the cultures of the humanities, which tend to attract minorities, and the sciences, she depicts all science disciplines as an "intensely collective team sport." Although it is common for dozens of scientists to take credit for a publication, essays in the humanities are solitary efforts (1997, 164). She adds,

Most faculty [academic] fields can be categorized as hard and applied, hard and pure, soft and applied, soft and pure. Good people in the hard/applied world (professors of medicine, business, law, molecular biology, engineering, and computer science, especially) must be kept sweet with bonuses, perks, and special deals, for their salaries would double or triple on the outside [of academia]. The hard/pure crowd has learned to bargain: give me a new atom smasher, or I call Berkeley. . . . Soft/applied fields are, like all academe's niches, at least 25 percent overpopulated: still, the commercial world, or other nonprofits, or government, continue to absorb a fair number of rural sociologists. . . . Like classicists and art historians, literature specialists are a hundred years behind the market, soft, pure, and in alarming over-supply. (1997, 173–74)

While binary opposites in traditional academic culture can affect some students adversely, binary systems in organizational infrastructures can confuse administrators as well, making culture change more difficult in higher education than in the private sector in some cases. In his book *How Colleges Work* (1988) Robert Birnbaum evokes a binary analogy and systems thinking to explain the dynamics of organizational structures in education. Like most organizations, colleges and universities consist of certain subsystems (technical, administrative), containing specific components (faculty, departments, students) that interact as either tightly coupled or loosely coupled systems. Tightly coupled systems have well-connected components with few inconsistent subsystems, and they function smoothly with predictable and efficient outcomes—good administrative support helps faculty graduate new doctoral students in a relatively short time. While tightly coupled systems are deterministic, loosely coupled systems, with weak or intermittent subsystem connections, are probabilistic. No one can predict with any certainty the outcome of an action or decision—tenure, faculty policy, student enrollment, or graduation rates (Birnbaum 1988, 30–40). Systems analysis is important for understanding how these institutions function, and having either tightly coupled or loosely coupled systems is neither entirely functional or dysfunctional in every case.

Birnbaum suggests that systems function has some bearing on institutional culture. College administrators and presidents cannot manipulate academic cultures; although cultural differences tend to disrupt the forces of cultural similarity, cultural differences between distinctive academic disciplines and departmental environments tend to balance out. Birnbaum believes that management cannot create a culture as much as it can sustain one once it is created. Presidents, he tells us, "can strengthen and protect the existing culture by constantly articulating it, screening out personnel who challenge it, and in other ways continually rebuilding it. Culture, like other aspects of organizations and all other systems, constantly loses energy and moves toward entropy and disorder. A major function of administrators is to prevent the organization's culture from falling apart" (1988, 81). This position is highly susceptible to encouraging administrators to respond to isolated incidents by simply altering a system or process. For example, to counteract and protect the system from institutional racism, one might think to simply add ethnic studies courses or requirements. This is a quick-fix solution that offers some benefits for students and the organization, but it fails to address systemic problems or forestall cultural entropy.

Sustaining and protecting academic culture, especially the traditions of education, from entropy, disorder, and falling apart is not only the antithesis of the image projected by many private-sector institutions, it is nearly impossible for almost any organization to accomplish. To be sure, if social systems are to endure, they must be protected and sustained. But "culture," organizational or otherwise, is a humanly constructed cognitive environment that evolves and changes but does not atrophy. Private enterprise must survive under market fluctuations and adverse socioeconomic conditions by seeking to adjust, adapt, and create anew, even if these are merely cosmetic changes in packaging or presentation. Across the country, and throughout the world, private sectors such as the automotive industry have genuinely tried to sharpen their focus on serving their customers by incorporating in their culture quality improvement processes and even reinventing themselves if necessary (Walton 1990). In most cases these transformations generate significant structural and cultural changes, like flattening management hierarchies and working in teams. Higher education, on the other hand, stubbornly refuses to even consider such cultural change. It accepts constant re-creation or revision of knowledge but not the constant renewing or reframing of its cultures. It is the "last great American institution, except for presidential campaigns, to dodge systemic downsizing and reform," Matthews tells us, "mostly because it has no system, no market laws, no set constituency to please. Manufacturing, the military, the health industry, the mainstream religions, even Congress, have all painfully acceded to some sort of change. The campus world claims privilege, resists accountability, fights limits of any kind" (1997, 113).

Professional Culture

How did U.S. campuses become so resistant to change? Hall (1984) believes the campus is overbureaucratized. Daniel Seymour (1996a, 1996b) thinks it is a unique adaptation of professional bureaucracy and culture that fully embraces the status quo. A professional bureaucracy is essentially built into the cultures of many complex organizations. Thus complex organizations prefer to emphasize governance by "authority of a professional nature—the power of expertise" (D. Seymour 1996a, 19). Hospitals and universities, for example, tend to lock on to a model of doing things that focuses on resources, reputation, and a fleeting notion of quality. As professional bureaucracies, they rely on the coordination of experts, physicians or faculty—and, more recently, business professionals—to standardize skills and to design relevant training and indoctrination and management practices. For instance, the health care industry relies on medical schools and hospital residency programs and even MBAs to produce its experts. Higher education relies on graduate schools and the departmental disciplines, the "invisible colleges," for indoctrination and on the professorship for training. However, it is rare to find business school faculty in top executive positions, at least at large research universities, and when nonacademic business executives are selected as college presidents, it is unsettling news in academic circles. Trained and indoctrinated specialists (professors) are given considerable individual control over their own work. These specialists become self-declared administrators. Because they are professors and specialists, the built-in assumption is that they know best how to manage higher education, even without formal training. Their dealings with administrators hired from the private sector are marked by conflict and distrust. Faculty and administrators in higher education tend generally to disdain the management style of the private sector.

The following are some of the essential points of Daniel Seymour's work (1995, 1996a, 1996b). They outline his ideas about professional academic bureaucracy and fundamental faculty principles, including his views on institutional academic culture:

- Colleges are functionally oriented, not process oriented.
- Universities are organized horizontally and consist of a cluster of highly specialized "functional silos" called schools and colleges.
- Personnel policies (tenure, staff contracts that run for more than one year) and norms such as "academic freedom" function as crossbeams in the structure of higher education and perpetuate the status quo.
- Coordination is accomplished by standardizing skills and knowledge.
- Power and authority originate from and are controlled by "trained experts" (faculty) who maintain the sole right to define their own professional responsibilities.
- Training and indoctrination rely on graduate or professional schools and the disciplines.
- Trained specialists, given individual control over their own work, become self-declared administrators who know best how to manage education (faculty governance).
- Faculty autonomy is paramount, and that they work alone is the central reality of academic life (especially in the nonscience fields).
- Protection of faculty autonomy is accomplished by administrators whose job it is to "buffer" the faculty from external pressures.
- Specialization is the route to publication and in turn to tenure, promotion, and raises.
- Conservative, decentralized organizational structures are extraordinarily well designed to resist and weather the most turbulent storms of change (state-legislated curriculum reform, federal affirmative action, etc.). Universities survive better than most other institutions the rise and fall of governments, wars, and social movements.
- Any incursions into faculty culture (e.g., accountability, unionized teach-

ing assistants, eliminating tenure, or creating a post-tenure review, etc.) are threats to academic freedom and are seen as blatant attempts to usurp the exclusive authority of faculty members to determine how, when, and where they provide their services.

• Such incursions should be identified, neutralized, and dispatched, because professionals know quality in education and are under no special obligation to explain either the processes or the outcomes to the unenlightened.

• Universities function with a "business-as-usual" attitude: great researchers still earn far more than great teachers, and the lecture format endures as the education delivery vehicle of choice.

• Universities have a disregard for any ideas that are not grown at the academy.

Professional bureaucracies, Seymour explains, are conservative bodies that run smoothly when it is business as usual. But problems surface quickly if socioeconomic conditions change. Then universities

are usually both unwilling and unable to respond to the demands of a dynamic environment. Their unwillingness stems from the universal nature of inertia and perceived threats to closely held beliefs and standard operating procedures. Their inability to respond to new conditions results from the organizational structure itself. Since there is virtually no control of the work except by the professionals themselves, the system has no way to correct deficiencies the professionals choose to ignore. (D. Seymour 1996b, 10)

Consequently, Seymour believes that higher education suffers from what he calls "paradigm paralysis," for it sees no alternative models to pursue (1996b, 11). St. Clair and Dow (1996) attribute this paralysis to a lockstep mentality within academic disciplines—the "invisible colleges" within universities (see also Becher 1984; B. Clark 1984). The departments within colleges and universities are discipline-based communities. They value their reputations and their ability to evaluate scholarship and research based on criteria established by their own research and publications. Thus "preservation of the strength of the discipline's knowledge base from intrusion by other disciplines is central to the survival of the reputation system" (St. Clair and Dow 1996, 161). In other words, departments are reluctant to permit entry by outsiders, including institution-based administrators who are implementing formalized program or student/faculty assessments. Only systems within the paradigm—peer accreditation systems, program reviews, academic quality reviews—will suffice.

Thus universities in general are hard to challenge because faculty are experts at resisting change. They are "very smart people in a very closed system" who become adept at defensive reasoning (D. Seymour 1995, 107). If faculty are defensive about university assessments, no wonder so many disciplines fend off any attempts they perceive as watering down scholarly standards. Transdisciplinary research, team-oriented studies, and collaboration can be unsettling for faculty, especially when new ideas shift academic culture from faculty-oriented teaching to student-oriented learning (see Daniel 1997). Changes associated with student-oriented teaching and learning are probably the most threatening because they undermine the primary faculty prerogative—being accountable to no one but themselves, which is the core principle of faculty governance. It also flies in the face of the most sacred of all principles: "Faculty, not students, know what knowledge is new, important, and deserving of inclusion in the course" (St. Clair and Dow 1996, 164).

Faculty face a deeply ingrained conceptual conflict involved with changing the student–teacher role. The premise that the customers (students) are always right conflicts directly with professorial beliefs that the person with the Ph.D. always knows best what is right in education. At the graduate level the priorities are clear: a professor's needs take precedence over the students' educational needs. The origins of academia are framed in the context of the student apprenticeship, which permits no questioning of the student's professor-mentor. Graduate students are apprentices, according to faculty mentors; if anything, they should behave like employees, not customers. Moreover, which has the bigger payoff: reflecting on the customers' needs or writing an article necessary for tenure? The cultural reward system suggests that the primary customers are the faculty, not the students (D. Seymour 1995).

Cultural Entrenchment

In the growing conflict about changing faculty roles, cultural entrenchment is an even greater danger than paradigm paralysis. An important underlying issue is the effect on values of cultural context and cognition of introducing change. Cultural entrenchment is indeed deepest at the departmental and disciplinary levels, the central stage for graduate education and the enculturation of new faculty into academe. Today departmental faculty are confronted by change from women and minorities who enter graduate education bent on pursuing new ideas and methods for teaching and research. And to those who might countenance an expansion of the traditional academic mission, the message from scholars like Burton Clark is to bolt the door, for academia is being eroded by a "downward slide" that could "deprofessionalize the professoriate" (1987a, 273).

Clark mirrors the beliefs of many traditional academics by suggesting that American higher education has proliferated far too much, with more than three thousand institutions, many of them community colleges, dispersed across the country. Clark fears that higher education, and especially community colleges, which focus almost exclusively on teaching, "risk becoming profoundly obsolete" and that academic work could become standardized and repetitive if faculty do not have an opportunity to enhance their knowledge through research (1987a, 100). He describes academic life as diffused and dispersed into small and different worlds, where the most perilous current trend is "open access[,] turning [the] purpose [of higher education] into all things for all people. Then the administrative need to adjust flexibly to floating clienteles becomes more important than the need to have faculty define dominant duties and develop in-house cultures rich in professional meaning" (1987a, 273). The main issue, he concludes by citing others, is that "the community college as an institution has eroded the essential intellectual core of faculty work. The perils of student-centeredness are greater [than] the dangers of professional dominance. In the shopping mall college, intellectual stagnation is a clear and present danger. For sure, the intellectual core runs down" (273). His recommendation is to balance the academic work of teaching with research because it "develops the system, first by appeasing the disciplines and rewarding disciplinarians for advancing knowledge and technique" (100).

Educational quality is everyone's concern, regardless of institutional type. And issues about content and systems for delivery of education are real. The danger here is the embedded academic cultural theme of entrenchment, which continues to reject the fundamental values of high-context, field-sensitive individuals. Clark's point, about higher educational systems that do nothing but teach, is well taken. Yet he misses the point about why community colleges are proliferating and popular. Community colleges are populated largely by ethnic minorities, predominantly Latinos. They are attracted to community colleges for a variety of reasons, including cost, proximity to home community, and their academic culture, which is more high context than most colleges—community and people oriented. The underlying theme of cultural entrenchment is that conditions that erode higher education—community and student/people–oriented high-context cultural values—are signs of intellectual stagnation, even danger. Though it is not Clark's intention to attack those who attend these institutions, the message is clear and the implication insidious. Attempts to introduce inclusive high-context ideas about research and/or teaching pedagogies are to be met with dedicated resistance, for traditionalists have an inherent fear that introducing these ideas will dilute "the work of American academics" even further (B. Clark 1987a, 141).

Academic cultural entrenchment and the reluctance of institutions or departments to accept alternative ways of doing things on campus seemed to be major concerns among those I interviewed for the Latino study. What caught my attention were the experiences of about a half-dozen new Latino and Latina faculty during the interviews. As could be expected of new faculty, they reflected feelings about their current status that originated in graduate school—feelings of exclusion, disinterest, and disapproval from colleagues. Boice (1992) found patterns among minority faculty in general that relate directly to the specific Latino and Latina faculty experience I encountered. Latinos and Latinas, for instance, described in their interviews with me the "pressures to give up racial and ethnic identities," how "they were discouraged from studying their own cultures," and "doubts their research was real" (1992, 257). They lacked role models and encountered extra burdens because they were called upon to serve as ad hoc counselors and advocates for minority students, without receiving even minimal collegial support in return.

Anglos have highly developed networks that facilitate hiring and career mobility, whereas the networks of minorities are more informal and limited. One example of the Anglo network is the preference for hiring internally from a pool of instructors, adjunct professors, or postdoctoral researchers. This tactic is not only cost effective but gives competitive advantage to certain inside candidates for the position. When a new position is advertised, it can be tailored to fit the characteristics of a favored internal candidate. Consequently, the new position can be "wired" for a specific individual, and if it does attract outside minority candidates, it is unlikely they will be offered the position.

According to Boice, some institutions and departments tend to create ambiguous job descriptions and expectations, as well as ambiguous processes for filling academic positions. Consequently, new minority hires, who often have limited social and professional campus contacts, receive only vague clues about what they should do. This ambiguity ultimately creates unnecessary anxiety and ineffective evaluations, especially during the tenure review process (1992, 260–65). However, differences in cultural context regarding self-assessments may contribute significantly to ineffective evaluations of minorities. For instance, the peer review for tenure at a research university requires the faculty member to submit a package of publications and letters from peers testifying to the candidate's research excellence in the discipline. In essence, this is an academic brag sheet that faculty members craft and assemble to demonstrate their scholarship among academic equals. In many cases minority faculty have scholarly networks that are not familiar to mainstream academics and that majority faculty may not recognize or value. In addition, high-context populations may not be accustomed to seeking attention for their accomplishments, whereas low-context individuals tend to seek recognition by trying to stand out among their peers (see table 3.1).

Many low-context faculty members value getting things accomplished by following policies and procedures and thus are likely to get ambiguous job descriptions and expectations clarified quickly. More high-context faculty members have a high commitment to people and prefer a process that depends on relationships with people and attention to group process to get things done. Consequently, many Latinos as well as other minority and women faculty rely heavily on more high-context personal standards rather than the low-context academic standards for evaluation. According to Boice, many minority faculty rely too heavily on evaluations from students and informal assessments by colleagues. If they are better known off campus than on campus because their research is nontraditional and attracts academics of similar ethnic background, minority faculty rely heavily on outside evaluations, which brings them up short on internal reviews (1992, 261–62).

Academia in Historical Context

We take for granted that nearly all our basic institutional structures in the United States originated in northern Europe. We also recognize the importance of historical events and the role that national cultures play in the creation of these institutions. But what we fail to observe and take into account are the implications of cultural origins that shape not only our structures but how we perceive the world and interact with one another when we are involved in these structures. Few of us are aware or have even observed how much all organizational cultures, especially academic cultures, are from the outset forged by ethnicity and cultural context. The implications of this simple construct may have profound but seldom recognized ramifications.

The history of graduate education in the United States, for example, reveals a process of repressing high-context academic cultural values while encouraging more and more low-context academic cultural values, thereby disconnecting many people, especially women and ethnic minorities, from higher education. What changed and when?

Graduate education as we know it today was imported from Germany to the United States in the early 1800s by American academics who returned from there excited about their experience with the German research model. In 1815 they introduced the German research and educational model, which focused on creating new knowledge, at Harvard, but it was slow to catch on there until the 1860s (Boyer 1990, 8). By then an influential number of scholars had returned to the United States after completing their education in Germany, and they began transforming some institutions in the eastern United States into science-based research schools. These were originally colonial colleges fashioned after the British model of small private liberal arts colleges. Though segregated by class and gender—the students were almost exclusively wealthy white males—

these institutions seemed to foster high-context learning environments that emphasized moral education over scholarly achievement, still an educational goal but poorly achieved today (Boyer 1990; B. Clark 1987a, 1987b, 1993, 1995).

However, rather than blend the new German educational model with the liberal arts model, some—for example, Johns Hopkins—decided to reframe the institution to establish the research component as a capstone experience. By capping the colonial college structure with a research arm, Hopkins created the first school in the country fashioned after the German model for graduate education in research.

According to both Boyer (1990) and Rice (1996), the original mission of the colonial colleges—to teach and serve their communities—became devalued within these new graduate institutions, and it was gradually replaced by a new mission to create knowledge with rigorous research, methodology, and experimentation. Moreover, Boyer claims the German research model demanded that the professors view the everyday world at a distance, a low-context cultural pattern that still permeates teaching and learning cultures today.

This concept of specialized research gained interest among academics in this country, and they slowly transformed many institutions into the "New American Research University" we are familiar with today (Rice 1996). That transformation—one of the most profound institutional transformations to take place in U.S. higher education—reshaped faculty priorities by replacing the original teacher-scholar role found at private liberal arts colleges with a new social identity, social meaning, and culture of professionalism in academic work (1996). Graduate education today is a product of that transformation.

German universities in the early nineteenth century were founded on the Humboldtian principles of freedom to teach and learn. Inquiry for its own sake was foremost. Professors selected the curriculum unconstrained by outsiders and kept an eye on the research topics pursued by students. In the last decades of the nineteenth century, German teaching professors and students had more intellectual freedom than did their counterparts in the United States (B. Clark 1995, 21). As inquiry and knowledge expanded, the disciplines gave way to the modern academic department with distinct research boundaries (Edwards 1999). Two new institutional forms emerged: the teaching-research laboratory and the teaching-research seminar. Knowledge from the outside world was brought into the lab, a closed and controlled environment, to be processed analytically and meticulously with rules of investigation, protocol, and technique prescribed by the discipline (B. Clark 1995, 26–27). But in the United States the delivery system of higher education—group work, discussion, and sharing—was still based on the colonial system inherited from the British, and it remained high context.

However, this was about to change. When the industrial revolution caused student enrollments to grow in the middle decades of the nineteenth century, U.S. higher education shifted its mission from training a very small, very select number of elite young men to serving up education for the larger number of elite students. But the Humboldtian German university model concentrated on research, teaching, and learning for a small number of students, and it could not handle the increased student demand (B. Clark 1995, 50). That role fell to the new land-grant institutions created in the mid-1800s and resulted in public institutions dedicated to offering both service to the community and applied research for the public mission of reshaping society. These developments represented the first steps in shifting the population of higher education from the elite to a more democratic system of higher education for the masses, as represented by community colleges today.

In the first half of the twentieth century, foundation funding and government research grants shifted universities' priorities toward graduate education. The importance of research during World War II and the war's aftermath ensured the trend would continue (Gumport 1993a, 1993b). But American higher education was not prepared for the rapid change that occurred at the end of World War II because of the GI Bill of Rights. By then the organizational structure of graduate institutions in the United States had been imprinted with what was essentially a German cultural context. Thus the culture and mission of higher education were not geared to broad-based community needs, and higher education was becoming less and less oriented toward applied research and more oriented toward theoretical research.

The GI Bill, enacted in 1944, blew open the doors to higher education, and throngs of eager scholars doubled, and even tripled, some campus enrollments within five years (Matthews 1997). Members of ethnic religious groups, as well as women, all of whom previously were shut out of college because of cost, discrimination, sexism, and elitism, were now swelling the ranks of the college educated. Despite the overt discrimination these groups experienced, no clamor for reform or battle to install a multicultural curriculum arose. Although people with different ethnic heritages (i.e., Irish, Italians, Greeks, and so on) and different religious beliefs (i.e., Catholics, Jews, and Moslems) were now attending colleges and universities, the climate of the mid-1940s was notably different than it is today. First, ethnic groups entering college after the war were predominantly European. And although some European Americans were from notably high-context cultures (i.e., Italians, Spanish, Greeks), they were more interested in obtaining access to and gaining acceptance in the once exclusive systems of graduate school and the professoriate than in reforming them. They were willing to adjust and adapt to low-context learning modes. The system of higher education, especially graduate education, remained relatively unchanged because there was no catalyst for immediate change.

However, I would posit that the GI Bill generated not just one but two significant changes. One had the immediate effect of sending people from different ethnic backgrounds and socioeconomic levels into higher education. The other set the stage for a delayed reaction. Although the direct beneficiaries of the GI Bill did not much rock the academic boat (other than by their mere presence), and relatively few stayed long enough to obtain advanced degrees, their children did. These were the college students in the huge cohort known as the baby-boom generation, vast numbers of high-context field-sensitive individuals who entered college and graduate school in the mid-1960s, at the height of the civil rights era (and some of whom undoubtedly stayed to avoid the draft during the Vietnam War). Significant numbers of women and ethnic minorities began entering graduate education for the first time, hoping to change forever some of the entrenched cultural ways of doing things at the academy.

There are a number of important reasons for tracing some of the transformation of American higher education from British private colleges to Germanic research institutions. It is probably the best example of organizational culture change in higher education, and it laid the foundation for a new academic culture that for the most part is still with us today. One of the most significant factors in this transformation was the imprinting by the cultural characteristics of Germany, the epitome of low-context national cultures, according to Edward T. Hall (1959; 1977; 1984).

Daniel Seymour believes the current structure of our colleges and universities reflects the characteristics and mechanical imagery of industrial age England in the seventeenth century. He finds that "colleges and universities have all the characteristics of a nicely dissected Newtonian organization"—segmented, fragmented, split into components of systems, layered, and organized in a machine-like way around a curriculum (1995, 148). As Seymour describes it, organizations tend to chop work processes and systems into pieces and place them in separate boxes with clear boundaries and rules to make certain things happen as they should. This image easily characterizes the low-context cultures of northern Europe as well as the cultural paradigm of Western analytical science.

If our graduate institutions evolved from a synthesis of British and German academic cultures, what are the implications for people from high-context cultures who try to teach, learn, or research there today?

Clearly, doctoral education and its Germanic and British origins are imprinted with a field-independent cognitive learning structure. Teaching and work are formal; doctoral education is private and task or goal oriented; communications are impersonal, to the point, and more verbal than nonverbal; vital relationships between faculty and students are reserved, cautious, distant, and formal; motivation for study and research comes from nonsocial rewards and self-advancement (M. Ramírez 1991). Hall's ideas about cultural context also fit: the low-context individuals emphasize quality performance, precision and efficiency, professional effectiveness, punctuality and timely performance of tasks, and a Western analytical approach that reduces concepts to understandable parts and fits them together. Acceptable ideas must be logical and rational, the teaching style technical. Graduate research and education are still Germanic, and this is the nexus of conflict for people from high-context cultures.

The implications for explaining behaviors with these ideas are tremendous—differences in standardized testing performance, teaching styles, attractions to certain disciplines, and more may all be associated with the lack of synchronicity between academic and ethnic cultural context and cognition. What also becomes clear is that, although every campus today has significant populations of women and minorities (at least in the aggregate), no one has looked at how their different perspectives and styles have affected the professional and intellectual lives of minorities and women in higher education. The first large wave of minorities and women in graduate education arrived only in the 1970s and 1980s, at the height of the affirmative action era, when the focus was on admitting underrepresented populations into academia. They demanded greater democratization of higher education than the academy would allow. But confrontations with the academic establishment over the failure of the undergraduate curriculum to reflect ethnicity and multicultural perspectives ultimately led to the creation of black studies and, later, women's studies programs, as scholarship that looks at a variety of subjects from far different perspectives than those of the hallowed "old dead white guys." The backlash from this intrusion into the curriculum grew into the liberal versus conservative battles about political correctness and the attempt to be sensitive to issues of multiculturalism on campus that consumed most of the 1990s (Bell 1997; Bloom 1987; Bork 1996; D'Souza 1991; Herrnstein and Murray 1994; Honan 1996; see Lederman 1997b; Levin 1996). Today women constitute the majority in our graduate schools, yet minority groups and women have been unable to instigate fundamental changes in the curriculum or culture of higher education.

Faculty Culture and Systems

It is probably not unreasonable to describe tenure as the Valley Forge of the academic cultural wars today. Most of those who teach at colleges and universities see tenure as their ultimate goal; it marks their arrival and acceptance into the ethnic group known as the professoriate. Yet minority faculty, in this case Latino faculty, recognize that tenure also is a political tool that can be used against them (see Mindiola 1995).

Daniel Seymour attributes the paradoxical nature of tenure to a process he calls "sort and shoot" (1995, 113–15). He views the tenure system as a standardization process that maintains the quality of faculty and staff by sorting out the "bad apples"—a quality-by-inspection mentality. Threshold tenure reviews are simply inspection systems designed to unearth deficiencies, he says. This process may eliminate people who are culturally different if they don't fit into the academy's definition of *quality*. For example, if a faculty member tends to publish coauthored articles, the academy that prizes sole authorship may count this as a demerit at tenure time. But a preference for sole authorship is culturally contrary to those whose ethnic backgrounds value true teamwork and collaborative engagement. Thus cultural differences can directly affect one's ability to attain the goal that the academy counts as the only real measure of success: tenure (D. Seymour 1995, 115–17).

Seymour points out that similar traps are embedded in many academic processes. Regional accrediting agencies, for example, use a peer review process to generate institutional rankings based on a series of quality indicators that may be culturally biased. Hiring practices acceptable to the accreditation team are merely systems of improvement-by-elimination, not unlike the "bad apple" strategy in the tenure process. The accreditation system has a limited ability to enhance the quality of the faculty or the institution because the overall level of quality is determined by the internal systems, not by outside systems like accreditation. Thus the hiring process, including procedures that create a pool of candidates for faculty positions, the various criteria used to screen candidates, and the voting procedures of the hiring committee, is designed to ensure that the position goes to the candidate with the best chance of gaining tenure—who may not be the best teacher or researcher in the pool (D. Seymour 1995).

Administrators also have a vested interest in seeing that the job goes to the person with the best chance of gaining tenure. It takes roughly seven years before a new faculty member is reviewed as a candidate for tenure. According to some estimates in the sciences, the cost to the institution of supporting the candidate to the point of tenure review (whether successful or not) may be at least $500,000 from date of hire. "It comes closer to $1 million in most lab sciences," says John Wiley, vice chancellor and provost for academic affairs at the University of Wisconsin–Madison. Salaries loaded with fringe benefits like health insurance and retirement, plus overhead costs, and around $500,000 in start-up and research money add at least that much and more (personal communication 1998). With those costs skyrocketing, denying tenure to faculty becomes a costly procedure, if not a bad investment (Tennant 1997).

Thus hiring decisions often hinge on ethnic preferences and cultural context. In any organizational system these are usually invisible to their originators. Teaching and learning systems, for example, are made even more invisible because language and culture imprint and shape our reality, our perceptions, and our cognitive understanding of the world. How can one change when the problem simply never registers?

I would argue that whether adoption of an organizational system from another culture succeeds may be highly dependent on whether the system is relatively compatible with essential patterns of cultural context. If competitive learning environments are irritating to or in conflict with the values of the adopting culture, the adopting culture can either modify its old ethnic markers—the visible and less visible ethnic group characteristics that tend to avoid competition—or imprint its own cultural markers to encourage membership in or association with the adopting culture, in this case, the professoriate.

Over time, ethnic markers may become less conspicuous or the host society may adopt the ethnic markers (witness the longevity of the term *kindergarten*). Unlike ethnic markers, cultural context within organizational structures and subsystems becomes invisible and less likely to be removed. With such structures left in place, the system appears to almost everyone to be unbiased by cultural values and, for graduate educational systems, unbiased by gender values as well. The implications are that conflicts will occur where gender differences are involved, and the same holds true for cultural differences, as previously stated.

Overcoming Paradigm Paralysis

The less obvious cultural context of an organization can explain why so many women and ethnic minorities encounter conflict with academic culture, but are they the only ones affected by the conflict? Or does cultural context affect majority males who may be caught in high-context/low-context issues and are unable to recognize the dynamics? Daniel Seymour's work suggests that it could. He believes that processes are likely to endure in a professional bureaucratic system like higher education. The faculty can guardedly preserve low-context academic value systems and subsystems, such as tenure, to ensure that their values are not lost or eroded by contradictory value systems. It is highly likely that low-context academic cultural values adversely affect high-context, field-sensitive individuals and some multicontextual individuals as well.

GRE results show that standardized testing evidences patterns of ethnic or gender disparity. If so, GRE scores may be hiding patterns among majority individuals who may also be high context.

As I contemplated these issues, I met with a professor, an Anglo male, who had recently been denied tenure at his university. Although he was a mainstream academician, he was describing circumstances that sounded exactly like the tenure stories I had heard from Latinos and Latinas across the country. John was an assistant professor at the time, involved in a professional discipline that requires both graphic talent and intellectual acumen. He was devastated to learn that, although he had the backing of his department, he had been denied tenure by an institutional committee of peers far removed from his department and with little information about him or the nature of his academic discipline.

He pieced together two events that show where the tenure process failed him. One resulted from carelessness in his department, which highlights the importance of good mentorship and the necessity of having safeguards for new faculty. He learned that his tenure package, though ready to be sent to the review committee, was not in order. The department's cover letter, which was supposed to review his accomplishments and organize his tenure package (all documents, publications, materials, and special letters or recommendations), was confusing and unclear, and he felt it detracted from the presentation of his credentials. This problem arose because key people were on academic leave and unable to help him ensure the package was put together properly. Although he complained, his material went to the committee without revision of the letter (a factor that later helped him in his successful appeal).

But the real stumbling block occurred at the divisional committee level. His research was reviewed by a committee of peers from departments that are clustered by similar academic field into a division (i.e., the divisions of humanities, physical sciences, social sciences, biological sciences). The problem, we concluded, was that John's tenure materials were packaged to emphasize high-context applications by practitioners or professionals in his field, and his negative reviews came from individuals who were associated with low-context basic research in disciplines within the same division. They apparently thought his work was too applied, or too practitioner oriented, and therefore judged his publications as lacking academic quality. Although his work had been published in journals highly regarded in his subfield, they were more oriented toward application than many other journals in his discipline overall. Finally, reviewers commented about the frequency and type of projects in which John had engaged outside the department, essentially his "service" to the community.

What troubled John the most was one reviewer's disregard for his type of research and work. This questioned the very essence and validity of his discipline, undermined his self-worth, and diminished the value of his expertise, which was the reason he was hired in the first place. John's tenure package was in fact outstanding for that particular portion of his discipline. His department recognized his valuable contributions and supported him for tenure. The reviewers, however, were following established guidelines based on criteria for tenure in that particular academic field. The essential problem seemed to be the disconnect that occurred between the low-context and high-context academic cultural perceptions of what constituted appropriate scholarship for granting tenure in that discipline. And, readers should note, his teaching evaluations were never called into question and seemed to have had no effect on the decision.

This major academic decision could have had devastating consequences. John's academic subfield is oriented toward high-context cultural methodologies, teaching, research, and service. He saw how inherent differences in context, even between colleagues in similar disciplines, could easily be misinterpreted. It simply reinforced what I knew was happening with greater frequency to Latino and Latina faculty around the country. But John was an Anglo, and though he was not necessarily culturally attracted to high-context, field-sensitive activities, his academic discipline naturally embraced these elements. He was not the only Anglo professor with tenure difficulties associated with academic disconnects (Davidoff 1996). In general, graduate students today seem to be more attracted to teaching and are less enchanted with the emphasis on research for gaining tenure. "If you spend all your time trying to solve the burning questions of society in order to impress some divisional committee, how much of your efforts are really going towards your responsibilities as a teacher?" (Tennant 1997, 3).

Certainly, cultural context goes a long way toward explaining the difficulties that Latinos, women, and other minorities have had with tenure committees. But as much as we might like to, we still cannot discount the possibilities that institutional racism also has played a role. If organizational culture and context are systemic, or perhaps even subsystemic, and if the culture and context are closely aligned with behaviors construed as institutional racism, then both racism and cultural context may play roles in causing negative consequences for minority candidates for tenure. The issue is how to convince others that both cultural context *and* racism are at work systemically in academia. So long as educators believe, for instance, that either unrecognized institutional racism (Tierney and Bensimon 1996) or "epistemological racism" (Scheurich and Young 1997) is the central, perhaps the only, cause for conflict with women and minorities in our educational systems, majority stakeholders (power holders?) will continue to pay little attention to the problem. However, majority stakeholders might take more interest in making the system more inclusive if they can be persuaded that high- and low-context organizational culture also negatively affects some majority individuals, creating academic conflict, causing poor test and class performance, and preventing majority faculty from achieving academic excellence.

I believe cultural context and cognition do affect majority individuals. But we have little data to demonstrate it because few, if any, researchers have looked at the problem in this way. Thomas Kuhn tells us that the nature of paradigms determines what people see and what they don't see. Kuhn, who defined the concept of scientific paradigms, discusses entrenchment in his book, *The Structure of Scientific Revolutions* (1996). Paradigms define boundaries of acceptable practices within frameworks of shared thought and ideas. Paradigms are useful so long as they continue to provide the answers to the problems being addressed. When that no longer happens, a new paradigm may emerge, but people are usually unable or unwilling to make a shift from an old paradigm to a new one, Kuhn points out.

In public presentations near the end of his career, Ernest L. Boyer tried to recover the concept of community from within the community of scholars. This meant forging a "new American college" with an "engaged campus" that "celebrates teaching and selectively supports research, while also taking special pride in its capacity to connect thought to action, theory to practice," Boyer said (Coye 1997, 23). Boyer's "scholarship of engagement" urged all faculty members to find connections to reality (Coye 1997). He wanted the new American college to be founded on three priorities: clarifying the curriculum, connecting to the world beyond the classroom, and creating a campus community. Addressing the role of graduate schools specifically, he called for "hiring and rewarding faculty who, in addition to research, are good at teaching, integrating scholarship, and applying scholarship" (Coye 1997, 28; see also Shulman 1990).

In a panel presentation at the 1996 conference of the Hispanic Association of Colleges and Universities in Washington, D.C., Gene Rice briefly defined a new kind of faculty scholar, touching on the academic cultural changes needed to create Boyer's new American college. Rice's new American scholar, the "complete, or inclusive scholar," values collaboration over autonomy and competition, is part of a "practitioner faculty" with a real ability to move in and out of academia, and contributes to both the private sector and research easily and without question (Rice 1996, 20–31).

Each characteristic of the new American scholar seems to mirror the research of Manuel Ramírez (1991) and Hall (1977). Rice's vision of scholarship matched the characteristics of a large portion of the Latino and Latina faculty I interviewed across the country, and his model helped explain why they are frustrated with the current academic system. They seemed out of sync, almost disconnected from the academic world that had in fact socialized them. The next chapter focuses almost exclusively on their encounters with academia, and they describe their issues, interests, and scholarship. As you will see, their academic abilities and levels of performance are high; they simply march to a different cultural drummer.

6

Latinos and Latinas Encountering the Professoriate

> But American academe is really two faculties. The tenured ranks are heavily male and middle-aged, and . . . below them lurk the tenure-track faculty, full-time but not yet permanent. On a parallel road to power are academics who take on administrative duties as a way to bring up a salary, lighten a teaching load, or make an honorable exit. . . . But operating beside and below this professorial cosmos is the shadow world of the adjuncts: all the campus instructors given the courtesy title of faculty member in return for handling much of the actual undergraduate teaching. . . . They are the temps and day-care workers and field hands of academe . . . invisible to real faculty.
>
> Anne Matthews, *Bright College Years*

Latino and Latina Faculty Today

Many Latino and Latina faculty told me they feel like second-class citizens in academia. Though not regarded as a "race" by the U.S. Census Bureau, Chicanas/os, Puerto Ricans, Cuban Americans, and other Latino ethnic groups have been amassed and counted so often with other ethnic and "racial" minorities, usually African Americans, that they have become lost in the numbers. A few ethnic groups feel ignored by academia. This recurring theme may have some basis in fact. Relative to other populations, Latino representation in the U.S. professoriate "remains the absolute lowest of all racial and ethnic groups when their proportion of the U.S. population is considered" (Garza 1993, 33). Despite steady increases in real numbers over the years, the ratio of Latinos receiving doctoral degrees to the total number awarded each year was 1 in 33 in 1998, still relatively low, and growth has remained relatively flat since 1990 (see table 2.1, and National Science Foundation et al. 1999). While academia continues to be the largest employer of Latinos who hold doctoral degrees, the tenure rate for Latino full-time faculty from 1989 to 1996 declined more than in any of the other underrepresented populations surveyed in higher education (D. Carter and Wilson 1997, 35). These statistics, coupled with a tight job market and fewer faculty retirements than expected during the 1990s (see Bowen and Rudenstine 1992), give more than a little credence to the impression that academia has ignored Latinos.

If they are to generate change in higher education, Latino faculty need to achieve a critical mass in the U.S. professoriate. While some see optimistic trends in the increasing number of minority faculty (Schneider 1997), other evidence shows that Latinos may actually be losing ground. For instance, data from the American Council on Education show that only 2.3 percent of all faculty in 1993 were Latino (D. Carter and Wilson 1997). The latest report on faculty shows little has changed. According to the National Center for Education Statistics, Latinos still comprised only 2.6 percent of all faculty in 1997 (Roey et al. 1999, 11).

According to Alicea, the highest percentages of Latino faculty are found among the growing number of lecturers and instructors, primarily adjunct teachers, on our campuses (1995). Data from the HERI survey of nearly thirty-four thousand faculty show that among Latinos surveyed in 1996, about 2.2 percent of all faculty surveyed, fewer were above the rank of assistant professor, and more Latino faculty were clustered at the lecturer and instructor levels than any other minority group except American Indians (H. Astin et al. 1997). Twenty-six percent of all Latinos in the survey were adjuncts, and 30 percent of all Latinas were adjuncts. Quite simply, it appears that more Latinos (more than 32 percent) hold nontenure-track positions than almost any other minority faculty in the survey (1997, 37).

Some of these figures could be attributable to a greater number of Latinos in the overall population. But this is not a major factor. The job market for tenure-track positions was tight in the 1990s, but the percentage of new Latino doctorates during that time was also relatively flat. The HERI survey provides a partial explanation for the figures: a large number of Latinos are teaching in two-year institutions, which tend to hire instructors and lecturers. Almost 33 percent of all Latino faculty and 48 percent of all Latina faculty work at two-year institutions; only Native American faculty hold more appointments at two-year colleges, and they are almost invisible at four-year institutions and universities (H. Astin et al. 1997, 4). Unfortunately, whether they cluster at two-year institutions by choice or necessity is a topic that requires extensive analysis and is beyond the scope of this book.

Among the different Latino ethnic groups surveyed, the situation is even more tenuous. Mexican American/Chicano faculty, the largest ethnic population among Latinos, were also the largest cluster at the instructor level (40.6 percent). Forty-one percent of all Chicanos and 48 percent of all Chicanas in higher education are nontenure-track faculty (H. Astin et al. 1997, 63, 89). By comparison, Anglo women surveyed by HERI hold about 26 percent of nontenure-track appointments, and Anglo men hold about 11 percent of those teaching jobs.

There is one bright spot. One-quarter to one-third of all Latinos in the HERI faculty survey, including Mexican Americans, were working on a doctoral degree. The question is whether the professoriate has enough full-time positions to absorb the potential increases. If colleges and universities continue to replace full-time faculty positions with part-time adjunct professorships, the future for more full-time, tenure-track Latino faculty looks grim. This of course generates some conflict for Latino and Latina faculty across the country (see Alicea 1995; Garza 1993).

The few data available on Latino administrators in higher education are also disturbing. Although since the early 1980s three out of five Latinos with a doctoral degree have consistently told annual surveys that they are committed to employment in academia, only a few become senior or executive-level administrators (D. Carter and O'Brien 1993). In 1991 fewer than 3 percent of all full-time administrators in higher education were Latino, representing an increase of only 2 percent since 1981 (D. Carter and O'Brien 1993). Data from 1996 show only 99 of the 2,939 college and university chief executive officers in the United States were Latino, and more than half were working at two-year colleges (D. Carter and Wilson 1997). These figures still trail far behind the 2,175 majority and 192 African American university CEOs in this country; 65 percent of the Anglos and 68 percent of the African American CEOs lead four-year institutions (D. Carter and Wilson 1997).

The Latino Study Group

Of the seventy-seven interviews I conducted, forty-six were with Latinos and Latinas who had completed their graduate work and moved on to faculty, administrative, or nonacademic positions.

Although I found subjects to interview somewhat at random, the combined sample of faculty, administrators, and nonacademics was fairly similar to the national profiles for Latinos in these groups: predominantly male (59 percent), Mexican American (52 percent), and in the social sciences and humanities.

Four individuals had master's degrees and for a variety of reasons had decided not to complete or had yet to complete a doctoral degree. Twenty-three faculty were in tenure-track positions, and six were newly hired junior faculty. The group included twelve administrators, nine of whom had risen through the faculty ranks, taking only thirteen years on average to reach their current position. Among the administrators were four CEOs and three college deans. For comparison, I interviewed eleven nonacademics: two had left academic positions for other opportunities, two were in the private sector but still pursuing traditional academic positions, and the remainder had never pursued academic work. (In fact, the nonacademics were people working for educational organizations as researchers and in other capacities; within their places of employment, their duties resembled those found in traditional academic institutions.)

I have separated the stories about the situations of ethnic minority faculty members, administrators, and nonacademics into roughly two parts. The first part begins with an overview of the major issues for Latino and Latina academics compiled from their answers to specific questions and from their discussions about academic life and culture. The second part of the chapter focuses on how academia intensifies interest in ethnicity, work conditions outside academia, and the high-context cultural patterns that predominate in my subjects' careers. Although the majority of respondents are faculty, I also am using the experiences of administrators and nonacademics, many of whom still teach or held faculty positions in the past. In addition, many have unique experiences relevant to their current positions as administrators and nonacademics. Those comments provide useful points and counterpoints.

The flexible, open-ended interview format generated discussions that sometimes explored new insights and expanded upon the issues.[1] Interviewees presented interesting new perspectives, especially in regard to ethnic and gender-related concerns. In fact, my initial interviews of Latinas yielded numerous descriptions of events involving ethnic and gender issues and bordering on discrimination. The dissonance between academic cultural values and the ethnic values that they described to me has been noted by other scholars as well (see, for example, Austin 1990; Gainen and Boice 1993; Meyers and Turner 1995; Moody 1997; Rice 1986). Let's examine these patterns, beginning with stories about how they became involved in academia.

Eight people described how they or other Latinos ended up in higher education, although half seemed to have little idea about how they became interested in academia.[2] They described how they "drifted" toward the idea of becoming a professor while in graduate school by having to teach or become jobless. Only one person viewed it as "the good life." But four had clear objectives, usually high-context reasons, and went to graduate school to pursue an academic career. Most participants, including scientists in academic fields not considered people oriented, said they were "always community service oriented" and felt academia would satisfy their interests.

Beto, a Mexican American newly appointed to the faculty at an eastern school, had also paid attention to his internal feelings in pursuing an academic career. He knew he was "bad at science and good at people." Beto's story offers some unusual insights into high-context culture and field-sensitive cognition and offers some evidence that Latinos are drawn to the humanities and social sciences because their high-context culture has given them exceptional people skills.

All my life I had spent understanding people who were the same and different than me, and that's essentially the basis of psychology. . . . I didn't know what was propelling me or what was drawing me—whether, indeed, something was pushing me into the field or whether I had been drawn into it. As I look back on it now, I think it was probably a combination. But I think I was being drawn into it because . . . to my mind when you grow up and you develop a bicultural confidence, you have a hypersensitivity to the feelings and understandings of people around you. I think largely because it's a survival mechanism. We in the field call it a paranoia. For example, African American males tend to look paranoid on personality tests. Hell, they're not paranoid, they have a hypersensitivity to the white culture—they have to in order to survive. I remember growing up, and all you have to do is make one or two mistakes on how to pronounce something, and you are on your toes all the time, and essentially that's what happened. I was on my toes all the time looking at the white people around me and their culture, trying to fit in.[3]

Beto's survival mechanism of "hypersensitivity to the feelings and understandings of people all around you" also suggests what Edward T. Hall called "interpersonal synchrony" (1984, 160–76). From his experiments comparing visual acuity in different cultures, Hall found that Latinos in the Southwest are exceptionally skilled, compared to Anglos, at reading nonverbal cues from other people. He also found that Latinos' lives tend to revolve around a special cultural rhythm—he called it a "dance of life." The biorhythm of polychronic people must stay in sync with others', or they are susceptible to dissonance and discord in their daily lives. Disynchronicity can even lead to illness.[4]

In fact, an underlying theme in many of the interviews I conducted was the need to link physical and psychological needs with group cohesion. My subjects, for example, described one aspect of this interpersonal synchrony as a force compelling them to pursue academics. Latinos and Latinas discussed it both directly and indirectly in their interviews. This could help explain why so many Latinos and others associated with high-context cultures in general choose the social sciences or humanities, both closely associated with high-context characteristics, over the hard sciences, which tend to appeal more to people with low-context attributes.

Daniel, originally from Colombia, is now a high-level administrator at an eastern university. Asked to describe his academic career path, Daniel chose to discuss instead his observations and theories about why only some Latinos choose academic careers. For example, some Latinos are not going into academe, he believes, because their parents push them toward lucrative professional careers in medicine and law, and the parents are unfamiliar with career options in academia. Consequently, the parents can't really help or encourage their offspring to pursue a graduate education toward a career as a faculty member.

Daniel has another theory, that administrative positions, especially those that involve work with minorities, can attract Latinos to careers in higher education. But that attraction has a downside that can quickly derail the careers of both faculty and administrators. Too many Latinas and Latinos make premature career moves, he believes, jumping too soon from the faculty to administration. He says this is a pattern he sees too often in Latinos and other ethnic minorities in academia.

I think to a certain extent many of the Latinos, as well as many African Americans, have been side-tracked in areas of student affairs and staff positions that do not necessarily lead to tenure or faculty rank. . . . When they want to move forward into a rank[ing] position within the faculty, be it a chair or a dean or vice president or something, they never learned about budgets or tenure and promotion, to make issues about policy and to get involved in the college issues or the university-wide issues. So people tend to categorize the many Latinos who are on that track as unable to understand the big picture.

Daniel's concern about upward mobility for Latino faculty relates to the type of administrative position that appeals to Latinos and other minorities. High-context, field-sensitive people are attracted to positions that are often community or people oriented. Without good mentoring, Latinos can end up in dead-end jobs. The consequences can be serious when, for example, Latinos take positions that do not carry a good measure of nonminority responsibilities, or they accept a directorship or assistant position that does not lead to promotion. The results are exactly as Daniel describes them.

Some Latinas and Latinos exhibited clear gender differences in describing their academic and nonacademic career choices. Although many of them said they were drifting in their careers, this was the prevalent pattern for women in particular. More than half the Latinas were unaware of how to effectively pursue an academic career. Unrealistic expectations were among the factors that created problems for them. However, all but one of the men described traditional academic career paths with very clear goals.

Drifting career patterns and related comments made by Latinos in the study could reflect a dominant pattern of polychronicity over monochronicity. If high-context cultures tend to be polychronic, pursuing multiple activities at the same time, and low-context cultures are monochronic, proceeding in linear fashion, cultural disasters can occur when monochronic and polychronic individuals collide (Hall 1984, 44–58). Hall compares academics in the United States and Latin America:

Some Americans associate schedules with reality, but M-time [monochronic time] can alienate us from ourselves and from others by reducing context. It subtly influences how we think and perceive the world in segmented compartments. This is convenient in linear operations but disastrous in its effect on non-linear creative tasks. Latino peoples are an example of the opposite. In Latin America, the intelligentsia and the academicians frequently participate in several fields at once—fields which the average North American academician, business, or professional person thinks of as antithetical. Business, philosophy, medicine, and poetry, for example, are common, well respected combinations. (1984, 49)

Multicontextual individuals learn to adapt to both high- and low-context and field-sensitive and -independent cultures. Despite outward appearances of adjusting to monochronic time conditions in educational settings, multicontextual people may find it difficult to shed polychronic time values imprinted as part of their ethnic identity with family and community. To think, learn, and act in school using low-context behaviors does not necessarily change the values and preferences for doing things on either flexible or restricted schedules and may influence their career choices. How an individual responds to new experiences reflects a default response preset within either a polychronic or monochronic time modality. Considering multiple ideas, shifting majors or fields of graduate study, trying out multiple careers, or drifting into career paths without considering the logical consequences of not getting tenure first could be subtle but expected outcomes for some multicontextual individuals. This is especially so if they are attracted to jobs and career options that are people-oriented high-context cultural opportunities that fit their cultural identities.

Latino Faculty Issues

In every interview I asked about the specific concerns of Latino faculty or administrators on campus or nonacademics at work. Thirty-seven described issues specific to their department, campus, or workplace. None of the participants included concerns usually associated with private-sector noncampus environments. Table 1 in appendix 3 contains all 120 responses sorted into four general categories and listed in order of frequency of response: campus culture and climate issues; recruitment; tenure and research; and governance.

For the most part the responses reflect persistent stressors associated with minority faculty. Although the groupings are subjective, the categories my subjects identified are not much different from those generated by other scholars. Moody, for example, lists a number of special stresses often faced by minority faculty—chilly climate, excessive committee assignments, excessive student demands, acute reactions to negative developments, internalization of failure, undervaluation of scholarship on minority issues, and being undervalued as an affirmative action hire (1997, 15–19). Focusing only on minority faculty in the Midwest, Meyers and Turner generated a list of chilly climate issues: racial, ethnic, and gender bias; isolation and unsupportive work environment; lack of information about tenure and promotion; language barriers; and lack of mentors (1995, 3). The stories and analysis here concentrate mainly on the top ten issues identified by my Latino and Latina faculty respondents by frequency of response (for additional detail, see table 1 in appendix 3):

1. Hiring problems—20
2. Gender issues—14
3. "Minority burden" (overcommitment to minority activities or teaching overload)—13
4. Tenure issues—11
5. Racism, classism, and tokenism—9
6. Retention issues—8
7. (Tie) Intracultural issues—5
   Lack of support groups—5
   Promotion problems—5
   Few or no Latinos in upper management—5

Hiring Problems

Researcher Darryl Smith sought to explore the truth about minority faculty hires and diversity in higher education. With her associates she set up an ambitious interview project that attempted to follow up on nearly three hundred minority scholars (32 percent were Latinos) to find out what they encountered in the job market after receiving their doctoral degree (see D. G. Smith 1996; D. G. Smith et al. 1997; D. G. Smith, Wolf, et al. 1996). Among a number of conclusions, her findings reveal a variety of myths: no hiring bias favors minority faculty over majority males; the so-called bidding wars for minority faculty are grossly overstated; the scarcity of minority faculty is not a problem because major universities, prestigious or otherwise, are not recruiting them; and minority faculty are not waiting for positions at only prestigious institutions (D. G. Smith, Wolf, et al. 1996, 3–4).

Others concur with these findings. For example, Ivy League schools and other prestigious institutions are not courting Latino faculty. According to Irene Thomas, Latino tenure-track faculty, "including both U.S.-born and foreign-born, comprise anywhere from about .01 to .025 percent at the eight Ivies" (Brown, Columbia, Cornell, Dartmouth, Harvard, the University of Pennsylvania, Princeton, and Yale); at Harvard "only one tenured Hispanic professor" can be identified despite institutional claims that others are in the ranks (1994, 19–22).

Smith and her colleagues did find a growing demand for faculty with expertise in areas associated with ethnicity, race, class, and gender—the new scholarship associated with efforts to diversify the curriculum by adding courses in ethnic and/or gender studies (D. G. Smith, Wolf, et al. 1996). Smith and her associates show that these jobs still tend to go to majority faculty with expertise in traditional fields like philosophy if they have been recognized as experts in the new scholarship; they are perceived as best qualified to teach in these emerging areas of study. Yet women and minority faculty are at a disadvantage in the job market if their expertise is in traditional academic areas because few departments take them seriously. In these fields "scholars who bring a different perspective still find it difficult to 'break in'" (D. G. Smith, Wolf, et al. 1996, 137). Thus majority faculty members have an advantage in the job market if they have combined expertise in traditional and new scholarship areas. "When push comes to shove," a majority male art historian told Darryl Smith's researchers, "they still hire white males" (1996, 117).

Although the job market has some encouraging signs for minority faculty seeking jobs in the future (Schneider 1997), they still face numerous problems in becoming part of the professoriate. These issues are related to conflicts involving high- and low-context cultural values, which were often at the heart of many comments made to Darryl Smith and her team. A Chicano molecular biologist noted how research priorities disregard high-context values: "The publish-or-perish 'myth' is not a myth. . . . You should not have to be a publishing machine. So much emphasis is placed on your ability to get grants, and the ability to get grants is based on how much you publish, and the human side is lost" (D. G. Smith, Wolf, et al. 1996, 85). Another (perhaps the same) Chicano scientist remarked on differences in academic style: "The thing they care about is the number of publications. They want your reputation. But if you are studying a nontraditional thing, then it is difficult to get published. They are after academics who study the subjects who are usually white. They like to see their dispassionate approach replicated and they don't want you to experience your work emotionally" (1996, 86). The issue today is not just a lack of critical mass (see Brown 1988); the essential problem, as some of Smith's respondents suggest, rests on the institution's inability to consciously and systemically change the academic culture.

Gender Issues

Latinas, like other women on the faculty, deal with sexism, stereotyping, multiple role conflicts, and other kinds of discrimination on a regular basis. But Latina faculty are encountering additional struggles for recognition and validation in academe (see Gainen and Boice 1993). The mounting stress for Latina faculty compounds the problems and can produce even greater internal obstacles. The following are selected issues described to me that specifically affect Latina faculty:

Gender politics and tensions (intracultural issues and hostile Latinos)
Combining motherhood and an academic career, a particularly sensitive issue in traditional Latino culture
The "solo phenomenon" (the unease associated with being the only Latina or female professor in the department)
Lack of Latina role models in the media
Latino/Chicana politics (political labels and the effect on tenure and promotion)

In talking with Latinas it quickly became apparent that a fundamental question for them is distinguishing gender issues from ethnic issues. Yolanda Garza's study of Latina administrators found that they, like many other minority professionals, face a "triple oppression from race, class and gender" differences in power (1996, 93–95). Other researchers (see Gloria and Pope-Davis 1997) have also recognized that this combination does much to explain why Latinas and minority females have more difficulties than other scholars in academia (Gloria Anzaldúa 1987, 1990).

Latinas in graduate education suffer from relative isolation, lack of faculty support for women students, and the lack of collegiality with other graduate students (see for example, Turner and Thompson 1993). Latinas and other women in the sciences face even greater difficulties. According to Elaine Seymour, what contributes to the greatest loss of women in science and engineering fields occurs earlier, during their undergraduate careers:

Young women tend to lose confidence in their ability to "do science," regardless of how well they are actually doing, when: they have insufficient independence in their learning styles, decision making, and judgments about their own abilities: to survive denial of motivational support and performance reassurance by faculty, the refusal of male peers to acknowledge that they belong in science. (1995, 469–70)

In my experience as an assistant dean in minority affairs, the loss of Latinas in the sciences is not something that occurs mainly at the undergraduate level. The most difficult and most painful experience I have encountered professionally has been watching absolutely bright, successful Latinas, in both engineering and science graduate programs, simply walk out the door. These Latinas had completed their master's degrees in their chosen fields, received honors or were active in the academic associations of their field, and were quite capable of completing their dissertations. When conditions became unbearable or the situation was urgent, they sought advice from other Latinos and Latinas because they felt more at ease talking about the issues within the Latino language and culture. They shared with me their decisions to simply discontinue the battle against an academic culture in a male-dominated arena that took no interest in mentoring or encouraging them. One Latina decided to try her skills in various research labs, something she had intended to do with her degree from the outset. Another found an excellent position with a well-known corporation and appears to be thriving. Neither is actually "lost" in terms of not completing a doctoral degree in her respective field. The real loss is for the faculty, their graduate programs, and for other researchers in their field—all have lost trained talent, cultural energy, and creativity.

Overcommitment to Minority Activities or Teaching Overload

The "minority burden" is a term that describes the extra work done by women and ethnic minority faculty. It represents the responsibilities associated with minority activities, which they usually shoulder in addition to their assigned duties. This could be described as a "push-pull" situation. For a variety of reasons minorities and women faculty feel pushed to accept additional obligations when asked, and, at the same time, they feel pulled into the commitment by their own cultural compassion and ethnic or gender loyalties. Administrators are well aware that these faculty members can be counted on to help minority students or to offer cultural advice to those requesting it. Mentoring new minority faculty wisely can protect this individualized resource and expertise from abuse.

The minority burden is also known as "cultural taxation." According to Amado Padilla:

"Cultural taxation" is the obligation to show good citizenship toward the institution by serving its needs for the ethnic representation on committees. Or to demonstrate knowledge and commitment to a cultural group, which may even bring accolades to the institution but which is not usually rewarded by the institution on whose behalf the service was performed. (1994, 26)

Padilla says cultural taxation occurs in a variety of ways. For example, someone may be called upon to act as an expert in diversity matters, to educate majority individuals and groups about diversity matters, or to serve on an affirmative action committee, a task force, or as a community liaison for the university. Sometimes administrators need a problem solver, troubleshooter, or negotiator to handle minority issues. Latinos are often asked to translate documents from Spanish or to interpret for non-English speakers (1994, 26).

A deep sense of personal "cultural obligation" is involved, says Padilla, and if the institution asks for the minority faculty's participation, Latinos can find themselves caught in a number of double binds. Declining to be of service can indirectly affect an individual's reputation, students' perceptions, and collegial relationships. Someone who declines more than once is likely to find that the negative perceptions accumulate. And the decision to serve "on behalf of cultural diversity . . . is not usually in the equation for promotion within academia" (1994, 26). Furthermore, "although diversity may be important, it is not a substitute for intellectual excellence," which reflects competencies other than ethnic training, such as research and publication (1994, 26). Yet when ethnic trouble appears, administrators may quickly turn to the ethnic faculty. Cultural taxation is a continuing problem for Latinos and any other underrepresented populations on campus.

A few subjects confided to me that they have contemplated leaving their jobs because of their minority burden. Virtually every faculty member I asked had served as a representative of his or her ethnic group and had recruited minorities to campus. Only two in twenty-six thought their careers had not been affected in any way. A majority of the other eleven faculty believed their careers had suffered because of these activities. Good mentoring of new faculty and fair departmental policies about service commitments can be effective in helping faculty to deal with this issue.

In general, faculty felt "used as a token minority." Many felt the pressure of being a token minority was placed on them immediately and remained constant. Some were acutely aware of being the only Latina professor and as such were experiencing the "solo effect"—other faculty tend to evaluate the behaviors of the token, novel, or solo person in an extremely positive or extremely negative way (see Moody 1997, 16).

Almost all the people I interviewed felt a subtle conflict between cultural taxation and their high-context cultural values. For example, some may feel an overload of committee assignments as a minority burden, but many committees are attractive to minorities because they offer opportunities for high-context interactions with students or related activities like building an inclusive campus environment for all. A few faculty were able to control their involvement in committee work or minority recruiting efforts and gained either personal or departmental benefits (e.g., recruiting students; instilling a new Latino consciousness in the department; helping to inform faculty and staff about Latino social/cultural issues).

Victor, a Cuban American, represents the new generation of more high-context Latino scientists. He believes that recruiting for the sciences today requires faculty to become involved with elementary and secondary schools and to go into the community to attract minority students. Still untenured, Victor is willing to balance the minority burden—carefully juggling his academic priorities for research and publication with recruiting—because it is so beneficial. "I'm trying to contain it in terms of not letting it totally dominate what I'm doing day to day. What I see is the opportunity, and that opportunity is to not just say that I'm doing research or that I'm only doing education, [and] I think there's a synergy that can be tapped. But it's a little bit of a juggling act."

Tenure Issues

Tenure issues pose vexing problems for Latinos around the country. The patterns of declining tenure rates and few Latinos in tenure-track positions confirm their concern. Roughly 20 percent of my informants complained bitterly about issues associated with academic activities like publication quotas and research priorities. But whether to continue tenure as a guarantee of "academic freedom" or to abolish it as an "insurmountable obstacle" in reforming higher education has been an ongoing (and sometimes heated) debate (see Arnold 1996; Chiat 1997; Leatherman 1996; Magrath 1997; Perley 1997).

Among the strongest advocates for tenure reform today is William Tierney (1990, 1997, 1998a). He and Estela Bensimon are authors of a controversial 1996 book that examines the current system of tenure and promotion and evaluates it against its effects on academic organizational cultures, especially women and ethnic minorities (1996). They find the system no longer meets the needs of higher education. While the authors assume the original reason for tenure is still valid, whether tenure actually protects academic freedom is questionable (1996, 27). The main reason is that not all faculty are tenured, and with the growing number of nontenure-track positions held mainly by minorities, the system designed to protect academic freedom in this country is now counterproductive and outdated. Like Tierney and Bensimon, I found that the tensions and turbulence encountered by women and ethnic minority faculty are related to the entrenched system of academic tenure.

How did tenure affect the Latino and Latina faculty I interviewed? Ten people answered the question directly, but nearly all mentioned tenure during the interview. In reviewing the transcripts, I found many respondents discussed tenure in a variety of contexts. Although I discerned no

Table 6.1. Latino study, 1994–1995: Profile of tenure problems by gender (12 male respondents; 14 female respondents)

	Left academe	No tenure problems	Witness to problems (none personally)	Had problems	Not yet tenured
Males	0	5	3	2	2
Females	3	3	0	6	2

patterns directly associated with ethnicity, I did find interesting differences related to gender. Table 6.1 shows that of twenty-six Latino and Latina faculty, almost evenly divided by gender, more women than men encountered problems at some point during their tenure process, but many of the men saw others run into tenure problems. Apparently none of the faculty I interviewed had been denied tenure themselves, yet this issue ranked high on their list of concerns and many discussed tenure as one of the more stressful experiences they encountered in higher education.

One interesting pattern about faculty members leaving academe apparently had little if anything to do with tenure. Of all those interviewed, only three individuals—all Latinas—eventually left or did not find a position after beginning their careers as full-time faculty or administrators in traditional academic institutions. One left to take a more attractive salary in the business sector, another was harassed and left because the traditional university environment was a "bad fit" for her, and the third, who had been teaching part time in a college and could not land a tenure-track position, vehemently refused to become an adjunct professor with no chance for tenure and left academia for work in organizations serving the higher education community.

One way to eliminate most of the problems faced by new faculty is to institute formal orientation, faculty development, and mentorship programs. At the very least, a faculty mentorship program is valuable, even in the absence of formal orientation and development programs, my respondents said. I asked them two questions about mentoring: Did you have a mentor on campus? If so, how did she or he help? My interviewees were split evenly: thirteen had no mentor and thirteen had faculty mentors. Of those without mentors, three encountered tenure problems, which they attributed directly to not having a mentor, and the other ten made no mention of tenure difficulties. But few of the women had mentors, and the majority of those who did were administrators. One creative new faculty member actually negotiated for a mentor as part of his employment contract.

Many respondents believe that without good advice from an experienced mentor, Latino faculty tend to get sidetracked more than do many other groups. This was only their collective opinion, not something the data substantiated. However, eight of twenty-six individuals, approximately 31 percent, mentioned they encountered problems personally or knew others who had problems—they got sidetracked, became frustrated, suffered mistakes in their tenure package, or had difficulty advancing—because they lacked a faculty mentor. One cause for concern is the poor advice they get from other faculty when they don't have a mentor to help them negotiate the tenure process. I asked Jaime, a Chicano professor in the Southwest, whether he could find no one to help him through the process. He responded:

Not really. That's my big complaint. I'm always looking for a mentor. Well, they [other faculty] help you through the process but not really, they talk to you. . . . I have some senior people who will listen to me, but what they keep telling me—and it's what I've been told since graduate school: "Just go and do your research, and just stay away from all these minority issues. Why do you have to carry the torch? Just settle down, teach your courses, let the university run." That's their advice. I think these mentors, if you want to call them that, like me, and they're genuine in their advice. But they can't understand why I'm so committed to Latino issues, and they don't really believe that there are issues about Latinos. They believe that we're playing on a level playing field.

Racism, Classism, and Tokenism

Although my respondents place racism, classism, and tokenism in the middle of their list of concerns, these certainly are major issues for women and minorities. The relative importance my respondents ascribed to such issues of discrimination probably is the result of their hesitation to suspect or label every negative act as racism. Tierney and Bensimon (1996) also noted this pattern of "hesitancy" in their chapter on the socialization of minority faculty. They found the "great majority of minority faculty did not allude to acts of overt racism" (1996, 121). Tierney and Bensimon's minority interviewees also described cultural taxation, discrimination, tokenism, issues related to ethnic research, cultural identity issues, and the like. As I discussed in earlier chapters, what others may attribute to racism, I see as dissonance in organizational cultural context and cognition; Tierney and Bensimon attribute such problems to climatelike conditions associated with a lack of a coherent academic community (1996, 103–23).

Let me expand on and clarify my point in some detail. Tierney and Bensimon note that minority faculty at one institution cited overt acts of racism and pointed to these events as contradicting the institution's claim of being sensitive to "multiculturalism" and "diversity." One professor claimed that what was being taught was at odds with the "social justice mission" of the institution. Another claimed the service he provided to

Latino students was "not recognized" by the department (1996, 121). One minority professor told the authors this was a "smoke screen" to cover up institutional racism, which professors could not discuss openly. Though the circumstances here are unclear, an alternative explanation is that low-context academic culture is clashing with high-context characteristics in the diversity mission or within the ethnic faculty culture or both.

According to Tierney and Bensimon, a primary example of unrecognized institutional racism is associated with interpersonal interactions and the lack of academic scholarly feedback. They cite as an example an African American woman, a junior faculty member who gave a lecture attended by several of her department colleagues, who then seemed to ignore her and failed to give her any feedback, although they offered feedback to two speakers from another department. Because she did not get feedback and could not tell, in general, "how people are reacting" to her or why, she was uncertain how to regard a broader set of negative reactions she observed from other faculty. She cited as examples being ignored when she said "Good morning" or when she saw people turn away from her as she tried to make eye contact. According to Tierney and Bensimon, the woman was reluctant to see or discuss these incidents as racism because she was under academic social pressures not to regard such slights as racism (1996, 121–22).

But I think there's another way to interpret the problems this faculty member was encountering—as a good example of academic high- and low-context cultural conflicts, as well as a mismatch of field-sensitive and -independent cognitive behaviors. A lecture is a form of academic social event, but it is not an open social event such as a party. The individuals involved are part of a formal and rigid hierarchy: junior faculty, senior faculty, ranked and unranked academic colleagues. Their interactions may or may not be highly structured, but the circumstances of a lecture are inherently critical, with senior members of the audience weighing the academic values of performance, evaluation, recognition of scholarship, and perhaps tenure worthiness. In such a situation the interactions, or the apparent lack thereof, are more important clues to one's academic status and level of acceptance, not evidence of racism and discrimination, even though discrimination may be present in those interactions.

My guess is that the academic style of this African American professor is more personal than that of the others, perhaps high context and field sensitive. That she seeks contact with colleagues suggests she is outgoing, and certainly interactive, and her academic values—she is concerned with getting feedback from colleagues after the lecture—appear to be driven by social rewards. But her colleagues and many other faculty are more likely to have been socialized by the low-context, field-independent academic style, which tends to favor or require a response that is more formal, distant, and reserved than what she expected or needed. The majority faculty, whom she perceived as cold or even rude, were assuming an academic style that they felt was appropriate. Regardless of circumstances, exhibiting such behaviors could reflect intentions that range anywhere from the extremes of simply being themselves to actually exhibiting racist reactions. Another explanation could be that the more senior faculty were using a demeanor that they have found to be appropriate when tenure and promotion are on the line: meeting the highly territorial and cutthroat tenure game with the low-context cultural response of avoidance. Is this sexism? Quite possibly, though senior female faculty play this game too. Is it discriminatory? Only against the academically weak, which may be how such faculty perceive high-context, field-sensitive individuals, who prefer informal personal interactions and associations with other academics. This could be especially true for new faculty members, such as this African American professor, who signaled her awareness of her newness and uncertainty about her surroundings.

That she was trying to understand why others react as they do to her suggests she probably needs more information than others, and her need probably was heightened because she was a junior faculty member. She also may seek short-term interpersonal feedback, constantly checking the status of others and expecting the same in return. Other faculty, however, may prefer long-term interpersonal feedback, to avoid interfering with or intervening in others' lives, and they may not be as sensitive to the information needs of an African American junior faculty member. She is concerned about personal commitment to people and is constantly trying to read her colleagues' nonverbal cues. That may make her colleagues uncomfortable with her, or they may simply be following the low-context social rules of respecting privacy and being considerate of others by not returning her gaze. Even she is not certain whether this is "the culture of the city, the college, or my being African American" (Tierney and Bensimon 1996, 121). Thus we can see that academic cultures and their organizational structures are riddled with certain conditions, values, and behaviors that can create severe problems with negative consequences for ethnic minority and women faculty.

The concepts of cultural context and cognition offer a more plausible explanation for what the African American professor and others experience than does the concept of unrecognized institutional racism presented by Tierney and Bensimon (1996). Suggesting that cultural context and cognition may be a good part of the problem does not, of course, preclude that faculty were, in fact, also reacting to the African American professor with discrimination and racist attitudes. But I would argue that she is not adequately served by a rationale that tends to use some form of racism to explain all cases of cultural conflict. As psychologists are fond of pointing out, when a particular behavior has more than one plausible explanation, why assume the worst motives are in play? Even if they are, it is often more productive—and certainly less stressful—to proceed under the assumption that a more benign explanation accounts for the behavior in question (see Sternberg 1996, 1997). Finally, it seems unlikely that social pressure is the reason so few academics are likely to label such dissonant behaviors as racism.

Unfortunately, we cannot altogether ignore racism as an explanation. But we would do well to remember that when the primary motivation for others' behavior is racism, there is no ambiguity. A Chicana professor recounted experiences from early in her academic career when she was a junior faculty at a large research university:

They did horrible things to me the first two years I was here. They wouldn't give me the security code to my classroom; instead they sent a staff member down to . . . [open] it for me. They wouldn't tell me things I was entitled to [know]. I was never introduced to the faculty. To this day, I have never been introduced. They know me now, of course. After I had been here a few weeks, I was walking into the faculty area where the mail boxes were, . . . I was stopped by another member of the faculty who told me only faculty were allowed there and I should stay out of the area. I was sent anonymous racist notes, and they were put in my faculty mailbox where only faculty could be.

On another occasion, as I was winding up an interview with a Latino administrator in which he spoke of the prevalent racism on campus, he pulled an anonymous hand-printed note from his desk drawer. The note contained a hateful and pointedly racist message. His comment was matter-of-fact: "I get these all the time."

Retention Issues

Latino faculty had such mixed feelings about campus conditions that they were uncertain they would remain in academia. Many felt comfortable on campus, yet most believed overall campus conditions were negative. In fact, more than half the respondents personally experienced serious problems on campus, and only two Latinos felt that campus attitudes were generally positive. But even they qualified their opinions by noting they had overheard snide offhand remarks from Anglo faculty about "minority hires."

These comments came in response to what most people refer to as "climate" questions about an organization, but I prefer to call them "cultural attitude barometers." I asked the faculty members in my study about the overall campus attitude toward Latino faculty and students, whether they feel comfortable on campus, and whether the campus has a revolving door for Latinos.

Their mixed feelings could reflect conflict between ethnic and academic cultures or even conflict over academic style. Diego, now a professor in California, understands that his high-context academic style—he tends to avoid feeding the bureaucracy—causes conflict with those whose communication style is more low context:

> I feel comfortable on campus and in the school. I play a pivotal role here right now, but I always feel the powers that be or my peers want things done a certain way, and I'm more offbeat than they are. I don't know. . . . I feel my style is a little bit different, and I think it's a stylistic difference that aggravates some of the people. I don't write a lot of memos and I don't put things down in black-and-white, and I'm not keen on being accurate on writing my minutes when I run a meeting.

Thus little things, like Diego's style, highlight the enormous cultural gaps that foster misunderstanding and even charges of discrimination on campuses today.

Intracultural Issues

Latino faculty from ethnic groups of diverse national origins inhabit many campuses across the country, but their numbers are so few and so spread out among various departments that distinctions along cultural or ethnic lines are sometimes blurred or nonexistent. When I asked respondents whether they could identify distinct subethnic groups among Latinos on campus, and, if so, whether they could discern any intragroup tensions, I received only twelve responses. Half said too few Latinos were on their campus to notice any tensions. One said, "There are too few Hispanic faculty to isolate ourselves. And we're so busy that the faculty never gets together. There is no interaction." The other six recognized other Latino groups on most of their campuses and mentioned significant differences between groups from around the Caribbean (Cubans, Puerto Ricans, Dominicans) and those who grew up in Mexico. Campuses with a variety of Latino groups apparently experience few interethnic conflicts or tensions. In fact, many participants commented that despite such diverse backgrounds, the Latino faculty tended to work together on Latino issues, especially to protect each other in personnel issues and from budget cuts. On campuses where Latino faculty or administrators are more numerous, cultural and ethnic distinctions are more evident and regional distinctions are more sharply defined. A few individuals said they feel some cultural conflict with other Latino individuals but saw little, if any, cultural tension between the various groups. Diego was able to find a few cultural distinctions among the Latino faculty on his campus: "Yes, there are culture variations. There's a group of people from New Mexico that are pretty strong here, and there's a strong *Tejano* contingent, people from Texas, [who] came as migrants to California. Then there's those of us from California like myself."

I asked how the groups differ and whether he distinguishes the Tejanos from the Chicanos in California. He replied:

They [Tejanos] are pretty much very politically involved in terms of the Chicano needs on campus. They're looking out for the Chicanos and the migrants especially. There's a real strong concern and support for the Chicano migrant, the Mexican migrant. Then there's the Chicanos from New Mexico: they're politically conservative, they're Republicans, and they're more into working with the system and doing the correct procedures. They're really an astute group of people too, in that sense.

Many participants believe that any tensions among Latino faculty of different national origins are not based on cultural or ethnic issues but rather stem from political differences distinguished by conservative and liberal viewpoints. For instance, the differences that exist between Puerto Ricans from the island and the various mainland Latino populations (e.g., Puerto Ricans, Cubans, or Dominicans) are centered around issues related to immigration (see Fitzpatrick 1971; Moore and Pachon 1985; Sánchez Korrol 1993), class and other socioeconomic differences (Moore and Pinderhughes 1993; Safa 1974), and even rural versus urban value systems (see Ibarra 1996).

Among Cuban Americans, including faculty, mainly in the Miami metropolitan area, the tensions center around personal and political opinions about Fidel Castro. This is a heated, contentious, and ongoing debate with serious consequences. It appears that the majority of Cuban American faculty on many campuses around Miami are, like the larger Cuban American community, politically conservative; they tend to be politically anti-Castro, and they steadfastly support current U.S. foreign policy, including the embargo of Cuba. Faculty with more liberal views on Cuba or Castro are cautious not to reveal them openly for fear of repercussions. Yet such political issues can directly affect academic life, making it easy or difficult, depending on which side you take. Roberto, a Cuban American professor in Florida, tells us about it in his response to my question about specific issues between the Puerto Ricans, the Cuban Americans, and Americans from Central and South America:

I think if there is an issue . . . it is the perception that Cuban Americans just network for themselves and support their own group, or they want only Cuban Americans to be hired. I think there's that sense of exclusivity. But there are other issues between Cuban Americans, political issues. And, the litmus test is where you stand on Cuba. The only other Hispanic member of my department didn't want to participate in my tenure vote. He didn't want to vote for, against, or abstain. He wanted to be totally removed from my tenure vote, because I conducted research in Cuba and for my position regarding Cuba.

The large majority see Latino cooperation as the norm and only during one-on-one interviews would individuals share their feelings about inter-ethnic tensions—"It's also the only university in the United States which is populated by the most affluent Hispanic group, the Cubans. I'm Hispanic so I have to suffer the consequences. I don't mind. It's alive and well, discrimination." There were only a few such faculty overall, and the issues they discussed were targeted primarily against particular individuals from other ethnic groups and rarely against a particular ethnic group in general.

Lack of Support Groups

A common assumption even among Latinos is that they lack the organizational ability and numbers to form coalitions and support groups. Other Latinos contend that this may be a self-fulfilling prophecy. Despite a documented history of strong, well-organized political and social movements, especially among Chicanos during the 1960s (see Acuña 1972, 1998; Menchaca 1997; Sánchez 1993; Vélez-Ibáñez 1996), their small presence and misperceptions about organizational skills within the Latino community continue to provide what I believe is a poor explanation for the apparent lack of academic support groups and coalitions created and sustained by Latinos on campus.

Promotion Problems

Scholarship, publication, promotion, and academic recognition are some key ingredients for academic success and form the basic criteria for gaining tenure at research universities. To achieve tenure remains quite an accomplishment in any department. It is even more difficult to achieve for faculty who are committed to research that is thought to be less mainstream, even marginal, within a demanding and intellectually rigorous discipline. This is what Latinos and other women and ethnic minority scholars face as they climb the tenure ladder, gain promotions, and seek notice in their fields. If their research interests are geared to ethnicity, diversity, or gender issues, what they accomplish is seen as somehow less worthy. Many faculty in the mainstream of their academic discipline consider it a "no-brainer" for a Chicano or a woman to study and publish books and papers about ethnic culture and women. Even though the work that they are doing is groundbreaking basic research, most of the academic mainstream crowd consider the topic too mundane or exotic, too commonplace or too obscure to merit attention. Consequently, women and minorities have a difficult time getting strong letters of support for their tenure packages from peers in their disciplines. It is still considered less rigorous work, although ethnic and gender research is inherently difficult because it is marginalized in academia. Ethnic scholars and Latina scholars must endure and persevere to gain even local campus recognition, much less the critical national or international notice that has become a prerequisite for tenure and promotion at many research universities.

According to Jaime, the Chicano professor in the Southwest, gaining tenure and promotion are much more difficult for Latinos who engage in ethnic and gender research than many majority professors recognize. The inherent obstacles become even larger when scholars encounter reluctance to publish their work, or they find resistance to promotions within their department. Looking back from his more senior faculty position, Jaime shared the following insights and comments:

I don't think we're playing on a level playing field. Let me give you this example. I got promoted to full professor last year. Because I am now more senior, I have more opportunities. The [major disciplinary association] calls me, I'm asked to review articles and that kind of stuff. I work with some faculty, and we've had articles sent back from, say, the [disciplinary] association, manuscripts that haven't even been read, that say things like . . . "This manuscript really is not appropriate for this journal." . . . That's one example. Then my wife did a review of the literature of that [disciplinary] journal for ethnic content [over the last] twenty years, and [that organization] writes back and says it's not appropriate for that particular journal. The methodology we know is sound because we had [a recognized scholar] consulting with us on that article. . . . I've had articles rejected because there's not a great deal of interest by the readership on assessment of minority students. I'm talking about an assessment journal. I see that as problematic in that the journals are not accepting the stuff, so how do you get the [appropriate] numbers [of articles published] to be tenured?

Administration

One theme throughout this book has been the polarization of Latinos within academia. Latino and Latina administrators experience another kind of "cultural gap"—more accurately, a gulf—related to the management experience they and their majority peers bring to administration. In higher education most majority faculty begin their administrative careers as department chairs. With their tenure as insurance and their department as a retreat in case of career difficulties, they may separate from the faculty ranks to accept more administrative responsibilities. If they like the work, and if they are willing to discontinue their major research projects and reduce their teaching load, they may choose to give up faculty life for upper-level administration in higher education. At some point in their careers they may even decide to return to the faculty.

But Latinos, like many ethnic minorities, tend to skip this long-term process and sometimes embrace administrative opportunities prematurely. They may be attracted by administrative positions that tend to be people or community oriented. Some may take lower-level positions that may not provide decision-making authority and upward mobility. Thus few have jobs that can shape academic organizational culture. Consequently, researchers find that women and minority administrators, even at the level of dean, are less likely to have appropriate academic credentials and profiles for achieving the highest levels of educational administration (M. Clark, Gill, and Duby 1991).[5] This creates a significant cultural gap both in regard to promotion and the administrative socialization process.[6] Except for certain pockets of institutions on the west coast and in the Southwest, this pattern even appears in predominantly Latino regions and at Hispanic Serving Institutions, including Catholic universities dedicated to serving Latinos.

One interesting but as yet undocumented finding about Catholic universities in the United States is that there may be a correlation between historical patterns and the low numbers of Latino executives. A few Latino faculty at Catholic universities commented that institutional racism in those institutions sometimes surfaces as an attitude of paternalism. These faculty had strong feelings about the paucity of Latino administrators on their campuses. This, they surmised, reflected the struggle between Anglos and Latinos for administrative control of institutions associated with a specific order of the Catholic Church. One order in particular is controlled by Anglos and tends to have a western European perspective, according to Alfonso, a Latino professor at a Catholic institution. If this is true, certain Catholic institutions are structured and imprinted by cultural perspectives that are both low context and peculiar to the particular religious missions and beliefs of the founding order. Alfonso claimed that the founding order is concerned about a growing Latino identification with that institution, even though it has few Latino administrators:

I know that there have been a lot of problems in getting a Latino into the administrative positions at this university, and there have been several recent cases where Latinos could easily have been chosen and were not. That's been the source of some concern, particularly for some of the Latino faculty. There is a power struggle at this university. This is a [specific Catholic order] university and [this] order is a very Anglo order. A handful of Latinos, at most, within the order, and the people who run the university at the administrative level, are all either of the order, are [viewed positively] by the order, or they have a certain traditional Catholic idea about what the university should do and what it should teach. While there is a sort of rhetoric about having [this institution] conform, be more connected, to be more in tune with its [predominant] Hispanic student population, there is a reluctance to go that way.

Career Trends and Patterns among Latino Study Administrators

Because they have not been socialized as tenure-track faculty, Latinos in administration may become further marginalized by their differences from faculty culture. Some Latinos and Latinas are unaware of the long-term implications for their careers.

Similar messages emerge from the sparse research literature on Latino administrators in higher education. Research surveys, such as Esquibel's work on career mobility among Chicano administrators (1992), are usually aimed at identifying the problems and improving occupational conditions with solid quantitative data to support their sage advice. Garza (1996), on the other hand, interviewed Latina administrators exclusively and selected sixteen from different ethnic subgroups for her study. The administrators were employed on four different campuses within the University of Wisconsin system of colleges and universities. Focusing on her subjects' notions of how retention and promotion issues affected their careers, Garza found three common problems or themes: a lack of mentoring, little professional development, and work environments that primarily fostered isolation and tokenism (1996, 20). She concluded that these institutions gave far more attention and consideration to the recruitment and retention of faculty and students than to the recruitment and retention of administrative staff members. The Latinos I interviewed echoed these patterns and themes, among others, in Garza's study.

My questions for Latino administrators covered three general areas: How did they became involved in administration? What problems did they encounter? What strategies help build successful administrative careers?

Seventeen of the seventy-seven people I interviewed were administrators who responded to most of these questions. Some overlap occurred with five faculty members who were trying out administrative positions or were moving toward new careers in administration. The remainder were twelve full-time nonfaculty administrators. The sample was balanced almost evenly by gender, with men representing slightly more that 50 percent of the group. Mexican Americans represented the ethnic majority at close to 56 percent, followed by Puerto Ricans (25 percent). Ten individuals, representing a little more than half the group (59 percent), were directly or recently involved with minority administrative activities (such as recruiting and outreach, community work, multicultural issues on campus, and directing English as a Second Language programs). The other seven administrators were not currently involved directly with minority issues, but many had been so involved in the past and were now high-level administrators. Even so, they talked about how they continued to enhance the minority presence on their campus, either through hiring faculty or by recruiting students. These seven included school or college deans, provosts or vice chancellors, presidents or chancellors; four were either current or past presidents or chancellors of their institutions or of other institutions.

Career histories revealed some variation in career mobility patterns. Academic career tracks fell into two types: ethnic specific or broad spectrum. Among the past and present CEOs, two had a broad spectrum of experiences rather than a focused emphasis on ethnicity, such as positions in minority student services or faculty positions in Chicano studies. Two others, equally successful, had pursued both general and ethnic interests. The latter realized early on in their careers that administrative success—reaching the highest levels of management—requires a significant record of research and publication. They learned that without those credentials they would be unlikely to move higher than associate dean or associate vice chancellor at any research university. They might be able to attain the presidency or vice presidency without the traditional credentials, but those instances are rare and usually occur at much less prestigious institutions. These respondents also noted that Latinos tend to do many things at the same time (polychronicity) and that they are willing to research, publish, and even teach while working as an academic administrator. But they also knew that publishing enough to gain tenure under these circumstances would be distracting, so they adjusted their strategy by concentrating on academic work at appropriate points in their careers.

Some Latinos tend to become seduced by administrative opportunities too early in their careers. If they accept an administrative position before they complete their doctoral degree, they are at high risk of never completing it. And if they accept an administrative position just after completing their doctoral degree, they run a fairly high risk of not getting teaching experience or a tenure-track position.

However, not all administrative careers contain the same level of risk. In fact, in some predominantly Latino areas, such as in Puerto Rico, administrative work is attractive and is less risky professionally within the island universities. According to Reinaldo, a faculty member and program administrator in Puerto Rico, administrative work actually carries little risk and more benefits than a faculty appointment. The faculty governance systems are considerably weaker at Puerto Rican public universities than at most U.S. mainland institutions. As he explained:

Since there are such few opportunities in terms of salary incentives for purely academic work, the real incentives that you have are in terms of administrative work. What happens is that a lot of people who are qualified academically end up doing administrative work simply because it's a way of increasing your income, on the one hand, and it's possibly the only channel for real input in terms of decision making too. . . . It's incredibly top-heavy here. . . . With our institutional bureaucracy . . . it seems that power is really in administration and not in academics.

Some careers tended to follow random paths that were seemingly un-planned or accidental. The accidental pattern is characterized by scattered career directions or frequent changes and career shifts, sometimes chang-ing radically, as in the following career trajectory: community work, community-based organizational positions, a directorship, an administra-tive position, teaching, law school, teaching. A career strategy that vacil-lates between academia and community-based organizations carries a higher risk than most, but it did not prevent some Latinos from achieving academic success. Even successful high-level administrators exhibited this rather high-context, people-oriented pattern.

Success entails avoiding the administrative "minority ghetto." Latino faculty are under a good deal of pressure if they are asked to direct minor-ity initiatives on campus. This often means curtailing a research/publica-tion agenda and may sidetrack a faculty career. People who are unaware of the potential hazards of pursuing an administrative career prematurely are even more vulnerable if they choose to jump from faculty to adminis-tration and back (see Garza 1996; Moses 1993).

Latino faculty members are sometimes asked to take on administrative responsibilities before they complete their tenure/promotion sequence. In addition to increasing the potential for a vacillating career path, two other problems can develop if they are not careful: one is a common pattern— the "overworked administrator syndrome." This pattern emerges among those who are both faculty and administrators in charge of campus re-search centers and institutes. As they notice their colleagues moving ahead in their research and promotions, they may attempt to catch up by jumping back and forth between academics and administration. This pattern can become a serious problem for directors and faculty for ethnic or gender studies programs who hold joint appointments from degree-granting de-partments and the ethnic center.

Ileana, a Puerto Rican professor still a few years from tenure, exempli-fies this problem. Her department had so few Latino faculty that it could not meet the linguistic demands from students enrolled in the English as a Second Language program her department runs for the university. With teaching and administrative duties made more difficult by recent faculty departures, the department chair was under pressure to ask Ileana whether she would continue teaching and run the ESL program for a year until the department could hire a tenured faculty member with the skills to take over the program. It was difficult for her to refuse his request because she knew that having no administrator in her program would make academic life more complicated. Besides, she confided, the chair was offering a boost in salary and a reduction in teaching load, attractive inducements to put her quest for tenure aside for a year and accept the offer. The chair had made the request for help three years before I interviewed Ileana, and she

163

was still running the program, her teaching load had increased, and a severe financial crisis at the institution meant it would not be hiring a permanent administrator for the program in the foreseeable future. Ileana felt trapped. What happened to her is a good example of being called upon to administer a program too early in one's career, thus jeopardizing progress toward tenure or certainly delaying it.

Latina administrators say they were naive and lacked experience when they took on management positions. Four of the ten administrators directly involved in minority administrative activities left academia, one for the private sector and another for a position in a large museum. The third Latina bypassed teaching at the university level and was attracted to administrative work very early in her career. She is now successful in a career associated with academia and says she may never complete her doctoral degree. With doctoral degree in hand, the fourth Latina abandoned her frustrating search for a tenure-track position and has turned her attention to nonacademic interests. The other six Latinas are still administrators in higher education. Three were on the faculty, were mentored by Anglos, and were encouraged toward administration by high-level administrators; three others followed traditional career paths to administration, by teaching, heading a department, or taking a directorship or deanship. They were not mentored or groomed for administration.

One recipe for success is to get as much broad experience a possible in academe. All seven high-ranking administrators commented that the crucial steps in their success were the broad experiences they gained while working as special assistants to presidents and/or from firsthand observation of top-level decision makers and their administrative approaches. For example, one ranking administrator was a fellow at the American Council on Education and two others had Ford Foundation Fellowships. One believed the secret to his success in administration was getting involved with mainstream issues and being in the right place at the right time. He became an assistant to the president, who soon resigned; the new president promoted him.

Finally, despite concerns about ghettoization, most Latino and Latina administrators kept close to their personal missions and interests. For the most part their interests were aimed directly at improving minority conditions on campus and helping other Latinos pursue an advanced degree. Even as high-level administrators and leaders, they continued to be part of the Latino community and maintained their interests in Latino/minority student concerns.

High Context and High Content: Latino Ethnicity and Research

Ethnic research interests mark the academic careers—and career problems—of the Latinos I interviewed. Though research is integral to the tenure process, the problems of ethnic research for ethnic minorities deserve special attention. In earlier chapters I discussed my research findings about ethnic transformations, academic cultural turbulence, and the notable increase in ethnic research among Latinos in graduate school (1996). In my first report I posited the idea that Latinos may be more high context culturally than other ethnic populations, but that does not appear to be the case.[7] I believe many of these patterns show a strong correlation with cultural context and cognition. For instance, ethnic research for Latinos represents more than an interest in studying one's community; it also reflects the high-context associations, like the strong personal commitments, deep involvements with people, and stable lifetime relationships that Latinos value highly (see table 3.1). Field-sensitive children function well when curriculum content is relevant to their personal interests and experiences. This is one reason why literature for minority children often sets story lines in familiar ethnic neighborhoods. Field-sensitive adults tend to personalize communications by referring to their own life experiences, interests, and feelings (see table 3.2). This helps explain the rise in ethnic research among Latinos in graduate education. In the general academic community and among some Latino scholars, ethnic research is still a controversial issue (A. Padilla 1994). Others, like Enrique Trueba, believe ethnic research is now more important among Latino scholars because it is constructing a new ethnicity and a new identity among Latinos nationwide (1999). Tierney and Bensimon (1996) found that minority faculty in the social sciences encountered so many obstacles in trying to do and publish ethnic research that one of their subjects called the problem "academic ethnocentricism" (1996, 112).

Among the Latino faculty I interviewed, ethnicity does play a large part in their academic interests. Latina and Latino scientists in my study demonstrated a strong pattern of ethnic activity outside the lab (see table 6.2). The overall cohort is relatively small, but the pattern is clear. All five scientists working in academic research labs are heavily involved in ethnic minority recruitment programs. These programs include, for example, those of the National Science Foundation (NSF), Society for the Advancement of Chicanos and Native Americans in Science (SACNAS), Society of Hispanic Professional Engineers, Hispanic Research Center at Arizona State University, and the Smithsonian Institution. Latino scientists may become very involved in their ethnic community and with other major

Table 6.2. Latino study, 1994–1995: Field of study of participants by gender (June 1995)

Field of study	Males $n=41$	Females $n=36$
Education	8[a]	10
Social science	19	13
Humanities	5	7
Physical science	6	2
Biological science	3	4

[a] Figures include both master's and doctoral degrees.

national Latino organizations such as the Hispanic Association of Colleges and Universities (HACU), National Council of La Raza, or the National Association of Chicano Studies. Many saw their involvement as a way to give back to the community. All saw their activities as an opportunity to recruit the cream of the crop among minority students in the sciences. This shows an intense commitment to ethnicity, although they are unlikely or unable to study an ethnic topic or project in their field of research.

Most nonacademics in the Latino study are involved in ethnic activities or research in both the private and public sectors. These included all three researchers with degrees in science, some with prior university research or teaching experience. One female entomologist volunteers to teach science each summer and encourages Chicanas enrolled in a special high school summer science program to consider science as a career.

Virtually all faculty and administrators in the Latino study were involved in some activity directly associated with Latino ethnicity. Moreover, twenty-eight of the thirty faculty and administrators I interviewed were either recently or currently involved in research and writing directly associated with ethnicity. Overall, a number of respondents in this group registered their concerns about ethnic research. At least three said they were shifting to more ethnic-oriented research, and one felt as if she were coming "out of the closet" about being a "Hispanic scholar" (see Ibarra 1996). Others held strong, sometimes negative, opinions about pursuing ethnic research. Some recognized that once scholars are committed to a particular research topic or area, including ethnicity, they risk "being tracked," "ghettoized," and marginalized by their research interests. These individuals recommend to other Latinos considering academics that, depending on what they want to study, it is important to think ahead and plan which direction one intends to go academically. Many participants simply wanted others to be informed about the issue and to avoid being labeled or ghettoized as an ethnic or Latino scholar if possible.

The questions about ethnic research generated different experiences that correlated with the individuals' backgrounds. For example, the quest for recognition and validation for ethnic or gender research has a downside. Leticia, a Latina professor now teaching at a university in Texas, was irritated that people assumed "that you're a woman, therefore you should know feminist theory, or you're Latina—you ought to be studying some aspect of Puerto Rican ethnicity." Generation can also make a difference. Francisco, an administrative leader at his institution, has seen changes regarding ethnic research in his field: "I was the first member of that department to get an article published in the prestigious [journal]. Once you do achieve whatever you're doing, then there is always the attitude . . . 'Well, the only reason it got published was because you are Chicano.' . . . But there is the other, positive side. You are a pioneer."

I asked several additional questions of Latino faculty members who said they were committed to combining ethnicity and scholarship: Are you involved with any academic or professional organizations? Are any of them ethnic-oriented organizations? Are you associated with any nonacademic but ethnic organizations in the community?

Of the eighteen faculty responding, half were involved with academic organizations in their disciplines. Most (about 89 percent), however, were involved with an ethnic-oriented academic organization, some even associated with their particular disciplines. Approximately one-third of the respondents were either leaders or founders of national Hispanic/Latino organizations focused on higher education (i.e., HACU, SACNAS, and the like). Others saw joining and becoming active in these organizations as important occasions for networking and as opportunities for improving their careers. Nearly 75 percent of those responding to the question were also active in an ethnic community organization in some fashion. The few not involved mentioned full academic agendas, prior commitments and responsibilities with academic organizations, and simply being new to the faculty as the main reasons for no current involvement.

Becoming involved in civic organizations, volunteering, even becoming active in one's academic or professional organizations are not activities associated only with ethnic minorities and women in our society. Many people are involved in their communities and feel it is important to offer their services or expertise. But professional service, defined as university outreach into community, has never been a high priority among the majority academics in this country (Lynton 1995). As Matthews describes it, "Campuses talk a lot about public service. Yet except for state extension efforts at the land-grant schools, faculty outreach to the larger world tends to be individual, sporadic, quixotic" (1997, 153). Among majority academics, who tend to interpret "service" as helping their college or university, even they dislike activities such as committee work, for they consider these obligations as taking time away from "real academic work." Thus community outreach is the least valued of all academic responsibilities, for it brings few, if any, rewards toward achieving tenure, promotion, or academic recognition. This academic cultural value may have some influence on the attitudes of high-context individuals. A case in point is that of the director of Latino Studies, whose experience, described in chapter 5, emphasized the importance of academic cultural values over the values of the Latino community.

For most Latinos and other ethnic minority faculty, "professional service" means something quite different, and they are quite willing to give the extra measure in both the academic and nonacademic communities. One of my interviewees, Beatriz, articulated it well: "I have always believed that what you study in a community you give back. It doesn't have anything to do with the trendiness in [social sciences today] as much as it has to do with me being a Latina and having the need to reflect that into the community. Who they are and who we are."

Of the ten Latino respondents involved with nonacademic ethnic organizations, half described an "intense feeling" about becoming involved, saw themselves "building bridges to the community," or said they were "giving back to the community." The widening gap and increasing tension between low-context academic culture and this high-context ethnic "intensity" toward community may even heighten the internal conflict they feel. Other researchers have noted that both women and minority faculty describe "a sense of 'gap' or 'chasm' that they feel or observed in their departmental environments . . . [an] absence of collegial connection and effective communication" (Spann 1990, 2). I alluded to this point in my preliminary report, which suggested that the "cultural gap" between academia and Latino graduate students precipitated in the students a greater interest in ethnicity and ethnic research that increased and intensified during their graduate careers (1996, 56–58). This same "ethnic intensity" seems to surface among Latino faculty as well, with consequences and outcomes similar to those encountered by graduate students.

For example, two administrators in the Latino study, who were not involved with ethnic organizations when they were working as faculty, became very involved with nonacademic ethnic organizations once they left the faculty for administrative work. Two others, one of whom is now a professor and the other a high-ranking administrator, actually left academe after completing their doctoral degrees to join or direct ethnic-oriented, community-based organizations. These are intensely committed activists. One Latino, the CEO of his corporation, commented how he became more aware and involved with ethnic organizations after receiving his doctoral degree. He attributed this to the "absence or invisibility of Latino identity in graduate school." Because he was the only Latino in graduate school, he focused on getting the degree and eventually the job.

Although professional service is not peculiar to Latino academics, they do tend to be more intense in their efforts, perhaps driven to improve the conditions of minority populations. Nearly all faculty or administrators who found themselves among highly concentrated Latino populations other than their own, or even among other entirely different ethnic minority groups, would become intensely involved with that minority community. Graciela, a full professor at a university along the east coast, believes in reaching out to other minority communities, in this case, African Americans:

Sometimes I feel that it's important to be those bridges . . . that bridge building is important with the larger communities whether it's with Latinos or blacks, like [a public university in the community] which was a lot of headaches. Being on the board of trustees of a public university anywhere is a headache. But a young public university, where the ethnic issues are there on the surface, being a Latina on that is hard.

Finally, I asked the group active in professional service about plans for the future. Despite their conflicts and tensions within academia, the twelve Latinos who responded to the question said they mainly planned to pursue academics. This was similar to the response Darryl Smith and her colleagues received from respondents in their study (Smith, Wolf, et al. 1996). Seven of my respondents, mostly women, "didn't know" much about future plans and offered some vague ideas and general directions. The other five, mostly men, had their sights set on administration. Only one Latino wanted to do research and teach. Not surprisingly, he was a new faculty member. Future goals seemed family oriented among the Latinas responding to the question. Four were married and had families. One Latina wanted to start a family, and she acknowledged that her interests toward children and family were winning out over her interest in continuing her career. Two women mentioned an interest in seeking promotion, but family was still a top priority. Among Latinos, current and future career opportunities dominated their plans.

Beyond Academe: The Nonacademics

Among the questions I wanted to answer is why so few Latinos are employed in academia. Thus I also sought to interview individuals who had obtained advanced degrees but had decided not to seek employment on campus. Tomás, a Puerto Rican who is a director in a federal agency, said he enjoyed teaching and research but decided against the academic life: "I think it's the sense of isolation of the academic. . . . It hits very deep in me. I don't want to be isolated. . . . I want

169

to be in the middle of everything and be involved in it with my hands. I don't want to write about the party, I want to be *in* the party."

Studies of people who drop out of graduate programs also shed light on why some people find academic life to be unattractive. Nerad and Miller (1996) found graduate students at Berkeley, who had obtained their master's, became "early leavers" for a variety of reasons. For some the Ph.D. was not the goal; others began switching their academic fields or institutions. Some left because they felt mismatched or frustrated with their program or adviser, and a number of students in professional school found their graduate program did not meet their expectations (1996, 68–69). Regardless of ethnicity or gender, Nerad and Miller found they could categorize most reasons for graduate student attrition as disconnects between the faculty or the program and the student.

Looking at ethnicity, they found increasing numbers of minority students were not completing their programs, and they had little substantial data that suggested why. Clearly, retention and completion rates are core issues for graduate programs around the country (see Baird 1983; Haworth 1996; Nerad and Cerny 1993). Despite that, faculty assume that attrition is somehow directly related to students. Nerad and Miller (1996) offer two views: students leave either because of external factors, such as financial reasons, or because they come to a graduate program with unreasonable expectations and do not find the "hand-holding" they needed or expected (1996, 66). Neither of these perspectives, however, considers the possibility that the departments or the faculty could be major factors in the problem of graduate student attrition.

Faculty attitudes and academic culture, however, may in fact play a larger and more direct role in attrition among "late leavers" than previously thought. According to Nerad and Miller, these are doctoral students who tend to leave in their third year because they are undecided and unclear about academic goals, experience poor adviser–student relationships, lack financial support, and, most important, find the departmental climate too "chilly" to continue. A "chilly climate," according to the authors, "was one especially salient attrition factor for women" but not as much for men (71). Education researchers consider these nonpersisters to be an elusive group. Because faculty assume that students leave for personal or external reasons, departments fudge their attrition rates by manipulating their admissions rates and hope to get enough students who "fit" into the department and eventually complete the program. Consequently, academic departments, and graduate schools as well, are notorious for not monitoring their students. Given these conditions, which are traditional, few students are likely to discuss their problems with faculty or departmental advisers. They stop out, and by the time the department realizes they are gone, the institution may not be able to trace them because too much time has passed (Nerad and Miller 1996).

In exploring this phenomenon, I decided to interview Latinos who had received their master's degree but had decided not to continue for a doctoral degree, as well as those who had completed a Ph.D. but did not select a career in academia. I was also interested in locating another, even more elusive group: Latinos with and without doctoral degrees who had taught at the college level and decided to leave academia.

Latinos in nonacademic occupations provided some interesting information. Nonacademics, who may or may not have held faculty positions, did not rule out seeking full-time faculty positions in the future. In some cases they chose to leave traditional academic occupations, whereas others had no choice. In most circumstances these nonacademics, or "nonfaculty," are now working in public or private organizations that are closely associated with higher education, or they are researchers and administrators doing work similar to their counterparts on traditional campuses.

Eventually, I was able to interview eleven Latinos in nonacademic positions that spanned a variety of occupations. To profile them briefly, they were seven Latinas and four Latinos. More than half the group was Mexican American; three were from other Latino groups; one was Puerto Rican; and one was Cuban American. Four nonacademics worked in federal agencies in the Washington, D.C., area, and three had completed doctoral degrees in the natural sciences, though only two were working as research scientists in nonacademic labs. Two others were public school teachers, and the other five nonacademics were administrators, program directors, researchers, or analysts. Of the entire group, eight individuals had taught at the college level or had administrative experience in higher education, and half showed interest in returning to a traditional academic teaching position.

Another pattern worth noting is this group's high level of interest in ethnic-related occupations. The majority (55 percent) were working in positions associated with minority/diversity issues; although the remaining five were working in other kinds of positions, two were scientists who were interested in obtaining minority-related positions but were unable to switch careers at that point. One of the scientists, who has a career in a private lab, was granted a leave by his employer and at the time of the interview was working in a Latino-oriented association related to higher education. Much like the Latino faculty and administrators, the nonacademics demonstrated high levels of interest in ethnic-oriented activities outside their work, and they apparently capitalized on such opportunities whenever they could.

I asked the nonacademics why they had not sought careers in academia and, if they had once held academic positions, why they had left.

Upon completing her or his degree, almost every nonacademic received several job offers, which happened not to be in academia. One Latino scientist said he had turned down a higher-paying offer to teach at a research university in Texas to accept a private-sector position for the better benefits it offered. But the pivotal factor in his decision was the complaints he overheard the more senior university faculty make about salaries that had not caught up with salary levels offered to newer faculty.

The reasons given for taking private-sector and government jobs instead of positions on campus were as varied as the interviewees' current occupations. Listed briefly here are several factors that directly or indirectly influenced their decisions:

Money—The salaries offered entry-level faculty were poor.

Bad departmental environment—They knew they would have conflicts with low-context culture.

No permanent positions available in academe—They refused to teach as adjunct faculty.

Private enterprise was more attractive than academe—The private sector was more serious than higher education about improving the diversity of the workforce and providing a working environment in which minorities could do their best work.

Distaste for college teaching—A research position in academia would have been attractive, had it been offered.

Isolation—They wanted to be "in the action."

Academic distractions—They were eager to do scientific research and received offers from several universities but decided the private sector offered fewer distractions.

The nonacademics stood out from their academic counterparts in two distinct ways: they had a clear sense of direction and a desire to apply their knowledge in their career. Felipe, a Chicano research analyst with clear aspirations to become an academic, did not consider a professorship after completing his doctoral degree because of market conditions. He entered into private research because, "if I wanted to go into the academy, I could have a stronger leverage position by doing this kind of work first and then going back to the university. . . . It was the job market, financial remuneration, and I didn't want an entry-level professorship."

A primary goal for those nonacademic Latinos and for the academic Latinos as well is to apply their knowledge and tools of their discipline to enhance their communities and the lives of the people in them. Academic disciplines, the "invisible colleges" of higher education alluded to in earlier chapters, have their own shared and sometimes differentiated culture and values that can clash with the values and goals of Latinos and other high-context, field-sensitive individuals. According to Becher (1984), the various disciplinary cultures may be shaped by what he calls "environmental" forces associated with national, institutional, and even organizational contexts. For example, political forces (i.e., guilt associated with weapons development), epistemological differences, ideologies, the focus of knowledge, and even the taint of amateurism (i.e., astronomy, archaeology, and other disciplines that attract amateur practitioners) all play a role in the development of the values, procedures, and characteristics that frame the disciplinary cultures. Comparing the methodologies of social/cultural anthropology and sociology, for instance, reveals distinctive values that hint at roots in high- and low-context cultural preferences. According to Becher (1989), in social/cultural anthropology, which focuses on an internal process of experiential fieldwork, relationships *are* data, and methodology is an introspective method of analyzing those relationships. In sociology, which is obsessed with obtaining scientific status, "methodology is external and technical and related to the possibility of objective knowledge" (1989, 39). However, I agree with Becher that the disciplines' characteristics are so variable that it is difficult to analyze these subcultures (1984, 179–86).

However, discipline-based culture may be a reason that Latinos eschew careers in academia. Many preferred careers and perhaps academic disciplines with characteristics that lend themselves to applied work. Some academic disciplines accommodate and even support applied fields of research as an inherent component of their academic culture, whereas others have historically maintained an academic core of traditional basic research, neither encouraging nor discouraging applied work. These cultural patterns among the disciplines, noted by Latino social scientists in their comments to me, make academic employment unattractive to people from high-context cultures, especially Latinos.

Carolina, a Mexican American with strong roots in Mexico, is an independent consultant for international development programs. She now prefers her applied work, but she would have accepted a research position in academia if one had been offered. She pursued an applied career, although she believes her discipline and department actively discourage applied work. Her comments express the feelings of many other Latinos and even majority academics who were turned off by negative aspects and attitudes they found within their discipline or department:

> I was not really thrilled by the thought of teaching. I felt that it was a tough job . . . but even then [in graduate school] I knew I was more interested in applied work than academic work. If anybody had offered me a research position in academia, I would have taken it. As it turned out, I was required to do research for most of the professional work I have done. I just put it in an applied context, and a lot of it was traditional anthropological research.

173

I pointed out that traditional anthropology prefers training students for an academic position and asked why she did not pursue that path, what made her decide to proceed differently.

Probably out of vindictiveness for the department, which actively discouraged their students in applied anthropology. I felt strongly about that. I always had a soft spot for doing applied work because, coming from Mexico and from a situation where you understand the poverty and the dispossession of so many people, I always felt that there had to be some usefulness to what you were doing. I wouldn't call it outright altruism or anything like that, but I felt there was a social responsibility that you did have to do something. I also think there was a little element of vindictiveness [on my part] because they [the department] didn't want to teach field methods, or to teach applied anthropology, because they don't like that. . . . It was closing up an avenue [of study] that shouldn't have been closed. . . . I was not off-track because people who went to school with me ended up in applied anthropology careers. If you define it in terms of a certain social conscience, or social makeup, or awareness because of my ethnic origin, then, sure, some cultural influence affected my decision. But I also think the bad job market at the time was part of it.

Carolina, who focused on cultural anthropology, was clearly upset by the department's attitude toward applied studies. I would add that this is an overall problem in the discipline, not just the department. Given the high number of minorities with doctoral degrees in the social sciences, and the high-context nature of cultural anthropology, one might expect to find a significant ethnic presence in the discipline. But faculty surveys show that anthropology does not seem to attract ethnic minorities. In 1996 the American Anthropological Association surveyed anthropology departments and found only 10 percent of all anthropology faculty are underrepresented ethnic minorities, a figure that has remained relatively unchanged since at least 1988 (Givens and Jablonski 1996b).

Given its emphasis on ethnicity and multiculturalism, why is anthropology apparently unable to attract ethnic minorities? One answer may simply be tradition. Despite some high-context characteristics, certain fundamental cultural traditions in anthropology are in direct conflict with the high-context values of some ethnic populations. One deterrent may be the discipline's habit of discouraging—and sometimes forbidding—its graduate students to study their own ethnic cultures or communities, claiming student bias can undermine an impartial analysis. Traditional anthropologists prefer that students test their skills in culturally different societies instead of their own. Undoubtedly compounding the problem is the dictate that scholars must not become involved with or inadvertently change another culture. There is no doubt that anthropology is attractive to some ethnic minority populations, as it is for me, but it may not be as attractive as other social science disciplines. Sociology, for example, focuses on ethnicity and poverty and other social problems and seeks community-based researchers, encourages problem solving, and has a sister discipline, social work, that is completely hands-on, interactive, and client oriented. Psychology, for similar reasons, is becoming more attractive to Puerto Ricans, and education remains the most attractive of the professional and "soft" sciences.

As I said earlier, choosing a discipline or career may be more bound up in issues involving cultural context and cognition than we first recognized. Disciplinary domains associated with terms like *hard, pure, soft,* and *applied* come from the work done by Biglan (1973), who compiled what academics perceived were characteristic of their disciplines. Kolb's work (1981, 1984; D. M. Smith and Kolb 1986) classified student learning styles as measured along two binary dimensions—active-reflective and abstract-concrete—to explain variations associated with the disciplines that emphasized conceptualization over experience or preferred active participation to detached observation. Both classification systems are reflections of cultural context and cognition; according to their designers and other researchers (Becher 1989), they also reflect a hierarchy of dominance, with hard sciences such as physics leading the group.

What is important here is not the pecking order but the dominance of the influence—the imprint—of the leading disciplines in the physical and natural sciences. Other disciplines mimic the leaders as best they can, demonstrating that even social sciences can be rigorous and "as good as" the others. This hierarchy of prestige is directly related to the importance of the disciplines in research universities and in graduate programs. This is not a trivial point. Gumport (1993a, 1993b) points out that graduate education and organized research became so interwoven in American higher education during the twentieth century that they are the major reasons for top-tier research institutions to exist. A research university is becoming "an increasingly noble aim for lower tiers to emulate" (1993a, 247). According to Rice (1996) and Boyer (1990), among others, departmental budgets that are skewed toward grant revenues rather than tuition drive the effort to become more scientific, and they claim the emphasis on research has been the primary cause for the narrowing of scholarly and creative faculty work in teaching and community service.

Borrowing from Kolb's concepts of learning styles (1981, 1984), Rice (1996, 14–18) demonstrates the growing imbalance in higher education that favors research over teaching. Over the years science has become more analytical and quantitative, abstract and detached, a more reflective science over concrete science. Meanwhile, science that is more connected to the community, experiential and applied, or one that is practiced actively, became increasingly less important in higher education. This trickle-down emulation pattern among disciplines is found not only in research universities but in the doctoral and master's-only institutions as well. And it seems to be causing havoc with scholarship priorities, which have shifted from teaching to research and publication. In essence, higher education, especially graduate education, is playing a cultural game of "follow-the-research-leaders" to the detriment of high-context cultures and those with field-sensitive cognitive preferences. When professional service takes a back seat in academia, and applied anthropology is not encouraged, we are not likely to see many changes in priorities in the near future. It is no wonder that Latinos and other ethnic groups, as well as women, have become increasingly unhappy in higher education.

This, I believe, is some of the evidence that demonstrates how the power of organizational academic cultures, and not racism per se, is one of the root causes for conflict between Latinos and academia. Judging from the preferences expressed by Latino faculty, administrators, nonacademics, and students, as well as from recent data in the discipline (Givens and Jablonski 1996a), anthropology and perhaps other social sciences may see a new surge of interest for real-world applications in graduate work. The profile of graduate students, now predominantly female, has changed, and on the horizon is an increasingly culturally diverse and, I contend, more multicontextual population with preferences for high-context approaches and interactions. They are likely to learn better if they can use a field-sensitive learning style. New types of student-oriented institutions that are focused on delivering graduate education are rapidly emerging to meet this new demand. Traditional academe, with subcultures and disciplines that tend to preserve cultural values unattractive to these populations, could find itself stalled at a cultural crossroads along with others who cannot read the early warning signs of demographic change.

One of these early signs may be warning that abrupt changes in student enrollment patterns could rapidly become a crisis for higher education. For example, what would happen to our research universities—our faculty factories—if international students, especially those from Asian nations, suddenly stopped coming to the United States for their education? As table 2.1 shows, noncitizens received nearly 28 percent of all doctoral degrees awarded in 1998, second only to the majority population, which received 57 percent of all the advanced degrees awarded that year (NSF et al. 1999). U.S. ethnic minorities *combined* received only about 10 percent of all doctoral degrees, mainly in the humanities and social sciences; Latinos took home only 3 percent of all doctoral degrees in 1998. A closer look at the data shows that almost the entire population of noncitizen degree recipients—about 93 percent—were international students, here on temporary visas. (The remaining 7 percent of that group were here on permanent visas and seeking U.S. citizenship.) Almost 69 percent of all doctoral degrees awarded in the sciences that year went to international students on temporary visas, mainly from Asian nations; nearly a third of those science degrees (31 percent) were clustered in engineering programs. In other words, doctoral education in many of the science disciplines at major research institutions in the United States trains more international students than U.S. citizens. Thus these disciplines rely on the flow of international students, mainly Asian nationals, to keep critical research projects moving along as they work toward their doctoral degrees.

If this student population flow suddenly ceased, as it can when national or international political and economic conditions deteriorate, and if U.S. citizens, especially the swelling numbers from ethnic minority populations, are not brought into the sciences relatively soon, the pool of science students could literally disappear, endangering both university programs and national research projects almost overnight. This is not unlike our national dependence on foreign oil-producing nations, which continually jeopardizes the economic well-being of this country. But unlike the U.S. oil crisis in 1973, and the even more recent dramatic oil price hikes in early 2000, the problem of dependence on international students has yet to be widely recognized as the Achilles heel of U.S. science research.

Although the science establishment is not alarmed, research institutes now developing in prime urban centers along the Asian/Pacific rim could attract faculty and students who historically attended or were employed by U.S. institutions (Nelson and Ibarra 1999). At the same time, globalization and the associated technological innovations now "put distance learning into the reach of students all over the world, perhaps ultimately undermining the more traditional methods of graduate education" that require campus residency to receive a degree (1999, 10). And all these developments are arising as the majority student population is constricting and the pool of minority students is increasing. In short, to ensure the continuing preeminence of U.S. research universities, we must reform academic culture to attract the talents of U.S. citizens who are multicultural.

In the end, we have more questions than answers for why so few Latinos, not to mention other minorities, are in graduate school or on the faculty. Interviewing nonacademics was valuable and relevant to the questions I was exploring, but the sample group was too small for any definitive conclusions. However, a few interesting patterns surfaced that should lead to future research. It seems that only a few Latinos in the sample left academe because they found it too uninviting. One newly minted Ph.D., for instance, could not find a full-time position and refused to be an adjunct professor. Others would be interested in returning to academe or entering it for the first time. But the essential findings are that other careers are more attractive because of the isolation of academia from the real world.

But long before they became faculty or administrators, Latinas and Latinos learned to survive and thrive in a multicontextual world, where adjustments to multiple cultural realities are a common occurrence. Renato Rosaldo and Gloria Anzaldúa agree that, as Rosaldo says, "because Chicanos have so long practiced the art of cultural blending, 'we' now stand in a position to become leaders in developing new forms of polyglot cultural creativity" (Rosaldo 1993, 216; see also Anzaldúa 1987, 1990).

Part III

The Engagement
of Cultural Context
in Academia

7

Teaching, Testing, and Measuring Intelligence

Uncovering the Evidence That Cultural Context Is Important

The greatest obstacle to well-intentioned efforts to expand educational opportunities for underrepresented groups, and to achieve greater equity in our society in general, may well be our obsession with *being* smart. The real problem is that we value being smart much more than we do *developing* smartness.

Alexander W. Astin, "Our Obsession with Being Smart"

Since the mid-1990s colleagues have increasingly been sharing with me their sense that something is missing from higher education, but they can't quite figure out what it is. The system has served us well, and we have produced a world-class educational model for research and scholarship. Graduate education, for instance, contributed directly to the phenomenal scientific and technological achievements we enjoy today. But it is both excellent and deficient. Like a slightly off-color thread woven into fabric, the defect is hard to detect. We lock our institutional cultures into a perspective that excels in the logical, rational, and analytical scientific domains, but they come up short in accommodating alternative approaches, for example. Cultural research by Hall (1977, 1984) and cognitive analysis by Manuel Ramírez and Castañeda (1974) are only a few of the strongest and most consistent studies that address this theme. Even the psychologist Robert Sternberg, who tends to ignore the importance of ethnicity in the cognitive arena, finds that most institutions in this country value certain ways of thinking more than others and that the institution often penalizes individuals whose thinking styles are different (1997, 8). This has been my perception of the situation for quite a long time.

Part III examines what higher education, more specifically, graduate education, can change (chapter 7). Applying the concepts of the multi-contextual model for enhancing educational systems, including diversity, requires finding evidence of the importance of cultural context within our traditional academic cultures. What, then, can we learn about our approaches to teaching, testing, and measuring intelligence that will give us clues to the patterns of cultural context and cognition? Moreover, how can we enhance and institute a new balance between these systems as the model suggests? Chapter 8 uses this evidence to consider ways to create a new framework to strengthen the current organizational infrastructure of higher education. Bringing about such change requires restructuring current educational systems, reconstituting diversity initiatives, and adapting these diversity initiatives throughout the system. This chapter begins with a discussion of learning to detect the latent conditions—the bits and pieces of cultural context and cognition—that are all around us.

Intelligence and the Effects of Cultural Context on Standardized Tests

When I first meet people who are thinking about attending graduate school, one of the questions they ask most frequently is, "How can I get into graduate school—what does it take?"* Faculty on graduate admissions committees ask each other the same question but from a different perspective: "What characteristics should we be looking for in a candidate for our department?" My response to both is that one or more of the following factors may determine the likelihood of success in graduate school: motivation, reasoning skills, interpersonal skills, per-

*Much of the next two sections is the result of my collaboration with Dr. Allan S. Cohen, director of the Office of Testing and Evaluation at the University of Wisconsin–Madison. This is especially true of the discussions of differential item functioning (DIF) and standardized testing and test development, none of which would have been possible had we not collaborated in an effort to determine whether cultural context, cognition, and DIF are somehow related. Portions of the section titled "The Enigma of DIF" are taken from Ibarra and Cohen (1999) and adapted from Fairness, Access, Multiculturalism, and Equity (FAME) material. Reprinted by permission of Educational Testing Service, the copyright owner.

sistence, creativity, prior achievement, cognition, and miscellaneous non-cognitive factors.

Gándara's study of low-income Chicanas and my own report on Latinos in graduate education found few, if any, academic predictors for success (Gándara 1995; Ibarra 1996). Although attending an integrated high school or taking college prep courses certainly enhances the potential for being admitted to college and eventually graduate school (see chapter 4), many college administrators agree that the most influential factors in the college admissions process are high school grades and transcripts (Owen and Doerr 1999). Even some officials from the Educational Testing Service (ETS), producers of the Graduate Record Exam (GRE) and other standardized tests, have made similar comments off the record about college grade-point averages. As one measure of academic success, Latinos in the study were completing advanced degrees regardless of preparation or privilege. Beyond academics, "the primary ingredients for success seem to be personal characteristics: persistence and determination, the willingness to surmount obstacles in completing advanced degrees and the ability to adapt to adversity" (Ibarra 1996, 26).

Because the studies seem to show that personal characteristics, including the willingness and ability to surmount obstacles, is a primary determinant of success in graduate school, it stands to reason that graduate schools would benefit greatly by asking potential students what barriers they had to overcome to prepare themselves for graduate work and by examining students' backgrounds for their experiences in overcoming adversity. That strategy was adopted as part of the admissions process for the 1998 medical school class at the University of Texas. Forced by the U.S. Court of Appeals for the Fifth Circuit to change its procedures for admitting minority students, the medical school revised its strategy; without compromising its standards, minority enrollments were expected to increase. Because the 1996 *Hopwood v. Texas* federal court decision prevented the medical school from considering race as a factor in admissions, minority enrollments dipped in 1997. Admissions committees could, however, consider the students' socioeconomic backgrounds, bilinguality, whether they come from an area of the state with few doctors, and "what obstacles they have overcome to pursue their studies" (Mangan 1998a, 1). Whereas admissions decisions once were determined mainly by grade-point averages and standardized test scores, in 1998 decisions committees could consider students' backgrounds as a criteria for admission. Using this strategy, the average GPA of those offered admission to the medical school at the University of Texas for the fall of 1998 barely changed, from 3.66 in the fall of 1997 to 3.64 in 1998, but the number of Latinos offered admission jumped from 108 in 1997 to 142, and the number of African Americans admitted rose from 29 to 50 students. Clearly, the medical school was able to admit more minority students without lowering its standards by selecting those candidates who had shown how well they could overcome obstacles to pursue their studies. The Medical School at Texas A&M will now admit some applicants without Medical College Admissions Test (MCAT) scores if these students participate in a program intended to increase the number of doctors in minority communities (Basinger 1998).

One ETS official is experimenting with a variant of the medical school model that considers the background of college-bound test takers. His version looks at "strivers," students who score more than two hundred points above the average Scholastic Aptitude Test (SAT) of students with similar backgrounds (Gose 1999). Instead of evaluating students by their positive individual characteristics (e.g., being bilingual) or by the obstacles they have overcome, such as poor schooling, the ETS model determines and measures how much "disadvantage" should be factored into a student's score. A striver is identified by first scaling a student's SAT score with fourteen variables that measure levels of disadvantage, such as family income, parents' education, rigor of high school courses, and so on. The adjusted score is compared with the average score of other similarly disadvantaged students. Students who score two hundred points above the average score for their peers are strivers with potential for success in college. Thus "students who earned 'striver' status could be given extra consideration in admissions" (Gose 1999, 1). Because ethnicity may be included as a factor in the striver index, the model has the potential for increasing minority student admissions in college, as well as in graduate school and professional schools by adjusting the weight given to GRE, MCAT, and LSAT test scores of identified strivers. But these developments in admissions criteria may be short lived for undergraduates. Many universities in states affected by assaults on affirmative action programs—California, Texas, and Florida, for example—are turning to class-ranked GPA-based systems that admit a top percentage (4 to 20 percent) of state high school graduates (Nickens 1999).

The *Hopwood* decision has adversely affected graduate education. For instance, medical school applications across the country decreased in the first two years after the decision was handed down. Instead of the enrollment increase expected in 1998, "since 1996, the number of minority applicants to medical school in Texas, Louisiana, and Mississippi [the states overseen by the Fifth Circuit] has dropped 22 per cent, while in California, the number of minority applicants to medical schools has dropped 19 per cent" (Mangan 1998b, 1).

While the process of graduate admissions is readjusting, renewed controversy surrounds traditional concepts of intelligence as well as traditional admissions criteria. The problem is that minorities and women have continuing performance problems on standardized tests (ETS 1995; Grandy

1994; Sacks 1997). Gándara suggests that "testing and assessment of individual students should be reconceptualized as diagnostic, not predictive" (1995, 121). A 1997 study of law school students admitted in 1990 found that their LSAT scores were "poor predictors of graduation and bar exam passage for both white and minority students" (Owen and Doerr 1999, 200). Many graduate school deans will tell you that, at best, the GRE can predict the grades of a first-year graduate student, but it cannot predict the student's overall performance in graduate school. Owen and Doerr analyzed the SAT specifically and found that this standardized test is seriously flawed and is still unfair to minorities despite company efforts to remove cultural bias (1999). Though some educators acknowledge that the SAT, GRE, and professional school tests remain culturally skewed, they still push for even greater reliance on standard admissions tests as one measure of preparedness for higher education (Stewart 1998).

The psychologists Robert Sternberg (1996, 1997) and Wendy Williams (1997) claim standardized admissions tests, like the GRE, are not good predictors of success in graduate school. They question what, in fact, the exams are testing. Is it aptitude, knowledge, or intelligence that predicts success, or all these? Their answers provide significant support for the fundamental concepts associated with cultural context and cognition. Sternberg's research focuses on the nature of intelligence and how it relates to standardized testing. He believes graduate school testing overvalues analytical abilities and undervalues creative and practical aptitudes. He finds that "IQ accounts for less than 10% of the variation among those people who are more successful by society's standards and those who are less successful. . . . Analyzing GRE scores of 167 Yale psychology students on the [standardized] graduate school entrance exam over a 12-year period found that scores predicted only first year grades but did not predict success—or failure—in grad school" (Morin 1996, C5). This is not surprising, because this is what the GRE is intended to do—predict first-year grades in graduate school. Correlation with subsequent success is a less well-defined criterion.

The GRE, according to Sternberg, "measures only a very narrow aspect of intelligence" (Basinger 1997, 1). As it turns out, among the analytical, verbal, and quantitative sections of the GRE, Sternberg and Williams both found that only the analytical section is a good predictor for first-year grades in graduate school, and it predicts well only for men (Basinger 1997). In fact, the best and worst correlations for men and women, respectively, were found in their scores from the ETS Advanced Achievement Test in psychology (Sternberg 1996). From their limited study of GPAs and doctoral dissertations among psychology students at Yale, Sternberg and Williams (1997) suspect that success in predicting first-year grades could reflect the way graduate-level psychology courses are taught. The courses require fairly abstract memorization and the attributes of ability and achievement that are being tested by the GRE (634). However, building a successful career as a psychologist, they argue, requires other, equally important creative and practical attributes that are not tested by the GRE exam.

In fact, Sternberg's reasoning is problematic in several respects. First, graduate students at Yale are a select group. As such, they are probably more homogeneous than the overall population of students that takes the GREs. The result is that correlations or predictions between GRE scores and first-year grades are likely to be depressed or lowered. If the Yale students do differ among themselves, it is probably not so much in their verbal or quantitative scores as in their analytic scores. Although Sternberg's ideas about testing are interesting, his attack on the GRE in this instance is not on target.

Sternberg advocates proactive solutions for the standardized testing problems that plague students throughout their educational careers. He suggests that school systems should be redesigned to embrace three distinct types of intelligence: analytic intelligence (the ability to solve academic problems and judge the value of ideas); creative intelligence (the ability to formulate good problems and ideas); and practical intelligence (the ability to use ideas and analysis effectively in everyday life—academic street smarts). "Typically only analytic intelligence is valued in the classroom," although it may be "less useful to many students in their adult lives" than the ability to "think creatively about problems or use common sense to arrive at solutions" (Morin 1996, C5). To make matters worse for students, research on the patterns of parental support for school achievement among Mexican Americans (Okagaki and Frensch 1995; Okagaki and Sternberg 1993) suggests that the more that parents emphasize competence in social skills as a component of intelligence—high-context values of the family and community—the less bright their children look by school standards. While Euro-American parents selected cognitive traits (e.g., problem-solving skills, verbal abilities, and creative abilities) as important measures of intelligence for their children, the groups of immigrant and native Mexican American parents selected noncognitive traits (e.g., social skills, motivation, and practical skills) as more important (Okagaki and Frensch 1995, 337). Parents from both Mexican groups believed social skills (such as playing well with other children, showing respect to others, being sensitive to other people's needs) are important components of what children need to know in order to demonstrate academic intelligence in school.

Characteristics that emphasize preferences for group learning processes, associations, and personal commitment to people lend support to the hypothesis that high-context cultural values are integral components not only of Mexican American and other Latino families but of African

American families as well. Many African Americans are as adept as Latinos at communicating with nonverbal cues in their own community but tend to use this skill less well in school, according to Shirley Brice-Heath, because nonverbal cues are less valued there (1983). Unfortunately, our K–12 school systems make little use of this knowledge to advocate for reform, as Sternberg recommends.

Sternberg believes that Anglo middle-class culture undervalues the importance of nonverbal communication, and he makes a strong argument for all educators to become adept at both understanding and transmitting nonverbal cues (1996). Sensitivity to nonverbal communication, he suggests, can be a key to success in professional or work-related interview settings, close interpersonal relationships, and for international or intercultural business interactions as well (1996, 144). A facility for interpreting nonverbal human behavior is an extremely important skill for psychologists to have and develop. Unfortunately, it is never a part of standardized testing for prospective teachers or practitioners.

According to Morin, Sternberg's own assessment test, the Sternberg Multidimensional Abilities Test (see also Sternberg 1988), measures all three types of intelligence and finds "notable abilities in students who 'previously had been viewed as not particularly bright'—including both minority and white students" (1996, C5). Learning increased significantly when students were taught in a style that matched their learning abilities (Morin 1996). The reason, Sternberg believes, is "that in everyone there is some combination of analytical, creative, and practical intelligence. We need to foster *all* these forms of intelligence, not favor just one" (Sternberg 1996, 146). Wendy Williams, in the Department of Human Development at Cornell University, is now trying to develop an alternative to the GRE for students in the social sciences (1997). Her vision of such an exam assesses the skills needed by that particular discipline, such as the ability to complete certain tasks that are relevant to that discipline but not derived directly from it. That would avoid handing an advantage to students with prior knowledge of the fundamentals of that discipline.

Sternberg's research examines what he believes are a number of fallacies built into our society that tend to drive our values in current testing designs. One is the misperception that "to be quick is to be smart" (1988, 22). Echoing Edward T. Hall's earlier pronouncements about the concept of time in our society, Sternberg says American culture values speed. It permeates U.S. social values—we admire people who are "quick studies," or learn quickly, make quick judgments, or are quick decision makers. This translates into the assumption that what a student can exhibit in a timed testing situation is an accurate measure of academic ability. Such an assumption, of course, is not necessarily accurate. As I noted earlier, the meaning of time and time limits involves a culture-based pattern of thinking. Students who are high context may not do as well on a test with a time limit simply because time limits have different meanings for them (R. Cohen 1969). Timed testing probably selects against high-context test takers who have a reflective cognitive style. Yet the impulsive style is more highly valued in our society and in our testing. Overall, his model has essential characteristics associated with multicontextual Latinos and other ethnic minorities and women.

A second fallacy, according to Sternberg, assumes that highly verbal people read everything carefully. Careful readers are flexible readers who can adjust to all types of material. But tests require "brute force"—meaning under pressure, timed conditions, an uncomfortable environment, and no outside help or resources—to solve problems, which is not realistic in everyday situations. Somewhat related to careful readers, according to Sternberg, is the false assumption that the size of one's vocabulary is a measure of intelligence. Vocabulary items, according to Sternberg, measure achievement rather than the ability to achieve—more intelligent people do tend to do better in school (e.g., learn more words, understand better what they read, solve more mathematics problems correctly) than less intelligent people. The problem for students, particularly some minority students, is that a vocabulary test may not be an appropriate surrogate for an intelligence test. This is what Boice (1992) refers to as a disconnect between minority students who are attempting to demonstrate the ability to develop intellect and academics who are looking for individuals who can demonstrate their fully developed intellect.

Finally, Americans harbor the fallacy that intelligent people solve problems the same way other people do, but they do it better. The fact is that some people solve problems in linear fashion, others use spatial strategies, and still others are effective with a verbal approach. To illustrate his point Sternberg describes how he learned to improve his scores on spatial ability tests, which he consistently failed in his youth. He simply learned how to verbally describe a particular object, then read the multiple-choice answers, and select the one most likely to be right. He was not always correct, but his scores improved and that was enough (1996, 101). What Sternberg describes is the conceptual equivalent of the learning process that high-context individuals must endure when they attend elementary and secondary school.

For Latinos such learning processes become even more challenging in college. As they tell it, if they survive college, graduate school is an entirely different adventure. Our schools gear nearly everything to low-context culture; as a result, high-context learners have a great deal more to learn than others. Latinos, for example, among other high-context people, learn to become multicontextual in the same way Sternberg "learned" to improve his spatial abilities. The result, however, is that high-context learners are often labeled as slow learners who "blossom later" in their academic careers than others, while people who learn useful but "noncritical skills," such as improving spatial ability test scores, are not necessarily penalized academically for their deficiencies.

But why do men perform better than women on analytical portions of standardized tests? Commenting about his research on gender differences in standardized testing, Sternberg speculates that "women's performance in graduate school might be more affected by such variables as role expectations or unjustified fears of incompetence" (Basinger 1997, 2; see also Sternberg and Williams 1997). This "unjustified fear" is very similar to what the psychologists Claude Steele and Joshua Aronson call "stereotype threat" found among African American test takers (1995). With a small number of subjects, and in laboratory conditions, Steele and Aronson found significant differences in test scores when they made only small changes in the directions for taking the test and in the explanations given to their subjects. Their research showed that when African American college-level students were asked to take a test that had no direct consequence for them, their performance was equal to or better than that of majority test takers in the same group. But when similar groups were told the outcomes of the same tests would affect them academically, performance levels among African American test takers dropped dramatically. The perceived stereotypes associated with testing and other lab or classroom performances of women and minorities created this effect, according to Steele and Aronson (1995). Although the differences between real testing situations and laboratory test situations are great, their findings show that hidden variables in the testing environment may have long-term effects on women and minority test takers.

When I began my Latino research project, I was well aware of the controversy about the GRE and low test performances of women and minorities. This widely used admissions test is a notorious academic gatekeeper because ethnic minorities and women generally do not perform as well as majority males, especially on the GRE's general test. To make matters worse, academic institutions and departments are known to abuse these tests by depending entirely upon test scores or by using cutoff scores as an admissions criterion (Ibarra 1996, 31–33). Yet critics of affirmative action admissions programs claim that standardized tests scores are valid measures of scholastic merit. They claim that test scores, combined with students' grades, should be the only criteria that qualify students for admission to higher education (Thernstrom 1997). ETS tries hard to fight testing abuse in general and to eliminate factors that may cause performance differences, especially the types of questions known to cause special problems for women and ethnic minorities (see Sacks 1997; Stricker and Emmerich 1997; Strosnider 1997a).

The Enigma of DIF

I had no idea when I started my research that I would soon become embroiled in the enigma called *differential item functioning,* or simply "DIF" analysis, as it is known to professional test developers. This arcane term refers to the performance problems of women and ethnic minorities who take batteries of standardized tests beginning in high school, throughout college, and even for graduate school admission. For more than thirty years researchers have shown that "test-takers of approximately equal ability" will "perform in substantially different ways" on particular test questions on standardized exams (ETS 1995, 3). Comparisons between women and men and/or minority and majority test takers usually reveal this differential is at work on particular test items. The problem is that no one has been able to adequately explain why this occurs.

The existence of DIF is a concern for test developers because it represents a serious threat to the validity of their tests (Ibarra and Cohen 1999). It may also represent a bias against those populations that, for still inexplicable reasons, perform poorly on the exams. For these reasons test developers have focused on trying to detect DIF and to determine why DIF occurs. One major obstacle has been the lack of a good theoretical framework for explaining it. Another problem is that multiple types of DIF exist, including gender DIF and ethnic DIF, each caused by one or more factors. Whatever it is, it probably contributes to the low test scores generated among women and ethnic minorities. Solving the enigma of DIF has been an elusive goal for both test developers and the quantitative researchers who are hired by institutions like ETS to resolve the problem. The quest for this Holy Grail is an important one, however, for whoever generates a rationale for predicting or understanding DIF will begin to unravel the mystery of how to control it in test construction. That could at least reduce, if not eliminate, the inequity associated with standardized tests.

It is hard to imagine that a qualitative researcher would become involved in this quantitative domain, but that is precisely what happened. While I was searching for quantitative evidence to establish the validity of my multicontextual theory, I was invited to present my views on graduate school, ethnicity, and testing issues at a conference cosponsored by ETS and Xavier University (Dwyer 1998; Ibarra and Cohen 1999). The goal of the conference was to explore issues related to access and assessment—standardized testing—for women and minorities in higher education. If cultural context and cognition were dynamic forces for ethnic conflict in academic organizational culture, could they be detected in quantitative domains such as standardized testing?

My hypothesis suggests that becoming multicontextual is a lifelong process of learning to accommodate or adopt appropriate forms of cultural context and cognition. Individuals who can shift strategies in this sense reflect the demands of a growing number of situations in our educational systems. Ethnic minorities and women are not necessarily the only people who can do this. Some majority males may demonstrate this ability as well (see M. Ramírez 1991, 1998). However, without further study much of this theory, including the actual proportions of multicontextual groups or individuals within the population, remains speculative.

Multicontextual individuals are equipped with a versatility to adjust or adapt at any time to a variety of activities, tasks, or social environments. This is not an easy transition, as it requires additional concentration and perhaps more academic work as well. Thus the process is subtle and often difficult to observe directly. For example, the learning modes and styles of some populations imprint cultural patterns of perceiving the world through more visual or auditory ways, whereas other populations are imprinted to perceive the world more verbally or through other symbolic cultural extensions, such as numbers and signs. The latter incorporate visual cues, but these carry less value than messages with words. The cultural differences constantly confront high-context individuals, who are taught and who must learn to interact within dominant low-context institutions. The consequent turbulence often interferes with the multicontextual learning process. Through trial and error high-context populations that learn multicontextual modalities are likely to be successful in elementary and secondary school and eventually successful in higher education. Our society infrequently tests or evaluates this part of the learning process.

Individuals raised in dominant low-context cultures have difficulty perceiving these different learning processes unless they encounter one personally. The process of learning a new language offers a good example of the conditions and problems high-context learners face in low-context learning institutions. For example, learning words in a foreign language and pronouncing them correctly requires transposing new material from visual and auditory channels, memorizing it, and then repeating it with some translated meaning. Our secondary schools have long used a fragmented and segmented low-context teaching process for foreign-language instruction: one must first learn individual words, then memorize grammar and verb tenses, and then begin to compile these constructs into meaningful phrases. In the United States, taking a foreign language is very similar to learning analytical Western logic via scientific methods. It is an individual, somewhat isolated, learning process that works best for low-context learners.

An ideal high-context mode for learning a new language would focus first on sets of actions, called *action sets.* Instead of learning the meaning of isolated words and the rules of grammar, students string together integrated, sometimes linear, activities such as preparing food, traveling somewhere, asking directions, and the like (action sets). These are interactive immersion techniques best suited for real-world conditions and involve interactive partners in a group-learning context. For low-context learners the rules of language come before effective language usage. For high-context learners real-world applications take priority over learning the rules. For example, pronunciation and meaning, generated by observation in an interactive context, come before learning the rules. The low-context learning mode produces individuals who can read and comprehend the language from books, but they lack a facility for using other modes of communication effectively. Attention to critical nonverbal cues, such as tonality, inflection, pronunciation, and even body language, may be missing entirely. High-context learners absorb these modes more quickly than low-context individuals because they are culturally trained to extract meaning from all these information streams. High-context learners take on the rules of grammar later in the process, when their meaning makes more sense contextually.

But what is the ultimate goal in language acquisition? Is it comprehension based on reading ability, effective communication, or both? Standardized tests in this country are primarily constructed to evaluate individual academic skills and ability in low-context learning modes. Test scores for verbal ability are quantitative measures of language comprehension and whether the student has first learned the rules. But passing such tests can often be accomplished by memorization. Learning to pass such tests in this context can be too fragmented a process for the more high-context field-sensitive learners. For individuals who are predominantly high context, memorization, or learning the grammatical rules without real application, has few lasting effects and leads to little real comprehension. The high-context learning mode, driven by people-oriented real-world application of language with few capabilities that are measurable, provides such individuals with significant retention and the ability to pick up new languages or other academic skills throughout their lives. What this suggests is that the skills of high- and low-context learners cannot be measured or standardized in the same way. Furthermore, not all measured or standardized skills are necessarily equally meaningful or important in every culture. This mechanism is what prevents many minorities and women from achieving recognition and success in higher education. Although many high-context skills cannot be measured as easily, they are quite valuable in real-world situations.

For example, the developed high-context skill of using nonverbal cues in human observation plays an important role in the training of intellectuals in a host of disciplines. Sternberg discusses this at length throughout his research (1996, 1997). Clinical psychologists, he tells us, must translate animal and human behavior into meaningful concepts and theories, and successful surgeons must know how to distinguish auditory, visual, tactile, even olfactory distinctions to diagnose human conditions. The most successful social scientists understand subtle body language in multiple cultural contexts within their own cultures and within nonliterate ones often studied by anthropologists throughout the world. Unfortunately, these vital skills are rarely, if ever, tested in the highly standardized selection process used for admission to academic and professional careers that ultimately require them in order to achieve minimal facility and success.

With these concepts firmly established in my mind, I plunged headlong into the latest findings about DIF for women and minorities in an attempt to correlate high- and low-context or field-sensitive and -independent characteristics with the results of the GRE (see ETS 1995). The ETS's findings focus on creating fairness, access, and equity for women and minorities taking the GRE. The patterns for DIF showed interesting relationships, with potential correlations of cultural context and DIF. For instance, ETS found that "analogies in verbal DIF cause more negative DIF for [African Americans] and [Latinos]. The wrap-around format (i.e., the horizontal display of answer choices) in analogies may also influence DIF" for these groups (Ibarra and Cohen 1999, table 1.2). High-context learners may be hampered by a conflict between gestalt learning patterns (from general to specific) and a more fragmented, compartmentalized low-context learning model of inductive thinking. Reading comprehension shows little DIF for women and minorities, but when it does appear, it is often positive DIF, meaning they performed better than others on passages with minority-oriented content. An interest in questions associated with people or community, especially their own, suggests that high-context, field-sensitive attributes play some role in this positive DIF pattern for women and minorities (1999). In math, differential performance seems to be associated with process or task orientation and nonverbal cues. There seems to be evidence that cultural context might help explain how the format of test questions can result in lower scores for women and minorities (ETS 1995; Gallagher 1998).

These were just my preliminary observations. It was Allan Cohen, director of the Office of Testing and Evaluation at the University of Wisconsin–Madison, who explained the enigma and how elusive test developers have found the reasons for DIF. He believed that the multicontextual model showed promise of offering an answer. But the only way to find out was to experiment—actually try to predict DIF on a set of test questions and results he had compiled.

Based on our initial research, we believe that multicontextuality shows potential for identifying some causes of gender and ethnic DIF. To date, we have examined DIF in two tests (see Zhu, Safrit, and Cohen 1997). The initial work enabled us to predict some DIF that occurred in the results of each test (Ibarra and Cohen 1999). Our procedure was quite simple. I was given copies of tests that Allan Cohen had administered to two different population samples. I attempted to predict which items would demonstrate specific gender or ethnic DIF and, if possible, the direction (positive or negative) of the DIF I had predicted. In one set of English placement exams I immediately saw the patterns that have led the anthropologist Mark Cohen to say that standardized tests "should be called, 'standardizing' tests ... because they force people into very narrow and unrealistic patterns of knowledge, thought, and behavior" (1998a, 236–37). Much later, when I was able to compare Mark Cohen's notes with my observations and reactions, it became clear that the problems encountered by ethnic minorities in the U.S. testing culture are multifaceted, multilayered, and multicontextual.

Mark Cohen describes the subtle and embedded test performance issues for ethnic minorities as a conflict with the cultural "grammar," or structure, of standardized tests, especially intelligence tests, which extend beyond the mere content of the items selected. The "biases also involve other arbitrary American cultural rules and assumptions about thought itself," which are built into the structure of the tests (M. Cohen 1998a, 220). Even when tests are designed for a particular ethnic culture, low-context cultural logic remains embedded in the construction of the test and the test items. Mark Cohen believes these cultural rules and assumptions, which heavily emphasize, for example, finding simple, clear-cut, right-or-wrong answers; finding those answers quickly (thus reflecting the tests' time limits); and demonstrating individuality and competitiveness, cause some of the major performance problems for ethnic minorities in this country (1998a, 233–36). These were some of the same issues I uncovered in my experiments with Allan Cohen, and, more important, they correlate with the differences in cultural context and cognition described by Hall (1977, 1984) and Manuel Ramírez (1991).

The success at predicting DIF in these items was encouraging, but sifting for specific clues that explain the importance of cultural context in DIF results in standardized testing is still a work in progress. We are developing criteria for predicting DIF and plan to examine a cohort of test takers to determine whether a correlation of factors can predict or eliminate certain kinds of DIF in the construction of standardized tests. Creating the set of criteria from a cohort of student test takers will be crucial to our progress (Ibarra and Cohen 1999, 28).

Teaching and Learning Styles

Teaching is so fundamental to academics that we scarcely think about it. That, unfortunately, is also a fundamental flaw in training graduate students. Traditionally, learning from the "master" meant acquiring knowledge, learning research analysis and methodologies, and—if the graduate student is lucky—perhaps trying to teach if a teaching assistantship is available. In the past this experience did not necessarily come with training or guidance, for learning to teach relied mainly upon knowing the academic discipline well. Today higher education is beginning to realize that knowing something well is simply not enough to teach it effectively. Thus graduate student programs, such as Preparing Future Faculty (PFF), sponsored by the Association of American Colleges and Universities and the Council of Graduate Schools, are being offered and are growing in both size and popularity at various graduate schools throughout the country. Long overdue, these programs are immensely important for recontextualizing academia. One goal is to change the pedagogy of teaching to match institutional types (i.e., two-year community colleges or four-year liberal arts schools) and thereby change academic culture. PFF programs can focus on the contrasts and "cultural gaps" encountered by junior faculty in both teaching and learning styles. Doing so reveals clues to what those differences in cultural context and cognition are.

Galloway (1996), perhaps unintentionally, effectively demonstrated some of these pedagogical differences in the published proceedings of a recent PFF symposium held for graduate students at Howard University. In her symposium presentation, "Coping with Cultural Differences in the Learning Process," Irelene Ricks, an African American graduate student in political science, commented on unexpected teaching situations she has encountered:

What I began to discern with growing unease was a cultural difference in how the students engaged in the learning process. Simply put, they were quiet, too quiet to my way of thinking. They were respectful and dutiful, but inactive participants. I like open exchange. I am an interactive person, so I found myself developing little strategies to draw them out (group presentations, debates) with little success. What this meant was that I had to modify my teaching style to fit their learning style— something I was unable to do easily. Somehow we completed the semester with both teacher and students trying to adjust. (Galloway 1996, 34)

PFF students learn to teach in different types of colleges, and to students from a variety of ethnic groups, and Ricks does not tell us what the different cultural backgrounds of her students were. She just thought they were too quiet and inactive. Regardless, Ricks has clear preferences for a more high-context teaching style—interactive, collaborative, group-oriented learning activities—and for students who are more active in the classroom, a learning style that researchers have found to be typical of African Americans (see also Brice-Heath 1983). Though one could argue this also could be a difference in the teaching styles and expectations at small colleges versus large universities, for African Americans something more may be involved. Confirming that African American schoolchildren tend to be cognitively field sensitive and highly interactive learners, Shade suggests that "the group consciousness, cooperative, sociocentric, and affective orientation that seems to underlie Afro-American culture has an effect on learning" as well (1982, 238). Chambers, Lewis, and Kerezsi (1995) reiterate the difficulties minority faculty encounter when teaching majority college students in this country. Evoking the findings of Rosalie Cohen (1969) and Hall (1976, 1984), among others, Chambers, Lewis, and Kerezsi point out that at all levels of education in the United States the predominant analytical style is that of the middle-class majority populations (1995, 48). They have found that conflicts between cultural context and cognition make faculty less effective and can generate negative racial attitudes among the students.

What Ricks is saying also points to another strategic mandate for high-context minority faculty—adapt to the culture of the students and abandon any attempt transform them to your cultural teaching perspectives. This is an uneasy lesson that minority faculty soon learn, revealed in Ricks's parting advice to others: "Don't try to change the culture—it isn't broken and you don't need to fix it" (Galloway 1996, 35).

Clearly, preparing graduate students for teaching requires more than preparing them to deal with different institutional settings and students; it requires crafting a training program that prepares them for different learning and teaching styles from many gender and ethnic perspectives—a veritable array of pedagogies. Because such training is probably the least developed component of higher education, programs like PFF are few. The American Association for Higher Education (AAHE) in Washington, D.C., is dedicated to advancing college-level teaching and learning programs. Historically, AAHE has fostered new initiatives for teaching, learning, faculty development, distance learning, and quality initiatives for learning more about what constitutes a learning-centered campus. The initiatives are not only innovative but aimed at reforming higher education in general (see E. Anderson 1993; Edgerton, Hutchings, and Quinlan 1991; Lambert and Tice 1993). Within a variety of new ideas on teaching and assessment, some, like peer collaboration and review of teaching (Hutchings 1996), are even headed in the direction of accommodating high-context learners.

But even the mixture of programs and goals at AAHE appears to be missing major ingredients in the recipe for enhancing faculty and student success—how cultural background affects teaching and learning. AAHE's programs never even mention ethnic cultures, context, or cognition. The organization is not alone in this omission, for other organizations that work to improve college teaching also do not incorporate these concepts in their programs.

This omission is not, however, the result of insufficient research on diversity and teaching/learning styles. In fact, quite a few scholars and teachers have incorporated and developed pedagogical models centered around the diverse learning styles of college students (see M. Adams 1992; Schmeck 1988; Tobias 1990). The problem is centered around the compartmentalized, fragmented, somewhat low-context approach used to institute cultural change by using these teaching and learning models.

Let me explain. A small portion of organizational initiatives and related literature on the topic acknowledges the importance of multicultural research and researchers (J. Anderson 1997; J. Anderson and Adams 1992; M. Ramírez 1991; M. Ramírez and Castañeda 1974). Felder (1993) and Felder and Silverman (1988), for example, have developed some very promising models that, although they may not highlight ethnic or gender diversity, incorporate college students' learning styles so inclusively that the models closely match the needs of all high- and low-context and field-sensitive and -independent students simultaneously.

The remarkable feature of Felder's "multistyle" approach is that it was created for teaching science, specifically, his (inherently low-context) chemistry and engineering courses. The problem, however, is that many organizational efforts, and much of the research on pedagogy mentioned earlier, fail to adequately address the core issue—how to change *all*, not just a few, of the components of academic organizational cultures. This means doing more than simply adding multicultural ideas piecemeal to a curriculum or to the pedagogy of teaching as if they were stand-alone components; it means changing them systemically and synchronously along with other components within the infrastructure of institutional culture itself. That is not an easy task.

Yet in a variety of ways educators can sense when the style of academic cultural systems is causing students to disconnect. Lani Guinier senses a disconnect between teaching and learning that unfairly discriminates against female students, especially in law school. Challenged because of her supposedly controversial views on minority voting rights after she was nominated to head the civil rights division of the Justice Department in 1993, Guinier is now challenging the traditional Socratic teaching style in law school classrooms (Mangan 1997). Her views reflect the same concerns evident when high-context Latinos and Latinas are subjected to learning in predominantly low-context educational environments. Hall (1977, 106–8) describes legal procedures and trial law in the United States as an illustration of how law has been overadapted to a low-context culture.[1]

The importance of Guinier's book, *Becoming Gentlemen: Women, Law School, and Institutional Change* (1997), is that she not only understands the problem but provides a way to create a more inclusive learning environment for women and ethnic minorities. Although her intent is to change the learning process, she appears to be suggesting a way of doing this that does not compromise the long heritage of legal education and training. Her insights reach far beyond gender differences.

Guinier illustrates the multiple teaching styles that can reframe the context of academia. (Guinier, of course, is writing about women, but what she says applies equally to men from high-context cultures.) She believes that women have difficulties in law school—more stress, lower grades, fewer honors than men—because the traditional Socratic method is designed to shape students into gladiator-like trial lawyers. In the classroom "a professor calls on students and asks them a series of questions about a court decision in order to extrapolate the underlying legal principles" (Mangan 1997, A12). The problem, Guinier finds, is that this method unnecessarily belittles and intimidates women in a combative, less-than-respectful atmosphere. Because the Socratic teaching method has become a deliberate one-on-one sparring match between a student and professor, its advocates believe it is ideal for preparing students to deal with the unexpected. It also favors majority males, who are low context and more aggressive. "Women," Guinier argues, "generally learn better through cooperative approaches [which are high context] than through adversarial ones," which are low context, and in an atmosphere of respect (i.e., student centered and high context) (1997, A12). In her book she describes women who "participate only after listening to what others are saying. They see conversation as a way of collaborating to synthesize information, rather than competing to perform or win" (in Mangan 1997, A12). The Socratic method forces women, she says, to act like males; when they do, their self-esteem suffers.

In a brief description of Guinier's class Mangan tells us that Guinier has students sit in a semicircle, and she encourages students with a number of high-context techniques and methods (1997, A13). She asks them to build upon other students' comments, compiling and extending ideas in a collaborative process and tracking arguments through what appears to be a comprehensive (rather than linear) thought process. In effect, her approach fosters a more conversational process of social interaction. When challenges arise—and they do—they are between students and not professor versus student. In a traditional classroom students usually sit in an auditorium facing the professor, with little or no interaction among students. Guinier claims that this environment favors men and affects women (and men from high-context cultures) adversely because they are reluctant to volunteer (1997, A13). Moreover, high-context individuals take longer to adjust to and participate in a confrontational atmosphere.

Multicultural or Multicontextual?

Thus the evidence points strongly to the importance of developing a multicontextual approach to teaching and learning styles. The high- and low-context cultural model offers a good explanation for why people do what they do. Guinier has tapped into an important characteristic that she correctly attributes to women; however, her thesis also successfully addresses a much larger problem, found among most ethnic minorities, including Latinos. Also, her teaching style has a positive effect on many different types of students. Women and ethnic minorities, and even some majority males, may be positively or negatively affected by lopsided or one-sided teaching and learning styles. This pattern may be difficult to discern among majority males because educators have not usually examined that population to determine to what extent they exhibit high-context or field-sensitive characteristics. Finally, if in fact a variety of populations share multicontextual patterns, the multicontextual model— the combination of high- and low-context cultures and field-sensitive and -independent cognitive styles that I have described—might function as a unified or shared cultural learning model as well. Manuel Ramírez has found, for example, that low-context Anglo men become bicognitive when they interact closely and consistently with Latinos (1991, 1998).

Institutions that lack diversity are likely to find that adding a multicontextual teaching approach to the pedagogy of higher education and the curriculum will begin to change the academic culture and thereby attract more students from a variety of ethnic backgrounds, especially those who prefer high-context, field-sensitive contexts and cognition.

Adding multicontextuality does not preclude using or supplanting a multicultural curriculum. In fact, it adds a cross-cultural and cross-gender dimension that enhances a multicultural perspective but makes reaching and teaching students easier. Instead of pushing institutions to add ethnic dimensions to the curriculum to attract a diverse student base (and avoid criticism), multicontextuality accommodates a variety of teaching and learning styles and both spurs and accommodates creativity (M. Ramírez 1991, 1998; M. Ramírez and Castañeda 1974).

Traditional and multicontextual teaching methods can coexist, as Guinier and others so clearly demonstrate (Felder 1993; Felder and Silverman 1988). In fact, having two or more teaching contexts better prepares students (future attorneys, in this case) to adopt a greater variety of legal strategies—or research methodologies—than does the Socratic method alone. These are good reasons to expand one's repertoire (Ford 1992), for they are inclusive and add value for all students.

The Effects of Adopting Multicontextual Characteristics

Those of us in higher education must identify and reconfigure the imbalances in our educational systems, or we may find our institutions are becoming increasingly less attractive to various ethnic populations in the future. While Latinos are best represented in fields like education and foreign languages, increasing numbers of Latinos are entering fields they formerly shunned or were shut out of in the United States, including engineering, medicine, and law. As consumers, if given a choice, they are likely to flock to those institutions that make them feel intellectually and socially welcome and shun those that do not. It doesn't take the expertise of a director of annual giving to see what will happen to the endowment of an institution that graduates large numbers of Latino doctors and lawyers. Nor does it take a crystal ball to see what will happen to the relative popularity of institutions that fail to attract high-context individuals—sooner or later their low-context graduates will figure out that their educations omitted a variety of techniques that boost professional creativity and that they are endowed with only a cookie-cutter approach to problem solving.

One way to observe the effects of acknowledging multicontextuality is by examining programs that adopt these techniques. In the physical sciences, for instance, the best example comes from the mathematician Uri Treisman, who made an important discovery in the mid-1980s by observing the study habits of a variety of minority students (see Fullilove 1986; Treisman 1988, 1989). From that he generated a model, the Emerging Scholars Program (ES), for teaching first-year calculus to African American students at the University of California, Berkeley. The model continues to be successful for students in other ES programs being developed nationwide.

Treisman's finding was based upon the quintessence of anthropological methodology—participant observation. He first noted sharp contrasts between academically capable African American students who were failing freshman calculus, and their Asian American counterparts, who usually received honors-level grades in the same courses. Curious about what could cause such a discrepancy, Treisman set out to observe student behaviors. He followed twenty Asian American and twenty African American students around the Berkeley campus for many months, watching how they did homework, socialized with friends, and adjusted to campus life (Fullilove 1986, 4). He found that the Asian American students had established effective informal study groups within which they shared vital information about course content, professors, and study skills while providing a mutual support system that helped ensure their success.

African American students, on the other hand, studied alone and, despite strong academic credentials, foundered on exams and quizzes and did not know what information the professor considered important. Confused and unable to catch up, many were so discouraged that they became academically traumatized by their failure in calculus, and a good number ultimately dropped out. Treisman also found that African Americans who never mastered the ropes of academic and social life were much less likely to survive their first college years (Fullilove 1986, 6). His study implies that students who learn about academic culture in conjunction with adaptive strategies for studying math or other difficult topics (like studying in groups) are more likely to succeed academically than those who are given mainly remedial help.

Based on his findings, Treisman created *nonremedial* math workshops with specific features that he felt contributed to Asian American students' success. His goal was to have students excel, not merely to avoid failure or having to play catch-up in a remedial fashion. In fact, the calculus problems in his workshops were complex exercises, and the problem-solving process of using small-group self-discovery methods was more challenging than first-year calculus courses usually are. Thus workshops emphasized collaborative learning and were student or learning oriented rather than teacher oriented. Students arrived with a variety of learning styles and could share or demonstrate different problem-solving strategies for their peers. The objective was to be less results oriented, or intent upon finding the answers, and more process oriented by learning *how* they obtained the answers. The most important feature of the workshops was that they were designed to encourage students to establish effective social networks that could become long-lasting friendship networks and provide vital group arenas for trying out newly developed social and academic skills. For both social and academic reasons the workshops met more hours per week than typical lecture or discussion sections. As Treisman says,

My idea, then, was to create a small and intimate setting—sort of an honors program—in which black and other students would work together on interesting and challenging mathematical exercises that would help them gain perspective on the central ideas of the course. The mathematician's role would be to construct these exercises and to be a resource for the students as they tried to solve them. If all went well, a community of students would develop, bound together by their enjoyment of mathematics and their interest in pursuing a career requiring a mathematics or science degree. (1989, 8)

The student outcomes were spectacular, and the program was a success, not only in California but nearly everywhere it has been established (Conciatore 1990). At the University of Wisconsin–Madison, the Wisconsin Emerging Scholars Program (WES) was fashioned after Treisman's model and has been part of selected introductory calculus courses since 1993. Program reviews show that WES scholars consistently outperform their counterparts in non-WES course sections by generating higher GPAs than other sections (see Alexander et al. 1997; Kosciuk 1997). The essential component of an ES program is building a core learning community based on integrating social, cultural, and academic principles. Community building becomes even more important on a predominantly Anglo student campus, such as the University of Wisconsin–Madison. Researchers observing the WES program at Wisconsin point out that the predominant U.S. culture of education rewards working independently toward a competitive goal, one objective of which is to outperform others (Alexander et al. 1997, 9; see also Fordham 1991); these are essentially low-context educational values. Building on the work of Fordham (1991), Alexander and colleagues point out that this fundamental cultural foundation is an "inversion of [the] indigenous cultural pattern" not only for African Americans but also for Latinos and other people from high-context cultures. They continue: "ES programs, through their emphasis on community and collaboration, create a group-centered ethos that may be more culturally appropriate for underrepresented ethnic minority students and thus may contribute to their success" (1997, 9). Treisman correctly assumed that learning the academic ropes was essential for minority students' success. He observed how peer groups are important for helping minority students figure out what they need to know and for providing them with a framework within which to test and validate their understanding of both the content of academic courses and the culture of educational institutions. Clearly, important factors for student success are eliminating isolation and alienation among minority students and creating a collective sense of ethnicity, which also serves to counteract negative attitudes toward low-context academics (Alexander et al. 1997, 9).

Kosciuk's 1997 report on the WES program reveals that it could benefit students even more if it were redesigned to be more systemic. In fact, if additional combinations of cultural context and cognitive characteristics are introduced into this or other similar programs, we could expect even better results or perhaps avoid unexpected problems.

For example, the WES program did not anticipate one result: that ethnic group behavior would interfere with the interactions of the study group and would generate interethnic conflicts. From reading the report and other publications about WES (Alexander et al. 1997) and a personal conversation with a former teaching assistant in the WES program, I surmise that tensions arose between African American and majority students under conditions that can be best explained as conflicts in cultural contexts and cognitive learning styles. Apparently, African American students in certain WES sections began to relate, that is, to talk openly with one another in more interactive (high-context) cultural ways, which tended to disturb majority students in these sections, according to the teaching assistant, and generated tensions that split the students along cultural lines. Though the behaviors were typical of high-context interactive behavior expected from African American faculty (see Ricks's comments earlier), they were not well understood by others, many of whom came from low-context cultures; students in the study sections clashed (for more explanation of conversation that distracts from group learning, see Brice-Heath 1983). Thus fine-tuning these programs for greater efficiency also means accommodating culturally different study habits and other high-context cultural behaviors so that all students understand them and can incorporate them in their group-learning effort.

However, factors that are important for ensuring minority students' success were built into the original design features of the ES program. Without realizing it, Treisman adopted a strategy for academic study generated by observing Asian American students with high-context culture. He then successfully applied those patterns to another, usually high-context, population of African American students who, at least culturally, were attuned to such concepts. Even if they have little direct experience with group-study patterns, African Americans are likely to react positively to the high-context features and would therefore be more likely to adopt such a context-compatible strategy. Treisman simply observed and absorbed the high-context cultural behaviors and packed them into a model that adapted to high-context, field-sensitive cognitive learning styles. The unique feature was that he modified the traditional academic approach to teaching math with an exceptionally rich set of high-context academic adaptations, as described earlier. In fact, features of the ES program's design correlate closely with the cognitive and cultural context characteristics generated from the models by Manuel Ramírez (1991) and Hall, as outlined in chapter 3. Treisman's design demonstrates quite clearly how to achieve a balance in which high-context students, who usually perform poorly in low-context math and science, can excel when the learning and academic culture have been modified to include field-sensitive, high-context learning techniques and strategies.

Treisman essentially modified the learning system—the academic organizational culture for teaching and learning mathematics—*without compromising the heritage and quality of the discipline or the field.* In fact, the Treisman model works quite well for majority students too, according to some reviewers and advocates (Alexander et al. 1997; Fullilove 1986).

The only concern with the data generated on students who have completed the program is that the emphasis has been on African Americans, with little information about other ethnic students such as Latinos. The early years of Treisman's ES program included Latinos, but no data or analysis were ever generated (Fullilove 1986). On predominantly majority campuses, such as the University of Wisconsin–Madison, the populations of ethnic minority groups are so small, especially in math and the sciences, that gathering any data on them means aggregating, or "lumping," them into one group (see Alexander et al. 1997). As discussed in chapter 2, analysis with aggregated minority student data is counterproductive and has little meaning unless couched as broad generalizations. It would be inappropriate to assume that aggregated minority behavior would be representative of behavior within the various Latino subgroups, such as Chicanos and Puerto Ricans, for example.

Cultural Context and the Pedagogy of College Teaching

Treisman's study focused almost exclusively on the problems of minority students. Although his research shows that group-study methods also help majority males to learn calculus better, his model is aimed squarely at helping minority students adapt to academic culture. What Treisman barely discusses is the pedagogy of teaching mathematics, and he ignores completely the dynamics of how math professors teach calculus. Guinier, on the other hand, demonstrates how to change the traditional system and the context of teaching law to produce positive effects for women and other students without compromising her objectives (Mangan 1997). How, then, do methodological differences in context and style affect the way women and minority faculty members teach? And how does the pedagogy of teaching in higher education contribute to the conflicts found among Latino and Latina faculty?

The 1995–1996 faculty survey generated by the Higher Education Research Institute (HERI) (H. Astin et al. 1997) is particularly good for showing methods, styles, and values in the teaching of undergraduates, with these factors differentiated by gender and multicultural perspectives and perhaps multicontextual perspectives. It is a relatively large survey—nearly thirty-four thousand faculty members responded nationwide—and it features data broken out by minority group, especially Latino faculty. I constructed an informal comparative study from a selected set of survey responses to see whether I could detect any pattern of cultural context, cognition, or multicontextuality.

The first steps were to determine what pedagogical differences existed between women and minorities compared to majority males and then to determine whether this initial comparison could be used for differences in cultural context. Table 7.1 (p. 210) highlights demographic characteristics that could influence the patterns of survey responses. I also selected three sequential tables from the 1997 HERI report that show how faculty evaluated undergraduate students (table 7.2), what instructional methods they prefer (table 7.3), and what they believe are important or essential goals for undergraduates (table 7.4). By coincidence, the question sets in tables 7.2 through 7.4 (pp. 212–17) were increasingly value driven, from the least value oriented to the most essential goals (values) for undergraduates; the contrasts helped to emphasize gender and culture differences.

Because majority males represent the prevailing teaching/learning pedagogy and they are more likely to reflect the voice of low-context academics, their responses (boxed in column 2) are natural benchmarks for comparison in each table. Each table also shows responses to the same questions broken out by gender and ethnicity. To show the differences in gender or culture, I compared responses by women and minorities to the majority male responses for each question. I calculated the differences either above or below the benchmarks in 10-point increments; shaded numbers vary from the majority male responses by at least 10 percent—and shaded numbers in bold underline vary by at least 20 percent. Numbers followed by a less-than sign highlight responses beneath the benchmark for majority males (see table legend). As expected, the patterns—especially among groups of minority women—reflect alternative and apparently conflicting views on important faculty practices and values compared to those held by majority males.

The results are exciting from a variety of perspectives: they verify what educators already know in general about the conditions women and minority faculty encounter in academia and help pinpoint some specific issues; more important, the tables reflect interesting comparisons of gender, multicultural influences, and multicontextual influences simultaneously. I originally turned to shading and other highlighting techniques to differentiate the responses of majority males from the responses of other groups and used these graphic devices mainly as a quick way to show a few patterns in the data. But this visual device revealed patterns that probably reflect multicontextual influences.

These tables yield enough interesting data to merit a chapter-length examination; here I will concentrate on a few important points. To begin with, the data are limited in some respects. For instance, it is nearly impossible to tell how different kinds of institutions, such as research universities and community colleges, influence faculty responses, and there is no way to know in which cultural regions or rural/urban areas of the country faculty members reside. However, the demographics in table 7.1 give us a number of clues to help weigh the responses. For example, the sample of Asian American faculty, especially males, is disproportionately larger than that for any other minority group, they have a greater percentage of doctoral degrees among them, and they are more heavily represented in the sciences, engineering, or math than even majority males. Consequently, the combined responses from minority faculty are skewed. We should consider this a good example of the need to be cautious when using aggregated data and in evaluating the responses by specific gender and ethnic group.

The differences between ethnic minorities, both males and females, and the majority males shown by the shaded areas in each table are quite striking. But the greatest differences clearly lie between majority male and minority female faculty members. Counting the differences among women by ethnic group only (columns 4 to 10) shows twice as many differences with majority males than do the minority male faculty by group, especially in areas of instruction and essential goals for undergraduates. Viewing the tables sequentially, differences for minority males tend to increase in number and percentages, but in the same comparison minority females show more differences and by greater percentages on most questions than minority males.

The only exceptions to this show up in the multicultural patterns tracked by the vertical columns of faculty responses. Looking at faculty responses by minority group (columns 4 to 10) in all three tables (7.2–7.4), African American faculty, men and women combined, show the greatest number of differences when compared to majority males, followed by Native Americans, all Latinos, and Asian Americans. However, the figures for all Latinos simply confirm that lumping data by groups can skew the results. When the category of "All Latinos" is broken out by specific ethnic group, we see significant differences between Mexican Americans/Chicanos, Puerto Ricans, and "Other Latinos" that could equal the differences found in other minority faculty responses. The response patterns among Asian Americans in general are not surprising; that they tend to follow the patterns of majority males probably reflects the strong academic cultural influences of the sciences, engineering, and math. But Asian American women faculty seem to break both gender and cultural stereotypes. In fact, on the questions of essential goals for undergraduates, Asian American women respond more like Native American women than any other group.

The patterns associated with particular questions are the most interesting features in the tables because they hint at the existence of multicontextual influences. That is, there seems to be some association between high-context, field-sensitive populations, mainly women and minority faculty in most ethnic groups, and certain questions in the tables that probably reflect high-context, field-sensitive cultural values—fundamental ingredients in the theory of multicontextuality. Even HERI takes note of this pattern, distinguishing particular questions by association with either majority or minority faculty in a section entitled "Student-Centered Pedagogy":

Although extensive lecturing is the second most popular instructional method for faculty, between 13 and 39 percent of all faculty are utilizing more student-centered instructional and evaluation methods in most or all of their undergraduate courses. In comparing faculty of color with [majority] faculty, percentage differences slightly favor faculty of color, but the margin is usually only two to three points. However, there does seem to be a tendency for faculty of color to utilize methods that are more likely to engage the group of students of the whole class in the learning process, while [majority] faculty seem to more often choose methods that are more individual in nature. For example, faculty of color are more likely than are their [majority] counterparts to have class discussions and to use cooperative learning, group projects, student presentations, and student evaluations of each others' work. [Majority] faculty in contrast are more likely to encourage independent projects, experiential learning/field projects, and recitals/demonstrations. (H. Astin et al. 1997, 22–23)

To check the validity of my interpretation of these patterns, I asked a small number of faculty to examine the questions and determine whether they recognized any characteristics of cultural context and/or cognition.[2] Although the survey is not complete, agreement among the faculty on question content is remarkably consistent so far.

For example, the questions in table 7.2 are the least value driven, and I found it difficult to determine agreement on context and cognition. Question 6, "student presentations," was one of two questions that garnered the most differences among all women and even some minority male faculty. However, for reasons that are unclear, nearly all faculty examining the questions found it to be high context and field sensitive. Examining faculty determined that the other question, number 9, "grading on a curve," is low context and field independent. It is often criticized as a notoriously unfair method that favors high performers—which may explain why none of the women preferred this as much as do majority males.

In table 7.3, questions registering the greatest differences for women and minorities and consistently identified as high context and field sensitive (questions 11 and 13) are associated with group interactive learning. Not surprisingly, questions identified as low-context field-independent instruction methods (13, 16, 18, and 19) also registered responses that tended to be high context and field sensitive because they were quite the opposite of responses from majority male faculty. Questions identified with high-context and field-sensitive characteristics in table 7.4 are closely associated with concepts of personal development—they are people oriented. These reflected development of character (questions 31, 32, and 33) or self-identity and citizenship by instilling a commitment to community (36, 37, 38, and 39). Though women and minority faculty believe in commitment to community more than do majority faculty, as shown in their responses to questions 38 and 39, they seem unable to incorporate these goals as required activities in their courses (see questions 25 and 26 in table 7.3). While the data on teaching undergraduates hint at multicontextual influences among women and minority faculty, is there any evidence of this among majority males? The comparisons here were made against majority males, and readers can find more information at the end of this chapter about the methods used. Yet multicontextual theory suggests some majority males tend to be high context and field sensitive too. How does the variability of preferences among women and minorities confirm multicontextual influences without further quantitative analysis? A host of other questions like these has never been explored.

However, the direction of analysis seems clear: cultural context and cognition play a vital role not only in teaching but also in test performance and the perception of intelligence in this country. The evidence is that cultural context and cognition, or multicontextuality, are shaping up as providing a viable model for reinterpreting the current paradigm for diversity in higher education. It is conceivable that this model could be the steppingstone to achieving even greater learning potentials than high-context individuals ever reached in higher education. If multicontextuality offers another perspective, perhaps another dimension, for better understanding what we know as affirmative action and equal opportunity programs, incorporating this diversity of perceiving and knowing—new areas of critical knowledge—into the mainstream of critical thinking and innovation in this country offers real opportunities for evolutionary social change and long-term economic benefits for everyone (see Hardi 2000; D. Thomas and Ely 1996). Equally important is that multicontexuality brings immediate benefits that may help proponents of affirmative action make the case that higher education has a compelling interest in continuing to diversify the populations of its college and university campuses. It will mean looking beyond the notion of valuing human diversity only by the number of women and ethnic minorities we recruit, employ, educate, and send out into the world. Academia, above all, must recognize a kind of diversity that is inclusive, that can be synthesized into our organizational cultures and structures, and that adds new insights and value to our way of creating knowledge. The final step, then, is to reframe the infrastructure of higher education to demonstrate how to activate latent academic cultural values associated with multicontextuality and to learn how to invigorate organizational culture change—not a trivial next step.

Those readers whose tolerance for statistical information is limited may wish merely to scan the tables and proceed directly to chapter 8. However, those who would rather examine tables than see Steven Spielberg's latest movie will want to read the following explanatory text for tables 7.1 to 7.4.

Tables 7.1–7.4: Methodology

The data presented here were not subjected to rigorous statistical analysis, so my methods and hypothesis are relatively simple. Table 7.1 is a demographic profile of survey participants designed to highlight such factors as highest degree earned, academic discipline, and primary academic interests, which could influence participants' responses. Tables 7.2 to 7.4 contain subsets of thirty-nine survey questions and were modified to compare faculty responses by gender and ethnicity. For the purposes of comparative analysis, I assume that in each table the percentage of majority male responses to each question (boxed in column 2) is a benchmark for that question. The responses of the majority men represent both the prevailing teaching/learning pedagogy and preferences that are likely to be predominantly low context. The remaining columns show the percentages of responses to the same questions broken out by gender and ethnicity. My suspicion was that the answers provided by minority and female faculty were likely to reflect alternative, and perhaps conflicting, views of the prevailing pedagogy when compared to the majority male responses.

To determine whether conflicting viewpoints could be the result of a culture or gender gap, I then compared responses from all minorities, minority males by ethnic group, and all females by ethnic group, including majority women, to the responses to each question from majority males. Any response that is off the benchmark by at least 10 percent is shaded.

However, it is difficult to conclude that these differences reflect differences in cultural context or cognition. Uncontrolled variables, such as the types of institutions at which respondents were employed (i.e., community college or research university I), the disciplines they teach, or regional urban differences probably have some undetected influence on the overall outcomes. However, the survey data show that among all the ethnic cohorts, a large percentage of Latino and Latina professors tend to be employed in adjunct positions at two-year institutions. This percentage is larger for Latinos and Latinas than for any other ethnic group. Survey data also show that the largest number of respondents are employed in the humanities and in education. Approximately one-third of all majority and African American faculty are employed in those two areas. Nearly half of all American Indian faculty are employed in the humanities, as are all the Latino faculty

Text continued on page 218

Table 7.1. Faculty survey, 1995–1996: Demographics of full-time undergraduate faculty (percentage distribution)

	Total responses (col. 1)	Total majority	Total minorities
	All faculty		
Number of respondents	**33,986**	**30,157**	**2,943**
From 4-yr. institutions	90.7	NA	NA
From 2-yr. institutions	9.3	NA	NA
U.S. citizens	95.3	97.2	81.3
	Male faculty		
Number of respondents	**21,959**	**19,497**	**1,804**
Male	64.6	64.7	61.2
Ph.D. highest degree	65.2	65.4	63.0
Master's degree only	21.9	22.0	22.3
Highest degree in bio/physical sci., engr., or math	30.0	29.0	31.0
Primary interest very heavily in teaching	33.5	34.7	24.9
Primary interest very heavily in research	3.1	2.9	4.4
	Female faculty		
Number of respondents	**12,027**	**10,660**	**1,139**
Female	35.4	35.3<	38.8<
Ph.D. highest degree	42.5	42.4<	42.0<
Master's degree only	40.9	41.1	40.3
Highest degree in bio/physical sci., engr., or math	12.0	13.0<	11.0<
Primary interest very heavily in teaching	46.6	47.9	39.1
Primary interest very heavily in research	2.0	1.9	2.3

African American (col. 4)	American Indian	Asian American	All Latinos	Mexican American Chicano/a	Puerto Rican	Other Latinos
All faculty						
684	423	1,075	761	290	111	360
NA	NA	NA	NA	NA	NA	NA
NA	NA	NA	NA	NA	NA	NA
91.9	99.7	61.4	86.3	94.9	99.0	71.2
Male faculty						
355	265	748	436	171	59	206
51.9<	62.6	69.6	57.3	59.0	53.2<	57.2
51.1<	42.3<	83.9	51.9<	34.9<	56.0	72.5
28.1	35.6	9.5<	30.1	40.8	27.1	17.3
18.0<	21.0	55.0	20.0	16.0<	19.0<	26.0
32.0	38.3	12.8<	30.0	35.9	29.9	22.5<
1.3	3.3	6.7	4.1	1.5	5.1	7.2
Female faculty						
329	158	327	325	119	52	154
48.1<	37.4<	30.4<	42.7<	41.0<	46.8<	42.8
33.5<	31.7<	59.0	42.1<	29.1<	43.4	58.4
48.3	45.0	28.2	39.5	54.6	33.0	22.6
4.0<	8.0<	23.0	11.0<	11.0	10.0	12.0
40.1	47.3	29.9<	41.6	50.6	42.0	29.9
1.1	2.7	2.7	2.9	1.5	2.7	4.7

Source: Data and table are adapted from H. Astin et al., *Race and Ethnicity in the American Professoriate, 1995–1996* (Los Angeles: Higher Education Research Institute).

Note: Boxed data in column 2 are the benchmark majority male responses. The shading shows responses that vary from those benchmarks by at least 10 percentage points, the sign < indicating responses beneath the benchmarks. The bold numbers that are underlined represent responses that vary from the benchmarks by at least 20 percentage points.

The "total responses" numbers in column 1 include individuals who did not identify their ethnic heritage on the HERI survey. These individuals and their responses were not included in columns 2 through 10, according to Bill Korn, HERI's associate director of operations.

Table 7.2. Faculty survey, 1995–1996: Evaluation methods used in most or all undergraduate classes (percentage distribution)

	Total responses (col. 1)	Total majority	Total minorities
	Male faculty		
Number of respondents	**21,959**	**19,497**	**1,804**
Multiple-choice midterms & final exams	28.1	27.8	30.4
Essay midterms & final exams	41.0	41.1	39.0
Short-answer midterms & final exams	34.2	34.4	31.7
Quizzes	35.4	35.1	37.1
Weekly essay assignments	13.5	12.9	18.1
Student presentations	26.2	26.0	28.1
Term/research papers	31.7	31.4	32.3
Student evaluations of each others' work	9.8	9.6	10.9
Grading on a curve	22.6	22.7	23.2
Competency-based grading	47.0	47.1	45.7
	Female faculty		
Number of respondents	**12,027**	**10,660**	**1,139**
Multiple-choice midterms & final exams	36.2	36.5	34.5
Essay midterms & final exams	38.2	37.3	43.5
Short-answer midterms & final exams	30.4	30.4	31.0
Quizzes	37.6	37.1	42.1
Weekly essay assignments	20.7	20.1	24.8
Student presentations	40.2	39.6	42.7
Term/research papers	35.1	34.5	36.4
Student evaluations of each others' work	19.0	18.8	19.5
Grading on a curve	10.3	10.2<	10.9<
Competency-based grading	51.2	51.2	50.8

African American (col. 4)	American Indian	Asian American	All Latinos	Mexican American Chicano/a	Puerto Rican	Other Latinos
Male faculty						
355	265	748	436	171	59	206
37.6	28.0	24.9	33.2	41.4	27.3	24.1
42.0	46.7	32.1	42.6	38.1	49.5	46.6
30.2	31.9	31.5	33.3	36.8	31.1	29.5
40.2	38.9	35.6	35.7	34.8	39.0	36.1
15.6	18.9	18.0	20.1	23.5	22.6	15.0
37.1	36.3	16.8	32.7	31.1	46.9	31.0
45.0	39.6	9.9<	35.8	30.2	48.9	39.4
12.4	16.6	6.3	13.3	13.3	21.5	11.2
13.4<	19.2	30.4	23.4	20.3	26.5	26.5
41.0	46.3	48.2	46.1	48.9	41.4	43.8
Female faculty						
329	158	327	325	119	52	154
43.9	28.0	28.1	32.5	44.2	24.4	20.3
44.2	35.2	38.0	50.4	45.4	59.3	53.3
28.1	30.1	34.0	32.1	30.5	28.5	35.6
35.3	42.3	44.6	46.9	43.7	49.8	49.8
24.4	23.8	17.0	31.5	34.1	25.1	30.6
50.2	41.1	34.1	42.2	38.3	31.6	52.2
42.7	34.6	30.7	35.0	33.2	35.1	37.4
22.6	25.6	13.1	18.7	23.8	13.0	14.4
7.2<	8.4<	19.8	9.0<	9.6<	9.8<	8.0<
44.6	53.3	59.3	49.6	54.6	33.9<	49.1

Source: Data and table are adapted from H. Astin et al., *Race and Ethnicity in the American Professoriate, 1995–1996* (Los Angeles: Higher Education Research Institute).

Note: Boxed data in column 2 are the benchmark majority male responses. The shading shows responses that vary from those benchmarks by at least 10 percentage points, the sign < indicating responses beneath the benchmarks. The bold numbers that are underlined represent responses that vary from the benchmarks by at least 20 percentage points.

The "total responses" numbers in column 1 include individuals who did not identify their ethnic heritage on the HERI survey. These individuals and their responses were not included in columns 2 through 10, according to Bill Korn, HERI's associate director of operations.

Table 7.3. Faculty survey, 1995–1996: Instruction methods used in most or all undergraduate classes (percentage distribution)

	Total responses (col. 1)	Total majority	Total minorities
Male faculty			
Number of respondents	**21,959**	**19,497**	**1,804**
Class discussions	63.8	63.4	66.4
Computer/machine-aided instruction	16.5	16.4	18.4
Cooperative learning	27.5	27.0	31.0
Experiential learning/field studies	15.2	15.3	13.6
Teaching assistants	10.8	10.8	10.4
Recitals/demonstrations	18.1	18.2	17.0
Group projects	19.0	18.8	21.0
Independent projects	29.9	30.1	28.2
Extensive lecturing	55.2	55.6	52.4
Multiple drafts of written work	12.8	12.9	11.2
Readings on racial/ethnic issues	11.3	10.5	16.9
Readings on women/gender issues	10.4	10.1	12.1
Student-developed activities	11.4	11.0	15.4
Student-selected topics	6.5	6.3	7.7
Community service in-course required	1.5	1.3	2.9
Community service as option in course	1.7	1.6	2.7
Female faculty			
Number of respondents	**12,027**	**10,660**	**1,139**
Class discussion	75.6	75.3	76.7
Computer/machine-aided instruction	22.4	22.0	25.3
Cooperative learning	50.0	**49.6**	**52.1**
Experiential learning/field studies	27.5	28.0	22.6
Teaching assistants	6.9	6.7	8.9
Recitals/demonstrations	21.3	21.4	18.8
Group projects	30.4	30.2	30.1
Independent projects	39.4	39.1	38.9
Extensive lecturing	35.1	35.8<	**30.3<**
Multiple drafts of written work	21.0	20.5	23.3
Readings on racial/ethnic issues	24.2	22.9	**31.6**
Readings on women/gender issues	24.1	23.3	28.3
Student-developed activities	16.3	15.2	23.5
Student-selected topics	11.0	10.5	13.5
Community service in-course required	4.6	4.4	6.0
Community service as option in course	3.2	3.2	3.1

African American (col. 4)	American Indian	Asian American	All Latinos	Mexican American Chicano/a	Puerto Rican	Other Latinos
Male faculty						
355	265	748	436	171	59	206
75.9	76.8	52.1<	73.8	77.2	84.1	66.5
15.1	14.1	21.3	19.4	23.8	17.6	14.1
32.1	40.4	21.5	39.0	42.2	47.1	32.6
14.0	22.5	8.8	15.7	18.1	15.1	12.8
8.9	6.3	13.7	9.0	8.0	8.7	10.4
17.9	22.7	14.6	16.8	19.3	13.7	14.5
22.7	29.9	16.8	21.0	20.9	35.3	17.2
31.5	39.1	21.8	29.2	28.3	31.4	29.8
47.6	42.6<	63.4	45.4<	40.3<	39.0<	53.8
10.7	20.9	5.6	14.8	13.8	18.5	15.0
22.4	18.2	6.3	26.4	30.9	36.0	18.0
14.6	15.1	4.5	19.1	19.7	32.3	14.5
11.6	16.5	15.9	17.4	18.5	22.3	14.7
9.1	15.6	3.4	8.8	10.2	12.1	6.1
4.6	5.7	0.7	3.0	5.1	1.8	0.6
2.4	3.4	0.9	5.1	6.9	1.4	3.8
Female faculty						
329	158	327	325	119	52	154
82.3	75.2	69.1	77.4	71.7	79.8	83.7
23.0	30.6	24.8	25.6	29.6	20.2	22.7
53.3	52.3	43.7	56.9	55.2	63.5	56.6
24.0	25.6	24.3	18.8	18.1	20.3	19.1
8.3	5.5	10.8	9.4	10.9	12.9	6.1
16.5	23.6	24.1	15.3	14.1	5.7<	20.6
31.2	36.2	27.6	28.3	32.3	29.2	22.9
44.4	43.5	33.8	35.5	27.3	39.0	44.8
29.4<	28.6<	40.7<	24.2<	25.7<	26.1<	21.6<
21.7	25.6	17.6	28.2	28.9	38.0	23.3
40.4	36.4	15.7	32.7	36.9	35.3	26.3
35.6	32.7	16.2	28.3	30.8	31.5	23.9
22.8	20.9	22.8	25.6	26.3	21.6	26.4
17.1	11.8	9.1	13.9	14.8	27.1	7.6
10.6	6.9	2.5	3.8	1.5	4.6	6.3
4.1	3.3	2.3	2.5	0.0<	2.8	5.6

Source: Data and table are adapted from H. Astin et al., *Race and Ethnicity in the American Professoriate, 1995–1996* (Los Angeles: Higher Education Research Institute).

Note: Boxed data in column 2 are the benchmark majority male responses. The shading shows responses that vary from those benchmarks by at least 10 percentage points, the sign < indicating responses beneath the benchmarks. The bold numbers that are underlined represent responses that vary from the benchmarks by at least 20 percentage points.

The "total responses" numbers in column 1 include individuals who did not identify their ethnic heritage on the HERI survey. These individuals and their responses were not included in columns 2 through 10, according to Bill Korn, HERI's associate director of operations.

Table 7.4. Faculty survey, 1995–1996: Goals for undergraduates noted as "very important" or "essential" (percentage distribution)

	Total responses (col. 1)	Total majority	Total minorities
	Male faculty		
Number of respondents	**21,959**	**19,497**	**1,804**
Develop ability to think clearly	99.3	99.4	99.2
Increase self-directed learning	90.0	89.9	91.9
Prepare for employment	66.3	65.5	73.5
Prepare for graduate education	52.2	51.2	60.5
Develop moral character	54.5	53.5	64.1
Provide for emotional development	33.0	31.9	42.6
Prepare for family living	15.1	14.4	22.3
Teach classics of Western civilization	29.6	30.1	23.7
Help develop personal values	56.6	56.2	61.3
Enhance out-of-class experience	38.5	37.2	49.6
Enhance self-understanding	56.7	55.8	65.1
Instill commitment to community service	30.6	29.3	42.1
Prep for responsible citizenship	58.2	57.3	65.6
	Female faculty		
Number of respondents	**12,027**	**10,660**	**1,139**
Develop ability to think clearly	99.6	99.7	99.3
Increase self-directed learning	94.8	94.8	95.0
Prepare for employment	77.2	76.7	82.5
Prepare for graduate education	56.0	54.5	65.7
Develop moral character	63.1	62.4	67.9
Provide for emotional development	46.1	44.8	**54.8**
Prepare for family living	21.3	20.6	25.5
Teach classics of Western civilization	25.7	25.3	27.9
Help develop personal values	65.2	64.8	67.6
Enhance out-of-class experience	47.0	45.5	**57.7**
Enhance self-understanding	70.7	70.2	74.7
Instill commitment to community service	42.6	41.6	49.2
Prep for responsible citizenship	67.8	67.4	72.1

African American (col. 4)	American Indian	Asian American	All Latinos	Mexican American Chicano/a	Puerto Rican	Other Latinos
Male faculty						
355	265	748	436	171	59	206
99.7	99.2	99.3	98.6	97.2	100.0	100.0
94.8	89.6	90.7	92.2	93.2	84.0	93.2
78.9	72.2	74.5	68.0	74.7	64.2	60.3
71.2	55.5	54.3	62.9	64.5	57.5	62.2
71.2	58.6	64.3	60.2	61.7	57.0	59.1
57.8	42.7	36.6	38.2	39.1	42.7	35.6
32.7	23.3	17.3	20.3	21.6	16.8	19.5
20.7	36.6	16.6<	30.3	24.5	20.8	40.6
67.0	66.8	57.8	58.7	61.5	62.7	53.9
60.1	46.4	45.3	48.4	54.7	55.2	38.3
74.7	72.2	59.3	61.5	62.0	69.4	58.7
53.5	44.4	31.9	45.9	49.0	47.2	41.4
69.4	70.3	62.4	64.5	66.5	61.5	62.7
Female faculty						
329	158	327	325	119	52	154
100.0	99.8	99.1	98.6	99.1	95.3	99.2
95.7	93.7	93.5	96.0	98.8	89.5	94.9
88.5	78.0	78.3	81.6	87.9	82.2	73.6
72.4	54.5	65.0	64.3	66.0	59.8	63.8
73.5	66.7	70.6	60.8	61.5	46.3	65.5
61.9	52.9	54.1	49.2	51.7	36.3	51.2
28.2	20.4	29.1	22.2	25.1	12.7	22.3
26.8	25.9	26.8	30.6	26.2	29.8	36.4
68.6	70.4	75.5	59.3	57.1	51.0	65.4
62.9	56.5	59.3	52.0	52.5	56.5	49.6
79.3	73.5	74.7	70.6	70.9	70.3	70.5
56.8	50.1	47.1	42.8	42.0	44.3	43.0
76.1	73.2	74.1	66.1	58.8	75.0	71.7

Source: Data and table are adapted from H. Astin et al., *Race and Ethnicity in the American Professoriate, 1995–1996* (Los Angeles: Higher Education Research Institute).

Note: Boxed data in column 2 are the benchmark majority male responses. The shading shows responses that vary from those benchmarks by at least 10 percentage points, the sign < indicating responses beneath the benchmarks. The bold numbers that are underlined represent responses that vary from the benchmarks by at least 20 percentage points.

The "total responses" numbers in column 1 include individuals who did not identify their ethnic heritage on the HERI survey. These individuals and their responses were not included in columns 2 through 10, according to Bill Korn, HERI's associate director of operations.

(combined), whereas only 19 percent of all Asian American faculty in the survey are employed in humanities or education. They comprise nearly 43 percent of faculty in the physical sciences, including engineering.

Context and cognition are not automatically assumed to be associated with greater or lesser point spreads or even with the frequencies of variance from the benchmarks. If these patterns are associated with cultural context or cognitive characteristics, the association probably is less a reflection of ethnicity and more a reflection of such additional factors as values, goals, methodologies, or preferences embedded in the questions. In other words, the evidence for cultural context and cognition will be associated with the embedded factors. Therefore, I chose which survey questions to examine by using a greater-to-lesser set of values embedded within related questions in the survey on undergraduate teaching and learning pedagogies. If the evidence for cultural context or cognition is present in the responses, and it is related to values embedded in the questions, under my working hypothesis we should first see gender and cultural values in the differences in the groups' responses. We may see additional evidence of the influence of context and cognition if we can identify and validate the individual questions as designed to yield answers reflective of high- or low-context or field-sensitive or field-independent factors.

Preliminary Results of Pilot Study of Inter-Rater Reliability

Although research to confirm this is still in progress, preliminary findings from a small number of faculty raters show that it may be possible to confirm that cultural context and cognition are present in these data.

Each question in tables 7.2 through 7.4 is being shown to faculty and staff to determine question content. As of the fall of 1999, fewer than twelve individuals had participated. Despite the small pool of participants, agreement among them on question content is remarkably consistent. Preliminary analysis of the question sets suggests that cultural context and cognition (fundamental principles in the theory of multicontextuality) may be detected in the faculty responses and could have some bearing on the variance uncovered. Because work on this project is still in progress, I can report only generalized findings here. However, in a pilot study with a small sample of male and female faculty and academic administrators of mixed ethnic groups, participants were asked to review the thirty-nine questions and identify which ones are high context or low context and which are field independent or field sensitive, which contain characteristics that are both high and low context or field independent and sensitive, and which questions do not appear to have any of those elements. All participants in the pilot study agreed that 49 percent of the questions are high context *and* field sensitive, 26 percent are low context *and* field independent, another 21 percent reflect both context and cognition, and fewer than 1 percent of the questions contain none of the elements.

I then compared the ratings from the pilot study—which categorized each question in the faculty survey by context and cognition—compared with the ethnic faculty's responses to each question in the survey. I then noted the pilot study rating for each question to which the answers from two or more ethnic groups (columns 4 through 10), whether men or women, differed by more than 10 percent from the majority male benchmark for that question. Preliminary findings seem to point to an association between HERI survey questions that show variance for ethnic minority faculty above the benchmark and the questions identified by participants in the pilot study as high context, field sensitive, or both. There also seems to be a similar association between HERI survey questions that show variance for ethnic minority faculty that falls 10 percentage points or more below the benchmarks (marked in tables 7.1–7.4 by < sign) and questions identified by participants in the pilot study as low context, field independent, or both. This suggests that in the survey data, many majority women and most minority faculty, especially minority women in most ethnic groups, demonstrated a high preference for high-context, field-sensitive evaluation methods, instructional methods, and educational goals for undergraduates in higher education. The responses of women, especially minority women, showed a pattern of 10- to 30-point differences from the majority male benchmarks on those questions that the pilot group designated as low context and field independent. The relatively large number of faculty responding to the HERI survey lends additional support to the assumptions that cultural context, cognition, and multicontextuality play a much greater role in higher education than many of us realized.

As expected, the three tables reflect a set of important differences in female and minority faculty practices and values and those for the benchmark majority males. In comparing faculty responses from only the four ethnic groups (columns 4 to 7 only) in table 7.3, for example, I found one problem that these data illustrate is the effect of combining or "lumping" categories together. Although different groups of minority male faculty (columns 4 to 7) and the majority faculty (column 2) show several differences of 10 points or more, the differences essentially disappear in column 3, which lumps the minority male data together. If one were to compare the data in columns 2 and 3, which is often done when data on minorities are presented, minority males and majority males would show virtually no differences. In fact, when the data in all three tables are combined in columns 2 and 3 (see H. Astin et al. 1997, 49), only five questions (30, 31, 32, 36, and 38) demonstrate a difference of 10 percentage points.

The lumping problem is also evident when we compare the aggregated data on Latinos and Latinas in column 7 with the data broken out by specific Latina/o groups in columns 8, 9, and 10. That is, the combined data on Latinos in column 7 reflect some of the differences between the three ethnic categories and the majority benchmarks, but aggregation tends to reduce the number and magnitude of these differences. This is consistent with the observation in chapter 2 that combining ethnic groups into one category tends to mask real differences between different Latino ethnic groups and the majority cultural benchmarks. In this case the amount of difference, and perhaps the conflicts associated with those differences as well, are masked not only in comparison to majority males but also in comparison to other groups of minority colleagues, including other Latino ethnic groups. Without breaking down the data, it would be hard to see that Puerto Ricans demonstrate a greater number of differences as well as a larger spread than any other group of minority males. Furthermore, this pattern is even more pronounced for Puerto Rican women.

Does the lumping effect also prevent us from detecting cultural context and cognition? If so, might that explain why question 13, on comparative learning, and question 19, on cooperative learning, show more 20- and 30-point differences than other questions? The response patterns for both questions clearly show agreement among female faculty members, and the questions certainly point to key conditions of high and low context as well as field-sensitive and field-independent cognitive styles. But does this pattern offer evidence for these conditions? The last table may offer some clues.

Table 7.4 contains a larger number of goal-oriented or value-driven questions than do tables 7.2 and 7.3, which focus more on preferences in teaching methods and practice. Furthermore, it appears that ethnic minorities and majority males have vastly different goals for their undergraduates (table 7.4) and are more different from majority males in this respect than they are in regard to evaluation methods (table 7.2) and methods of instruction (table 7.3). These general patterns point to high-context and field-sensitive preferences for women and minorities. In addition, this is the first set of questions in which Asian Americans, particularly women, show a large number of differences from majority males. In tables 7.2 and 7.3, Asian American faculty tend to respond much like the majority males. In fact, except for Asian American males, the pattern toward high-context cultural preferences is evident across the spectrum of ethnic populations and women in the survey. According to Helen Astin and her colleagues, ethnic minority faculty value the practical side of higher education and, as discussed earlier in this chapter, they tend to use methods that engage groups of students or the whole class in the learning process (1997, 22). According to the authors, African American and Latino faculty are far more likely than other professors to choose an academic career because they see it as an opportunity for generating social change (H. Astin et al. 1997, 34).

If evaluation methods for undergraduates are any measure of academic culture, pedagogical styles do not reflect major differences, although some differences between ethnic groups and majority males are evident. Gender differences are also quite evident among majority professors. Minority women show even greater differences in their responses about what they consider to be important goals for undergraduates. Asian Americans, however, seem in general to have preferences close to those expressed by majority males. The data in table 7.4 suggest that, as ethnic faculty, both male and female Asian Americans are group oriented and high context and tend to emulate or conform to the preferences expressed by majority male faculty, but they are also becoming more and more multicontextual.

8

Reframing the Cultural Context of the Academy

*A New Infrastructure
for Teaching, Learning,
and Institutional Change*

Graduate education in America is now a little more
than a century old. It has received much less searching attention, many fewer proposals for real reform,
than undergraduate education. In my experience, it is
the most bureaucratized, lockstep, and unimaginative
sector of the university. Since it's clearly in crisis, let's
apply to it some imaginative rethinking.
Peter Brooks, "Graduate Learning as Apprenticeship"

A deep interest in reforming higher education
simply has not caught fire with most faculty and administrators. Despite
the efforts of some of the best educators in the country, supported by the
best-led organizations at the National Center for Higher Education in
Washington, D.C., reform has yet to begin. To be sure, numerous educational institutions around the country have recognized and rewarded the
efforts at One Dupont Circle, but among teaching faculty at large research
universities, our nation's "faculty factories," little has changed. Reform has
not caught on because no incentive for instituting fundamental change
exists.

My primary objective here is to plant a theoretical model that will help build a more inclusive learning community, one that involves everyone in higher education without dismantling the successful infrastructures. This reframing process begins by examining the principles of organizational cultural change associated with four specific questions:

Why should academic cultures change?
Which components of higher education need to change?
How can the transformation of higher education occur dynamically and effectively?
What is an appropriate model for higher education?

Why Should Academic Cultures Change?

The call for changing higher education has been eloquent and persistent for decades, but the response from academics has been less than enthusiastic. Growing concerns about changing socioeconomic and political conditions have also failed to push higher education to institute reform. Even the sometimes fiery president of George Washington University, Stephen Trachtenberg (1997), stirs little interest among academics when he advocates developing new educational opportunities to attract the aging baby-boom generation. Franklin Raines, director of the federal Office of Management and Budget (OMB), warned research universities in 1997 that they need to redefine their missions and change their public image. If they continue to focus only on research, which directs the creation of knowledge, and ignore the other core functions—teaching as well as the integration of that knowledge in society—Congress will increasingly perceive them as just another economic sector seeking to increase their consumption from the public trough. If they are treated like all other business enterprises, the result could be fewer federal research dollars (Metheny 1997).

Levine (1997) offers one explanation for the perception of higher education as intransigent: its new status as a mature industry. Considered a growth sector throughout the twentieth century, higher education has matured and a certain lethargy toward change has set in. Not surprisingly, then, the impending demographic changes associated with minority population growth, also called "Tidal Wave II" in the California State University systems, are generating a wait-and-see response from academics. Meanwhile, political groups and factions across the country are scrambling to dismantle civil rights–era programs in order to establish what they would perceive as a new kind of equal rights. The increasing number of Latinos entering higher education today hides the fact that their ratio to total Latino population growth is becoming smaller and thus generates little concern among college and university administrators. The prevailing argument remains: creating diversity in U.S. institutions is the right thing to do. However, the rationale for building a diversified campus—that is, one that promotes multicultural awareness and understanding in society—has come under direct attack by those who believe that European American culture is the only standard that "can hold our society together and keep us a competent nation" (Bork 1996, B7).

"Mission Creep"

The late Ernest Boyer frequently spoke against "mission creep," the growing trend of smaller liberal arts colleges and universities to emulate the missions and visions of our larger research-driven universities throughout the country by emphasizing research over teaching and service. This was, in fact, a central thesis in his now classic book, *Scholarship Reconsidered* (1990), and his warning call for reform was directed at that growing imbalance. As described in chapter 5, Boyer tracked the historical growth of the Germanic research model in graduate education as a major force in tipping the balance. His underlying theme is that the research culture—a model that demands that "professors view the everyday world from a distance"—has seriously eroded the basic principles of academic culture (1990, 9). This shift in emphasis has greatly diminished the role of teaching in the academy, and service has become less important and less valued among scholars; in fact, some academics consider service "a violation of the integrity of the university" (1990, 9). According to Boyer, an even greater danger is the degree to which the academic values associated with the research culture have affected liberal arts colleges. His conclusions were simple and direct:

What we urgently need today is a more inclusive view of what it means to be a scholar—a recognition that knowledge is acquired through research, through synthesis, through practice, and through teaching. We acknowledge that these four categories—the scholarship of discovery, of integration, of application, and of teaching—divide intellectual functions that are tied inseparably to each other. Still, there is value, we believe, in analyzing the various kinds of academic work, while also acknowledging that vision of scholarship, one that recognized the great diversity of talent within the professoriate, also may prove especially useful to faculty as they reflect on the meaning and direction of their professional lives. (1990, 24–25)

As for graduate education, he added:

Graduate schools must continue to be a place where students experience the satisfaction that comes from being on the cutting edge of a field, and the dissertation, or a comparable project, should continue to be the centerpiece—the intellectual culmination of the graduate experience. However, it is our conviction that if scholarship is to be redefined, graduate study must be broadened, encompassing not only research, but integration, application, and teaching too. It is this vision that will assure, we believe, a new generation of scholars, one that is more intellectually vibrant and more responsive to society's shifting needs. (74)

Boyer opposed the narrow definition of faculty roles vis-à-vis the research model, and he was deeply committed to the belief that "teaching was crucial, that integrative studies [transdisciplinary studies] are increasingly consequential, and that in addition to research, the work of the academy must relate to the world beyond the campus" (75). He embraced the "community" model, which was embodied in the structural development of his "new American college," his most active project before his untimely death in 1995 (Coye 1997). Boyer suggested that the new scholarship and the new academic community would come about only if the various components of higher education work together for change—through persuasive presidents, faculty that change the curriculum, accrediting bodies that redefine scholarship—a *team* approach (1990, 76–80). The parallels between Boyer's vision of scholarship and community and the clear, preferential cultural patterns of multicontextual Latinas, Latinos, and other ethnic populations in academia are direct.

Boyer was aware of the importance of diversity on campus, and though he recognized that faculty must reach beyond the classroom into minority communities, he did not connect—or, perhaps, had not yet connected—his vision to cultural context and ethnic minority culture. Without qualitative research to confirm the necessity to implement his reform concepts, Boyer could only try to persuade higher education that this was the right approach. Without clear values and a purpose for change and reform, instigating the process of adopting such new ideas is made more difficult and time consuming.

The Value Added by Enhancing Diversity

Has graduate education absorbed or implemented any of Boyer's ideas? Probably not. U.S. institutions today remain committed to diversity because it is the right thing to do. What they have failed to see is that reform that accommodates and embraces diversity will bring very practical benefits to the academy. In my opinion, one reason reform has not taken hold in higher education is both an institutional sense of invulnerability and a lack of incentives for the faculty.

New research findings on the benefits of diversity in the private sector offer some powerful reasons for academics to reform their institutions in a way that, by fostering diversity, increases the value of education. In an article entitled "Making Differences Matter: A New Paradigm for Managing Diversity" (1996), business professors David Thomas at Harvard University and Robin Ely at Columbia University argue that some organizations have experienced a three-stage evolution in recognizing the importance of ethnic and gender diversity in the work force. Each stage represents a new paradigm for diversity: the discrimination-and-fairness paradigm; the access-and-legitimacy paradigm; and the learning-and-effectiveness paradigm.

The Discrimination-and-Fairness Paradigm

This could be characterized by the phrase "it's the right thing to do." This still-dominant paradigm represents what is usually the first step institutions take after they conclude that increasing their ethnic and female populations is morally correct. This philosophy emphasizes a need for a greater critical mass of ethnic minorities and women. It also focuses on equal opportunity, fair treatment, recruitment, and compliance and in that respect resembles traditional affirmative action initiatives and programs. The benefits are increased diversity for the institution, but the limitations are that everyone must assimilate a gender- and "color-blind conformism" that is closely aligned with the prevailing organizational culture (D. Thomas and Ely 1996, 81).

The Access-and-Legitimacy Paradigm

The second step is characterized by market-oriented multiculturalism associated with demographic change. The objective is to introduce diverse cultural ideas and concepts into the organization. The benefits are greater access for women and minorities and legitimacy for their ethnic and gender differences. A major limitation is the greater potential for exploitation. Individuals are valued mainly for their experiences as women and/or minorities, and they may be called upon to help organizations gain access to their communities for the purposes of recruiting others in the community and penetrating new consumer markets (D. Thomas and Ely 1996, 84).

The Learning-and-Effectiveness Paradigm

This is a new perspective, only now emerging in a handful of organizations. It is directed toward opening up new sources of knowledge—finding other ways of thinking and learning—that are derived from the diverse cultural and gender perspectives of the world. It is characterized as "connecting diversity to work perspectives," which is achieved by incorporating those perspectives in the mainstream of the way the organization does business (D. Thomas and Ely 1996, 85).

The emerging learning-and-effectiveness paradigm essentially taps into the benefits to be realized by incorporating cultural context and cognition in organizational culture. The rewards from doing this flow both ways— the organization values diverse ideas and perspectives based on ethnicity for their intrinsic cultural capital, while diversity generates its own intrinsic value and becomes part of the organization's culture. Thomas and Ely found a good example of this positive-flow model that was thriving in a public interest law firm. In the late 1980s the all-majority legal staff recognized that its female clients in employment-related disputes were "exclusively white." The principals in the firm viewed this not only as a deficiency but also a bad business strategy in general. Driven by their experiences in embracing the first two diversity paradigms—discrimination and fairness, and access and legitimacy—the partners decided to hire a Latina attorney. Her skills not only increased their business and encouraged them to hire other minority lawyers but also quickly made the partners realize she, like the other new "diversity hires," brought to cases fresh perspectives that other staff "never thought relevant or appropriate" (D. Thomas and Ely 1996, 85).

The new links between the firm's mission and its hiring strategies were all but invisible to longtime staff members. But the new connections influenced the partners to "pursue precedent-setting litigation" within completely new areas. Many new hires remarked how "their perspectives are heard with a kind of openness and interest they have never experienced before in a work setting. Not surprisingly, the firm has had little difficulty attracting and retaining a competent and diverse professional staff" (D. Thomas and Ely 1996, 85–86). According to Thomas and Ely,

Women, Hispanics, Asian Americans, African Americans, Native Americans—these groups and others outside the mainstream of corporate America don't bring with them just their "insider information." They bring different, important, and competitively relevant knowledge and perspectives about how to actually *do work*—how to design processes, reach goals, frame tasks, create effective teams, communicate ideas, and lead. When allowed to, members of these groups can help companies grow and improve by challenging basic assumptions about an organization's functions, strategies, operations, practices, and procedures. And in doing so, they are able to bring more of their whole selves to the workplace and identify more fully with the work they do, setting in motion a virtuous circle. Certainly, individuals can be expected to contribute to a company their firsthand familiarity with niche markets. But only when companies start thinking about diversity more holistically—as providing fresh and meaningful approaches to work—and stop assuming that diversity relates simply to how a person looks or where he or she comes from, will they be able to reap its full rewards. (80)

As colleagues and I have described elsewhere, the new knowledge and fresh perspectives that Thomas and Ely describe may in fact be a hidden resource in our organizations even now. These "critical knowledge areas" are often associated with individuals or groups that have been marginalized in their organizational activities (Ibarra and Thompsen 1997; Thompsen and Ibarra 1997). Individuals with thinking styles and worldviews derived from different cultural or gender contexts are often misunderstood. For example, Mexican Americans or Chicanos may adopt social and educational strategies (behaviors) that may be less valued or even considered confrontational in certain cultural contexts and may thus become marginalized in our society. Yet their critical knowledge and their adaptive strategies may prove essential to our society.

This scenario is all too familiar when someone's valuable ideas are declared to be ahead of their time. As this book clearly demonstrates, critical knowledge can also lie dormant in our academic institutions. Physics professor Barbara Whitten, for example, believes that physics as an academic discipline is constrained by gender-oriented models that are unnecessarily hierarchal (low context) and consequently are biased against applied science (1996). Physics can play a significant role, she believes, in raising the level of applied science from a second-class status by connecting it positively with the rest of society. However, she and other women scientists are concerned that science may be intrinsically antifemale and hopelessly male oriented, or "androcentric." Sandra Morgen, an anthropologist, offers a more critical view. She believes that "Euro-American men are incapable of making a significant contribution to our understanding of these [gender, ethnicity, and sexuality] areas of new knowledge. . . . They just did not see many of the issues or did not experience the marginalization and injustices that were front and center for their colleagues of color and many women" (1997, 4). Tapping these hidden critical knowledge areas requires rethinking how we acquire and disseminate new knowledge and how we can generate it by embracing the perspectives of women and ethnic minorities. Rather than increasing diversity simply for the sake of having diversity, the learning-and-effectiveness model recognizes that diversity can provide new ideas *and* advance our current academic knowledge.

A good demonstration of diversity that generates new knowledge is the Emerging Scholars Program (ES) described in chapter 7. Founded by the mathematician Uri Treisman, its success came from observing the most effective learning styles found among ethnically diverse students and applying these as innovative methods for teaching math and calculus. If Treisman and the ES program can achieve these results by closely observing ethnic learning styles, what other techniques might we discover that will enhance our institutions and advance our current knowledge? Clearly, the benefits of encouraging ethnic and gender diversity can open up vital new ways for creating knowledge and making signficant contributions to higher education in general.

My research among Latinos in academia verified that higher education has yet to catch up with the paradigm emerging in the corporate sector. In fact, academic cultures may be so complacent that they will never catch up with the private sector. As we have seen, it is one thing for Latinos and

Latinas to gain access to graduate education, but it is quite another matter to make high-context, field-sensitive approaches part of traditional faculty culture.

Does higher education in general seem concerned? Not really, according to my research. Even worse, the traditional strategy of the academy could quickly become a maladaptive strategy. As stated earlier, one reason Latinos are not entering academia is that academic careers are less attractive than other activities and opportunities. The majority of Latinos in higher education attend community colleges today, but only a relative few complete professional degrees in law, medicine, or even in the more traditional areas such as education. Graduate schools, however, may soon find themselves competing with the corporate sector. If the learning-and-effectiveness paradigm takes hold in the corporate sector, as is likely, colleges and universities will almost certainly suffer a Latino brain drain. Why should they enter academia when corporate life beckons, with its significantly larger salaries, respect, creative freedom, and seemingly unlimited opportunities for promotion?

Which Components of Higher Education Need to Change?

Though my comments in the last section end on a gloomy note, some interesting developments are on the horizon. Mathematics, for instance, may be on the threshold of genuine curriculum reform (Wilson 2000). As this book went to press, members of the Mathematical Association of America were conducting a major review of the undergraduate curriculum, changing content and methods to incorporate elements that turn out to be high context and field sensitive. Some math programs have already replaced the typical practice of memorization and repetitive manipulation of formulas with more story problems, oral presentations, and student papers in an attempt to attract students who are mathematically inclined but prefer to apply it in disciplines, such as business, English, and anthropology, that are outside the traditional sciences (Wilson 2000).

The trend in math is the "mathematicization of society" to make math more universal and useful for everyone, according to Thomas Berger, professor of mathematics and computer science at Colby College (Wilson 2000, A14). This trend was fueled by developments in computer technology that created mathematical models that now can test real-world applications of theoretical concepts. Before these programs were developed, students were limited mainly to calculating and manipulating formulas. Today computer modeling is making it easier for almost everyone to test ideas by simulating machines or replicating the effects of, say, changing health insurance benefits or environmental conditions in ways that affect social and ecological systems.

In essence, these changes represent a new way of thinking and processing information. High-context field-sensitive concepts, such as modeling of practical applications, teach by presenting people-oriented problems in combination with traditional low-context calculations and formulas. This is one way of creating a multicontextual learning environment. If successful, these reforms could attract multicontextual students to math and science disciplines. The real question in all of this is whether mathematicians will recognize the powerful implications of multicontextual concepts—can they see that these changes reach beyond the curriculum and into the academic culture of mathematics as a discipline? Is it enough to merely introduce these concepts and methods without fully understanding why they work and therefore help all students to learn and how they could be used as a marketing tool to attract diverse student populations to math? I argue that without fully understanding the dynamics of academic cultures, applying new approaches to the curriculum is only a half-measure of change. If higher education fails to connect these reforms to the knowledge of multicontextual thinking styles, or to the bigger picture of institutional organizational change, it will continue to run the risk of coming up short on fundamental reforms that could significantly advance current knowledge and provide new opportunities for funded research.

Scholars like Boyer and Eugene R. Rice have certainly guided sectors of higher education in the right direction. I have reviewed some of the new programs (described later in this chapter), and I think that those at the undergraduate level have clearly heeded Boyer and others by focusing on improvements in some aspects of teaching, learning, research, and community orientation. In 1997 *Change* magazine dedicated an entire issue, "Rebuilding a Civic Life in Higher Education," to an examination of this phenomenon (see Gamson 1997).

One of the latest and most promising entries in the arena of higher education reform is William G. Tierney's edited collection of articles that seek to prescribe how to restructure our universities to become more responsive to the changing social, demographic, and political forces in the United States today (1998b). Couched in Boyer's terms of "engagement" and "connectedness to the community," the track for systemic change laid down by Tierney's contributors suggests that universities need to become more responsive to "students as customers" (Chaffee); create alternatives to faculty tenure systems (Tierney 1998a); devise new ways to form lasting and effective partnerships with public school systems and community-based organizations (Braskamp and Wergin); and, ultimately, develop new governance structures and policies that are in sync with both internal and external communities (Benjamin and Carroll). These new models are designed to stimulate institutional change by using high-context cultural principles—collaboration, inclusiveness, community involvement, an orientation to students (people), comprehensive/systemic thinking, and so on. Equally important is the emphasis on the need to redefine the epistemology of faculty work in the context of academic culture change (Braskamp and Wergin 1998, 83).

How Can the Transformation of Higher Education Occur Dynamically and Effectively?

Although Boyer and others offer a clear rationale for why reform of higher education is necessary, and even highlight what needs to be accomplished, they are not always clear about how to transform institutional structures and cultures. Scott and Awbrey (1993) believe higher education is on the threshold of a self-transformation, from a "multiversity" (a rather low-context model that fragments knowledge and other learning components into disaggregated parts) into Boyer's model of a new scholarly community, which they call a "connected university." Society, according to Scott and Awbrey, is prepared to help shape the new model, which again connects teaching, research, and service as a unified whole (1993, 40–41).

Guskin (1996), on the other hand, offers some basic rules along with his recipe for implementing a process of change. The most important is to be alert for resistance to change. For instance, some faculty devote their entire careers to maintaining old systems and are notorious for resisting change. They bristle at being told to reform, whether the message comes from other colleagues or from administrators. Daniel Seymour, working alone (1993) and with his colleague Satinder K. Dhiman (1996), notes how easily organizational cultures can create barriers for change. How well "a new idea or innovation is adopted by an organization is a function of how well that idea fits into that organization's life" (D. Seymour and Dhiman 1996, 72). Organizational identity, or the shared meanings that people use to define the nature of the institution, plays an equally important role in facilitating or impeding the process of change, according to the authors (1996). For example, research universities are not likely to find faculty pushing for reforms that transform their institution into a national leader in job training, and community college faculty would unlikely to try to remake their campus as a leading institution in pure research.

From an anthropological perspective, Barth reminds us that internal change has both internal and external aspects. When viewed as external, change becomes a function of the boundary maintenance between various groups, whether they are faculty and administrators, or Latinos and Anglos (1969). Thus change will be reflected in the kinds of transactions and negotiations that take place between various groups. Individuals and groups are more likely to change if they perceive that doing so will maximize their interests financially, socially, politically, or in some other way (Barth 1967). Within-group change can also be entrepreneurial, but in this instance leadership becomes the critical factor in whether an adaptive strategy is successful. If executive decision makers show group members that outcomes favorable to them are likely to result, other individuals will follow their lead. This is essentially what Guskin suggests with his five elements for successful change: use internal experts as much as possible; support risk takers; form partnerships with other institutions undergoing change; invest in faculty development; and invest in technology (1996, 37). Thus entrepreneurial leadership becomes a critical factor in effective organizational change (Barth 1967; Guskin 1996; Scott and Awbrey 1993).

Thomas A. Angelo's 1997 article, "The Campus as Learning Community," is more specific than Guskin's about which components need to change in order to make colleges and universities learning-centered environments. Angelo is convinced "that developing a cooperative academic culture is vital for our survival" in higher education (4). Essentially, doing this calls for shifting the current paradigm. He recommends improving both instructional productivity and learning quality. Angelo suggests that using powerful levers, mainly educational tools, methods, and new teaching or learning practices that can facilitate fundamental shifts in standard operating procedures (1997, 2–6).

Both Angelo and Guskin offer dynamic models they predict will lead to cultural change. Both models embody concepts of cultural context or elements of the entrepreneurial incentives that Barth advocates. But are they changing the system fundamentally, or are they just changing components of the system?

According to Richard Edwards, a senior vice chancellor at the University of Nebraska at Lincoln, one way to effect systemic change is to abolish academic departments (1999). His bold and articulate suggestions invite a closer look. Edwards believes that reforms in higher education have been underway since the 1980s and that these reforms are having some effects at the institutional and individual levels but have not changed midlevel university structures, namely, the academic departments. I would agree that research universities are paying more attention to teaching undergraduate curricula, learning assessments, and campus life, but I am not convinced that these reforms and others, such as post-tenure faculty review, will really catch on without a significant change in the academic culture as well.

I do agree with Edwards that genuine reform must take place on a larger, more systemic scale and that academic departments are the most resistant and the least changed structures on our campuses because they are the citadels of the traditional academic professional (Edwards 1999, 21). Edwards refers to the work of Boyer (1990) and especially to Rice's model of "the new American scholar" (1996) and explains that faculty members "hold tight to their departments as the most congenial arena for their traditional understanding of what is important in academic work and for the power of enduring disciplinary affiliation that is independent of the institution" (1999, 21). Departments are stumbling blocks to change because departmental status is a key signifier that the discipline is taken seriously; colleagues around the world, including members of the disciplinary association, will protect these bastions of traditional faculty ways, a culture that Edwards profiles accurately in his article.

Faculty members also dig in their heels because their department is "the only front-line operating unit of a complex bureaucratic organization" (1999, 19). They feel pressure from all sides to shoulder the ever-growing and increasingly burdensome management and administrative duties—business functions—that include legal, personnel, efficiency, accountability, and diversity issues (I will return to this point later). All these functions eat into the time, attention, and resources available for the more traditional functions of faculty hiring, considering for tenure, promoting, and training graduate students, as well as the basics—teaching and producing scholarship of the highest quality. The crucial question is how can higher education strike a balance with reform and still maintain the best traditions of academe?

Edwards advocates organizational structural change combined with new or stronger leadership roles for department chairs and offers some interesting but radical solutions. Foremost among them is to reorganize all departments by abolishing "all departmental lines and simply appoint professors to the university faculty" (1999, 22–23). Another is to redefine the department's functions by, in effect, redefining "the work for which departments are responsible" (24). One way to do this, he says, is to outsource business functions if necessary and acknowledge interdisciplinarity in faculty work. The least radical solution is basically to change or strengthen the role of departmental leadership. Edwards's recommendations reflect a great deal of innovation and merit but other aspects of what he says are problematic.

For instance, although Edwards advocates systemic change, he either ignores cultural change or assumes that restructuring will bring about change in the faculty culture. But will abolishing departments, redefining their functions, or strengthening the roles of departmental leaders change the traditional academic culture and faculty mind-set that Edwards so accurately depicts? In my opinion, restructuring without a plan to deal with academic culture either simultaneously or (preferably) before initiating structural change could invite disaster or, at best, resistance. The danger in abolishing departments and then reappointing all faculty to the university, for example, is that this tactic does not prevent strong departments and faculty from forming alliances and becoming stronger while weaker departments and faculty become weaker because they have no choice in the process.

Such a plan could further marginalize minority faculty and nondegree programs such as ethnic or women's studies. Interdisciplinary programs based on emerging new scholarship could literally become lost in the shuffle. How could colleges and universities convince disciplinary associations to become allies in dismantling the departments? Dismantling departments would be even more difficult for professional disciplines, like psychology and nursing, in which licensing is essential.

Finally, Edwards claims that reform must not exclude faculty participation and must build upon campus traditions of shared governance, must not jeopardize the tenure system, and must recognize the faculty need for disciplinary scholarship (22). His model stops short of reframing overall academic culture, not just the faculty culture in departments. If the inherent academic culture, which Edwards claims must not be jeopardized by reform, does not become more inclusive of multicontextual principles, for example, the structural change he advocates would amount to little more than reshuffling the faculty into new packages, and the traditional work would continue with business as usual. An alternative is one that strikes a balance in reform and accounts for both structural and cultural change. Before I discuss it, readers need to be familiar with the concepts of systems thinking and systemic change.

Systemic Change and Shifting Models

The key to implementing organizational change effectively is systems thinking. Nearly every work cited here that focuses on creating institutional change agrees on the importance of entrepreneurial leadership. They also agree on two other significant points: effecting organizational change requires working on multiple components of an institution simultaneously, and change is more likely to succeed if it is implemented systemically (Benjamin and Carroll 1998; Ewell 1998). A colleague of mine at the University of Wisconsin–Madison, Maury Cotter (1996), describes the benefits of systems thinking for implementing change in the processes used by a large research university. By focusing on processes within academic units, the entire mission of the university can be advanced while maintaining the integrity, autonomous structure, and culture of the departments (1996, 29; see also Cotter, Simmons, and Paris 1997).

Perceiving and understanding the world systemically is not something that comes easily to people who have been imprinted by a society steeped in low-context culture. Working systemically is truly an art that needs practice. According to Peter Senge, author of *The Fifth Discipline: The Art and Practice of the Learning Organization,* the essence of systems thinking lies in the ability to shift one's mind to see interrelationships rather than linear cause-and-effect chains and to see processes of change rather than snapshots (1990, 73). "Practice" in shifting our thinking involves understanding the concept of "feedback," which demonstrates how actions reinforce and counterbalance each other. It requires learning to recognize types of "structures" that recur repeatedly. The examples I emphasize here are cultural conflicts associated with organizations and ethnicity and academic cultures that reinforce low-context scientific values and other low-context constructs. To recognize recurring types of structure may require shifting our vision from seeing things in straight lines (low context) to visualizing things as moving dynamically in circles, as recurring forces that are either interacting with other dynamic forces (systems) or are nested (enclosed) in layers (73–75).

It should be evident by now that systems thinking is the dynamic underlying structure of this book. The problems encountered by Latinos within academic organizations, for instance, cannot be attributed to a single factor or event. Such problems and their solutions are driven by multiple systemic forces. In systems thinking, every influence or force is both cause *and* effect, for nothing is ever influenced in only one direction (Senge 1990, 75). Because our society is so ingrained with a linear language for describing the world, to understand higher education in a systemic way it is important to keep in mind that dynamic systems are constantly reinforcing (amplifying) or balancing (stabilizing) feedback. Some reinforcing systems that begin with small influences can grow to become what Senge calls "virtuous cycles," or processes that reinforce in desired directions. Other reinforcing systems can grow into "vicious cycles," which start off badly and get even worse (1990, 81). These are often escalating events driven by fear, such as the arms race or a run on a bank.

However, some virtuous cycles can become limited over time and will appear to have achieved a state of balance. This is deceiving, for what appears as inactivity from the outside is in fact a system of "hidden balancing processes" that is spending a great deal of energy just trying to keep up. It is like watching a duck gliding effortlessly across a pond. What we fail to see are the rapidly paddling webbed feet churning up the water and causing significant turbulence just below the water line. Whenever there is resistance to change in a system, "it almost always arises from threats to traditional norms and ways of doing things" (Senge 1990, 88).

The best illustration of these principles is an analysis of the prevailing system for enhancing diversity in higher education—the pipeline model. As described briefly in the introduction, the current system for ensuring diversity focuses on creating better "access" to a college education. It is based on the assumption that normal channels for access to a college are blocked for ethnic minorities and other underrepresented populations. To alleviate the problem, colleges and universities must either eliminate the barriers in the current pathway to college or create new pipelines into the affected communities to give them greater access and support.

Limitations of the Current Infrastructure for Diversity Programs

Now more than thirty years old, the infrastructure of minority programs in higher education has changed little since it was first created after passage of the Civil Rights Act of 1964. The first programs around the country were devised to create better access for "educationally disadvantaged" populations. Their missions were often fourfold:

- To increase the number of minority students on campus. In the beginning these programs targeted African Americans primarily. The driving force was "parity," or equity in the numbers of individuals admitted to a campus; parity was often defined by the institution's embryonic affirmative action plans. This mission evolved to include recruiting students from certain minority groups.
- To offer remedial courses, workshops, or tutorial support for underprepared minority students. The assumption was that all minorities were educationally underprepared and needed tutoring in most academic areas. This evolved to include other components designed to keep these students from dropping out, including freshman orientation programs, seminars to teach research skills, writing workshops, and other language support units (e.g., English as a second language).
- To assist in meeting the financial, academic, and sociocultural needs of minority students. On some campuses minority students were given full financial aid benefits; in the pipeline model this functioned as both a recruitment tool and a way to retain these students. Providing scholarships emerged slowly over time. Academic advising was a primary function that was only offered to majors in a school or college; for undeclared majors the advising usually was generic. Small program budgets supported a few social events, also seen as a mechanism for retaining students.
- To offer academic advice and, if possible, counseling on campus cultural issues. The assumption was that minority students were the first generation in their families to attend college and that they therefore had little

concept of what a university education entailed. In some college programs academic advising across all or most schools and colleges was available from trained minority staff as another way to try to retain students.

The first minority programs were often created and directed by majority individuals simply because campuses had so few members of ethnic minorities who could develop and staff them. The urgency to create these programs was motivated either by moral obligation or by the mandate to comply with the new federal legislation; the programs were supported by meager funding from federal or state agencies and sometimes the institution.

Pipeline programs continue to carry a burden that was foisted on them at their inception but that should never have become part of their mission. Historically, they were created as a quick fix to deal with the fundamental problems of increasing the number of minorities on campus and of complying with the legislative mandates that, in effect, changed the nature of minority access to higher education literally overnight. When first implemented, these programs were enormously successful. How could they not succeed? Very few, if any, ethnic minorities were on campus in the first place, and the campus remained a male bastion. Any boost in the presence of minorities and women from recruiting efforts would be instant success.

However, the management and administrative principles behind these pipeline programs are a classic example of not recognizing, or not wanting to deal with, the full extent of the problem at the outset. Senge would give to higher education the same advice he gave to the business sector: "Focus on the fundamental solution. If a symptomatic solution is imperative and there are delays in the fundamental solution (it takes a long time to increase the number of minorities with degrees), use it to gain time while working on the fundamental solution" (1990, 381).

So let's focus on what has been the fundamental solution to the problem of too few minorities on campus: pipeline programs. As we have discussed, these programs work, but over time their effects tend to level off. If most pipeline programs in existence today originated as quick fixes, these are essentially fragmented components, patchworks, if you will, that look deceptively like a system. They are focused on academic deficiencies, underpreparedness, and remediation and are modeled after the personnel, training, and other kinds of employee relations or assistance offices found in most organizations. Certainly, these are important problems, as well as legitimate ways to address them, but they are not the essential systemic problems with regard to the main business and core academic cultures of higher education. The only systemic issue that these programs address is access—the admissions process—which is influenced by recruitment and financial support systems. Beyond that, admissions is a process that consists mainly of criteria and standards for accepting or rejecting students. In other words, with a quick fix in place that was generating positive results, no one ever returned to reexamine the fundamental problem of the lack of diversity in the first place. No one ever pointed out that the pipeline was a temporary solution. No one has rethought this model to come up with the "fundamental long-term corrective measures" that Senge recommends.

Most minority programs are fashioned after undergraduate student service programs. Consequently, they are often housed near or within student service units, such as financial aid, career counseling, or student affairs, for these units seemed best suited to fulfill the fourfold mission of minority programs. Lacking an academic home, minority programs are usually not connected to or are only indirectly connected to the institution's schools, colleges, departments, or faculty. Minority programs are essentially ad hoc, add-on programs with low-priority missions at the periphery of student services. Consequently, they have been marginalized from the beginning.

The 1980s and 1990s witnessed a fine-tuning of the primary mission to diversify campus life, with increasing emphasis on retention, funding, and academic preparation. New developments included extending the pipeline in both directions. Pipeline programs were expanded into the primary and secondary school systems or given broader outreach, like the nationally recognized TRIO programs that "provide low-income, first-generation college students and students with disabilities the services they need to enter and succeed in college" (Council for Opportunity in Education 2000, 30). Dubbed "TRIO" programs after the first three projects—Upward Bound, Talent Search, and Student Support Services—that were created during the late 1960s, the U.S. Department of Education now offers eight programs, including the Ronald E. McNair Postbaccalaureate Achievement Program, created in 1990. Modeled after undergraduate research programs that emerged in the late 1970s and early 1980s, the McNair program encourages and prepares high-risk students, including a large number of ethnic minorities, to attend graduate school (U.S. Department of Education 2000). These programs expanded the core mission with more outreach and recruitment programs, mentoring programs that focused on retaining students, and increased interaction of students and faculty. Graduate minority programs evolved slowly and only after the first undergraduate programs emerged on campus. Their infrastructures and formats were fairly similar to most undergraduate programs, changing only on certain campuses to accommodate decentralized departmental admissions processes.

When analyzing the pipeline model systemically using Senge's systems archetypes (1990, see appendix 2, 378–90), two problems emerge. The first, mentioned earlier, is a problem in the balancing process. Because the pipeline model represents a process that occurs over a long period of time, it may take years for colleges and universities to see any positive outcome from their minority programs. Feedback is slow to arrive, and if problems arise, institutions have no way to determine what appropriate corrective action to take or where to introduce it in the process.

A greater concern for diversity programs in higher education is the systemic problem that Senge calls "shifting the burden." This is a system in which "a short-term 'solution' is used to correct a problem, with seemingly positive immediate results. As this correction is used more and more, more fundamental, long-term corrective measures are used less and less. Over time, the capabilities for the fundamental solution may atrophy or become disabled, leading to even greater reliance on the symptomatic solution" (1990, 381). Shifting the burden is endemic to diversity programs in colleges and universities throughout the country. What we generally hear on campus is "our minority student initiatives [pipeline programs] have worked so far. We just need to redouble our efforts, and put more money into scholarships and fellowships so that our folks can afford to get their degrees. We need to extend recruiting and reach out to potential students in public schools and prepare them for college and graduate school." There is nothing wrong with these methods or objectives; they have been the foundation of minority activities in our institutions for more than thirty years. But these are based on a "short term solution to correct a problem with seemingly immediate positive results," and Senge tells us that verbal messages like these contain an early warning signal that flags a source of some of the problems (1990, 381).

A 1997 article by David R. Burgess on eliminating barriers to graduate school for minorities articulates the issue quite accurately and illustrates the systemic problem of shifting the burden. He concludes that "perhaps the dearth of minority graduate students *is* one of supply," and "it is clear that this problem can be solved. Minority students *can* be encouraged to seek advanced education in biomedical or other areas if they are made to feel welcome" (1997, B7). The rest of the article describes what barriers to remove: cut federal funds that support international students and redirect the money to minorities; institute fair and responsible admissions processes, a change that will require the involvement and more direct responsibility of university leaders; reward faculty and departments for doing the right thing by admitting more minority students; ensure that faculty understand that minorities do not lack interest in scientific careers, they just lack opportunities to participate in graduate school; and, finally, ensure that the faculty eliminate inaccurate assumptions about why so few minorities enter graduate school and the sciences and require faculty to help recruit, inform, and mentor these students by all available means (1997, B7–8).

His advice is excellent, but it rests on the well-worn principles of pipeline programs—recruitment, access, and retention—and a virtuous circle with a hidden balancing system that has become limited over time. The "dearth of minority students" is really a *symptom* of the problem. The central problem is that minority students are not attracted to graduate school or the sciences for a much greater variety of reasons than Burgess suggests. But the pipeline model has always aimed at healing the symptoms by removing the painful barriers to getting into and through graduate school. The solution appears to be simple: redouble our efforts and "minority graduate students will feel welcome," but this merely masks the core problem. It is in fact shifting the burden away from problems embedded in academic cultures and the essential "academic business" of higher education to the important but less essential "business functions" of higher education, which focus almost exclusively on recruiting and retaining minority students and faculty.

This shift is easy to spot because of the traditional ways faculty continue to do their work. Teaching, scholarship, discipline-oriented research, and outreach to the community have changed little over the years. The reason for this is simple: diversity plans and initiatives send out mixed messages. Advocates for enhancing diversity, usually high-context field-sensitive individuals, pick up on the implicit message that diversity initiatives can also function as models for changing the culture and climate of the institution. But because the plans contain no explicit instructions for interesting majority faculty in, for example, community outreach, the advocates of diversity continue to rely on access and retention activities. This leaves the rest of the faculty with a false impression that the diversity plan has addressed the problem, while high-context individuals exclaim to one another in frustration, "The faculty just don't get it!"

Many faculty members do get it but in an entirely different way. They operate in traditional low-context field-independent cultures, which have long viewed the explicit message of diversity initiatives as just another business function of the institution that has little to do with the core features of faculty work. At best, department chairs and their faculty recognize the need to incorporate multicultural perspectives and courses in their curricula. But most view diversity initiatives primarily as important administrative functions with potentially favorable social outcomes (see Edwards 1999), akin to faculty orientation, training, and development, recruiting, or hiring. They even tend to compartmentalize personnel issues such as discrimination as a direct part of affirmative action. All are important activities that could have long-term ramifications for the department, but departments still tend to cede these duties to others because their faculty are preoccupied with running an academic program and see diversity initiatives as secondary to their mission of academic research and publication.

Consequently, they have shifted the burden to university administrators, thus preventing the development of diversity initiatives or plans that are closely related to the core of academic work and faculty culture. As a result, we have come to rely more and more on the pipeline model, but it is only a half-measure. Over time, our institutions and academic cultures have remained blind to the necessity for a long-term solution to a fundamental problem.

Others recognize the limits of the current diversity model and, well aware of the unfriendly fire leveled at affirmative action programs, know that institutions must devise other approaches. They complain that higher education still suffers from too little diversity of people and cultures, despite the years of financial support and effort. Student recruitment programs would, over many years, have to take on the sophistication and complexity of athletic recruitment programs to achieve an appropriate level of diversity in higher education. Efforts to hire minority faculty would have to increase significantly, and the number of appropriate hires would have to increase even more. My research on Latinos suggests that many components of the classic pipeline diversity programs are still viable and that recruiting and retention programs may reduce some of the impediments faced by minority students, but colleagues who share their personal concerns with me say something is clearly still missing.

Senge reminds us that *"everyone shares responsibility for problems generated by a system"* (1990, 78). Not everyone in higher education, however, is sharing responsibility for the problems generated by the current diversity system. The inability to find unique solutions to the problem of diversifying our campuses may prove devastating. The consequences of our complacency are twofold: we have tried to heal the symptoms and not the disease, and the disease has changed over time, from discrimination and racism to underrepresentation. The attempt to heal the symptoms has led higher education into a conflict with an organized movement to rescind—not rethink—affirmative action initiatives across the country. Instead of setting an agenda to create fundamental corrective measures, educators and administrators now find that agenda being set by others—judges, legislators, and voters—nonacademics for the most part, who are fashioning their own notion of equity and fairness by creating a patchwork of alternatives like the class-ranking systems in Texas and Florida or by banning affirmative action initiatives altogether (see chapter 7). The task before us is still the same, only now it is more urgent: how can we include and reach beyond affirmative action initiatives today to ensure that our campuses reflect the general population?

What Is an Appropriate Model for Higher Education?

Academia is stalled at a cultural crossroads because we are still trying to define the problem. We have yet to overcome our misperception that diversity systems are separate from the primary academic systems in higher education. We fail to think systemically. Minority recruitment and retention programs, now called diversity initiatives, emerged from well-established academic cultures already imprinted with the German research model. Consequently, diversity, as we currently understand it, is an adjunct, ad hoc system that never was made part of the fabric of our colleges and universities. Now, when systemic change is necessary, our ability to move quickly and effectively is impaired. We have so marginalized and undervalued cultural and gender diversity that we have little motivation to understand the systems involved. Yet those systems contain the essential components for change—veritable gold mines of critical knowledge that offer beneficial new ideas for academia. Failing to understand this, we have also failed to absorb any new ideas about our learning organizations (Ibarra and Thompsen 1997).

Today, the effectiveness of minority programs has leveled off. The programs are still necessary and viable; they simply are not capable of addressing the systemic changes and developments (i.e., new financial and political realities) that have taken place in higher education over the years. The critical mass of underrepresented minority students has yet to reach expected levels on our campuses simply because the issues and systems driving diversity initiatives have shifted and changed.

The best analogy I can use to explain this relates to engineering automotive systems. Imagine, if you will, that our higher education system works as effectively as the power train system within our automobiles. Each component, from the entry and ignition systems to the acceleration and deceleration systems associated with the wheels, is interlinked. The traditional minority pipeline models are like the rear-wheel-drive trains of cars built in the mid-1960s. The engineering objective is to increase the car's energy efficiency and its torque and then to apply the right amount of power to gain traction from the wheels. But what if engineers had spent the last thirty years focused almost exclusively on refining all automotive systems and designs to the exclusion of this particular rear-wheel system? You'd have a car with high-tech electronic steering, braking, engine, and other systems, all redesigned together to accommodate external conditions that range from aging roadways to baby boomers' spreading hindquarters to rising fuel prices to the mandates of the Clean Air Act of 1990 . . . and a rear-wheel-drive system that hasn't changed since the 1960s. And without concurrent changes to the drive train, the car is unable to gain forward momentum.

Some educators might argue that academic culture has always been the central problem for ethnic minorities in higher education, and they would be correct. The difference is that today we must rethink and reframe the operative paradigm to address the real problem, which is academic organizational cultures that prefer to confront, not collaborate.

And in no way are the pipeline programs born in the 1960s capable of dealing with the growing problem of high-context, field-sensitive students who are abandoning (or never entering) graduate schools, which are dominated by low-context, field-independent professors.

A Multicontextual Theory and Model for Change

I believe the theory of multicontextuality fits the parameters that Tabachnik and Bloch call for in their 1995 essay, "Learning in and out of School." They propose that

A new theoretical framework is needed that incorporates powerful elements of cultural compatibility theory but that goes beyond these. For example, such a theoretical framework would honor knowledge from multiple sources, language, community, and cultural backgrounds . . . ; it would not force a model of cultural and linguistic assimilation, thereby losing the wealth of cultural/language practices and traditions that communities can offer to each other. At the same time, a new theory is needed that recognizes the range and variety of differences within groups and across gender and class and that responds to the dynamic qualities of culture as expressed in multiple contexts. (206)

I postulate that a growing number of individuals now entering higher education bring with them a mix of characteristics that Hall would describe as their "cultural context" (high and low) and Manuel Ramírez and Alfredo Castañeda call "bicognition" (field sensitive and field independent). Bicognition represents the variety of personality, culture, and learning styles generated by two distinct cognitive conditions associated with majority and minority individuals in this country. As such, it is a micromodel that transposes the characteristics of individuals onto the characteristics of larger groups and populations within which individual identity is validated. Cultural context represents the binary continuum of a range of cultural characteristics that we can use to identify and measure differences between various cultural groupings. As such, it is a macromodel that transposes the characteristics of larger groups and populations onto the characteristics of individuals who consider themselves members of those groups.

The theory of multicontextuality is an amalgamation of these two basic constructs. It is neither a process of acculturation nor one of assimilation. Those processes suggest cultural displacement, the requirement that individuals from less-dominant groups subsume their cultural behaviors to adopt the cultural patterns of the dominant group. Multicontextuality suggests cultural inclusion by assuming that individuals and groups of individuals learn and formulate strategies of cultural adjustment that help them adapt to their current circumstances. Given that culture is the primary context for learning, the theory postulates that organizational cultures too may be imprinted with a variety of cultural patterns. The points that follow frame the historical and conceptual assumptions underpinning the new construct.

Historical Assumptions

The U.S. model of higher education was created and imprinted with both high-context and low-context cultural patterns as well as field-sensitive and field-independent perspectives. After the mid-nineteenth century, graduate education in the United States was established and fashioned after the German research model created by and for low-context, field-independent people and culture in Europe. It is successful because it focuses on combining Western analytical thinking with hard scientific teaching and research. That graduate school structure was imposed on the liberal arts college (a British colonial import with its own mix of cultural contexts) and evolved into the vertical university infrastructure we are familiar with today. The graduate educational setting and learning mode initially contained high-context, field-sensitive principles—a teaching seminar or research lab consisting of a small group of graduate students serving a one-to-one apprenticeship. The setting and modes were transformed over time into what we have now.

The first notable high-context, field-sensitive populations in graduate education were probably men who originated from southern European Mediterranean groups. For example, high-context Italian and Jewish men entered academia and eventually the faculty with the aid of the GI Bill in the 1940s. It opened admissions to ethnic populations previously denied access to academia, and their arrival on campus began changing the Anglo-European culture associated with the professoriate and higher education. These early populations were satisfied with being able to join and become accepted into academia, but for the most part they were not intent upon changing academic culture to suit their needs.

High-context, field-sensitive immigrant populations have steadily increased in the United States since the mid-1940s. The grandchildren of these early voluntary immigrant groups, now entering higher education in greater numbers, are beginning to have a contextual influence on graduate education and beyond. The historical events that led the Mexican Americans in graduate school today to higher education began with the Bracero

Program of World War II. The program, which encouraged Mexicans to immigrate to the southwestern United States, was instituted by the federal government as a means to ensure that U.S. food growers would have an adequate work force to tend their fields. Many Mexicans stayed after the program ended, and their grandchildren and great-grandchildren account for a large percentage of the high-context, field-sensitive Latinos and Latinas in this country today.

Involuntary in-migration by new refugee groups has introduced populations that are less interested in acculturating and more interested in maintaining their ethnic identity. The more recent Latino immigrant populations, also from Mexico (e.g., Chiapas), as well as Guatemala, El Salvador, Cuba, and the Dominican Republic, tend to favor their national culture over their adopted North American culture because they expect to return to their homeland. Maintaining their high-context, field-sensitive cultures provides continuity for these patterns. This in turn means that unless higher education finds a way to embrace these populations, the discord with low-context faculty is likely to become even more serious.

Enrollment of high-context, field-sensitive populations (women and ethnic minorities) in higher education began to accelerate in the mid-1960s. The Civil Rights Act of 1964 and associated affirmative action programs opened up the pipeline for women and minorities to enter higher education in greater numbers. Since the mid-1970s women have had the greatest influence in changing the academic climate by introducing more high-context values into higher education.

Changes in academia after 1964 focused primarily on ad hoc student services programs designed to fit the needs of new kinds of ethnic students. None of these programs included changing the core academic cultures. Building programs for "disadvantaged minorities" was a double-edged sword for many colleges and universities. These programs were effective in creating greater access to higher education, but they also tended to separate, polarize, and marginalize ethnic minorities and others from mainstream student life and the core learning systems in academia. Many institutions perceived the conflict that arose between these populations and academic cultures as a consequence of acclimating the "educationally disadvantaged." Others saw the conflict as resulting from racism and/or sexism. The general turbulence of the late 1960s and the 1970s exacerbated sociopolitical divisiveness among ethnic minorities on campus. Political protests fostered ethnic centers and women's studies courses or departments. These catered to the needs of high-context, field-sensitive students by providing demarcated ethnic boundaries and enclaves, allowing members of these groups to physically and culturally recharge in the presence of others with similarly high-context, field-sensitive backgrounds (interpersonal synchronicity).

245

By the mid-1980s a different cohort of high-context, field-sensitive populations was beginning to enroll in higher education and continues to enter graduate school today. These high-context, field-sensitive women and ethnic individuals are less traditional than earlier student cohorts and share concerns about the low-context insularity of academic culture, which is becoming more obvious. These are the clusters of women, ethnic minorities, and even some majority males, all of whom tend to gravitate toward academic fields and issues where high-context, field-sensitive backgrounds are especially valuable. This cohort includes growing numbers of recently arrived immigrant Latino groups as well as members of long-established majority populations with high-context cultures rooted in southern Europe.

Conceptual Assumptions

Although the population cohort that began higher education in the 1980s comes from a variety of national origins, these students tend to share preferences, such as high-context academic fields. They seem unified by contextual commonalities that surface as mutual conflicts with academic cultures. For instance, these diverse populations may encounter similar performance problems on standardized tests or share similar preferences in other cognitive areas that have been hidden by identity systems that tend to pigeonhole and stereotype cultures, ethnicity, and gender. Outwardly, each group maintains distinct sociocultural patterns relating to gender and ethnicity (they are multicultural). Inwardly, these populations are also closely associated with more than one cultural context and cognitive orientation (they are multicontextual).

No single high-context, field-sensitive group or individual has all the characteristics associated with any one cultural context or cognitive orientation. If individual women and ethnic minorities were measured and plotted along a continuum of context preferences, we probably would find that they would select from both high-context, field-sensitive and low-context, field-independent categories. Plotted as groups of significant size (e.g., Mexican Americans, African Americans, women), they would tend to demonstrate more high-context, field-sensitive than low-context, field-independent characteristics with varying intensity, depending on such variables as generation or immigrant experience, gender or ethnicity, intra- and interethnic variations, class, socioeconomic status, and so on. The Fairness, Access, Multiculturalism, and Equity (FAME) analysis conducted by the Educational Testing Service in 1995 on its new testing initiatives for the GRE may hold clues to the association of cultural context and performance on standardized testing for women and certain high-context, field-sensitive ethnic minority populations. The HERI faculty survey (H. Astin et al. 1997) offers another extensive set of questions with measurable responses that may be determined by high-context, field-sensitive or low-context, field-independent characteristics.

The degree of tension and conflict with low-context, field-independent academic culture may be related to the degree of multicontextuality found in the other cultures. More tradition-laden high-context, field-sensitive cultural populations are likely to suffer more adverse effects than less tradition-laden groups. These dynamics could be described as degrees of absorbing (assimilating) or adopting (acculturating) other cultural ways, but such concepts must also account for how cultural context and cognition may permit or prevent these dynamics to take place. Context and cognition function the same way for multicontextual individuals when they adopt multiple identities (Chicana, professor, community leader) or compile appropriate behavioral episodes (teaching undergraduates, planning a fiesta, preparing for tenure review)—they filter our perception of the world. Note that the more tradition-laden high-context, field-sensitive individuals, such as Native Americans, do indeed have the greatest difficulty with the culture of higher education. Tribal populations have the lowest enrollments in higher education. This may also account for the relative paucity of Latinos in higher education in proportion to the total U.S. population of Latinos.

Clearly, socioeconomic conditions influence these dynamics, but other factors may also be in play. In *The Shape of the River,* Bowen and Bok's study relating affirmative action to minority student success, there are few explanations for why the most academically talented African American students, with the fewest reasons to feel threatened intellectually, generally underperform the most, regardless of academic potential or background (1998, 262). I believe that multicontextuality is involved. If this is true for African Americans, whose culture is less tradition laden than the cultures of Native Americans, it is plausible to assume that this is why Native Americans are less attracted to higher education than any other group. There may be a correlation between cultural context, cognition, academic conflicts, and patterns of success among various high-context groups in higher education.

Conflict between high-context, field-sensitive populations and the low-context, field-independent culture of academia has probably always been a hidden issue in higher education, albeit one attributed to other factors, such as racism and sexism, in the past. Despite cultural variations among high-context, field-sensitive populations, these groups have often been recognized by the issues they share and, for better or for worse, lumped together in generic categories. These people have not been clearly identified for at least two reasons: there were fewer of these populations in higher education before the 1980s, and the potential for seeing the influence of cultural context or cognition was masked by the dominant theoretical perspective that some kind of discrimination was the major source of conflict.

High-context, field-sensitive populations tend to choose fields of study in the humanities or social sciences more often than in the physical or biological sciences. This is not associated with inability or lack of interest in studying science, engineering, or mathematics. Poor elementary and secondary school preparation of certain socioeconomic groups may be one cause. But another reason may relate to the degree to which a given field attracts high-context, field-sensitive individuals. Clinical psychology is popular among high-context, field-sensitive people because, as an applied field, its practitioners interact with the community. For similar reasons some fields in engineering tend to attract people with ethnic backgrounds. Many fields in the humanities or social sciences are more people oriented, or are aimed more toward applied or community study (e.g., social work), than those that tend to be purely intellectual, such as philosophy. Consequently, the people-oriented fields tend to attract more high-context, field-sensitive individuals. Some evidence even suggests that multicontextuality may explain why some minority undergraduates leave their science, engineering, and math majors to complete a degree in the social sciences or humanities (Ibarra 1999).

Not all social sciences are attractive to high-context, field-sensitive populations, however. Anthropology, for instance, could attract more high-context, field-sensitive personalities because the field has, for a variety of reasons, discouraged ethnic minorities from studying their own communities. Also, it has historically valued observational research over research aimed at supporting or driving change. Professions such as law, medicine, and business are notoriously low context by design. Yet they attract high-context, field-sensitive populations in surprisingly large numbers because they offer upward mobility, prestige, and high income and have long been traditional career paths for Latin Americans. The professions also are highly people oriented, with tremendous potential for working on behalf of the community.

Studies have shown that high-context, field-sensitive populations are not leaving graduate education in large numbers. Either they are simply not attracted to it in the first place or they are only attracted to certain high-context, field-sensitive academic programs for a variety of reasons. Low-context academic cultures, and graduate education specifically, are more resistant to change than organizations in the private sector. The private sector is moving much faster and more deliberately toward diversity. As a result, high-context, field-sensitive people are lured to the private sector not only by its higher salaries and other benefits but also by the likelihood that they will have greater opportunities to influence the corporate culture, advance in their careers, and inhabit a more culturally comfortable working environment. The issue of concern for higher education, especially its nonprofessional graduate programs, is the loss of talent, which ultimately will have a detrimental effect on academia.

Higher education in the United States must prepare for the rapidly increasing numbers of high-context, field-sensitive people with undergraduate degrees. But it must first recognize, and then adjust to, the real world, which is becoming increasingly multicontextual. To survive this challenge institutions must seek ways to correct imbalances in their academic cultures and realign educational priorities in ways that will build a new and inclusive community of scholars based upon equal measures of comprehensive knowledge (concrete connected knowing and active practice) and analysis-based knowledge (abstract analytical knowing and reflective observation).

Reframing Higher Education for a Multicontextual World

If the new mission of higher education is to create a more inclusive community of scholars, we need a model for adapting to the changing cultural and demographic conditions. The following outline suggests one possibility for creating such a model, one that moves beyond the quick fix of affirmative action programs. And rather than tack it onto our institutional structures, we should use it to reframe the context of higher education to meet the needs of an emerging multicontextual world.

This model incorporates the threads of multicultural and multicontextual diversity that have never been fully integrated into academic organizational culture. Diversity is built into and incorporated systemically in this model. One important feature is its focus on academic organizational culture; it includes an interlocking involvement of the faculty, the department and/or the discipline, and student services support systems and units.

A department or program must strive to create a total environment—academic culture and tradition—that is balanced contextually and functions like a magnet to attract diverse or high-context, field-sensitive students, faculty, and staff.

The goal is to create an inclusive community of scholars by activating, expanding, and encouraging development of high-context, field-sensitive values and perspectives throughout the department, program, or institution. The guiding principles for implementing these changes require that we examine

- Academic systems to understand the cultural context of what and why people do what they do

249

- Relationships between the way academic systems are expressed (their meanings and values) and how well they are organized according to those expressed meanings and values
- Academic systems for ways to expand multicontextual experiences of teaching, learning, researching, and doing (working, managing, or administrating)
- System failures by looking first at what may be wrong with the systemic or institutional design and not by looking at what is wrong with people or their social systems
- Opportunities to put academic theories into practice in a comprehensive, systemic way by avoiding compartmentalized thinking

The process, which I would describe as "contextualizing" academic cultures, identifies or creates awareness of the concepts of multicontextuality and introduces these into appropriate academic systems without dismantling successful low-context, field-independent academic cultures or ongoing minority programs.

To contextualize an academic culture, it is first necessary to establish and initiate a campuswide process for determining the kinds or patterns of academic culture.

This process should identify departments and programs with latent potential for introducing high-context cultural values, especially in academic fields that are perceived to be low context. Good examples are traditional science departments that take self-assessment seriously and successfully strive for improvement or whose faculty are willing to try novel ideas for teaching, research, or program improvement. The process should also identify high-context–type projects or programs that can be initiated, then used as models and resources for change on campus (e.g., initiatives for renewing the civic mission of research universities; collaborative or community-based teaching and learning environments). The final part of this process is to identify departments, faculty, and programs with the abilities or the skills for developing high-context pilot projects within or even across departments and disciplines.

The second step is to recruit entrepreneurial departments, programs, and faculty willing to review and rethink both their educational tradition and faculty priorities to include high-context cultural values as much as possible. The priorities may include but are not limited to the following policies and practices:

Tenure review—Include or prioritize high-context values such as community or professional service.
Teaching and learning styles and curriculum content—Expand these to include high-context learning modes.

Research and application—Expand this area to include high-context research interests or applied research opportunities, especially in disciplines or departments that do not typically offer this (e.g., English, history, and other humanities programs).

The third step is to create or adapt successful high-context–oriented projects and implement them in appropriate academic departments and programs. For example, sociology's Minority Opportunities through School Transformation Program (MOST II) was developed and managed by the American Sociological Association, the discipline's major organization, to help change faculty culture in sociology departments around the country (the next section of this chapter provides additional details of this program); Uri Treisman's Emerging Scholars Program could be adopted, modified, and expanded for other science programs, or a school or college could apply to the U.S. Department of Education to establish and fund a Ronald E. McNair Postbaccalaureate Achievement Program, or they could create their own version of undergraduate research opportunity programs modeled after McNair programs.

The fourth step is to identify and establish contact with discipline-focused minority organizations to coordinate collaborative initiatives with departments and their major disciplinary associations. Among the most active such organizations are the Society of Hispanic Professional Engineers (SHPE); National Action Council for Minorities in Engineering (NACME); American Sociological Association (ASA); National Holmes Scholars (education); Society for the Advancement of Chicanos and Native Americans in Science (SACNAS); and the National Consortium for Graduate Degrees for Minorities in Engineering and Science (the GEM program).

Yet another step is to use ethnic studies programs (e.g., Chicano/Latino, African American, Asian American, Native American) and student service programs as learning resources and sources for developing critical knowledge. The directors of these programs can collaborate with various academic departments to introduce multicontextual awareness and needs.

It is also important to close the cultural and structural gap between minority student service programs—often identified as recruiting, retention, or remedial programs—and the departments or disciplines. These minority programs tend to reflect high-context cultures and can serve as useful new knowledge resources for instituting changes in academic culture within departments. Another tactic is to revamp add-on or ad hoc minority student service programs and other student service apparatus toward a more decentralized model by

Aligning them within the schools and colleges, or creating a semicentralized infrastructure that aligns minority student service programs and ethnic studies units within the institutional academic divisions. For example, pairing an ethnic studies program with academic divisions or departments associated with information technology could bring multicontextual influences to bear in shaping technology.

Encouraging minority student service programs to increase their involvement with faculty, departments, and the associated disciplines by using discipline-oriented minority programs, such as the MOST program, developed by other organizations.

Incorporating, linking, or interlocking community or professional service components into faculty/student programs that always combine both faculty and student cultural domains (i.e., precollege programs, summer research programs, federal TRIO programs, and so on).

Developing a checklist for high-context cultural inclusiveness in all programs and activities. The intent is to develop campus-wide expectations for cultural improvements and to begin standardizing proposal requests for projects and improvements with built-in assessments and measurable outcomes. These measures might include a determination of whether the proposal (1) is community-oriented, (2) includes multidimensional thinking, (3) is multi-contextual, and (4) is connected with the faculty, as well as how it affects academic culture, whether it includes minority student support programs and other units, and how it involves off-campus partnerships.

Encouraging transdisciplinary programs in which faculty from various disciplines and students interact with high-context culture (e.g., a biosciences and humanities forum on biotech ethics).

Involving students in these new processes and talking about their gender/culture contributions.

Fortunately, college and university campuses need not reinvent the wheel. Most institutions provide a number of offices with techniques for facilitating change.

Continuous quality improvement (CQI) models are useful for implementing systemic change, not just process change. Many institutions use or have an office or program that deals with quality improvement (QI). These concepts and associated models for strategic planning, assessing the quality of a process, and so on, contain team-oriented techniques and methods that are ideal for analyzing academic or department/discipline cultures effectively. Many talented facilitators are available to help departments and institutions determine what high-context activities they can develop. The primary objective is to determine how high-context values can be incorporated into the faculty domain of academic culture in order to enhance tenure, teaching, distance education, and methods.

Most campuses also have many talented individuals on their human resources staff or in their training and development offices that they can use wisely and proactively. These individuals or units can be essential in efforts to coordinate the critical knowledge areas (e.g., ethnic studies, minority student services programs, and other student services components), faculty, and academic staff, as well as provide necessary training.

We also need to recontextualize current initiatives and existing minority programs by

- Developing student follow-up and tracking mechanisms
- Making current minority programs a formal consideration in institutional and departmental missions, goals, and objectives
- Formalizing the developmental sequence of campus minority programs and initiatives
- Seeking ways to collaborate on administration, recruiting, programming, and assessment across the campus
- Engaging the faculty and the community in planning, instruction, and assessment
- Seeking creative suggestions and approaches to win funding for the various initiatives
- Concentrating on the establishment of quality improvement programs
- Creating strategies and multicontextual departments that offer programs not found at other similar institutions, and then advertising these advantages and cultural changes effectively to prospective students and new faculty

Finally, institutions should adopt strategic marketing and advertising plans that publicize both internally and externally the results of specific pilot projects or the changes made by specific departments that have embraced multicontextuality. The key to this strategy is to heavily promote the institutional commitment to systemic change, and that can begin with renewing institutional mission statements and strategic plans that reflect multicontextual changes. Departments or programs should be encouraged to highlight their multicontextual activities through informational channels or networks, including their own disciplinary associations. Encourage faculty to showcase their accomplishments whenever possible and encourage departments to become adept at academic promotion and publicity to specifically attract high-context populations. Create a new promotional strategy designed to publicize the "new institutional mission" and the multicontextual department as an enlightened academic culture and climate that genuinely embraces high-context values. The goal is to attract high-context students, parents, faculty, and staff to the new academic community. Redesign publications, such as recruiting materials and brochures, to appeal to high-context students, faculty, and staff. In other words, make these cultural changes a source of pride, not a necessary evil.

Emerging Academic Models for Change

As I worked on the Latino study, I introduced my preliminary ideas about multicontextuality to colleagues, whose reactions of recognition and agreement were extremely encouraging. I was especially encouraged by other Latinos in higher education who sensed these ideas hold promise for cultural understanding and change. Those discussions helped me to construct the outline for the model of multicontextuality, which also brought positive feedback. This convinced me that I was at least headed in the right direction.

At the time I thought one or two programs on other campuses had the right idea, but I could find no departments or service units that even came close to using the inclusive concepts I have described. Fortunately, things are changing and not as a result of my presentations. A handful of pilot programs, represented by academic departments, service units, and minority programs, are now emerging with what I think are the active ingredients for organizational change. These seem to have developed serendipitously, as if the time was ripe. I mention two of these briefly and offer a final story about a successful academic department to show that becoming culturally inclusive is not only possible but that it is being done right now.

The Equity, Diversity, and Resource Center

Soon after one of my early presentations to colleagues at the University of Wisconsin–Madison, Greg Vincent, an assistant vice chancellor, pulled me aside to share a similar vision for reorganization. He agreed with the idea that diversity initiatives, in this case the Affirmative Action Office, could no longer function as entities outside the mainstream of faculty culture and the professors' departmental homes throughout the schools and colleges on our campus. The Affirmative Action Office has offered professional development training opportunities for faculty, staff, graduate assistants, and students since 1980. For a long time it had been the legal arm for affirmative action compliance and equal opportunity laws.

Now Vincent was expanding the office to provide an intercultural approach to enhancing diversity that went beyond awareness and into action (Vincent et al. 1998, 1–2). Even before Vincent heard my presentation, he had set in motion a strategic plan not only to rename the office but also to reshape its vision and mission. He was about to remake the mission of the

Affirmative Action Office and weave it into the everyday life of academic departments and programs. He was planning to instill equity and diversity as core values of the university by offering to become a different kind of resource center for faculty. In fact, he wanted to rename the unit the "Equity, Diversity, and Resource Center" and henceforth use its acronym, EDRC. The goal would be diversity rather than enforcing affirmative action rules and regulations to ensure the equitable treatment of employees and students. The redesigned office and staff would also be proactive by providing training and support in these areas for offices of human resources on campus. The unit's new name would reflect

an equitable balance between [the] compliance and consultative role. This is a natural evolution from Affirmative Action, which is temporary, remedial, and artificial, to Diversity, which is natural, permanent, and organic. In the short run, however, Affirmative Action is still a necessary and effective strategy. The name change also reflects a change in focus from the tool, Affirmative Action, to the end product, Diversity. It transcends recruitment, hiring, and selection of protected group members and focuses on the development of all faculty, staff, and students. (Vincent et al. 1998, 15)

The concept was a radical redesign in two ways: it was a shift in approach from the traditional as-needed sensitivity training to faculty development that would emphasize, as the staff put it, personal reflection, viewing higher education systemically, and encouraging faculty collaboration. But the plan also represented a shift in the office's mission, from regulatory compliance to assistance and guidance, unusual even for the normally decentralized University of Wisconsin–Madison campus (1998, 7). Because these services do not usually work from within academic programs, the proposal needed a favorable vote by the Faculty Senate, which it eventually received but not without heated discussion.

Recently, EDRC has proposed to expand by developing a leadership institute that would hold workshops on intercultural communications; develop a program called "Creating a Collaborative Learning Environment" (Sanders and Carlson-Dakes 1997) to assist faculty and graduate teaching assistants; provide an arena for prospective leaders to learn new skills; and foster research that leads to academic cultural change. As the saying goes, the jury is still out on its efficacy and effectiveness, but the center gets my support as innovative and headed in the right direction. In fact, because it is the only office of its kind among peer institutions, it is already on its way to becoming a national model.

The MOST II Program

Minority Opportunities through School Transformation, better known as MOST II, began in 1990 and has been funded for a third time, through 2003. It was designed and administered by the

ASA to enhance diversity in higher education, especially graduate education and the faculty, by increasing the number of minority college graduates who enroll in graduate school. But unlike other programs with a similar mission, its basic premise is that the success of traditional pipeline models rests on the ability to create institutional transformations. That is accomplished by changing the academic culture of a discipline, by working with the department's faculty.

MOST has three objectives to help the faculty in participating sociology departments accomplish their goals: to introduce undergraduate students to research and other core activities associated with graduate education and academia as a career; to prepare each undergraduate student for graduate work in sociology and for successful admission to a graduate program; and to change academic cultures and environments (e.g., faculty, department, discipline, and institution) by transforming departments of sociology into learning communities that are diverse and diversity sensitive. This requires concentrating on five essential elements that affect institutional diversity: creating a departmental climate that is sensitive to diversity and promotes the development of all students; evaluating and redesigning the sociology curriculum in order to prepare diverse students for careers in sociology; providing all students with hands-on research experience under the guidance of faculty mentors; increasing the number of minority scholars throughout the academic pipeline and preparing minority sociologists for future leadership roles in the academy; and building department-wide mentoring systems that can enhance students' intellectual and social skills and develop their professional identity.

A number of ongoing activities engage departments and prepare them for change and transformation: an annual conference during which faculty who coordinate the program on each participating campus share information and work together to identify opportunities for and constraints in implementing MOST; workshops for faculty on developing and implementing systemic research training and mentoring of undergraduates; site visits by trained ASA staff to address unique department challenges and impediments to change, enhance common goals, clarify plans to make midcourse changes, and highlight areas of progress (1998 MOST Coordinators Conference, personal communication).

The Department of Counseling Psychology

The Department of Counseling Psychology at the University of Wisconsin–Madison has grasped the inherent concepts of the model of multicontextuality quite effectively. While visiting the department to discuss research with some faculty members, I learned that the department had been successfully trying out new ideas on its own. Soon after, an article in the official campus newspaper, *Wisconsin Week,* revealed the whole story. Almost all of what I share and quote directly comes from that piece by Jeff Iseminger (1997), an anthropologist who tells it much better than I do.

As often happens in organizations, the impetus for change came from a few key individuals. In 1992 the faculty in graduate student admissions for the Department of Counseling Psychology began talking to their colleagues about serving the growing ranks of underrepresented populations in the United States. At their annual retreat in 1995 the psychology professors decided to refocus their mission to prepare their graduate students to deliver mental health services to an increasingly diverse population, according to Bruce Wampold, then chair of the department and one of the key faculty initiators. The purpose of the retreat was to set a new strategic plan and build an infrastructure in three specific areas: curriculum, climate, and selection (of both students and faculty).

These represented significant changes to the department's structure and cultural context. It was not enough to simply add a diversity dimension to existing courses. Iseminger reports that "faculty members looked at the curriculum to see how diversity issues could be integrated into all courses, not just an isolated class on multicultural counseling." Wampold incorporated diversity in his seminar on research techniques. "One of the things I ask students is how research design is complicated by factors of ethnicity," he said. In a recent conversation he added that rather than have his students consider whether research studies are valid across ethnic cultures, he has them examine each study design to consider the influence of Western teaching values. Some students are surprised by what they find because they never viewed research this way, whereas others find validation in the exercise because it meshes with their own perspective. Further curriculum changes have meant faculty members have to share details of their courses with each other, an act almost unheard of because most faculty defend their autonomy with their lives. "To nurture a climate as fluid and dynamic as diversity itself," Iseminger reports, "an outside facilitator helps faculty address diversity issues before the start of each school year."

The new process for selecting graduate students and hiring new faculty requires that all applicants demonstrate their eagerness to serve and study a diverse population, regardless of their age, gender, or ethnicity. Anyone not prepared to do so may not be selected by the department. The final and most important change was to emphasize and promote the department's uniqueness. The department's new brochures proclaim that its doctoral programs place "more emphasis on the multicultural aspects" of counseling psychology than other doctoral programs in the field.

The result of the new strategic plan has been that in 1997 the department's graduate program was ranked fifth nationally by *U.S. News and World Report* (by 1998 it was ranked third and has remained in the top six ever since—see "The Best Graduate Schools" 1997–2000.) The department claims it has become more diverse: by 1997, 24 percent of the students were minority; 5 percent had disabilities; students' ages ranged from twenty-two to fifty-five; two out of nine faculty were African American and two others were Latino. While some of these figures, such as the faculty profile, have not changed since 1997, others have changed dramatically, according to the department. By early in the year 2000, 42 percent of the graduate students were members of minority groups. Best of all, the faculty says, the quality of its graduate students has risen. The department chooses only six to eight doctoral students and twenty to twenty-five master's candidates each year, but its huge applicant pool of three to four hundred suggests that each student finalist is highly qualified and that the number of students who want to serve and study diverse populations appears to be increasing. Meanwhile the national pool of students seeking to enter graduate programs in counseling psychology has shrunk for all programs, but the program at Wisconsin has not seen any decrease in the number of minority applicants. "People want to come here," says Wampold. According to Iseminger, "The department has attracted so much national attention that faculty are asked to speak at conferences as representatives of a model program." New minority faculty in the department seem to agree. One described conditions that stand in stark contrast to what most Latino faculty members told me about their various departments around the country. At Madison this new faculty member could see diversity reflected in the faculty and students and see faculty open to change. She could teach new courses and would be encouraged to pursue new research on ethnicity as well. The highest compliment came when I asked a member of the department for a confidential assessment of the accuracy of Iseminger's article. The answer: "Yes! Every bit of it is true."

To what does the department attribute its success? According to Hardin Coleman, an associate professor, the faculty was aware that its critics thought the new approach would hurt the department, but Coleman believes it actually has enhanced its reputation: "We were successful because we did not set out to fill a quota, but focused on how we could create a department that prepared counselors to work with diverse populations and therefore became a magnet for students and faculty committed to these concerns." In other words, it is attracting more high-context, field-sensitive students and faculty.

These are only a few of the alternatives to the traditional ways of doing things that are now materializing from our traditional academic cultures. In each case individuals have been motivated to increase diversity by changing academic culture in a specific way: by creating a resource center for the academic departments that emphasizes equity and diversity; by inviting the faculty to interact and redesign a systemic model for preparing students for graduate schools; or by simply deciding to change the cultural values and the mission of a department to meet the future demands of the population its discipline serves. But making the curriculum more attuned to ethnic and gender values does not need to be the prime objective. Simply rethinking how to prepare for the new kinds of students now entering our graduate and undergraduate programs is enough to begin reframing the context of how we teach and learn and do research. It is not a question of whether form follows function or function follows form; either way will achieve the same results—organizational cultural change. Given the short time it took for each of these examples to achieve some significant results, it may not even be the slow process I have always assumed it would be.

The answers are all around us, but they are hidden by the larger, more entrenched mental maps about how we should view the world and what we think higher education should be. Taking the time to observe carefully what we have accomplished with our graduate research model is important. Our advanced technology, medicine, and science are still marvels of Western analytical thinking. Equally important, however, is what we do not see, or what does not appear to be there between the words, within the white spaces of academia. We are caught at a cultural crossroads with a one-dimensional vision of the future. We have yet to comprehend the multicontextual world that looms out there and exists in shadows all around us. That concept could unlock enormous untapped potential in human diversity and new critical knowledge. I believe this will happen when academia sees how different thinking and learning styles contribute important variations of scientific knowledge and understanding.

Appendixes
Notes
References
Index

Appendix 1

Institutions Attended by Interviewees

American University
Arizona State University
Bowie State College
Brown University
California State University at Fresno
California State University at Los Angeles
Catholic University of America
Claremont Graduate University
Columbia University
Florida State University
George Washington University
Georgetown University
La Salle University
Lehigh University
Long Island University, Brooklyn Center
Louisiana State University–A&M College (Baton Rouge)
Marquette University
North Texas State University
Pan American University
Pennsylvania State University–Capitol
Pennsylvania State University
Princeton University
San Jose State University
Southwest Texas State University
Stanford University
State University of New York at New Paltz
State University of New York at Stony Brook
Stetson University

Teachers College
Texas A&M University
Texas A&M University–Corpus Christi
Texas A&M University–Kingsville
Texas Woman's University
University of Arizona
University of California, Berkeley
University of California, Davis
University of California, Los Angeles
University of California, Santa Barbara
University of California, Santa Cruz
University of Colorado at Boulder
University of Colorado at Colorado Springs
University of Florida
University of Houston
University of Iowa
University of Maryland, College Park
University of Miami
University of New Mexico
University of Pittsburgh
University of Puerto Rico
University of Southern California
University of Texas at Austin
University of Texas at San Antonio
University of Virginia
University of Wisconsin–Madison
Yale University
York University (U.K.)

Appendix 2

Graduate Enrollment
1986–1996

Graduate enrollment by ethnicity, 1986–1996 (U.S. citizens and permanent residents only)

	1996	% of total	% change 1995–1996	Average annual % change 1986–1996
Total U.S.	951,750	100	−1	1
Men	383,044	46	−3	1
Women	515,167	54	−1	2
African American	73,635	8	2	6
Men	23,045	6	0	5
Women	47,086	9	3	6
American Indian	5,638	1	3	4
Men	2,238	1	3	4
Women	3,056	1	2	5
Asian	51,132	5	4	7
Men	24,644	6	2	6
Women	23,522	5	8	10
Hispanic/Latino	47,699	5	5	7
Men	18,235	5	2	6
Women	26,182	5	7	9
White	773,646	81	−2	1
Men	314,882	82	−4	0
Women	415,321	81	−2	1

Source: CGS/GRE Survey of Graduate Enrollment, modified from Syverson and Welch (1997), *Graduate Enrollment and Degrees, 1986–1996,* table 1.5, p. 10, and table 2.4, p. 28.

Note: The Council of Graduate Schools and the Graduate Record Exam surveyed approximately 680 member institutions representing 71 percent of all U.S. graduate student enrollment. Because not all institutions responded to all items, variables may not total 100. Percentages are based on total of U.S. citizens and permanent residents.

Appendix 3

Latino Faculty Issues

Major concerns of Latino faculty

Issue	Responses (120)	Description
Campus culture & climate	**44**	(Men tended to use the word *culture,* and women tended to use the word *climate.*)
Gender issues	14	Various personal issues (e.g., hostile Latino males; most Latino faculty are male) and academic/personnel issues (e.g., women had lower salaries than men).
Racism, classism, and tokenism	9	Others "made life difficult"; overt and covert discriminatory activities persist.
Intracultural issues	5	Issues between Latino groups (e.g., Puerto Ricans are not considered minorities in California; citizens are mistaken for immigrants; Puerto Ricans feel dominated by Cubans; Cubans are divided by their stance on Castro).
Lack of support groups	5	Latinos are not supportive of each other; lack department support; are discouraged from meeting by administrators who feel threatened; feel uncomfortable or do not feel welcome among senior faculty; may feel disconnected from the institution.

Issue	Responses (120)	Description
Interethnic issues	4	Cultural conflicts that occur mainly between non-Latino minority groups and Latinos (can include Anglos); a frequent concern is that only African Americans are considered minorities on campus.
Concerns about affirmative action	4	Twenty-one participants mentioned the term *affirmative action,* but only four discussed this issue of concern.
Internationals versus U.S. Latinas/os	2	Misperceptions between international faculty and U.S. minority populations.
Struggles for Chicano or Latino studies programs	1	Issues involving ethnic identity and preserving or maintaining recognition on campus, in the curriculum, and in academe.
Recruitment	**37**	
Hiring problems	20	The number of Latinas/os on the faculty is disproportionately lower than that of other minorities and student enrollments; low or negligible institutional commitment; conservative departments that do not believe in hiring minority candidates.
Retention issues	8	Not enough department or institutional money to retain Latinos; budget problems that affect retention; observing a "revolving door" with Latinos leaving; morale issues: Latinos believe that in comparison to Anglos they are grossly underpaid and/or receive significantly lower salaries for doing the same job.
Promotion problems	5	Latinos have to work harder for promotions than other faculty, including some minority faculty.

Continued on next page

Latino Faculty Issues

Issue	Responses (120)	Description
Mentoring	3	Lack of faculty mentoring, advice, information, or experience.
Part-timers	1	Too many part-time Latina/o faculty, and they are abused; concerns about rising number of adjuncts.
Tenure & research	**31**	
The "minority burden"	13	Latino professors are overloaded with minority academic activities (e.g., committee work, advising) or courses.
Problems in the tenure process	11	Not enough Latinos are getting tenure or promotions; too many denials of tenure or promotions.
Self-defeating issues affecting research and tenure	4	Concerns that Latina/os have low or no research/publication activity; Latinos place too much emphasis on teaching or community work, or they get side-tracked too soon into minority affairs or administration.
Problems concerning ethnic research	3	Ethnic or minority journals are rejected or discounted by mainstream faculty; Latinos avoid being labeled "Hispanic scholars"—stigma associated with minority scholarship.
Governance	**8**	
Few or no Latinos in upper management	5	This pattern also occurs at some Hispanic Serving Institutions and at many Catholic universities.
Latinos lack political power	3	Little influence internally (e.g., Latinos are infrequently selected for search committees) or externally in the community.

Note: Table formatting by John Center, St. Thomas University

Notes

1. Critical Junctures for Change

1. The Spanish term *Latino* refers to people who represent a superset of nationalities originating from, or having a heritage related to, Latin America. Though most individuals in the United States use a pan-ethnic or pan-national identifier to identify themselves by a specific U.S. ethnic category (e.g., Mexican American, Puerto Rican, etc.), most use the term *Latino* rather than *Hispanic,* a term made up by the Nixon administration for ethnic, political, and bureaucratic reasons. Many authors use variations, such as "Latinos/as" or "Latinas/os" to reflect gender-based inclusiveness, which they even incorporate in direct quotes. However, for linguistic consistency and ease of reading, I will use plurals where possible, as well as both masculine and feminine forms of the word in the singular.

2. Unless I am quoting someone directly, I use the term *majority* rather than *white.* Unless I specify otherwise, the term *minority* represents the following terms: *African American; Native American* or *Alaskan Native; Asian American* or *Asian Pacific American; Hispanic,* or *Latino.* Furthermore, unless I am quoting directly, I will not use the terms *black, brown,* or *people of color*—or any other terms that refer to racial or skin-color distinctions. I avoid using these distinctions because they contribute to the continuation of misguided assumptions that certain groups of people are inherently genetically superior or inferior based on the color of their skin.

The term *minority,* as I use it here, "refers to an ethnic group occupying a subordinate position in a multiethnic society, suffering from the disabilities of prejudice and discrimination, and maintaining a separate group identity" (Gibson 1997, 318). Though I use this term frequently, I do so with some reluctance. In our society it is a ubiquitous generic term that delineates and allocates power and status between dominant privileged ethnic groups of people, in the so-called majority, from less-dominant, underprivileged ethnic groups, in the so-called minority. As such, the term carries an inherent social stigma of disadvantage. Unfortunately, it also has become a euphemism for the concept of *ethnicity* as used by nearly everyone, and it is frequently misused by interchanging it with terms for particular ethnic groups, mainly African Americans. However, I use the term *minority* rather than terms that differentiate people by so-called skin color. Although the term does not adequately describe people who are not in the majority, and it inherently aggregates ethnic groups, it is most commonly understood to mean people not of the majority.

3. Data taken from D. Carter and O'Brien 1993; D. Carter and Wilson 1995, 1997; de los Santos and Rigual 1994; Hodgkinson and Outtz 1996; Ibarra 1996; National Science Foundation et al. 1999; O'Brien 1993; Ottinger, Sikula, and Washington 1993; President's Advisory Commission 1996; Wilds and Wilson 1998.

4. The term *Anglo,* according to the tenth edition of *Merriam Webster's Collegiate Dictionary,* is a shortened version of *Anglo-American* and refers to "a white inhabitant of the U.S. of non-Hispanic descent." I use the term as a synonym for *majority* and *white.*

5. The fieldwork and data collection were funded by the Ford Foundation and the postfieldwork phase was supported by both the Council of Graduate Schools and my home institution, the University of Wisconsin–Madison. I interviewed seventy-seven individuals in person or by telephone in two separate but interrelated studies completed between 1994 and 1997. I recorded all interviews on audiotape and promised that I would disguise participants' identities. The interviews were conducted in English; only a few participants responded in Spanish during portions of their interview. The study used two types of interview formats: individual private interviews and focus groups. The private interviews involved sixty-seven participants in private sessions that lasted ninety minutes or more with a primary set of seventy questions. I interviewed in two separate locations the remaining ten individuals in two-hour focus groups that I conducted with a much smaller subset of the seventy primary questions that I administered to graduate students. The questions were designed to obtain both qualitative and quantitative information to generate profiles on family and educational experiences from kindergarten through college graduation and graduate school. Full-time faculty, administrators, and non-academics were asked additional sets of questions depending on their career path. Unless otherwise indicated, the numerical data on interview subjects come from the sixty-seven individual interviews collected in the study (see Ibarra 1996).

In my 1996 monograph I included large portions of interview responses in order to highlight participants' concerns about graduate school in general and Latino culture in particular. I forgo that format here because of space limitations. Although I use some exchanges from the interviews verbatim, albeit sparingly, I change the participants' names and alter other information about them to protect their anonymity. As an additional safeguard, none of the fictitious names duplicates the real name of any participant.

6. This study uses specific terms to denote the relative size of a group of respondents who expressed particular perspectives or described similar experiences. These terms, called verbal quantifiers, are *a few*—up to 10 percent; *some*—10 to 25 percent; *many*—25 to 50 percent; *a majority*—50 to 75 percent; *most*—75 to 90 percent; and *virtually all*—90 percent or more. This format is fashioned after a similar model used by the Learning through Evaluation, Adaptation, and Dissemination (LEAD) Center at the University of Wisconsin–Madison.

2. The Latino Study

1. For readers who want more in-depth social profiles of Latino populations, a variety of excellent sources cover a range of literature, from popular studies (for example, Augenbraum and Stavans 1993; Heyck 1994; Santiago 1993; Shorris 1992; Stavans 1995; Suro 1998) to more academic social science (for example, Firmat 1994; Keefe and Padilla 1987; Limón 1994; Moore and Pachon 1985; Saldívar 1990; Sánchez Korrol 1993; Zambrana 1995), among others.

2. "The Women's Movement among Latinos has created additional permutations. Women activists have insisted on reading the term *Latino* in a very narrow sense as referring only to the male members of the species. They have thus forced a change in general usage and in the names of many programs to *Latina/o, Latina/Latino* and to *Chicana/o* or *Chicana/Chicano.* Males who resist the change on the basis that the original term is comprehensive and inclusive (the way that *Mexicano* refers to all Mexicans, including the females) are considered retrograde male chauvinists by the more feminist females" (Cuello 1996, 4). Thus I will use the terms *Chicano, Chicanola,* or *Chicana/o* interchangeably here to represent the current transition from gender-fixed terms to gender-inclusive terms in English. Except when quoting other authors, I will use the term *Mexican American* to denote this ethnic cohort. Calling oneself Mexican American or Chicana/o depends largely upon individual preference, as determined by such factors as political viewpoint, geographic location, generation, or social context. In general, the term *Mexican American* reflects ethnic culture and national origin, whereas *Chicano* or *Chicana* adds the ingredients of political awareness and socioeconomic struggle. For some Mexican American respondents in the study, the terms were so highly contextual that usage verged on identity switching. Among all Latinos I interviewed, a few described shifting ethnic terms to accommodate the situation. A majority were Mexican American. This is a salient point, for the chameleon-like behavior may reflect survival strategies under challenging conditions for Mexican Americans as well as "Other Latinos" (Ibarra 1996).

3. One problem in comparing data in higher education is the time it takes to collect, analyze, and publish the data. For instance, data on total student enrollment figures in higher education are subject to so many variables, such as different timing for semester and quarter systems, that they are not useful for reporting national patterns or trends during the year. Consequently, institutional data collected by various federal reporting agencies are not analyzed until complete, which may take some time after the end of each academic year. Because organizations need time to analyze and produce their reports, by the time the latest data are available, they can be at least two years old.

4. *Current Population Reports,* the Census Bureau publication that describes the U.S. population statistically, uses information collected in the fifty states and the District of Columbia but excludes data from Puerto Rico and other U.S. protectorates.

5. Hiring minorities with master's degrees also helps to increase faculty diversity, especially at community colleges and some four-year teaching institutions. But

tracking master's degree recipients is not a traditional way to gauge faculty diversity. At research universities, where the bulk of faculty members receive their advanced degrees, master's degrees are simply a step toward achieving the doctoral degree. In fact, until the 1990s, when graduate schools recognized that the new popularity of master's programs offered a fresh source of revenue, most doctoral programs considered the master's a consolation prize for those who were unsuccessful in the quest for a doctoral degree (Conrad, Haworth, and Millar 1993). Because the master's degree was traditionally not considered a final or terminal degree, and it was not considered a measure of success, the systems for tracking master's recipients are still an unreliable way to measure faculty diversity.

6. "Immigrant Norwegian" culture, which I would directly compare with the different ethnic groups of Latinos today, is usually associated with an older generation of retired farmers and families living in or near the city of Westby. Their lives reflect nearly all the cultural artifacts, symbols, and activities associated with the early immigrant culture in the community. "Rural American" culture is predominantly English, as is the common language driving all the social, educational, government, and economic systems, including agricultural activities typical of modern dairy farms across the Midwest. The most concentrated celebration of rural American culture is best represented by the annual county fairs. In addition to the rides and entertainment, fairs offer a full schedule of competitive events in which judges select the best of everything produced locally, from food to farm animals. Other contests pit individuals against one another in strength of their tractors, horses, and even the beauty of local young women in the traditional pageantry of rural America. "Commercialized Norwegian" culture is a fairly recent transformation that emerged roughly in the late 1960s during a renaissance of ethnic celebrations in this country. This transformation was spotlighted locally by community efforts to remodel all city storefronts with stylized Norwegian trappings to attract tourism and boost the local economy. The highlight of it all is Syttende Mai, an annual ethnic folk festival that is still being held in the community each May 17 and showcases all three cultural adaptations simultaneously.

3. Multicontextuality

1. In the historical context Edgar Beckham (1997) makes the only convincing argument for continuing the use of the term *race*. He writes: "What needs to be remembered, or perhaps learned for the first time, is that the biology of race has little relevance today. But race, like sex and ethnicity, has been used to construct history, and the constructed history remains and continues to exert influence on identity and culture even after the notion of race that originally informed it has lost credibility" (58). However, although I agree that the constructed historical context set the original debate about race in regard to African Americans, the term remains encased in biological determinism. In other words, race has also been used to construct a biological/historical context in which the concept of race, and the biological determinism associated with it, is still embedded in the social context of the term used today. Therefore, race is assumed to be genetically determined and thus incapable of change. The debate, or agenda, was not set by the "racial/

ethnic" populations involved. Therefore, it would be more fruitful to shift the debate, and simultaneously the agenda, away from a loaded term that has no actual meaning today and toward cultural concepts, which are amenable to change, are not biologically determined, and are not an agenda for anyone.

2. The American Anthropological Association (AAA) has even challenged the federal government regarding the recent redefinition of racial and ethnic categories and the continued misuse of the term *race* in the census (see American Anthropological Association 1997; Moses 1997; Mukhopadhyay and Moses 1997; Overbey 1997). The AAA challenge came in response to a report from the Office of Management and Budget (OMB 1997). AAA recommended further that "ethnic origin," or another similar phrase, be used in lieu of the term *race* to categorize and track U.S. populations (AAA 1997). In its final report, OMB, which became involved in the controversy at the behest of Congress, recommended that Hispanics/Latinos be permitted to identify themselves by national origin (e.g., Mexican, Puerto Rican, Cuban), *and* by racial heritage (e.g., white, black, and so on) (U.S. Census Bureau 1999). The final report recommended that the current racial and ethnic distinctions be continued.

3. Pedro's example, "the bullet fell," in fact shows he prefers to write in the third person rather than in the first person to describe action, not in the passive voice. But his grammatical style reveals hidden cultural differences that have important implications for Latino success in academia. Like many Latino populations in this country, most Mexicans believe that fate is a strong influence in the course of people's lives and that individuals have little control when fate intervenes. According to Heusinkveld, "This concept is reinforced linguistically with an interesting grammatical construction that shifts the blame away from the speaker in cases of carelessness or forgetfulness. In Spanish, there is no way to say, 'I ran out of milk.' Rather, Hispanics say, 'The milk ran out on me.' . . . There is no verb in Spanish meaning 'to drop' (as in, 'Whoops—I dropped the vase'). The closest one can come is to say, 'I let the vase fall'" (1994, 22). Though Pedro learned how less visible Mexican cultural values can cause him serious academic harm, it is not clear whether he understood how cultural differences in language go well beyond differences in grammar.

4. Both Edward Hall and Mildred Reed Hall greatly expanded this avenue of research by working outside the United States, especially among Asian and Japanese cultures (Hall and Hall 1990). In fact, Hall's popularity soared among American business executives, who found his work in Japan invaluable for preparing themselves and their organizations for doing business there during the early 1980s (see Djursaa 1994; Gesteland 1996; Ting-Toomey 1985). Training executives for international business, and his related research and publications from that activity, may have reduced his popularity among traditional anthropologists, who typically shunned applied work, especially in the multinational corporate world.

5. Hall lists ten primary message systems:

Interaction—Refers to various forms of communication such as speech, tone of voice, gesture, writing, and so on
Association—Defines the various ways in which societies and their components are organized or structured

Subsistence—Reflects more than just food: implies social values and message systems regarding the nature of labor and work

Gender—Describes sexual differentiation; reflects group beliefs about masculinity and femininity (Instead of the term *gender,* Hall actually uses *bisexuality,* which in 1959 was commonly used to mean "sexual dimorphism or differentiation" between the two sexes. Today, its common usage has shifted almost entirely to refer to people who have sexual relationships with both men and women. Because I believe this was not Hall's original meaning, I will substitute *gender* wherever he uses *bisexuality.*)

Territoriality—Encompasses the use of space in all aspects life: status, work place, play, defense, and the like

Temporality—Incorporates the concepts of time, including speech tempos, social cycles, life rhythms, and so forth

Learning and acquisition—Means "learning how to learn" processes, principles, values, beliefs, assumptions, cognitive styles, and the like embedded within cultures

Play—Reflects values regarding time and place, relationships, learning, humor, competition, defense, and so on

Defense—Refers to mechanisms for survival, coping, warfare, beliefs systems; religion, laws, medicine, and other professional specialities

Exploitation—Refers to the material extensions of the body, such as tools, clothes, houses, technology, goods, and so forth (1959, 45–60)

6. However, when Latinos choose to be become more aggressive in academic settings, the results can be overpowering. Enrique, a Latino professor in the Southwest, attributes his overly aggressive approach to graduate school as an attempt to overcome the "passive Latino" stereotype. He said he buried himself in his work and criticized colleagues "with a vengeance" until someone told him to take it easy (Ibarra 1996, 41–42).

7. During the 1960s, "low income" referred mainly to ethnic minorities before that phrase became popular.

8. Although the authors do not delve deeply into the subject of right- and left-brain studies and bicognition, it is apparent that the attributes of brain hemispheres in humans are directly associated with learning and education (see Hall 1977, 1984; L. Williams 1983). Although the topic is interesting and relevant, it can lead the discussion far off the main point and into neuroscience and brain physiology, so I will make only a few comments about it here. Briefly, we know that the left cerebral hemisphere of the human brain controls the right part of the body and perceives the right visual field, while the right hemisphere controls the left part of the body and perceives the left visual field. We also know that each hemisphere has a different point of view, so to speak. Individuals with a damaged or disabled right side of the brain can still see a picture with their left side and identify an image as a car or a dog. But individuals who can use only the right side of their brain could only identify the car or the dog visually, for the left side of the brain contains the ability to speak (1983). We have also learned that the left hemisphere is involved in tasks that require memorization, rote learning, analytical

reasoning, and linear logic, characteristics associated with low-context cultures and/or field-independent individuals, whereas the right hemisphere is associated with intuition, visualization, spatial manipulation of objects, organizing and synthesizing scattered bits of information, and spontaneity, all characteristics associated with high-context cultures and/or field-sensitive individuals.

My view is that bicognition and cultural context go hand in hand with right- and left-brain attributes, "each working in quite a different way, but in tandem; each supplying an essential element in virtually any communication" (Hall 1984, 60). Learned patterns of behavior or stimuli, imprinted perhaps even before birth, develop or facilitate the dominance of one side over the other. I would argue that the physiological characteristics associated with brain hemispheres are the biological foundations for exhibiting and storing learned patterns of cultural behavior that, compared to brain hemispheres, have broader and more far-reaching influences on individual preferences. Cultures with values that tend to favor high-context, field-sensitive attributes will likely imprint or shape to a relatively large degree those same values in individuals who are raised by parents, families, and communities that share and reinforce those values and beliefs in daily life. This does not mean, however, that every individual will share or continue to hold all these same values and beliefs, for I argue here that individuals can change their value systems to some greater or lesser extent. In the same way that individuals can change to some extent the functioning characteristics of brain hemispheres when one is disabled, the dominant characteristics of brain hemispheres can be changed or enhanced by learning and practicing to perceive and do things with both brain hemispheres equally. This combination of physiological and culturally learned characteristics, I believe, is the basis of multicontextuality.

Discoveries in the neurosciences in the 1990s have given us an enormous and important body of literature on the functioning of the brain. The problem with pursuing this discussion here is that despite all the findings, we have little theory that connects or interprets them for educators. "No scientist has yet come up with a coherent set of ideas about how the brain works that would be persuasive and usable for those of us who teach" (Marchese 1997, 4).

9. Many educators can identify patterns of cultural context as learning styles from the works of James Anderson and Maurianne Adams (1992), Howard Gardner (1983), David Kolb (1981), and others. But the application of cultural context here extends far beyond the concepts contained in learning styles described by these scholars. The goal here is to closely examine new applications of these concepts to our academic and organizational cultures. One observation about educational research in general is that the scope of theoretical applications is usually limited to specific learning environments in our educational systems. Cultural context and cognitive differences, for instance, have been recognized in the classroom and in student learning, yet these ideas are rarely applied beyond the classroom or lecture hall. My question is, why has this knowledge not been expanded or extrapolated for dealing with these issues in our communities or in other institutions? Women and ethnic populations, such as Latinos, have struggled through our educational systems in part because few researchers have recognized that such patterns also govern social discourse and that they could be embedded in our organizational systems, causing other problems as well. That blind spot in American

higher education has contributed to significant problems for women and minorities as they adjust to our campus environments and our seminar rooms. Some educators try to redesign their educational environments to accommodate the strengths and weaknesses of different types of learners—auditory, visual, abstract, concrete, group or individual, and so on. But when class is over, Latinos, among others, find themselves in a world of academic systems that is structured to accommodate low-context cultures rather than their own.

4. The Graduate School Experience

1. The terms *climate* and *culture* are often used interchangeably, and from an anthropological perspective they are almost always used inaccurately. According to Sandler, Silverberg, and Hall, the term *climate* came from a report on women in education published by the National Association of Women in Education (NAWE): "In 1982, Roberta M. Hall and Bernice R. Sandler wrote the first comprehensive report on women who are often treated differently than men in the classroom. They coined the term 'chilly climate' to describe the myriad small inequities that by themselves seem unimportant, but taken together create a chilling environment" (1996, 1).

Trice and Beyer tell us that in the early 1970s *organizational climate* originally referred to psychological environments in which human behaviors occurred and that climate studies were meant to measure cognitive attitudes but not necessarily structures, values, norms, or beliefs (1993, 19). Today, *climate,* as defined by Peterson and Spencer, is "the current common pattern of important dimensions of organizational life or its members' perceptions of and attitudes toward those dimensions" (1990, 7). Climate studies (see Baird 1990) gauge how individuals perceive the social interactions in an organization and are especially important on a campus, where volatile situations can surface quickly and cause lasting repercussions, even irreparable social damage. The differences between *culture* and *climate* lie between deeply held meanings, beliefs, and values versus current perceptions and attitudes. It becomes a matter of values versus atmosphere or style. The distinction is important in creating institutional change. Climate is simply a manifestation of often deeply ingrained cultural values. To create fundamental organizational change, you change the values that generate the atmosphere, a simple and logical approach that many people overlook when seeking to institute reforms.

2. Although I did not intend this project as a comparative study of Latino and majority graduate students, a handful of relatively recent publications, such as Melvin Williams and Brian Price (1993) and especially Weisbard (1997) offered examples of majority graduate student experiences for comparison with Latinos. I also found a few limited and informal opportunities to make these comparisons using material from my 1996 monograph on Latinos in graduate education and from a chapter in progress for this book. After I completed the monograph, I invited two majority graduate students to read and comment upon the Latino and Latina experiences described in that manuscript. King Alexander, then a doctoral student who was finishing his dissertation in higher educational administration at

the University of Wisconsin–Madison, and Tona Williams, a UW–Madison candidate for a master's degree in education with an interest in ethnic and gender groups, read a final draft. I encouraged both to comment about the cultural or gender differences they saw between the Latino experiences and their own. Although Williams found more common ground with the gender issues described by Latinas in graduate school, both she and Alexander said that Latinos in the study had encountered a variety of cultural differences that they did not.

3. I have negotiated a number of conflicts between Latino undergraduates and Latino faculty. One Latino professor, born and raised in Spain, would occasionally contact me. In impeccable Spanish he would share his frustration and show his disdain for "those island Puerto Rican students" in his course who couldn't speak the language properly, let alone use it to pass his language class. Shortly after I would hear from the professor, an angry student would come to my office and claim this professor was racist, hated all Puerto Ricans, and failed them every time they took his course. The problem, as I saw it then, was really a mismatch in class, culture, and academic backgrounds. This situation was not unlike what would undoubtedly result if an Oxford don were hired to teach grammar to an American freshman raised in the Bronx. The University of Wisconsin–Madison learned over time that, just as many Americans find the rules of English grammar and usage to be utterly mystifying, Latinos fluent in Spanish can become quite lost in upper-level Spanish classes. Today the university offers Spanish classes for native Spanish speakers that are similar to the English language and composition classes designed to provide students with a minimum level of proficiency and that are required of almost all first-year undergraduates.

5. "They Really Forget Who They Are"

1. Hispanic Serving Institutions (HSIs) are accredited colleges and universities at which Latinos comprise at least 25 percent of the total enrollment at the graduate or undergraduate level. Although the Hispanic Association of Colleges and Universities (HACU), a nonprofit national association, was founded in 1986 to represent HSIs, it was not until the 1992 reauthorization of the Higher Education Act that the federal government, through the U.S. Department of Education, formally recognized HSIs. HSI status now qualifies these institutions to apply for special federal grants and related assistance to improve and expand their capacity. By the end of 1999 approximately 145 HSIs were located in ten states, primarily in the Southwest and Puerto Rico.

2. Colleges and universities in the United States are categorized under the Carnegie Classification system. Adopted nationally, the system "groups institutions into categories on the basis of the level of degree offered, ranging from prebaccalaureate to the doctorate, and the comprehensiveness of their mission" (Boyer 1990, 129–30). The nine categories in descending order are Research Universities I; Research Universities II; Doctorate-granting Universities I; Doctorate-granting Universities II; Comprehensive Universities and Colleges I; Comprehensive Universities and Colleges II; Liberal Arts Colleges I; Liberal Arts Colleges II; Two-

Year Community, Junior, and Technical Colleges. Because of changes in institutions of higher education (for example, virtual universities, or cyberschools), the classification system was being revised as this book went to press.

6. Latinos and Latinas Encountering the Professoriate

1. The frequency or number of responses in this chapter reflect a small but representative sample of Latino and Latina faculty from across the country whose answers may or may not correlate with the findings of other quantitative studies. Although these responses may well be representative of a majority of Latinos and Latinas in academia and beyond, the small size of the sample means we cannot use them as quantitative benchmarks for measuring and gauging a Latino point of view in general.

2. Readers should note that, unlike the questions I asked about graduate school experiences, I did not consistently ask all respondents, nor did each specifically respond to, every question about faculty, administrative, or nonacademic experience. Consequently, my calculations reflect the actual number who responded to a particular question, with the percentages generated accordingly. There are two reasons for this shift in protocol: first, because the intention of the study was to gauge graduate students' experiences, interviews of faculty and administrators were mainly for the purpose of obtaining feedback about their postgraduate years and for obtaining a more cross-generational perspective wherever possible. Therefore, the questioning was not specifically focused on collecting all the details about Latino or Latina faculty, administrative, or nonacademic experiences. Also, interviewing of faculty and administrators required additional sets of questions that expanded the primary focus and tended to extend interviews beyond the allotted time. Thus the second reason for skipping questions intermittently during this portion of the interview was to allow for flexibility to pursue other directions or interesting information as it surfaced yet remain within a reasonable time limit for the interview.

3. What Beto describes here as "hypersensitivity to white culture" is also being studied as a phenomenon called "stereotype threat." Research by Steele and Aronson (1995) shows that minority student achievement can be influenced negatively and standardized test performance can drop specifically for African American students simply as a result of reinforced negative self-fulfilling stereotypes that one's group is commonly perceived as incapable of performing well compared to others.

4. On our campuses the phenomenon of interpersonal synchrony manifests in a variety of ways. The most common are associated with student demands that authorities provide multicultural centers and separate residence halls. Misunderstanding these unconscious needs for culturally synchronizing body rhythms, Anglos interpret what they observe as an inordinate need for "groupness" among ethnic minorities. The danger is that ethnic segregation and balkanization will occur on our campuses if authorities misinterpret the importance of interpersonal synchrony, or they fail to adequately accommodate the needs of high-context ethnic populations.

5. The authors' unpublished results were compiled from a mailed survey of

deans listed in the 1991 *Council of Graduate Schools Directory.* The 310 respondents represented an 85 percent response rate. Among them, 267, or about 81 percent, were Anglo, 36 were African American (11 percent), 1 Native American (0.05 percent), 9 Asian American (3 percent), and 12 (3.5 percent) Latino. Some of their findings on minorities showed the following patterns:

- Minority deans are more likely to be found at the assistant dean level, and they are likely to have student service functions rather than academic functions.
- Minority deans are less likely to have doctoral degrees.
- Minority deans tend to be appointed rather than the product of a "search" process. Majority deans tend to be hired as the result of an "in-house search."
- Minority deans are less likely to have faculty rank and tenure.
- Minority deans' salaries tend to be lower, a function of their years in higher education and the lack of doctoral degree and/or faculty rank.
- Majority deans are less sure of their end-of-career position aspirations, and they have greater desire than minority deans to return to faculty positions. (M. Clark, Gill, and Duby 1991, 2)

6. Tierney and Bensimon suggest that faculty socialization has four binary dimensions (1996, 38–42): faculty autonomy versus administrative teamwork; faculty specialization versus administrative generalization; academic affairs versus student affairs; fixed versus variable promotional events.

7. My 1996 publication on Latinos in graduate education referred to a special run of unique faculty survey data generated by the Higher Education Research Institute (HERI). It suggests that between 1989 and 1990 Latino undergraduate faculty across the country were more involved in ethnic research and studies than any other population in academia (see Ibarra 1996). I thought the data could help gauge cultural context and said so in the Latino study I published in 1996. But I subsequently learned it could not be used to gauge cultural context. A new HERI faculty survey for 1995–1996 (H. Astin et al. 1997) showed that my statement was premature. The Latino and Latina faculty surveyed in 1995–1996 were still highly involved with research and writing on ethnicity; nearly 28 percent more Latino faculty were involved in ethnic research than were majority faculty (1997, 42). However, Latinos no longer posted the highest percentage in ethnic research of any cohort surveyed, for the survey showed that 58 percent of African American faculty were involved in research or writing on race or ethnicity, and more than 34 percent of all African American faculty respondents had taught an ethnic studies course in the previous two years, compared to almost 25 percent of Latino and Latina faculty (1997, 46).

7. Teaching, Testing, and Measuring Intelligence

1. Hall's comparisons (1977) actually demonstrate mixtures of high- and low-context trial procedures that clearly show agreements between legal culture and national cultural contexts. In the United States the largest part of trial law is rigorously constrained by rules, and it is dependent upon meticulous step-by-step analytical procedures for compiling data to make a case. This exceedingly low-context

process is further fragmented by stylized segmented questioning protocols aimed at extracting surgically precise (i.e., short yes or no) responses and little more. The system permits no evidence based on hearsay or conjecture, and the U.S. legal system follows its procedural rules so strictly that it has become quite bogged down. In an odd reversal of cultural context, the tightly constructed case is put to a jury, which must work as a group and may or may not always follow the rules. In fact, despite the court's instructions to disregard certain testimony, jurors informally consider all kinds of conjecture and hearsay as part of the context of events to reach a verdict. Some might argue that informal considerations during jury deliberations ran amok in the O. J. Simpson trial or in the first trial of Los Angeles police officers accused of beating Rodney King. But this high-context decision-making process can uncover what actually occurred in particular cases if intelligent and skeptical jurors are allowed to bring context into the process. Hall offers an example from the Watergate era. Judge John Sirica rejected an offer from White House staff to review only the "summaries" of President Nixon's Watergate tapes in lieu of the real ones. Sirica's choice "shows that occasionally an American jurist recognizes the need for contexting information in order to make a judgment" (1997, 250). Other nations with cultures that are more high context than that of the United States, such as France and even Japan, have legal systems that work in opposite fashion. For the most part, attorneys in those legal systems present information—such as hearsay, conjecture, rumor, and the facts in the case—to a magistrate, who is then obligated to follow strict rules and guidelines in reaching a final decision.

2. I wish to thank Dr. Alberta Gloria, assistant professor in counseling psychology at the University of Wisconsin–Madison, for her advice and feedback on the survey data here and for her assistance in designing a pilot inter-rater reliability survey of high- and low-context content and field-independent and -sensitive content in the HERI question sets (H. Astin et al. 1997).

References

Acuña, Rodolfo F. 1972. *Occupied America: The Chicanos' Struggle toward Liberation.* San Francisco: Canfield.

Acuña, Rodolfo F. 1998. *Sometimes There Is No Other Side: Chicanos and the Myth of Equality.* South Bend, Ind.: University of Notre Dame Press.

Adams, Howard G. 1993. *Focusing on the Campus Milieu: A Guide for Enhancing the Graduate School Climate.* South Bend, Ind.: National Consortium for Graduate Degrees for Minorities in Engineering.

Adams, Maurianne, ed. 1992. *Promoting Diversity in College Classrooms: Innovative Responses for Curriculum, Faculty, and Institutions.* San Francisco: Jossey-Bass.

Adizes, Ichak. 1988. *Corporate Lifecycles: How and Why Corporations Grow and Die and What to Do about It.* Englewood Cliffs, N.J.: Prentice-Hall.

"Affirmative Action on the Line: A Special Issue of Multiple Articles." 1995. *Chronicle of Higher Education,* April 28, pp. A12–33.

Agar, Michael. 1994a. *Language Shock: Understanding the Culture of Conversation.* New York: Morrow.

Agar, Michael. 1994b. "The Intercultural Frame." *International Journal of Intercultural Relations* 18 (2): 221–37.

Alba, Richard D. 1985. "The Twilight of Ethnicity among Americans of European Ancestry: The Case of Italians." *Ethnic and Racial Studies* 8 (1): 134–58.

Alexander, Baine B., Anne C. Burda, and Susan B. Millar. 1997. "A Community Approach to Learning Calculus: Fostering Success for Underrepresented Ethnic Minorities in an Emerging Scholars Program." *Journal of Women and Minorities in Science and Engineering* 3 (2): 145–59.

Alicea, Ines Pinto. 1995. "Are Latino Faculty Second-Class Citizens?" *Hispanic Outlook in Higher Education* 6, no. 9: 8–9.

Alicea, Ines Pinto. 1997. "ACE and UCLA Survey 350,000 First-Year Students: Latinos Cite Money as Major Concern." *Hispanic Outlook in Higher Education* 7, no. 17: 4.

Almanac Issue, 1997–1998. 1997. *Chronicle of Higher Education,* August 29.

References

American Anthropological Association. 1997. "American Anthropological Association Response to OMB Directive 15: Race and Ethnic Standards for Federal Statistics and Administrative Reporting." *American Anthropological Association* <http://www.aaanet.org/gvt/ombdraft.htm> (9/6/97).

American Council on Education. 1992. *Environments of Support.* Washington, D.C.: Office of Minorities in Higher Education.

Anderson, Erin, ed. 1993. *Campus Use of the Teaching Portfolio: Twenty-five Profiles.* Washington, D.C.: American Association for Higher Education.

Anderson, James A. 1997. "Faculty Development and the Inclusion of Diversity in the College Classroom: Pedagogical and Curricular Transformation." In Deborah DeZure, ed., *To Improve the Academy,* vol. 16, pp. 41–52. Stillwater, Okla.: New Forms Press and the Professional and Organizational Development Network in Higher Education.

Anderson, James A., and Maurianne Adams. 1992. "Acknowledging the Learning Styles of Diverse Student Populations: Implications for Instructional Design." In Maurianne Adams, ed., *Promoting Diversity in College Classrooms: Innovative Responses for Curriculum, Faculty, and Institutions,* pp. 19–33. San Francisco: Jossey-Bass.

Angelo, Thomas A. 1997. "The Campus as Learning Community: Seven Promising Shifts and Seven Powerful Levers." *American Association for Higher Education Bulletin* 49, no. 9 (May): 3–6.

Anzaldúa, Gloria. 1987. *Borderlands/La Frontera: The New Mestiza.* San Francisco: Spinsters/Aunt Lute Books.

Anzaldúa, Gloria, ed. 1990. *Making Face, Making Soul Haciendo Caras: Creative and Critical Perspectives by Feminists of Color.* San Francisco: Aunt Lute Books.

Aponte, Robert, and Marcelo Siles. 1996. "Latinos to Emerge as Largest U.S. Minority in the Coming Decade." *NEXO, Newsletter of the Julian Samora Research Institute* 4, no. 2 (winter): 1–3, 8–10.

Appiah, K. Anthony. 1997. "The Multiculturalist Misunderstanding." *New York Review of Books,* October 9, pp. 30–46.

Aquilera, Francisco E. 1996. "Is Anthropology Good for the Company?" *American Anthropologist* 98: 735–42.

Arnold, Bill. 1996. "Ward: Tenure Central to the Soul of Universities." *Wisconsin Week* (University of Wisconsin–Madison), October 9, pp. 1–3.

Astin, Alexander W. 1985. *Achieving Academic Excellence: A Critical Assessment of Priorities and Practices in Higher Education.* San Francisco: Jossey-Bass.

Astin, Alexander W. 1997. "Our Obsession with Being Smart Is Distorting Intellectual Life." *Chronicle of Higher Education,* September 26, p. A60.

Astin, Helen S., Anthony L. Antonio, Christine M. Cress, and Alexander W. Astin. 1997. *Race and Ethnicity in the American Professoriate, 1995–1996.* Los Angeles: Higher Education Research Institute, University of California.

Augenbraum, Harold, and Ilan Stavans, eds. 1993. *Growing Up Latino: Memoirs and Stories.* New York: Houghton Mifflin.

Austin, Ann E. 1990. "Faculty Cultures, Faculty Values." In William G. Tierney, ed., *Assessing Academic Cultures,* pp. 61–74. San Francisco: Jossey-Bass.

Baba, Marietta L. 1986. *Business and Industrial Anthropology: An Overview.* National Association for the Practice of Anthropology, Bulletin No. 2. Washington, D.C.: American Anthropological Association.

Baba, Marietta L. 1989. "Organizational Culture: Revisiting the Small-Society Metaphor." *Anthropology of Work Review* 10 (3): 7–10.

Baird, Leonard L. 1990. "Campus Climate: Using Surveys for Policy Making and Understanding." In William G. Tierney, ed., *Assessing Academic Climates and Cultures,* pp. 35–47. San Francisco: Jossey-Bass.

Baird, Leonard L., ed. 1983. *Increasing Graduate Student Retention and Degree Attainment.* San Francisco: Jossey-Bass.

Banks, Marcus. 1996. *Ethnicity: Anthropological Constructions.* New York: Routledge.

Barth, Fredrik. 1967. "On the Study of Social Change." *American Anthropologist* 69: 661–69.

Barth, Fredrik. 1989. "The Analysis of Culture in Complex Societies." *Ethnos* 54, no. 3–4: 120–42.

Barth, Fredrik, ed. 1969. *Ethnic Groups and Boundaries.* Boston: Little, Brown.

Basch, Linda G., Lucie Wood Saunders, Jagna Wojecicka Sharff, and James Peacock, eds. 1999. "Transforming Academia: Challenges and Opportunities for an Engaged Anthropology." American Ethnological Society Monograph Series, No. 8. Washington D.C.: American Anthropological Association.

Basinger, Julianne. 1997. "Graduate Record Exam Is Poor Predictor of Success in Psychology, Scientists Say." *Academe Today,* web site of the *Chronicle of Higher Education,* August 6 <http://www.chronicle.com/che-data/news.dir/dailarch.dir/9708.dir/97080603.htm> (8/6/97).

Basinger, Julianne. 1998. "Texas A&M Medical School Will Allow Some Applicants to Avoid Admission Test." *Academe Today,* web site of the *Chronicle of Higher Education,* February 5 <http://www.chronicle.com/che-data/news.dir/dailarch.dir/9802.dir/98020504.htm> (2/5/98).

Becher, Tony. 1984. "The Cultural View." In Burton R. Clark, ed., *Perspectives on Higher Education: Eight Disciplinary and Comparative Views,* pp. 165–98. Berkeley: University of California Press.

Becher, Tony. 1989. *Academic Tribes and Territories: Intellectual Enquiry and the Cultures of Disciplines.* Bristol, Pa.: Society for Research into Higher Education, Open University Press.

Becker, H. S., Blanche Greer, E. C. Hughes, and A. L. Strauss. 1961. *Boys in White: Student Culture in Medical School.* Chicago: University of Chicago Press.

Beckham, Edgar F. 1997. "Diversity Opens Doors to All." *New York Times,* January 5, sec. 4A, p. 58.

Bell, Derrick. 1997. "Protecting Diversity Programs from Political and Judicial Attack." *Chronicle of Higher Education,* April 4, pp. B4–5.

Benjamin, Roger, and Steve Carroll. 1998. "The Implications of the Changed Environment for Governance in Higher Education." In William G. Tierney, ed., *The Responsive University: Restructuring for High Performance,* pp. 92–119. Baltimore, Md.: Johns Hopkins University Press.

Bennett, John W. 1969. *Northern Plainsmen.* Chicago: Aldine-Atherton Press.

Bennett, John W. 1975. "A Guide to the Collection." In John W. Bennett, ed., *The New Ethnicity: Perspectives from Ethnology,* pp. 3–10. St. Paul, Minn.: West.

References

Bensimon, Estela Mara. 1990. "The New President and Understanding the Campus as a Culture." In William G. Tierney, ed., *Assessing Academic Cultures,* pp. 75–86. San Francisco: Jossey-Bass.

"The Best Graduate Schools." 1997–2000. *U.S. News and World Report,* March 10, 1997, pp. 96–97; March 2, 1998, pp. 91–92; March 29, 1999, pp. 111–12; April 10, 2000, pp. 91–93.

Biglan, Anthony. 1973. "The Characteristics of Subject Matter in Different Scientific Areas." *Journal of Applied Psychology* 57 (3): 195–203.

Birnbaum, Robert. 1988. *How Colleges Work: The Cybernetics of Academic Organization and Leadership.* San Francisco: Jossey-Bass.

Bloom, Allan. 1987. *The Closing of the American Mind: How Higher Education Has Failed Democracy and Impoverished the Souls of Todays Students.* New York: Simon and Schuster.

Boice, Robert. 1992. *The New Faculty Member: Supporting and Fostering Professional Development.* San Francisco: Jossey-Bass.

Bork, Robert H. 1996. "Multiculturalism Is Bringing Us to a Barbarous Epoch." *Chronicle of Higher Education,* October 11, p. B7.

Bowen, William G., and Derek Bok. 1998. *The Shape of the River: Long-Term Consequences of Considering Race in College and University Admissions.* Princeton, N.J.: Princeton University Press.

Bowen, William G., and Neil L. Rudenstine. 1992. *In Pursuit of the Ph.D.* Princeton, N.J.: Princeton University Press.

Boyer, Ernest L. 1990. *Scholarship Reconsidered: Priorities of the Professoriate.* Princeton, N.J.: Carnegie Foundation for the Advancement of Teaching.

Braskamp, Larry A., and Jon F. Wergin. 1998. "Forming New Social Partnerships." In William G. Tierney, ed., *The Responsive University: Restructuring for High Performance,* pp. 62–91. Baltimore, Md.: Johns Hopkins University Press.

Brice-Heath, Shirley. 1983. *Ways with Words.* New York: Cambridge University Press.

Briody, Elizabeth K. 1989. "Organizational Culture: From Concept to Applications." *Anthropology of Work Review* 10 (4): 4–10.

Brooks, Peter. 1996. "Graduate Learning as Apprenticeship." *Chronicle of Higher Education,* December 20, p. A52.

Brown, Shirley Vining. 1987. *Minorities in the Graduate Education Pipeline.* Princeton, N.J.: Minority Graduate Education Project, GRE and Educational Testing Service.

Brown, Shirley Vining. 1988. *Increasing Minority Faculty: An Elusive Goal.* Princeton, N.J.: Minority Graduate Education Project, GRE and Educational Testing Service.

Burgess, David R. 1997. "Barriers to Graduate School for Minority-Group Students." *Chronicle of Higher Education,* October 10, pp. B7–8.

Burgess, M. Elaine. 1978. "The Resurgence of Ethnicity: Myth or Reality?" *Ethnic and Racial Studies* 1 (3): 265–85.

Carlson, Scott. 1999. "Minority Students Post Slight Increase in College Enrollment, Report States." *Chronicle of Higher Education,* December 17, p. A53.

Carroll, Thomas G., and Jean J. Schensul, eds. 1990. *Cultural Diversity and Ameri-*

can Education: Visions of the Future, special issue of *Education and Urban Society* 22, no. 4 (August): 339–433.

Carter, Deborah J., and Eileen M. O'Brien. 1993. "Employment and Hiring Patterns for Faculty of Color." *Research Briefs* (American Council on Education, Washington, D.C.) vol. 4, no. 6: 1–14.

Carter, Deborah J., and Reginald Wilson. 1995. "Minorities in Higher Education." *Thirteenth Annual Status Report.* American Council on Education, Washington, D.C.

Carter, Deborah J., and Reginald Wilson. 1997. "Minorities in Higher Education." *Fifteenth Annual Status Report.* American Council on Education, Washington, D.C.

Carter, Thomas P., and Roberto D. Segura, eds. 1979. *Mexican Americans in School: A Decade of Change.* Princeton, N.J.: College Entrance Examination Board.

Chacón, Maria, Elizabeth G. Cohen, and Sharon Strover. 1986. "Chicanas and Chicanos: Barriers to Progress in Higher Education." In Michael A. Olivas, ed., *Latino College Students,* pp. 296–324. New York: Teachers College Press.

Chaffee, Ellen Earle. 1998. "Listening to the People We Serve." In William G. Tierney, ed., *The Responsive University: Restructuring for High Performance,* pp. 13–37. Baltimore, Md.: Johns Hopkins University Press.

Chambers, Tony, Jacqueline Lewis, and Paula Kerezsi. 1995. "African American Faculty and White American Students: Cross-Cultural Pedagogy in Counselor Preparation Programs." *Counseling Psychologist* 23, no. 1 (January): 43–62.

Chapa, Jorge. 1988. "The Question of Mexican American Assimilation: Socioeconomic Parity or Underclass Formation?" *Public Affairs Comment* 35, no. 1 (fall): 1–15.

Chapa, Jorge et al. 1993. "Recruiting and Retaining Students of Color at the LBJ School: A Preliminary Analysis." Unpublished paper presented for discussion during the session called "Increasing Diversity in the Public Policy Profession," at the spring conference of the Association of Public Policy Analysis and Management, April 23–24.

Chiat, Richard. 1997. "Thawing the Cold War over Tenure: Why Academe Needs More Employment Options." *Chronicle of Higher Education,* February 7, pp. B4–5.

Clark, Burton R. 1984. "The Organizational Conception." In Burton R. Clark, ed., *Perspectives on Higher Education: Eight Disciplinary and Comparative Views,* pp. 106–31. Berkeley: University of California Press.

Clark, Burton R. 1987a. *The Academic Life: Small Worlds, Different Worlds.* Princeton, N.J.: Carnegie Foundation for the Advancement of Teaching.

Clark, Burton R. 1995. *Places of Inquiry: Research and Advanced Education in Modern Universities.* Berkeley: University of California Press.

Clark, Burton R., ed. 1987b. *The Academic Profession: National, Disciplinary, and Institutional Settings.* Berkeley: University of California Press.

Clark, Burton R., ed. 1993. *The Research Foundations of Graduate Education: Germany, Britain, France, United States, Japan.* Berkeley: University of California Press.

References

Clark, David L. 1985. "Emerging Paradigms in Organizational Theory and Research." In Yvonna S. Lincoln, ed., *Organizational Theory and Inquiry: The Paradigm Revolution,* pp. 43–78. Beverly Hills, Calif.: Sage.

Clark, Mark, Roger Gill, and Paul B. Duby. 1991. "Myths and Realities: Backgrounds and Aspirations of Assistant and Associate Deans in Higher Education." Unpublished manuscript, courtesy Mark Clark.

Cohen, Mark Nathan. 1998a. *Culture of Intolerance: Chauvinism, Class, and Racism in the United States.* New Haven, Conn.: Yale University Press.

Cohen, Mark Nathan. 1998b. "Culture, Not Race, Explains Human Diversity." *Chronicle of Higher Education,* April 17, p. B4–5.

Cohen, Rosalie A. 1969. "Conceptual Styles, Culture Conflict, and Nonverbal Tests of Intelligence." *American Anthropologist* 71: 828–56.

Conciatore, Jacqueline. 1990. "From Flunking to Mastering Calculus: Treisman's Retention Model Proves to Be Too Good on Some Campuses." *Black Issues in Higher Education* 6 (22): 5–6.

Conrad, Clifton F., Jennifer Grant Haworth, and Susan Bolyard Millar. 1993. *A Silent Success: Master's Education in the United States.* Baltimore, Md.: Johns Hopkins University Press.

Cotter, Maury. 1996. "Systems Thinking in a Knowledge-Creating Organization." *Journal of Innovative Management* 2 (1): 15–30.

Cotter, Maury, Jessica Simmons, and Kathleen A. Paris. 1997. *Administering a Department: A Guide for Identifying and Improving Support Processes in an Academic Department.* Maryville, Mo.: Prescott Publishing.

Council for Opportunity in Education. 2000. "Taking Good Care of TRIO." *Hispanic Outlook in Higher Education* 10, no. 1: 30–32.

Coye, Dale. 1997. "Ernest Boyer and the New American College." *Change* 29 (May–June): 20–29.

Cuádraz, Gloria Holguin. 1992. "Experiences of Multiple Marginality: A Case Study of Chicana Scholarship Women." *Journal of the Association of Mexican American Educators,* special edition: *Chicanos in Higher Education,* September, pp. 31–43.

Cuádraz, Gloria Holguin. 1993. "Meritocracy (Un)challenged: The Making of a Chicano and Chicana Professoriate and Professional Class." Ph.D. diss., University of California, Berkeley.

Cuello, José. 1996. "Latinos and Hispanics: A Primer on Terminology." Rev. November 19. Prepared for the Midwest Consortium for Latino Research, a listserve at <jcuello@cms.cc.2wayne.edu> (12/22/96).

Daniel, John S. 1997. "Why Universities Need Technology Strategies." *Change* 29 (July–August): 10–17.

Davidoff, Judith. 1996. "Tenure on Trial: Business Professor Denis Collins Says His Battle for Tenure Exposes a System in Need of Reform." *Isthmus* (Madison, Wis.), December 6–12, pp. 10–13.

Davis, Stanley M. 1971. *Comparative Management: Organizational and Cultural Perspectives.* Englewood Cliffs, N.J.: Prentice-Hall.

Davis, Stanley M. 1984. *Managing Corporate Culture.* Cambridge, Mass.: Ballinger.

Deal, Terrence E., and Allen A. Kennedy. 1982. *Corporate Cultures: The Rites and Rituals of Corporate Life.* Reading, Mass.: Addison-Wesley.

References

de Anda, Diane. 1984. "Bicultural Socialization: Factors Affecting the Minority Experience." *Social Work* 29, no. 2 (March–April): 101–7.

de los Santos, Alfredo G., Jr., and Antonio Rigual. 1994. "Progress of Hispanics in American Higher Education." In Manuel J. Justiz, Reginald Wilson, and Lars G. Björk, eds., *Minorities in Higher Education,* pp. 173–94. Phoenix, Ariz.: Oryx.

de Vos, George, and Lola Romanucci-Ross, eds. 1975. *Ethnic Identity: Cultural Continuities and Change.* Palo Alto, Calif.: Mayfield.

Díaz-Guerrero, Rogelio. 1977. "Mexicans and Americans: Two Worlds, One Border . . . and One Observer." In Stanley R. Ross, ed., *Views across the Border: The United States and Mexico,* pp. 283–307. Albuquerque: University of New Mexico Press.

Djursaa, Malene. 1994. "North European Business Cultures: Britain Versus Denmark and Germany." *European Management Journal* 12 (2): 138–46.

D'Souza, Dinesh. 1991. *Illiberal Education: The Politics of Race and Sex on Campus.* New York: Free Press.

Dwyer, Carol Anne, ed. 1998. "New Directions in Assessment for Higher Education: Fairness, Access, Multiculturalism, and Equity (FAME)." The GRE, FAME Report Series, vol. 1. Educational Testing Service, Princeton, N.J.

Edgerton, Russell, Patricia Hutchings, and Kathleen Quinlan. 1991. *The Teaching Portfolio: Capturing the Scholarship in Teaching.* Washington, D.C.: American Association for Higher Education.

Edwards, Richard. 1999. "The Academic Department: How Does It Fit into the University Reform Agenda?" *Change* 31 (September–October): 17–27.

Esquibel, Antonio. 1992. *The Career Mobility of Chicano Administrators in Higher Education: The Chicano Administrator in Colleges and Universities of the Southwest—A Fifteen-Year Replication Study.* Boulder, Colo.: Western Interstate Commission for Higher Education.

ETS (Educational Testing Service). 1995. *Graduate Record Examinations FAME Report (Fairness, Access, Multiculturalism, Equity, and the New Testing Initiatives).* Princeton, N.J.: Educational Testing Service.

Ewell, Peter T. 1998. "Achieving High Performance: The Policy Dimension." In William G. Tierney, ed., *The Responsive University: Restructuring for High Performance,* pp. 120–61. Baltimore, Md.: Johns Hopkins University Press.

Felder, Richard M. 1993. "Reaching the Second Tier: Learning and Teaching Styles in College Science Education." *Journal of College Science Teaching* 23, no. 5: 286–90.

Felder, Richard M., and Linda K. Silverman. 1988. "Learning and Teaching Styles in Engineering Education." *Engineering Education,* April, pp. 674–81. As reproduced in Katherine Sanders and Chris Carlson-Dakes, eds., *Creating a Collaborative Learning Environment: Faculty Resource Book, 1997–1998,* Madison, Wis.

Firmat, Gustavo Pérez. 1994. *Life on the Hyphen: The Cuban-American Way.* Austin: University of Texas Press.

Fitzpatrick, Joseph P. 1971. *Puerto Rican Americans: The Meaning of Migration to the Mainland.* Englewood Cliffs, N.J.: Prentice-Hall.

Ford, Martin E. 1992. *Motivating Humans: Goals, Emotions, and Personal Agency Beliefs.* Newbury Park, Calif.: Sage.

References

Fordham, Signithia. 1991. "Peer-Proofing Academic Competition among Black Adolescents: Acting White, Black American Style." In Christine E. Sleeter, ed., *Empowerment through Multicultural Education,* pp. 69–93. Albany: State University of New York Press.

Fox, Geoffrey. 1996. *Hispanic Nation: Culture, Politics, and the Constructing of Identity.* Secaucus, N.J.: Birch Lane Press.

Fullerton, Howard N., Jr. 1999. "Labor Force Projections to 2008: Steady Growth and Changing Composition." *Monthly Labor Review* 122, no. 11 (November): 19–32.

Fullilove, Robert E. 1986. "Sealing the Leaks in the Pipeline: Improving the Performance and Persistence of Minority Students in College." Unpublished manuscript and personal correspondence, Merck Sharpe & Dohme minority recruitment meeting, February 1987, San Francisco.

Gainen, Joanne, and Robert Boice, eds. 1993. *Building a Diverse Faculty.* San Francisco: Jossey-Bass.

Gallagher, Ann. 1998. "Gender and Antecedents of Performance in Mathematics Testing." *Teachers College Record* 100 (2): 297–314.

Galloway, Phyllis H., ed. 1996. *Reflections of the Professoriate: Proceedings of the Preparing Future Faculty Fellows Symposia, Howard University, 1995–1996.* Washington, D.C.: Graduate School of Arts and Sciences, Howard University.

Gamson, Zelda F. 1997. "Higher Education and Rebuilding Civic Life." *Change* 29 (January–February): 10–13.

Gándara, Patricia. 1982. "Passing through the Eye of the Needle: High-Achieving Chicanas." *Hispanic Journal of Behavioral Sciences* 4, no. 2: 167–79.

Gándara, Patricia. 1993. "Choosing Higher Education: The Educational Mobility of Chicano Students." *California Policy Seminar Brief* 5, no. 10 (April): 1–6.

Gándara, Patricia. 1995. *Over the Ivy Walls: The Educational Mobility of Low-Income Chicanos.* Albany: State University of New York Press.

Gardner, Howard. 1983. *Frames of Mind.* New York: Basic.

Garza, Hisauro. 1993. "Second-Class Academics: Chicano/Latino Faculty." In Joanne Gainen and Robert Boice, eds., *Building a Diverse Faculty,* pp. 33–42. San Francisco: Jossey-Bass.

Garza, Yolanda. 1996. "Critical Reflections on Oppression of Latina Administrators in Higher Education and the Role of Adult Continuing Education in Their Empowerment Amidst Diminished Opportunities." Ph.D. diss., Department of Leadership and Educational Policy Studies, Northern Illinois University.

Geertz, Clifford. 1973. *The Interpretation of Cultures.* New York: Basic.

Gesteland, Richard R. 1996. *Cross-Cultural Business Behavior: Marketing, Negotiating, and Managing across Cultures.* Copenhagen: Munksgaard International.

Gibson, Margaret A. 1997. "Exploring and Explaining the Variability: Cross-National Perspectives on the School Performance of Minority Students." *Anthropology and Education Quarterly* 28 (3): 318–29.

Gilliland, Martha. 1997. "Organizational Change and Tenure: We Can Learn from the Corporate Experience." *Change* 29 (May–June): 30–33.

Giovannini, Maureen J., and Lynne M. H. Rosansky. 1990. *Anthropology and Management Consulting: Forging a New Alliance.* National Association for the

Practice of Anthropology, Bulletin No. 9. Washington D.C.: American Anthropological Association.

Givens, David B., and Timothy Jablonski. 1996a. "Applied/Practicing Anthropology: 1996–2000." *Anthropology Newsletter,* November, p. 5.

Givens, David B., and Timothy Jablonski. 1996b. "1996 Survey of Departments." *Anthropology Newsletter,* September, p. 5.

Gloria, Alberta M. 1997. "Chicana Academic Persistence: Creating a University-Based Community." *Education and Urban Society* 30, no. 1 (November): 107–21.

Gloria, Alberta M., and Donald D. Pope-Davis. 1997. "Cultural Ambience: The Importance of a Culturally Aware Learning Environment in the Training and Education of Counselors." In Donald D. Pope-Davis and Hardin Coleman, eds., *Multicultural Counseling Competencies: Assessment, Education and Training, and Supervision,* pp. 242–75. Thousand Oaks, Calif.: Sage.

Gloria, Alberta M., and Sharon E. Robinson-Kurpius. 1996. "The Validation of the Cultural Congruity Scale and the University Environment Scale with Chicano/a Students." *Hispanic Journal of Behavioral Sciences* 18, no. 4: 533–49.

González, María Cristina. 1995. "In Search of the Voice I Always Had." In Raymond V. Padilla and Rudolfo Chávez Chávez, eds., *The Leaning Ivory Tower: Latino Professors in American Universities,* pp. 77–90. Albany: State University of New York Press.

Gose, Ben. 1996. "Minority Students Were Twenty-four Percent of College Enrollment in 1994." *Chronicle of Higher Education,* May 24, p. A32.

Gose, Ben. 1997. "Minority Enrollments Rose in 1995, A Study Finds." *Chronicle of Higher Education,* May 23, p. A38.

Gose, Ben. 1999. "More Points for 'Strivers': The New Affirmative Action?" *Chronicle of Higher Education,* September 17, p. A55.

Grandy, Jerlee. 1994. *Trends and Profiles: Statistics about General Test Examinees by Sex and Ethnicity.* PR/94/1, Supplementary Tables, PR/94/1A. Princeton, N.J.: Educational Testing Service.

Granfield, Robert. 1992. *Making Elite Lawyers: Visions of Law at Harvard and Beyond.* New York: Routledge, Chapman, and Hall.

Greeley, Andrew M. 1972. *That Most Distressful Nation: The Taming of the American Irish.* Chicago: Quadrangle.

Gregory-Huddleston, Kathleen. 1994. "Culture Conflict with Growth: Cases from Silicon Valley." In Tomoko Hamada and Willis E. Sibley, eds., *Anthropological Perspectives on Organizational Culture,* pp. 121–32. New York: University Press of America.

Guba, Egon G. 1985. "The Context of Emergent Paradigm Research." In Yvonna S. Lincoln, ed., *Organizational Theory and Inquiry: The Paradigm Revolution,* pp. 79–105. Beverly Hills, Calif: Sage.

Guinier, Lani. 1997. *Becoming Gentlemen: Women, Law School, and Institutional Change.* Boston: Beacon.

Gumport, Patricia J. 1993a. "Graduate Education and Organized Research in the United States." In Burton R. Clark, ed., *The Research Foundations of Graduate*

Education: Germany, Britain, France, United States, Japan, pp. 225–60. Berkeley: University of California Press.

Gumport, Patricia J. 1993b. "Graduate Education and Research Imperatives: Views from American Campuses." In Burton R. Clark, ed., *The Research Foundations of Graduate Education: Germany, Britain, France, United States, Japan*, pp. 261–96. Berkeley: University of California Press.

Guskin, Alan E. 1996. "Facing the Future: The Change Process in Restructuring Universities." *Change* 28 (July–August): 27–37.

Hale-Benson, Janice E. 1986. *Black Children: Their Roots, Culture, and Learning Styles*. Rev. ed. Baltimore, Md.: Johns Hopkins University Press.

HACU (Hispanic Association of Colleges and Universities). 1996. "How to Close the Hispanic Faculty Gap." *HACU—The Voice of Hispanic Higher Education* 5 (10): 1, 7.

Hall, Edward T. 1959. *The Silent Language*. Greenwich, Conn.: Fawcett.

Hall, Edward T. 1966. *The Hidden Dimension*. 2d ed. New York: Anchor.

Hall, Edward T. 1974. *Handbook for Proxemic Research*. Washington, D.C.: Society for the Anthropology of Visual Communication.

Hall, Edward T. 1977. *Beyond Culture*. 2d ed. New York: Anchor.

Hall, Edward T. 1984. *The Dance of Life: The Other Dimension of Time*. 2d ed. New York: Anchor.

Hall, Edward T. 1993. *An Anthropology of Everyday Life*. 2d ed. New York: Anchor.

Hall, Edward T., and Mildred Reed Hall. 1990. *Hidden Differences: Doing Business with the Japanese*. 2d ed. New York: Anchor.

Hamada, Tomoko. 1994. "Anthropology and Organizational Culture." In Tomoko Hamada and Willis E. Sibley, eds., *Anthropological Perspectives on Organizational Culture*, pp. 9–56. New York: University Press of America.

Hamada, Tomoko, and Willis E. Sibley, eds. 1994. *Anthropological Perspectives on Organizational Culture*. New York: University Press of America.

Hardi, Joel. 2000. "Education of Hispanic Americans Is Crucial to U.S. Economic Success, Panel Says." *Chronicle of Higher Education*, March 17, p. A36.

Haworth, Jennifer Grant, ed. 1996. *Assessing Graduate and Professional Education: Current Realities, Future Prospects*. San Francisco: Jossey-Bass.

Healy, Patrick. 1999. "University of California Broadens Admissions to Top Four Percent of Graduates from Each High School." *Academe Today*, web site of the *Chronicle of Higher Education*, March 22 <http://chronicle.com/daily/99/03/99032201n.htm> (3/22/99).

HERI (Higher Education Research Institute). 1991. "1989–1990 Higher Education Research Institute Faculty Survey." Unpublished data tabulations, November.

Herrnstein, Richard J., and Charles Murray. 1994. *The Bell Curve: Intelligence and Class Structure in American Life*. New York: Free Press.

Heusinkveld, Paula. 1994. *Inside Mexico: Living, Traveling, and Doing Business in a Changing Society*. New York: Wiley.

Heyck, Denis Lynn Daly. 1994. *Barrios and Borderlands: Cultures of Latinos and Latinas in the United States*. New York: Routledge.

Hobsbawm, Eric. 1992. "Introduction: Inventing Traditions." In Eric Hobsbawm and Terrence Ranger, eds., *The Invention of Tradition.* pp. 1–14. New York: Cambridge University Press.

Hobsbawm, Eric, and Terrence Ranger, eds. 1992. *The Invention of Tradition.* New York: Cambridge University Press.

Hodgkinson, Harold L., and Janice Hamilton Outtz. 1996. *Hispanic Americans: A Look Back, a Look Ahead.* Washington, D.C.: Institute for Educational Leadership, Center for Demographic Policy.

Holtzman, Wayne H. 1977. "Personality Development and Mental Health of People in the Border States." In Stanley R. Ross, ed., *Views across the Border: The United States and Mexico,* pp. 308–29. Albuquerque: University of New Mexico Press.

Honan, William H. 1996. "Curriculum and Culture: New Round Is Opened in a Scholarly Fistfight." *New York Times,* August 24, p. A14.

Hu-DeHart, Evelyn. 1995. "The Undermining of Ethnic Studies." *Chronicle of Higher Education,* October, 20, pp. B2–3.

Hurtado, Aída, David E. Hayes-Bautista, Robert Burciaga Valdez, and Anthony C. R. Hernández. 1992. *Redefining California: Latino Social Engagement in a Multicultural Society.* Los Angeles: UCLA Chicano Studies Research Center.

Hutchings, Pat. 1996. *Making Teaching Community Property: A Menu for Peer Collaboration and Peer Review.* Washington, D.C.: American Association for Higher Education.

Ibarra, Robert A. 1976. "Ethnicity Genuine and Spurious: A Study of a Norwegian Community in Rural Wisconsin." Ph.D. diss., University of Wisconsin–Madison.

Ibarra, Robert A. 1996. *Latino Experiences in Graduate Education: Implications for Change.* Enhancing the Minority Presence in Graduate Education, No. 7. Washington, D.C.: Council of Graduate Schools.

Ibarra, Robert A. 1999. "Multicontextuality: A New Perspective on Minority Underrepresentation in SEM Academic Fields." *Making Strides* (American Association for the Advancement of Science) 1, no. 3 (October): 1–9.

Ibarra, Robert A., and Allan S. Cohen. 1999. "Multicontextuality: A Hidden Dimension in Testing and Assessment." In *New Directions in Assessment for Higher Education: Fairness, Access, Multiculturalism, and Equity (FAME) Conference,* vol. 3, pp. 16–30. Princeton, N.J.: Educational Testing Service.

Ibarra, Robert A., and Arnold Strickon. 1989. "The Norwegian American Dairy Tobacco Strategy in Southwestern Wisconsin." In Odd S. Lovoll, ed., *Norwegian American Studies,* vol. 32, pp. 3–30. Northfield, Minn.: Norwegian-American Historical Association.

Ibarra, Robert A., and Joyce Thompsen. 1997. "Mining Organizational Culture: Critical Knowledge Areas and Breakthrough Concepts." In Dundar F. Kocagolu and Timothy R. Anderson, eds., *Innovation in Technology Management: The Key to Global Leadership,* pp. 349–52. Proceedings of the Portland International Conference on Management of Engineering and Technology Management, July 27–31, Portland, Ore.

Iseminger, Jeff. 1997. "Counseling Psychology's Success Is No Accident." *Wisconsin Week* (University of Wisconsin–Madison), December 10, p. 6.

References

Jones, Robert A. 1980. "Myth and Symbol among the Nacirema Tsigoloicos." *American Sociologist* 15 (November): 207–12.

Jordan, Ann T. 1994. *Practicing Anthropology in Corporate America: Consulting on Organizational Culture.* National Association of Practicing Anthropology, Bulletin No. 14. Arlington, Va.: American Anthropological Association.

Justiz, Manuel J. 1994. "Demographic Trends and the Challenges to American Higher Education." In Manuel J. Justiz et al., eds., *Minorities in Higher Education,* pp. 1–21. Phoenix, Ariz.: Oryx.

Justiz, Manuel J., Reginald Wilson, and Lars G. Björk, eds. 1994. *Minorities in Higher Education.* Phoenix, Ariz.: Oryx.

Keefe, Susan E., and Amado M. Padilla. 1987. *Chicano Ethnicity.* Albuquerque: University of New Mexico Press.

Kegan, Spencer, and G. Lawrence Zahn. 1975. "Field Dependence and the School Achievement Gap Between Anglo-American and Mexican American Children." *Journal of Educational Psychology* 67 (5): 643–50.

Kerlin, Roberta-Anne. 1997. "Breaking the Silence: Toward a Theory of Women's Doctoral Persistence." Ph.D. diss., Faculty of Education, University of Victoria, Canada.

Kerlin, Scott P., and Bobbi Smith. 1994. "Electrifying Stories: Virtual Research Communities in Graduate Education." Paper presented at the annual meeting of the Pacific Northwest Association for Institutional Research and Planning, October 19–21, Portland, Ore.

Kim, Don. 1997. "Social Support and Cognitive and Cultural Flexibility in the University of Texas Environment." Paper presented at the Texas Association of Chicanos in Higher Education (TACHE), July, Laredo.

Klamer, Arjo, and David Colander. 1990. *The Making of an Economist.* Boulder, Colo.: Westview.

Kolb, David A. 1981. "Learning Styles and Disciplinary Differences." In A. W. Chickering and Associates, eds., *The Modern American College: Responding to the New Realities of Diverse Students and a Changing Society,* pp. 323–55. San Francisco: Jossey-Bass.

Kolb, David A. 1984. *Experiential Learning: Experience as the Source of Learning and Development.* Englewood Cliffs, N.J.: Prentice-Hall.

Kosciuk, Steve. 1997. "Impact of the Wisconsin Emerging Scholars First-Semester Calculus Program on Grades and Retention from Fall 1993–1996." Program evaluation report. Learning through Education, Adaptation, and Dissemination Center, University of Wisconsin–Madison.

Kuh, George D. 1990. "Assessing Student Culture." In William G. Tierney, ed., *Assessing Academic Cultures,* pp. 47–60. San Francisco: Jossey-Bass.

Kuh, George D., ed. 1993. *Cultural Perspectives in Student Affairs Work.* Lanham, Md.: American College Personnel Association, University Press of America.

Kuh, George D., and Jenness E. Hall. 1993. "Cultural Perspectives in Student Affairs." In George D. Kuh, ed., *Cultural Perspectives in Student Affairs Work,* pp. 1–20. Lanham, Md.: American College Personnel Association, University Press of America.

Kuhn, Thomas S. 1996. *The Structure of Scientific Revolutions.* 3d ed. Chicago: University of Chicago Press.

Lambert, Leo M., and Stacey Lane Tice. 1993. *Preparing Graduate Students to Teach: A Guide to Programs That Improve Undergraduate Education and Develop Tomorrow's Faculty.* Washington, D.C.: American Association for Higher Education.

Lango, Deborah Ramírez. 1995. "Mexican American Female Enrollment in Graduate Programs: A Study of the Characteristics That May Predict Success." *Hispanic Journal of Behavioral Sciences* 17, no. 1: 33–48.

Larmer, Brook. 1999. "Latino America." *Newsweek,* July 12, pp. 48–51.

Lave, Jean. 1993. "The Practice of Learning." In Seth Chaiklin and Jean Lave, eds., *Understanding Practice: Perspectives on Activity and Context,* pp. 3–34. New York: Cambridge University Press.

Lave, Jean, and Etienne Wenger. 1991. *Situated Learning: Legitimate Peripheral Participation.* New York: Cambridge University Press.

Lave, Jean, Michael Murtaugh, and Olivia de la Rocha. 1984. "The Dialectic of Arithmetic in Grocery Shopping." In Barbara Rogoff and Jean Lave, eds., *Everyday Cognition: Its Development in Social Context,* pp. 67–94. Cambridge, Mass.: Harvard University Press.

Leatherman, Courtney. 1996. "More Faculty Members Question the Value of Tenure." *Chronicle of Higher Education,* October 25, pp. A12–13.

Lederman, Douglas 1997a. "Backers of Affirmative Action Struggle to Find Research That Will Help in Court." *Chronicle of Higher Education,* May 23, pp. A28–29.

Lederman, Douglas. 1997b. "Sole Black Student in Entering Class at University of Texas Law School Withdraws." *Academe Today,* web site of the *Chronicle of Higher Education,* May 23 <http://www. chronicle.com/che-data/news.dir/dailarch.dir/9705.dir/97052301.htm> (5/27/97).

Leijonhufvud, Axel. 1973. "Life among the Econ." *Western Economic Journal* 9 (3): 327–37.

Leland, John, and Veronica Chambers. 1999. "Generation Ñ." *Newsweek,* July 12, pp. 52–60.

Levin, Lawrence W. 1996. *The Opening of the American Mind.* Boston: Beacon.

Levine, Arthur. 1997. "Higher Education's New Status as a Mature Industry." *Chronicle of Higher Education,* January 31, p. A48.

Limerick, Patricia Nelson. 1997. "The Startling Ability of Culture to Bring Critical Inquiry to a Halt." *Chronicle of Higher Education,* October 24, p. A76.

Limón, José. 1994. *Dancing with the Devil: Society and Cultural Poetics in Mexican American South Texas.* Madison: University of Wisconsin Press.

Lincoln, Yvonna S., ed. 1985. *Organizational Theory and Inquiry: The Paradigm Revolution.* Beverly Hills, Calif.: Sage.

Lovell, Anne M. 1997. "The City Is My Mother: Narratives of Schizophrenia and Homelessness." *American Anthropologist* 99: 355–68.

Lynton, Ernest A. 1995. *Making the Case for Professional Service.* Boston: American Association for Higher Education Forum on Faculty Roles and Rewards and the New England Resource Center for Higher Education, University of Massachusetts.

Macunovich, Diane. 1997. "Will There Be a Boom in the Demand for U.S. Higher Education among Eighteen-to-Twenty-four-Year-Olds?" *Change* 29 (May–June): 34–44.

Magrath, C. Peter. 1997. "Eliminating Tenure without Destroying Academic Freedom." *Chronicle of Higher Education,* February 28, p. A60.

Mangan, Katherine S. 1997. "Lani Guinier Starts Campaign to Curb Use of the Socratic Method." *Chronicle of Higher Education,* April 11, pp. A12–14.

Mangan, Katherine S. 1998a. "Texas Turnaround in Minority Enrollment at Medical Schools." *Chronicle of Higher Education,* February 6, p. A35.

Mangan, Katherine S. 1998b. "Medical School Applications Are Down for the Second Year in a Row." *Academe Today,* web site of the *Chronicle of Higher Education,* October 29 <http://chronicle.com/search97cgi/s97_cgi?. . .rder= desc&ViewTemplate=ArchiveView%2Ehts&> (12/28/99).

Mangan, Katherine S. 1999. "Minority Numbers Down Sharply at California Medical Schools, Report Says." *Chronicle of Higher Education,* April 2, p. A50.

Manning, Kathleen. 1993. "Properties of Institutional Culture." In George D. Kuh, ed., *Cultural Perspectives in Student Affairs Work,* pp. 21–36. Lanham, Md.: American College Personnel Association, University Press of America.

Marchese, Theodore J. 1997. "The New Conversations about Learning: Insights from Neuroscience and Anthropology, Cognitive Science, and Work-Place Studies." *American Association of Higher Education,* November <http://www. aahe.org>. To access the article, click on "AAHE Members Only," then "Assessing Impact: Evidence and Action" (11/7/97).

Marklein, Mary Beth. 1997. "Minority Gains in College Lose Steam." *USA Today,* May 19, 1997, p. 1D.

Martell, Chris. 1997. "Women's Studies Now: It's Not Your Mother's Program." *Wisconsin State Journal,* March 30, p. 1G.

Martin, Joanne. 1992. *Cultures in Organizations: Three Perspectives.* New York: Oxford University Press.

Matthews, Anne. 1997. *Bright College Years: Inside the American Campus Today.* New York: Simon and Schuster.

McCall, John C. 1996. "Discovery as a Research Strategy." *Anthropology Newsletter,* October, p. 44.

Menchaca, Martha. 1997. "History and Anthropology: Conducting Chicano Research." Julian Samora Research Institute occasional papers No. 11, January, Lansing, Mich.

Metheny, Bradie. 1997. "Research Universities Must Change Image, OMB Director Says." *Washington FAX,* December 17 <subscriptions@washington-fax.com> (12/19/97).

Meyers, Samuel L., Jr., and Caroline Turner. 1995. "Midwest Higher Education Commission Minority Faculty Development Project." Final Report. Midwest Higher Education Commission, Minneapolis, Minn.

Miller, Lawrence M. 1989. *Barbarians to Bureaucrats: Corporate Life-Cycle Strategies.* New York: Clarkson N. Potter.

Mindiola, Tatcho, Jr. 1995. "Getting Tenure at the U." In Raymond V. Padilla and Rudolfo Chávez Chávez, eds., *The Leaning Ivory Tower: Latino Professors in American Universities,* pp. 29–52. Albany: State University of New York Press.

Mitchell-Kernan, Claudia. 1995. "Culture as a Frame of Reference in Higher Education: An Anthropological Perspective." *Culture of Graduate Education Communicator* (Council of Graduate Schools) 28, no. 5 (April): 2–6.

References

Moffatt, Michael. 1989. *Coming of Age in New Jersey: College and American Culture.* New Brunswick, N.J.: Rutgers University Press.

Moody, Joann. 1997. *Demystifying the Profession: Helping Junior Faculty Succeed.* New Haven, Conn.: University of New Haven Press.

Moore, Joan, and Harry Pachon. 1985. *Hispanics in the United States.* Englewood Cliffs, N.J.: Prentice-Hall.

Moore, Joan, and Raquel Pinderhughes, eds. 1993. *In the Barrios: Latinos and the Underclass Debate.* New York: Russell Sage Foundation.

Morgen, Sandra. 1997. "Shaping the Constitution of Knowledge-Producing Communities." *Anthropology Newsletter,* May, pp. 4–5.

Morin, Richard. 1996. "Those Dumb Intelligence Tests." *Washington Post,* December 29, p. C5.

Moses, Yolanda T. 1990. "The Challenge of Diversity: Anthropological Perspectives on University Culture." *Education and Urban Society,* special issue: *Cultural Diversity and American Education: Visions of the Future* 22, no. 4 (August): 402–12.

Moses, Yolanda T. 1993. "The Roadblocks Confronting Minority Administrators." *Chronicle of Higher Education,* January 13, p. B4.

Moses, Yolanda T. 1997. "An Idea Whose Time Has Come Again: Anthropology Reclaims Race." *Anthropology Newsletter* October, pp. 1–4.

Mukhopadhyay, Carol C., and Yolanda T. Moses. 1997. "Reestablishing Race in Anthropological Discourse." *American Anthropologist* 99: 517–33.

National Research Council. 1996a. *Excellence through Diversity: Profiles of Forty-two Ford Foundation Fellows.* Washington, D.C.: National Academy Press.

National Research Council. 1996b. *Status of Ford Foundation Postdoctoral Fellowship Recipients, 1980–1993.* Washington, D.C.: National Academy Press.

National Research Council. 1996c. *Status of Ford Foundation Predoctoral and Dissertation Fellowship Recipients.* Washington, D.C.: National Academy Press.

National Science Foundation. 1994. *Women, Minorities, and Persons with Disabilities in Science and Engineering.* NSF 94–333. Arlington, Va.: National Science Foundation.

National Science Foundation. 1996. *Women, Minorities, and Persons with Disabilities in Science and Engineering, 1996.* NSF 96–311. Arlington, Va.: National Science Foundation.

National Science Foundation. Division of Science Resources Studies. 1997. *Science and Engineering Degrees, by Race/Ethnicity of Recipients, 1989–1995.* NSF 97–334. Arlington, Va.: National Science Foundation.

National Science Foundation. 2000. *Science and Engineering Doctorate Awards: 1997.* Detailed Statistical Tables, NSF 00–304. Arlington, Va.: National Science Foundation.

National Science Foundation, National Institutes of Health, National Endowment for the Humanities, U.S. Department of Education, and U.S. Department of Agriculture. 1999. "Summary Report 1998: Doctorate Recipients from United States Universities." *National Science Foundation,* Survey of Earned Doctorates, Publication Tables <http://www.nsf.gov/sbe/srs/srs00404/start/htm> (11/16/99).

NCES (National Center for Education Statistics). 1995. *Minority Undergraduate*

Participation in Postsecondary Education. Statistical Analysis Report. June. Washington, D.C.: Office of Educational Research and Improvement, U.S. Department of Education.

Nelson, Helene, and Robert A. Ibarra. 1999. "Forward Wisconsin: Demographic Changes and Wisconsin Choices." The Robert M. La Follette Institute of Public Affairs, Sesquicentennial Paper Series, July 1999, University of Wisconsin–Madison.

Nerad, Marisi, and Joseph Cerny. 1993. "From Facts to Action: Expanding the Graduate Divisions' Educational Role." In Leonard L. Baird, ed., *Increasing Graduate Student Retention and Degree Attainment,* pp. 27–40. San Francisco: Jossey-Bass.

Nerad, Marisi, and Debra Sands Miller. 1996. "Increasing Student Retention in Graduate and Professional Programs." In Jennifer Grant Haworth, ed., *Assessing Graduate and Professional Education: Current Realities, Future Prospects,* pp. 61–76. San Francisco: Jossey-Bass.

Nettles, Michael T. 1990. *Black, Hispanic, and White Doctoral Students: Before, during, and after Enrolling in Graduate School.* Princeton, N.J.: Minority Graduate Education Project, GRE and Educational Testing Service.

Neville, Gwen Kennedy. 1975. "Kinfolks and the Covenant: Ethnic Community among Southern Presbyterians." In John W. Bennett, ed., *The New Ethnicity: Perspectives from Ethnology,* pp. 258–344. St. Paul, Minn.: West.

Nickens, Tim. 1999. "Bush's Move Fails to Dampen Race Debate." *St. Petersburg Times,* November 14, p. 13A.

Nieves-Squires, Sarah. 1991. *Hispanic Women: Making Their Presence on Campus Less Tenuous.* Washington, D.C.: Project on the Status and Education of Women, Association of American Colleges.

O'Brien, Eileen M. 1993. "Latinos in Higher Education." *Research Briefs* (American Council on Education, Washington, D.C.), vol. 4, no. 4.

Okagaki, Lynn, and Peter A. Frensch. 1995. "Parental Support for Mexican American Children's School Achievement." In Hamilton I. McCubbin, Elizabeth A. Thompson, Anne I. Thompson, and Julie E. Fromer, eds., *Resiliency in Ethnic Minority Families: Native and Immigrant American Families,* vol. 1, pp. 325–42. Madison: Center for Excellence in Family Studies, University of Wisconsin.

Okagaki, Lynn, and Robert J. Sternberg. 1993. "Parental Beliefs and Children's School Performance." *Child Development* 64 (1): 36–56.

Oltman, Philip K., Donald R. Goodenough, and Herman A. Witkin. 1973. "Psychological Differentiation as a Factor in Conflict Resolution." *Journal of Personality and Social Psychology* 32, (4): 730–36.

OMB (U.S. Office of Management and Budget). 1997. "Recommendations from the Interagency Committee for the Review of the Racial and Ethnic Standards to the Office of Management and Budget Concerning Changes to the Standards for the Classification of Federal Data on Race and Ethnicity." *Federal Register* 62, no. 131 (July 9): 36874–946.

Orfield, Gary. 1999. "Affirmative Action Works—but Judges and Policy Makers Need to Hear That Verdict." *Chronicle of Higher Education,* December 10, pp. B7–8.

Ottinger, Cecilia, Robin Sikula, and Charles Washington. 1993. "Production of

References

Minority Doctorates." *Research Briefs* (American Council on Education, Washington, D.C.), vol. 4, no. 8: 1–12.

Overbey, Mary Margaret. 1997. "AAA Tells Feds to Eliminate Race." *Anthropology Newsletter,* October, pp. 1–6.

Owen, David, and Marilyn Doerr. 1999. *None of the Above: The Truth about the SATs, Revised and Updated.* Lanham, Md.: Rowman and Littlefield.

Padilla, Amado M. 1994. "Ethnic Minority Scholars, Research, and Mentoring: Current and Future Issues." *Educational Researcher* 23 (4): 24–27.

Padilla, Felix M. 1997. *The Struggle of Latinola University Students: In Search of a Liberating Education.* New York: Routledge.

Padilla, Raymond V., and Rudolfo Chávez Chávez, eds. 1995. *The Leaning Ivory Tower: Latino Professors in American Universities.* Albany: State University of New York Press.

Parker, Rebecca Lee. 1997. "Why Special Housing for Ethnic Students Makes Sense." *Chronicle of Higher Education,* September 12, pp. B6–7.

Patterson, James. 1979. "A Critique of the New Ethnicity." *American Anthropologist* 81: 103–5.

Perley, James E. 1997. "Tenure Remains Vital to Academic Freedom." *Chronicle of Higher Education,* April 4, p. A48.

Peters, Thomas J., and R. H. Waterman, Jr. 1982. *In Search of Excellence: Lessons from America's Best-Run Companies.* New York: Harper and Row.

Peterson, Marvin W., and Melinda G. Spencer. 1990. "Understanding Academic Culture and Climate." In William G. Tierney, ed., *Assessing Academic Climates and Cultures,* pp. 3–18. San Francisco: Jossey-Bass.

Pettigrew, Andrew M. 1979. "On Studying Organizational Cultures." *Administrative Science Quarterly* 24 (December): 570–81.

President's Advisory Commission on Educational Excellence for Hispanic Americans. 1996. *Our Nation on the Fault Line: Hispanic American Education.* Washington D.C.: President's Advisory Commission on Educational Excellence for Hispanic Americans.

Price, Hugh B. 1998. "Fortifying the Case for Diversity and Affirmative Action." *Chronicle of Higher Education,* May 22, p. B4.

Puente, Maria, and Sandra Sanchez. 1995. "School Dropouts, Crisis for Hispanic Kids." *USA Today,* September 6, 1995, p. 1A.

Ramírez, Albert. 1988. "Racism toward Hispanics: The Culturally Monolithic Society." In Phyllis A. Katz and Dalmas A. Taylor, eds., *Eliminating Racism: Profiles in Controversy,* pp. 137–58. New York: Plenum.

Ramírez, Manuel III. 1983. *Psychology of the Americas: Mestizo Perspectives on Personality and Mental Health.* New York: Pergamon.

Ramírez, Manuel III. 1991. *Psychotherapy and Counseling with Minorities: A Cognitive Approach to Individual and Cultural Differences.* New York: Pergamon.

Ramírez, Manuel III. 1998. *Multicultural/Multiracial Psychology: Mestizo Perspectives in Personality and Mental Health.* Northvale, N.J.: Jason Aronson.

Ramírez, Manuel III. 1999. *Multicultural Psychotherapy: An Approach to Individual and Cultural Differences.* 2d ed. of *Psychotherapy and Counseling with Minorities* (1991). Needham Heights, Mass.: Allyn and Bacon.

References

Ramírez, Manuel III, and Alfredo Castañeda. 1974. *Cultural Democracy, Bicognitive Development, and Education.* New York: Academic Press.

Raspberry, William. 1998. "Enemies Won't Help You Solve Problems." *Washington Post,* January 2, p. A23.

Rice, Eugene R. 1986. "The Academic Profession in Transition: Toward a New Social Fiction." *Teaching Sociology* 14 (January): 12–23.

Rice, Eugene R. 1996. *Making a Place for the New American Scholar.* New Pathways Working Paper Series. Washington, D.C.: American Association of Higher Education.

Richardson, Richard C., Jr. 1989. "If Minority Students Are to Succeed in Higher Education, Every Rung of the Educational Ladder Must Be in Place." *Chronicle of Higher Education,* January 11, p. A48.

Roey, Stephen, and Rebecca Rak Skinner, Rosa Fernandez, and Sam Barbett. 1999. "Fall Staff in Postsecondary Institutions, 1997." National Center for Education Statistics, NCES 2000–164, November, Department of Education, Washington, D.C.

Rosaldo, Renato. 1993. *Culture and Truth: The Remaking of Social Analysis.* 2d ed. Boston: Beacon.

Sachs, Patricia, ed. 1989. "Special Issue: Anthropological Approaches to Organizational Culture." *Anthropology of Work Review* 10 (3).

Sacks, Peter. 1997. "Standardized Testing: Meritocracy's Crooked Yardstick." *Change* 29 (March–April): 25–31.

Safa, Helen Icken. 1974. *The Urban Poor of Puerto Rico: A Study in Development and Inequality.* New York: Holt, Rinehart and Winston.

Saldívar, Ramón. 1990. *Chicano Narrative: The Dialects of Difference.* Madison: University of Wisconsin Press.

Sánchez, George J. 1993. *Becoming Mexican American: Ethnicity, Culture, and Identity in Chicano Los Angeles, 1900–1945.* New York: Oxford University Press.

Sánchez Korrol, Virginia E. 1993. *From Colonia to Community: The History of Puerto Ricans in New York City, 1917–1948.* Westport, Conn.: Greenwood.

Sanders, Katherine, and Chris Carlson-Dakes. 1997. *Creating a Collaborative Learning Environment, A Faculty Resource Book, 1997–1998.* Madison: Creating a Collaborative Learning Environment Program, University of Wisconsin–Madison.

Sandler, Bernice Resnick, Lisa A. Silverberg, and Roberta M. Hall. 1996. *The Chilly Classroom Climate: A Guide to Improve the Education of Women.* Washington, D.C.: National Association for Women in Education.

Santiago, Esmeralda. 1993. *When I Was Puerto Rican.* New York: Vintage.

Schein, Edgar H. 1985. *Organizational Culture and Leadership: A Dynamic View.* San Francisco: Jossey-Bass.

Scheurich, James Joseph, and Michelle D. Young. 1997. "Coloring Epistemologies: Are Our Research Epistemologies Racially Biased?" *Educational Researcher* 26 (4): 4–16.

Schmeck, Ronald R., ed. 1988. *Learning Strategies and Learning Styles.* New York: Plenum.

Schneider, Alison. 1997. "Proportion of Minority Professors Inches Up to About 10 Percent." *Chronicle of Higher Education,* June 20, pp. A12–13.

References

Schwartz, Peter, and James Ogilvy. 1979. "The Emergent Paradigm: Changing Patterns of Thought and Belief." Analytic Report 7. Values and Lifestyles Program, Stanford Research Institute, Menlo Park, Calif.

Schwartzman, Helen B. 1993. *Ethnography in Organizations.* Qualitative Research Methods Series Vol. 27. Newbury Park, Calif.: Sage.

Schweitzer, John H. 1993. "Graduate Admissions at MSU: An Affirmative Action Investigation." Report for Urban Affairs Programs, Owen Graduate Center, Michigan State University, East Lansing.

Scott, David K., and Susan M. Awbrey. 1993. "Transforming Scholarship." *Change* 25 (July–August): 38–43.

Selingo, Jeffrey. 1999. "Minority Applications Plummet at University of Washington Law School." *Academe Today,* web site of the *Chronicle of Higher Education,* March 17 <http://chronicle.com/daily/99/03/99031703n.htm> (3/17/99).

Senge, Peter M. 1990. *The Fifth Discipline: The Art and Practice of the Learning Organization.* New York: Doubleday/Currency.

Seymour, Daniel. 1993. *On Q: Causing Quality in Higher Education.* Phoenix, Ariz.: Oryx.

Seymour, Daniel. 1995. *Once upon a Campus: Lessons for Improving Quality and Productivity in Higher Education.* Phoenix, Ariz.: Oryx.

Seymour, Daniel. 1996a. "Introduction: Another Paradigm, Another Plan." In Daniel Seymour and Associates, eds., *High-Performing Colleges: The Malcolm Baldrige National Quality Award as a Framework for Improving Higher Education,* vol. 1: *Theory and Concepts,* pp. 18–25. Maryville, Mo.: Prescott.

Seymour, Daniel. 1996b. "The Baldrige in Education: Why It Is Needed, and What the First Pilot Year Produced." *American Association of Higher Education Bulletin* 48, no. 8 (April): 9–14.

Seymour, Daniel, and Satinder K. Dhiman. 1996. "Baldrige Barriers." In Daniel Seymour and Associates, eds., *High-Performing Colleges: The Malcolm Baldrige National Quality Award as a Framework for Improving Higher Education,* vol. 1: *Theory and Concepts,* pp. 72–106. Maryville, Mo.: Prescott.

Seymour, Elaine. 1995. "The Loss of Women from Science, Mathematics, and Engineering Undergraduate Majors: An Explanatory Account." *Science Education* 79 (4): 437–73.

Seymour, Elaine, and Nancy M. Hewitt. 1997. *Talking about Leaving: Why Undergraduates Leave the Sciences.* Boulder, Colo.: Westview.

Shade, Barbara J. 1982. "Afro-American Cognitive Style: A Variable in School Success?" *Review of Educational Research* 52, no. 2 (summer): 219–44.

Sharff, Jagna, and Lucie Wood Saunders, eds. 1994. "Demystifying the Changing Structure of Academic Work." *Anthropology of Work Review* 25 (1): 1–31.

Shorris, Earl. 1992. *Latinos: A Biography of the People.* New York: Norton.

Shulman, Lee S. 1990. *Paradigms and Programs: Research in Teaching and Learning.* Vol. 1. New York: Macmillan.

Smith, Darryl G. 1996. "Faculty Diversity When Jobs Are Scarce: Debunking the Myths." *Chronicle of Higher Education,* September 6, pp. B3–4.

Smith, Darryl G., and Associates. 1997. *Diversity Works: The Emerging Picture of How Students Benefit.* Washington, D.C.: Association of American Colleges and Universities.

Smith, Darryl G., with Lisa E. Wolf, Bonnie E. Busenberg, and Associates. 1996. *Achieving Faculty Diversity: Debunking the Myths.* Washington, D.C.: Association of American Colleges and Universities.

Smith, D. M., and Kolb, D. A. 1986. *Users' Guide for the Learning Style Inventory: A Manual for Teachers and Trainers.* Boston: McBer.

Smith, Thomas M., et al. 1996. *The Condition of Education, 1996.* Table 4.5, p. 52, and table 4.7, p. 92. Washington, D.C.: U.S. Government Printing Office.

Sollors, Werner. 1989. "Introduction: The Invention of Ethnicity." In Werner Sollors, ed., *The Invention of Ethnicity,* pp. ix–xx. New York: Oxford University Press.

Solorzano, Daniel G. 1993. *The Road to the Doctorate for California's Chicanas and Chicanos: A Study of Ford Foundation Minority Fellows.* Berkeley: California Policy Seminar.

Solorzano, Daniel G. 1995. "The Baccalaureate Origins of Chicana and Chicano Doctorates in the Social Sciences." *Hispanic Journal of Behavioral Sciences* 17, no. 1: 3–32.

Spain, David H. 1995. "On the Culture of Graduate Education: Critical Commentary by a Psychocultural Anthropologist." *CGS Communicator* 28 (5): 7–10.

Spann, Jeri. 1990. "Retaining and Promoting Women and Minority Faculty Members: Problems and Possibilities." Office of Equal Opportunity Programs and Policy Studies, University of Wisconsin–Madison.

Spradley, James P., and David W. McCurdy. 1980. *Anthropology: The Cultural Perspective.* 2d. ed. New York: Wiley.

Stanton-Salazar, Ricardo D. 1997. "A Social Capital Framework for Understanding the Socialization of Racial Minority Children and Youths." *Harvard Educational Review* 67 (1): 1–40.

Stavans, Ilan. 1995. *The Hispanic Condition: Reflections on Culture and Identity in America.* New York: HarperCollins.

St. Clair, Gloriana, and Ronald F. Dow. 1996. "Strategic and Operational Planning: The Glue of the System." In Daniel Seymour and Associates, eds., *High-Performing Colleges: The Malcolm Baldrige National Quality Award as a Framework for Improving Higher Education,* vol. 1: *Theory and Concepts,* pp. 145–68. Maryville, Mo.: Prescott.

Steele, Claude M., and Joshua Aronson. 1995. "Stereotype Threat and the Intellectual Test Performance of African Americans." *Journal of Personality and Social Psychology* 69 (5): 797–811.

Steinberg, Stephen. 1989. *The Ethnic Myth: Race, Ethnicity, and Class in America.* Rev. ed. Boston: Beacon.

Sternberg, Robert J. 1988. *The Triarchic Mind: A New Theory of Human Intelligence.* New York: Viking.

Sternberg, Robert J. 1996. *Successful Intelligence: How Practical and Creative Intelligence Determine Success in Life.* New York: Simon and Schuster.

Sternberg, Robert J. 1997. *Thinking Styles.* New York: Cambridge University Press.

Sternberg, Robert J., and Wendy M. Williams. 1997. "Does the Graduate Record Examination Predict Meaningful Success in the Graduate Training of Psychologists? A Case Study." *American Psychologist* 52, no. 6 (June): 630–41.

Stewart, Donald M. 1998. "Why Hispanic Students Need to Take the SAT." *Chronicle of Higher Education,* January 30, p. A48.

Stricker, Lawrence J., and Walter Emmerich. 1997. "Possible Determinants of Gender DIF on the Advanced Placement Psychology: Familiarity, Interest, and Emotional Reaction." Draft report for Educational Testing Service, Princeton, N.J.

Strickon, Arnold, and Robert A. Ibarra. 1983. "The Changing Dynamics of Ethnicity: Norwegians and Tobacco in Wisconsin." *Journal of Ethnic and Racial Studies* 6 (2): 174–97.

Strosnider, Kim. 1997a. "A Controversial Study of Testing Finds the Gap between Boys and Girls Is Shrinking." *Chronicle of Higher Education,* May 16, p. A34.

Strosnider, Kim 1997b. "University of Michigan Says It Won't Report Some Statistics on Race." *Chronicle of Higher Education,* September 5, p. A58.

Suro, Roberto. 1998. *Strangers among Us: How Latino Immigration Is Transforming America.* New York: Knopf.

Syverson, Peter D. 1997a. "How Are We Doing? Benchmarking the Progress of Minority Students in Graduate Education." *CGS Communicator* 30 (6): 4–6.

Syverson, Peter D. 1997b. "The New Majority: CGS/GRE Survey Results Trace Growth of Women in Graduate Education." *CGS Communicator* 30 (5): 8–10.

Syverson, Peter D., and Stephen R. Welch. 1997. *Graduate Enrollment and Degrees, 1986–1996: Data Release for the 1996 CGS/GRE Survey of Graduate Enrollment.* Washington, D.C.: Council of Graduate Schools.

Szapocznik, José, M. H. Scopetta, William Kurtines, and Maria D. Arnalde. 1978. "Theory and Measurement of Acculturation." *Inter-American Journal of Psychology* 12 (2): 113–30.

Tabachnick, Robert B., and Marianne N. Bloch. 1995. "Learning in and out of School: Critical Perspectives on the Theory of Cultural Compatibility." In Beth Blue Swadner and Sally Lubeck, eds., *Children and Families at Promise,* pp. 187–209. Albany: State University of New York Press.

Tannen, Deborah. 2000. "Agonism in the Academy: Surviving Higher Learning's Argument Culture." *Chronicle of Higher Education,* March 31, pp. B7–8.

Tennant, Christopher. 1997. "Professors Question Tenuring." *Badger Herald* (University of Wisconsin–Madison), October 29, pp. 1–3.

Thernstrom, Abigail. 1997. "End the Double Standard." *USA Today,* May 22, 1997, p. 12A.

Thomas, David A., and Robin J. Ely. 1996. "Making Differences Matter: A New Paradigm for Managing Diversity." *Harvard Business Review,* September–October, pp. 79–90.

Thomas, Irene Middleman. 1994. "The Big Chill: The Ivy League Turns a Cold Shoulder toward Hispanic Professors." *HISPANIC,* December, pp. 18–22.

Thompsen, Joyce, and Robert A. Ibarra. 1997. "Extending Critical Knowledge Areas: Learn, Innovate, Propagate." In Dundar F. Kocagolu and Timothy R. Anderson, eds., *Innovation in Technology Management: The Key to Global Leadership,* pp. 353–58. Proceedings of the Portland International Conference on Management of Engineering and Technology Management, July 27–31, Portland, Ore.

Thurgood, D. H., and J. E. Clarke. 1995. *Summary Report, 1993: Doctorate Recipients from U.S. Universities.* Washington, D.C.: National Academy Press.

301

References

Tierney, William G. 1997. "Organizational Socialization in Higher Education." *Journal of Higher Education* 68, no. 1 (January–February): 1–16.

Tierney, William G. 1998a. "Tenure Is Dead; Long Live Tenure." *The Responsive University: Restructuring for High Performance,* pp. 38–61. Baltimore, Md.: Johns Hopkins University Press.

Tierney, William G., ed. 1990. *Assessing Academic Climates and Cultures.* San Francisco: Jossey-Bass.

Tierney, William G., ed. 1998b. *The Responsive University: Restructuring for High Performance.* Baltimore, Md.: Johns Hopkins University Press.

Tierney, William G., and Estela Mara Bensimon. 1996. *Promotion and Tenure: Community and Socialization in Academe.* Albany: State University of New York Press.

Ting-Toomey, Stella. 1985. "Toward a Theory of Conflict and Culture." In William B. Gudykunst, Lea P. Stewart, and Stella Ting-Toomey, eds., *Communication, Culture, and Organizational Processes,* pp. 71–86. Beverly Hills, Calif.: Sage.

Tobias, Sheila. 1990. *They're Not Dumb, They're Different: Stalking the Second Tier.* Tucson, Ariz.: Research Corp.

Trachtenberg, Stephen Joel. 1997. "Preparing for Baby Boomers: Older Students Will Bring New Opportunities to Colleges." *Chronicle of Higher Education,* March 21, p. B7.

Traweek, Sharon. 1988. *Beamtimes and Lifetimes: The World of High Energy Physicists.* Cambridge, Mass.: Harvard University Press.

Treisman, Uri P. 1988. "A Study of the Mathematics Performance of Black Students at the University of California, Berkeley." In N. D. Fisher, H. B Keynes, and P. D. Wagreich, eds., *Proceedings of the Mathematicians Education Reform Workshop,* vol. 5, pp. 33–46. Washington, D.C.: Conference Board of the Mathematical Sciences, American Mathematical Society, and Mathematical Association of America.

Treisman, Uri P. 1989. "Mathematics Workshop Revamped." *UME Trends,* March, pp. 8 and 4.

Trice, Harrison M., and Janice M. Beyer. 1993. *The Cultures of Work Organizations.* Englewood Cliffs, N.J.: Prentice-Hall.

Trueba, Enrique (Henry) T. 1999. *Latinos Unidos: From Cultural Diversity to the Politics of Solidarity.* Lanham, Md.: Roman and Littlefield.

Turner, Caroline Sotello Viernes, and Judith Rann Thompson. 1993. "Socializing Women Doctoral Students: Minority and Majority Experiences." *Review of Higher Education* 16, no. 3 (spring): 355–70.

University of Wisconsin–Madison. Office of the Chancellor. 1988. "The Madison Plan." February 9.

University of Wisconsin–Madison. Office of the Chancellor. 1991. "The Madison Plan Three Years Later."

Upham, Steadman. 1994. "Fandangos and Thermostats: A Twenty-first–Century Landscape for Public Higher Education." Unpublished paper.

U.S. Census Bureau. 1995. "Population Profile of the United States: 1995." *U.S. Census Bureau, Current Population Reports,* Series P23–189, July <http://www.census.gov/prod/1/pop/profile/95/21_ps.pdf> (3/18/00).

U.S. Census Bureau. 1996. "Population Projections of the United States by Age,

References

Sex, Race, and Hispanic Orgin: 1995 to 2050." *U.S. Census Bureau, Current Population Reports,* Series P25–1130, February <http://www.census.gov/prod/1/pop/p25–1130> (November 1999).

U.S. Census Bureau. 1999. "Revisions to the Standards for the Classification of Federal Data on Race and Ethnicity by the Office of Management and Budget." *U.S. Census Bureau,* April 1 <http://www.census.gov/population/www/socdemo/race/Ombdir15.html> (3/18/00).

U.S. Census Bureau. 2000. "The Hispanic Population in the United States: March 1999." *U.S. Census Bureau, Current Population Reports,* Series P20–527, February <http://www.census.gov/prod/www/abs/hispanic.html> (3/18/00).

U.S. Department of Education. Office of Postsecondary Education. 2000. "Federal TRIO Programs: Higher Education Programs." *U.S. Department of Education* <http://www.ed.gov/officesOPE/HEP/trio/> (1/5/00).

Vélez-Ibáñez, Carlos G. 1996. *Border Visions: Mexican Cultures of the Southwest United States.* Tucson: University of Arizona Press.

Viadero, Debra. 1997. "Hispanic Dropouts Face Higher Hurdles, Study Says." *Education Week,* August 6, p. 3.

Vincent, Gregory J., Katherine Sanders, Seema Kapani, Luis A. Piñero, and Christopher Darlson-Dakes. 1998. "An Expanded Intercultural Development Approach for UW–Madison Faculty, Staff, and Students: Creating Multiple Avenues for Intense Reflection and Supported Action to Meet Critical Campus Priorities." Proposal by the Equity, Diversity, and Resource Center to the federal Fund for the Improvement of Post-Secondary Education (FIPSE), March 20.

Wagener, Ursula. 1991. "How to Increase the Number of Minority Ph.D.s." *Planning for Higher Education* 19 (summer): 1–7.

Wagener, Ursula. 1992. "Increasing Minority Representation in Higher Education: What Works." Paper prepared for the Minority Faculty Pipeline, the interregional meeting on minority faculty development held by the Council of Graduate Schools, December 1992.

Walens, Stanley G. 1975. "Ethnicity and Collective Identification: The Old West." In John W. Bennett, ed., *The New Ethnicity: Perspectives from Ethnology,* pp. 275–82. St. Paul, Minn.: West.

Walton, Mary. 1990. *Deming Management at Work.* New York: Putnam.

WCER (Wisconsin Center for Educational Research). 1996. "Hispanic Student Dropout Rate a National Crisis." 1996. *WCER Highlights* 8, no. 2 (summer): 6–9.

Weber, David J. 1993. "Our Hispanic Past: A Fuzzy View Persists." *Chronicle of Higher Education,* March 10, p. A44.

Weisbard, Eric. 1997. "Sucker Ph.D.s." *Spin,* October, pp. 20–127.

Whatley, Warren C. 1996. "Affirmative Action and Institutional Change in Graduate Education: The University of Michigan's Rackham Merit Fellowship Program." Research report. University of Michigan, Ann Arbor.

Wheatley, Margaret J. 1992. *Leadership and the New Science: Learning about Organization from an Orderly Universe.* San Francisco: Berrett-Koehler.

Whitten, Barbara L. 1996. "What Physics Is Fundamental Physics? Feminist Implications of Physicists' Debate over the Superconducting Supercollider." *National Women's Studies Association Journal* 8 (2): 1–16.

References

Wiedman, Dennis. 1990. "University Accreditation: Academic Subculture and Organizational Shifts—Responses to Directed Change." In Tomoko Hamada and
Ann Jordan, eds., *Cross-Cultural Management and Organizational Culture,* pp.
227–46. Williamsburg, Va.: Department of Anthropology, College of William
and Mary.

Wiedman, Dennis. 1992. "Effects on Academic Culture of Shifts from Oral to
Written Traditions: The Case of University Accreditation." *Human Organization* 51 (4): 398–407.

Wilds, Deborah J., and Reginald Wilson. 1998. "Minorities in Higher Education,
1997–1998." *Sixteenth Annual Status Report.* American Council on Education,
Washington, D.C.

Wilkins, Alan L., and W. Ouchi. 1983. "Efficient Cultures: Exploring the Relationship between Culture and Organizational Performance." *Administrative Science Quarterly* 28 (September): 468–81.

Williams, Linda Verlee. 1983. *Teaching for the Two-Sided Mind: A Guide to Right
Brain/Left Brain Education.* New York: Simon and Schuster.

Williams, Melvin D., with Brian Price. 1993. *An Academic Village: The Ethnography of an Anthropology Department, 1959–1979.* Ann Arbor, Mich: Melvin D.
Williams.

Williams, Wendy M. 1997. "Reliance on Test Scores Is a Conspiracy of Lethargy."
Chronicle of Higher Education, October 10, p. A60.

Wilson, Robin 2000. "The Remaking of Math." *Chronicle of Higher Education,*
January 7, pp. A14–16.

Witkin, Herman A., and Philip K. Oltman. 1967. "Cognitive Style." *International
Journal of Neurology* 6 (2): 119–37.

Witkin, Herman A., Donald R. Goodenough, and Philip K. Oltman. 1979. "Psychological Differentiation: Current Status." *Journal of Personality and Social
Psychology* 37 (7): 1127–45.

Witkin, Herman A., Carol Ann Moore, Philip K. Oltman, David R. Owen, Donald R. Goodenough, Florence Friedman, and Evelyn Raskin. 1977. "Role of
the Field-Dependent and Field-Independent Cognitive Styles in Academic
Evolution: A Longitudinal Study." *Journal of Educational Psychology* 69 (3):
197–211.

Wuthnow, Robert, J. D. Hunter, Albert Bergesen, and Edith Durzweil. 1984. *Cultural Analysis: The Work of Peter L. Berger, Mary Douglas, Michel Foucault,
and Jürgen Habermas.* London: Routledge and Kegan Paul.

Wyche, James H., and Henry T. Frierson, Jr. 1990. "Minorities at Majority Institutions." *Science* 290 (August): 989–91.

Zambrana, Ruth E., ed. 1995. *Understanding Latino Families: Scholarship, Policy,
and Practice.* Thousand Oaks, Calif.: Sage.

Zeira, Yoram, and Joyce Avedisian. 1989. "Organizational Planned Change: Assessing the Chances for Success." *Organizational Dynamics,* spring, pp. 31–45.

Zhu, Weimo, Margaret J. Safrit, and Allan S. Cohen. 1997. *Technical Manual:
Physical Fitness Knowledge Test.* Urbana, Ill.: Human Kenetics Press.

Zwick, Rebecca. 1991. *Differences in Graduate School Attainment Patterns across
Academic Programs and Demographic Groups.* Princeton, N.J.: Minority Graduate Education Project, GRE and Educational Testing Service.

Index

academic culture: and change in higher education, 224–25, 234, 243, 246, 248, 249–54, 256, 258–59; and contextualizing, 249–54; and current infrastructure for diversity programs, 241; influence on graduate students of, 95–106; and multicontextuality, 246, 248, 249–54, 256, 258–59; and reconceptualizing culture, 29–30; research as eroding of, 224. *See also specific subculture or topic*

academic organizational culture: and academic organizations, cultures, and systems, 114–16; and administration, 160; and adoption of organizational system from another culture, 133; binaries and hierarchy of, 106, 119–20; and change in higher education, 120–27, 223–43, 244, 249–54, 259; and cognition, 109, 124, 131, 133, 136; and cultural context, 124, 126, 131, 133, 135, 136; and cultural entrenchment, 124–27; and definition of organizational culture, 115–16; and democracy, 129–30, 131; domains of, 118; and faculty, 114, 118, 122–23, 126–27, 128, 130–33, 150, 154; and governance, 111, 124; and graduate education, 105–6, 107–8, 124, 126, 127–31, 136; and historical context of academia, 127–31; and Latino studies programs, 109–14; and multicontextuality, 66–68, 114, 244, 249–54, 259; and multiculturalism, 131; and nonacademics, 176; and organizational structures, 118–21; and paradigm paralysis,

9, 123, 124, 133–37; and professional culture, 121–24; questions concerning change of, 223–43; and racism, 135–36, 154; and revolution in organizational theory, 116–18; and socialization, 117–18; and status quo, 112–14. *See also* academic culture; *specific topic*

academic performance gaps, 5–7, 13

access, 8, 226, 227, 236, 240, 245. *See also* admissions

access-and-legitimacy paradigm, 226, 227

acclimation. *See* climate

accreditation, 132, 225

acculturation, 38, 39, 46, 47, 61, 62, 65, 82, 114, 244, 245, 247

achievement, 22–23, 186–87

action sets, 191–92

Acuña, Rodolfo F., 158

Adams, Howard G., 8, 9

Adams, Maurianne, 17, 197

Adizes, Ichak, 115

adjunct faculty, 138, 139, 140, 151, 172, 177

administration/administrators: and academic organizational culture, 110, 111, 118, 120, 122, 125, 132, 160; career trends and patterns among Latino, 161–64; in Catholic universities, 160; and change in higher education, 222, 224, 250; and community outreach, 169; and cultural gap, 159–64; and current infrastructure for diversity programs, 237, 240, 241; by departments, 233; faculty as, 138, 163–64, 233; faculty relations with,

and historical context of academia, 128; and teaching and learning styles, 202, 207–8. *See also* community service

community colleges, 124–25, 229, 231. *See also* two-year institutions

community outreach. *See* community service

community service: and change in higher education, 224, 230, 231, 248, 250, 252; and current infrastructure for diversity programs, 240; and graduate school experience, 102; and high- and low-context characteristics, 165–66; and Latino ethnicity and research, 167–69; and multicontextuality, 248, 250, 252; and nonacademics, 175; research as diminishing emphasis on, 175

Conciatore, Jacqueline, 202

connected university, 231

Connerly, Ward, 3

context: and academic organizational culture, 109; definition of, 52, 66; and interrater reliability, 218–21; and Latino study scope, 15, 18, 19; and reconceptualizing ethnicity, 32–39; and teaching and learning styles, 18, 218. *See also* cultural context

continuous quality improvement (CQI) models, 252–53

Cornell University, 146

corporate sector/culture, 114–15, 228, 229

Cortez, Jaime, 62

Costa Ricans, 14

Cotter, Maury, 234

Council for Opportunity in Education, 238

Council of Graduate Schools (CGS), 12, 13, 20, 21, 23, 43, 107, 195

counseling, 236–37. *See also* student services

Counseling Psychology Department (University of Wisconsin–Madison), 256–58

Coye, Dale, 136, 225

Creating a Collaborative Learning Environment program, 255

creative intelligence, 185, 187

Cuádraz, Gloria, 11, 21–22, 23, 82

Cuban Americans: and change in higher education, 245; ethnic and minority status of, 95; as faculty members, 157, 158; and graduate education, 24, 95, 105; and intracultural issues, 157, 158; and Latino study overview, 14, 15; and multicontextu-

ality, 59, 245; as nonacademics, 171; and reconceptualizing ethnicity, 33, 39

cultural blending, 38–39, 41, 47, 82, 178

cultural context: and academic organizational culture, 124, 126, 131, 133, 135, 136; and change in higher education, 223–36, 242–49, 254–59; and cognition, 49; conceptual assumptions about, 246–49; and current infrastructure for diversity programs, 236–41; definition of, 66; and definition of context, 52; and DIF, 190–94; and diversity, 225–29, 236–41, 254–55; dynamic nature of, 66, 231–36; and ethnic research, 165; and faculty, 154–55; and graduate education, 97–98, 100, 106; Hall's development of concept of, 43, 49–55, 63, 181–82; and historical context of academia, 131, 244–46; and how change can occur, 232, 233–34; and inter-rater reliability, 218–21; and Latino study scope, 15–16; models for change of, 234–36, 242–49, 254–59; and multicontextuality, 49–55, 59–60, 62, 63, 64–68, 243–49, 257; and nonacademics, 175; and racism and classism, 154–55; and reasons for change, 223–29; reframing of current, 62, 66–68, 222–59; and standardized tests, 182–89, 190–94; and synchronicity, 54–55; systemic change of, 234–36; and teaching and learning styles, 195–99, 202, 203, 204–18; and which components of higher education need to change, 229–31

cultural democracy, 60, 62

cultural entrenchment, 124–27

cultural events, 32

cultural gap, 46, 159–64, 168

cultural research, 181–82. *See also* ethnic research

cultural taxation, 148–50

culture: Barth's views about, 31–32; and challenges for increasing diversity, 8–9; corporate, 114–15; definition of, 29, 30, 114, 115–16; dissonance between ethnic values and, 141–44; and graduate education, 22–23; and Latino study, 15–16, 21; reconceptualizing, 29–32; and reconceptualizing ethnicity, 32–39. *See also* academic culture; academic organizational culture; cultural context; *specific subculture*

Index

faculty/teachers (*continued*)
152–55; in two-year institutions, 139–40.
See also hiring issues; professional bureaucracy; promotion; teaching; tenure;
specific topic
Fairness, Access, Multiculturalism, and
Equity (FAME) analysis, 246
family: and academic organizational culture, 114; and academic performance
gaps, 6; and bicognition, 57, 58; and climate, 94; and cultural context concept,
52, 54; effect on school achievement of,
186; and graduate education, 21, 22, 84,
89, 92, 94, 100, 169
federal government, 129, 223, 237, 245
Felder, Richard M., 197, 199
Felipe (Chicano nonacademic), 172
field-dependent. *See* field-sensitive
field-independent: and academic organizational culture, 130; and bicognition, 57,
59; and change in higher education, 243,
244, 246–48, 250; characteristics of, 56,
77–78; and current infrastructure for diversity programs, 240; development of
concept of, 55–56; and faculty, 153; and
graduate school experience, 99, 100, 101,
102; and historical context of academia,
130; and inter-rater reliability, 218–21;
and multicontextuality, 59–60, 61, 64, 65,
66, 144, 243, 244, 246–48, 250; and racism and classism, 153; and teaching and
learning styles, 199, 207, 218
field-sensitive: and academic organizational
culture, 125, 135; and bicognition, 57–58,
59; and change in higher education, 229,
230, 243, 244, 245, 246–49, 258; characteristics of, 56, 77–78; development of
concept of, 55; and ethnic research, 165;
and faculty, 142, 143, 144, 153, 154; and
graduate school experience, 99, 100,
101, 102, 106; and inter-rater reliability,
218–21; and multicontextuality, 59–60,
61, 64, 65, 66, 144, 243, 244, 245, 246–
49, 258; and nonacademics, 172–73, 176;
and racism and classism, 153, 154; and
teaching and learning styles, 199, 203,
206–7, 208, 218
financial aid, 12, 84, 92, 93, 236, 237, 238
Fitzpatrick, Joseph P., 157
Florida, 3, 13, 62, 85, 184, 241
Ford, Martin E., 40, 83, 100, 101, 200

Ford Foundation, 28, 164
Fordham, Signithia, 202
foreign languages, 191–92
Fox, Geoffrey, 32, 35–36, 37–38
Francisco (administrator), 167
Frensch, Peter A., 186
Frierson, Henry T., Jr., 26
Fullerton, Howard N., Jr., 61
Fullilove, Robert E., 200, 201, 203, 204

Gainen, Joanne, 141, 147
Gallagher, Ann, 193
Galloway, Phyllis H., 195, 196
Gamson, Zelda F., 230
Gándara, Patricia, 11, 21, 22–23, 83, 183,
185
Garza, Yolanda, 139, 140, 147, 161, 163
Geertz, Clifford, 30
GEM program (National Consortium for
Graduate Degrees for Minorities in Engineering and Science), 251
gender: and academic organizational culture, 133; and administration, 147, 161,
164; and alternative perspective of higher
education, 46–47; and change in higher
education, 226, 228; and climate, 94; and
cognition, 56; and cultural context concept, 51, 52, 53, 55; and DIF, 190; and
disciplines, 147–48; and faculty, 143–44,
147–48, 151; and graduate education, 22,
94, 105; and high- and low-context characteristics, 72–73; and multicontextuality,
65; research about, 158–59; and sciences,
147–48, 228; and standardized tests, 184–
85, 189; and support networks, 147; and
teaching and learning styles, 197–99, 205,
206, 212–17, 221; and tenure issues, 151;
and undergraduate education, 147–48
Generation Ñ, 62
George Washington University, 223
Germany: and historical context of academia, 16–17, 86, 127–28, 129, 130, 131,
224, 242, 244
GI Bill of Rights, 129–30, 244
Gill, Roger, 160
Gilliland, Martha, 118
Giovannini, Maureen J., 115
Givens, David B., 174, 176
Gloria, Alberta M., 44, 85, 147
González, María Christina, 107
Goodenough, Donald R., 55

Index

National Science Foundation (NSF), 24, 25, 28, 139, 165, 176
Native Americans. *See* American Indians
Nelson, Helene, 177
Nerad, Marisi, 170–71
Nettles, Michael T., 26, 28
Neville, Gwen Kennedy, 39
new American college/scholar, 136–37, 225, 231, 233
Newsweek magazine, 62
Nickens, Tim, 85, 184
Nieves-Squires, Sarah, 21
nonacademics, 14, 90, 108, 141, 164, 166, 169–78, 241
nonverbal communication, 50, 54, 69, 78, 142, 154, 187, 192–93
Norwegian Americans, 36–37, 38, 39

object-oriented testing, 55–56
O'Brien, Eileen M., 21, 27, 140
Office of Management and Budget, U.S. (OMB), 45, 223
Ogilvy, James, 116
Okagaki, Lynn, 186
Oltman, Philip K., 55
Orfield, Gary, 7
organizational culture, 114–16. *See also* academic organizational culture
organizational structure, 63, 225, 232–36. *See also* academic organizational culture
organizational theory: revolution in, 116–18
organizations: academic and professional, 103, 167, 222, 233, 234, 251, 253; anthropological assumptions about, 115. *See also* academic organizational culture; organizational structure; organizational theory; *specific organization*
Ouchi, W., 114
Outtz, Janice Hamilton, 12
overworked administrator syndrome, 163
Owen, David, 183, 185

Pablo (Chicano scientist), 112–13
Pachon, Harry, 157
Padilla, Amado, 38, 148–49, 165
Padilla, Felix M., 27
Padilla, Raymond V., 11, 21
paradigm paralysis, 9, 123, 124, 133–37
parents. *See* family
Paris, Kathleen A., 234
Parker, Rebecca Lee, 55

Patterson, James, 32
pedagogy, 18, 195–99, 204–21. *See also* teaching
Pedro (Mexican American graduate student), 47–49, 50–51, 63–64, 66
performance gaps, academic, 5–7, 13
Perley, James E., 150
perseverance/persistence, 84–85, 103, 104
personal characteristics: as measure of academic success, 183–84
Peters, Thomas J., 114
Peterson, Marvin W., 30, 115
Pettigrew, Andrew M., 115
physics, 175, 228
pigeonholes, identity, 40–42, 105, 246
Pinderhughes, Raquel, 157
pipeline. *See* educational pipeline
polychronicity, 54–55, 71, 72, 144, 162
pools, identity, 40–42, 105, 246
Pope-Davis, Donald D., 44, 85, 147
practical intelligence, 185, 187
Preparing Future Faculty (PFF), 195–96
President's Advisory Commission (1996), 23, 83
Price, Brian, 30
Price, Hugh B., 7
Princeton University, 146
private colleges, 127–28, 130
private sector, 248–49
problem solving: and standardized tests, 188
professional bureaucracy, 17, 123, 133. *See also* administration/administrators; faculty/teachers
professional culture, 121–24
professional education, 22–23, 248
professional service, 167–69, 176. *See also* community service
programs. *See* curriculum; departments; disciplines; *specific discipline or program*
promotion, 122, 126–27, 158–59, 161. *See also* tenure
psychology, 57, 175, 185–86, 248
public service. *See* community service
publish-or-perish myth, 146
Puente, Maria, 83
Puerto Ricans: as administrators, 161; and climate, 94; ethnic and minority status of, 95; as faculty members, 157, 211, 220; and graduate education, 24, 94, 95, 105; and inter-rater reliability, 220; and intra-

Index

cultural issues, 157; and Latino study overview, 14, 15; as nonacademics, 171, 175; and teaching and learning styles, 206, 213, 215; and undergraduate goals, 217
Puerto Rico: administrators in, 162

quality: definition of, 132
quality improvement (CQI) models: continuous, 252–53
Quinlan, Kathleen, 196

racism: and academic organizational culture, 135–36, 154; and administration, 155, 160; and alternative perspective of higher education, 46; in Catholic universities, 160; and challenges for increasing diversity, 8, 10; and change in higher education, 13, 245; and climate, 93, 94; and cognition, 154–55; and common assumptions about higher education, 44, 45; complexity of defining, 45–46; and cultural context, 154–55; and current infrastructure for diversity programs, 241; and faculty, 152–55; and graduate school experience, 83, 93, 94, 96; and Latino study scope, 16, 18; and multicontextuality, 15–16, 45–46, 67, 245; and nonacademics, 176
Raines, Franklin, 223, 224
Ramírez, Albert, 59
Ramírez, Manuel: and academic organizational culture, 131, 136; and cognition/bicognition, 15, 49, 57, 58–60, 63, 67, 100, 181–82, 194, 199, 243; and cultural context, 194; and DIF, 191, 194; and field-sensitive and -independent characteristics, 56, 60, 77–78; and historical context of academia, 131; and Latino study scope, 15; and motivation of Latinos, 99; and multicontextuality, 59–60, 63, 64, 65–66, 67, 199; and new American scholar, 136; and teaching and learning styles, 15, 191, 197, 203
Ranger, Terrence, 42
Raspberry, William, 67
Raul (graduate student), 97–98, 99, 100
recruitment: and academic organizational culture, 109, 110–11, 120–21; and change in higher education, 226, 242, 250, 251, 253, 254, 255; and current infrastructure

for diversity programs, 236, 237, 238, 239, 240, 241; and high- and low-context characteristics, 165–66; and Latino ethnicity and research, 165–66; and Latino faculty issues, 145, 150; and Latino studies programs, 109, 110–11; and Latino study, 21; and multicontextuality, 250, 251, 253, 254, 255; in sciences, 150
Reinaldo (faculty member/administrator), 162
relationships, interpersonal: and academic performance gaps, 6; and field-sensitive and -independent characteristics, 77, 78; and graduate school experience, 105–6; and high- and low-context characteristics, 70; and multicontextuality, 60. See also faculty/teachers: student relationships with
reliability: inter-rater, 218–21
remedial programs, 201, 236, 251
research: and academic organizational culture, 111, 125, 126, 127, 128, 129, 134–35; and administration, 162; and change in higher education, 224, 225, 230, 231, 244, 250, 251, 256, 257, 259; and current infrastructure for diversity programs, 240; and graduate school experience, 102; and high- and low-context, 165–69; and historical context of academia, 128, 129; and Latino faculty issues, 145; and multicontextuality, 244, 250, 251, 256, 257, 259; and nonacademics, 175–76; and undergraduate education, 251, 256. See also ethnic research
research universities: and academic organizational culture, 109, 112, 122, 126, 128; and change in higher education, 222, 223, 224, 231, 232, 234, 250; and climate, 94–95; faculty in, 222, 231; goal of, 91; and graduate school experience, 86, 88, 89, 91, 94–95; and historical context of academia, 128; international students in, 176, 177; mission of, 223, 234, 250; and multicontextuality, 250; public image of, 223; as role model, 175
retention: and academic organizational culture, 110–11; and administration, 161; and challenges for increasing diversity, 7–8, 9; and change in higher education, 12, 242, 251; and climate, 155; and current infrastructure for diversity pro-

Index

Weisbard, Eric, 86
Welch, Stephen R., 11, 12, 23
Wenger, Etienne, 87, 88, 101
Wergin, Jon F., 230, 231
Whatley, Warren C., 9
Wheatley, Margaret J., 116
Whitten, Barbara, 228
Wiedman, Dennis, 30
Wilds, Deborah J., 10, 83
Wiley, John, 132
Wilkins, Alan L., 114
Williams, Melvin D., 30
Williams, Wendy M., 185–86, 187, 189
Wilson, Reginald, 4, 10, 12, 26, 83, 139, 140
Wilson, Robin, 229
Wisconsin: Norwegian Americans in, 36–37, 38, 39
Witkin, Herman A., 55, 57
Wolf, Lisa E., 145, 146, 168
women: and academic organizational culture, 127, 131; as administrators, 164; and alternative perspective of higher education, 46, 47; Asian American, 206; and challenges for increasing diversity, 8–9; and change in higher education, 226, 227, 228, 245, 246; and cognition, 55, 56, 57; demographics about, 61; and DIF, 190; as faculty members, 140; as field sen-

sitive, 56; and graduate education, 22, 23, 90, 105; as high-context population, 53; and historical context of academia, 131; and inter-rater reliability, 220; and multi-contextuality, 61, 66, 245, 246; Native American, 206; and nonacademics, 170; and racism and classism, 153–54; and teaching and learning styles, 197–99, 204, 205–9, 221; and timed-testing situations, 188; and undergraduate goals, 221. *See also* Chicanos/as; gender; Latinos/as
women's studies programs, 131, 146, 234, 245
work ethic, 98, 99
Wuthnow, Robert, 30
Wyche, James H., 26

Xavier University, 190

Yale University, 146, 185–86
Yolanda (graduate student), 104–5
Young, Michelle D., 8, 135

Zahn, G. Lawrence, 57
Zeira, Yoram, 115
Zhu, Weimo, 193
Zwick, Rebecca, 26, 28

323

DATE DUE

JAN 0 6 2017			
DEC 21 2019			
JUN 0 3 2020			
MAY 1 3 2020			